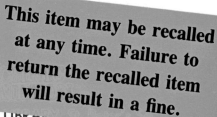

# Understanding Popular Culture

## Europe from the Middle Ages to the Nineteenth Century

Edited by
Steven L. Kaplan

MOUTON PUBLISHERS · BERLIN · NEW YORK · AMSTERDAM

Steven L. Kaplan
Director
Western Societies Program
Center for International Studies
Cornell University
Ithaca, New York 14853
USA

*Library of Congress Cataloging in Publication Data*

Main entry under title:

Understanding popular culture.

(New Babylon : 40)
Includes index.
1. Europe – Popular culture – History – Addresses,
essays, lectures. 2. Europe – Religious life and customs –
Addresses, essays, lectures. 3. Folklore – Europa –
Addresses, essays, lectures. I. Kaplan, Steven L.
CB 203.U54 1984      306'.4'094           84-1001
ISBN 3-11-009600-5

*CIP-Kurztitelaufnahme der Deutschen Bibliothek*

Understanding popular culture / Steven L. Kaplan (ed.).
– Berlin ; New York ; Amsterdam : Mouton, 1984. –
(New Babylon ; 40)
ISBN 3-11-009600-5

NE : Kaplan, Steven [ Hrsg. ] ; GT

This book is dedicated to

BRONISLAW GEREMEK

whose absence from these pages attests to his passionate
involvement in the popular culture of
contemporary Poland

# Contents

Preface                                                                    1

Chapter I.
David Hall
    Introduction                                                            5

Chapter II.
Jacques Le Goff
    The Learned and Popular Dimensions of Journeys in the
    Otherworld in the Middle Ages                                         19

Chapter III.
Carlo Ginzburg
    The Witches' Sabbat: Popular Cult or Inquisitorial Stereo-
    type?                                                                 39

Chapter IV.
Mary R. O'Neil
    *Sacerdote ovvero strione*. Ecclesiastical and Superstitious
    Remedies in 16th Century Italy                                        53

Chapter V.
Clive Holmes
    Popular Culture? Witches, Magistrates, and Divines in Early
    Modern England                                                        85

Chapter VI.
H. C. Erik Midelfort
    Sin, Melancholy, Obsession: Insanity and Culture in 16th
    Century Germany                                                      113

Chapter VII.
Günther Lottes
Popular Culture and the Early Modern State in 16th
Century Germany                                              147

Chapter VIII.
Richard C. Trexler
We Think, They Act: Clerical Readings of Missionary
Theatre in 16th Century New Spain                            189

Chapter IX.
Roger Chartier
Culture as Appropriation: Popular Cultural Uses in Early
Modern France                                                229

Chapter X.
Jacques Revel
Forms of Expertise: Intellectuals and "Popular" Culture
in France (1650–1800)                                        255

Chapter XI.
Hans-Ulrich Thamer
On the Use and Abuse of Handicraft: Journeyman Culture
and Enlightened Public Opinion in 18th and 19th Century
Germany                                                      275

Notes on the Contributors                                    301

Index                                                        305

*White Magic: An Introduction to the Folklore of Christian Legend,* 9
Wild Hunt, 47
Winterthur, Chonrad Von, 43
Witchcraft, 5, 6, 14, 179; English Witchcraft, 10, 85–111; Medieval European, 86; Sex-Linked, 94; Kinships, 96; Connection to Animals, 97

Witches' Sabbat, 9, 39–52
Wordsworth, William, 7

Zani, Teofilo, 61, 62, 64, 65, 66, 68, 71, 74
Zempoala, 191, 203, 204
*Zutrinken,* 170, 171, 172

Understanding Popular Culture

Europe from the Middle Ages
to the Nineteenth Century

# New Babylon

*Studies in the Social Sciences*
## 40

MOUTON PUBLISHERS · BERLIN · NEW YORK · AMSTERDAM

# Preface

STEVEN LAURENCE KAPLAN

In recent years, the historical study of popular culture has flourished within several different academic disciplines. Yet the notion of popular culture itself remains clouded by conceptual uncertainties. What is signified by the "popular" in popular culture? Is it fruitful simply to identify (or perceive) it by juxtaposing it to, and thereby distinguishing it from, the dominant culture? Or does such an approach imply an uncritical adoption of the category of "domination"? Are binary formulations such as high/low and learned/unlearned compelling? Does the frontier between high and low remain an analytically useful line of demarcation?

Is it sufficient to define "popular" in terms of the artifacts in which the quality is supposed to inhere – in a given body of texts, values, modes of behavior? Or is an approach that stresses the diffusion of these cultural objects through their societies better suited to locating and labeling the "popular"? Might it not be more illuminating to shift our emphasis away from the objects themselves, and their dissemination, to the diverse ways in which, by accident and by design, they are perceived, used, and transformed? What is the relation between the way in which a society is stratified, on the one hand, and the provenance and dissemination of popular culture, on the other? Similarly, what is the relationship between political consciousness and action, on the one hand, and popular culture, on the other?

How can we best articulate connections among the diverse ways in which popular culture manifests itself (for example, the relation between oral and written discourse)? How should we

2 *Preface*

conceive the relations among popular, folk, mass, and high culture? How does the process by which popular culture is transmitted across time — what some scholars call "reproduction" — differ from that of elite cultures? How should the study of popular culture be related to other kinds of historical inquiry in more or less contiguous areas such as social history, or the history of collective mentalities, or intellectual history, or political history?

Convinced that it was a propitious time to reappraise our understanding of popular culture, Michael Kammen and I convened an international conference at Cornell University at the end of April 1982. The conference ranged widely across Europe and America, from medieval times through the mid 20th century. This book consists of ten of the papers presented at the conference. Focusing on Europe before 1815, these essays address many of the questions on our agenda in a fresh and stimulating manner. Combining theoretical reflection with original empirical research, they suggest new ways to apprehend and to interpret popular culture. The authors are English, French, German, and American scholars specializing in European history. David Hall, who participated in the conference as a commentator, brings an Americanist's perspective to the Introduction.

This book owes a great deal intellectually to the other conference participants, absent from this volume, whose papers and critical comments enriched the discussion and led the authors of these essays to rethink certain assumptions and to sharpen their arguments. The authors join me in acknowledging our debt to James Boon (Cornell), Stuart Clark (University of Wales College at Swansea), Herbert J. Gans (Columbia University), Davydd Greenwood (Cornell), Neil Harris (University of Chicago), Temma Kaplan (University of California at Los Angeles), John Kasson (University of North Carolina at Chapel Hill), Dominick LaCapra (Cornell), Yves Lequin (Université de Lyon II), Emmanuel Le Roy Ladurie (College de France and Cornell), Hans Medick (Max-Planck-Institut für Geschichte, Gottingen), and Jonathan Wylie (Cambridge, Massachusetts). All of us at the conference felt impoverished and outraged by the involuntary absence of the eminent Polish historian Bronislaw Geremek, incarcerated for his heroic combat as a member of Solidarity.

Neither this book nor the conference that spawned it would have seen the light of day but for the dedicated labor of my colleague Michael Kammen. Cosmopolitan, sensitive, and resourceful, he was an ideal collaborator. Nor could we have held the conference without the financial support of the following agencies, to whom we are deeply grateful: the Western Societies Program of the Center for International Studies at Cornell University; the Ecole des Hautes Etudes en Sciences Sociales, Paris; the Maison des Sciences de l'Homme, Paris; the French-American Foundation; the Society for the Humanities at Cornell; the Office of the Dean of the College of Arts and Sciences at Cornell; and the Cornell departments of History, German Literature, and Romance Studies. We thank Ms. Pam Lane for her skillful assistance in organizing the conference. It was a pleasure to work with our copy editor, Roger Haydon, whose urbanity and good sense improved this book in sundry ways. We are obliged to Professor Jane P. Kaplan of Ithaca College and Professor James J. John and Mr. Robert Whalen of Cornell University for vetting several of the translations. Ms. Pat Carlson did a superb job of typing. Dr. Gerard Moran of Amsterdam provided expert counsel both as a historian and as an editor.

Ithaca, New York                                         S. L. K.

June 1983

# Introduction

DAVID HALL

The historian of popular culture is in pursuit of an elusive quarry.[1] No one knows exactly what this quarry looks like, or even who "the people" are whose culture is at issue. Anyone who intervenes to serve as guide is suspect; the intermediary is by definition different from the subject.

The essays in *Understanding Popular Culture* are exemplary in their awareness of the problems that beset the historian. These essays are useful as description, since they enrich in many ways our knowledge of the past. Some take up such classic topics as witchcraft and the *livrets bleus*; others move in new directions. In their range these essays serve as illustrations of the wealth of sources that lie open to investigation. But their special merit is their spirit of reflection. Each one is an exercise in self-criticism, for the history of popular culture has reached a point where we must think anew about the premises on which the field is founded.

The history of popular culture grows from the perception of division or difference: the culture of "the people" differs from the culture of "elites." There is no lack of efforts to draw a line between these types, or to declare that such a line functioned as a real boundary. But it is characteristic of our present situation that we seek more nuance than may have been the case before. Thus, the contributors to *Understanding Popular Culture* agree in recognizing that artifacts of culture cannot be automatically distributed among the social groups or classes that make up society. Culture has a social basis, but the relationship of culture to society is more fluid than the very phrase "popular culture" may permit.

The rethinking that these essays represent proceeds in four directions. The first is to describe how representations of popular

culture, representations that have at best a problematic bearing
on the thing-in-itself, emerged in the past. Peter Burke began his
*Popular Culture in Early Modern Europe* with a chapter on "The
Discovery of the People" in late 18th and early 19th century
Europe. That event hardly marked the first representation of
popular culture, however. Jacques Revel and Roger Chartier
carry the story back to the 16th and 17th centuries, when clerical
reformers tried to liberate the Christian church from certain
"false" beliefs. Even this great movement had antecedents in the
church of the middle ages, and the distinction between true belief
and "superstition" dates back to late antiquity.[2] In 17th century
France, the animus toward superstition arose anew in Jean-
Baptiste Thiers, who collected examples of the errors he condemned in the *Traité des Superstitions* (1679; 1702). Across the
Channel, Henry Bourne, a Church of England clergyman, was
assembling the materials for *Antiquitates Vulgares; or, The Antiquities of the Country People* (1725). In retrospect, we recognize
the politics that Bourne brought to his sources even as we use
them for our own devices.[3]

Everywhere in early modern Europe, the authorities were out
to reform popular culture in the name of their own values. In
16th century Germany, as Erik Midelfort and Hans-Ulrich Thamer
note, the efforts of the clergy were supplemented by secular
authorities and academic specialists. By the close of the 17th
century a coalition of clergy, freethinkers, philosophers, and
scientists was seeking to emancipate mankind from beliefs in
witchcraft, apparitions, portents, prophecy, special providence,
and miracles. On the whole, these critics were successful in achiev-
ing the disenchantment they sought.[4]

In 18th century Europe, the rise of classicism stimulated
another round of attacks on certain social practices and customs.
The situation changed once again, and decisively, in the early
19th century, as popular culture, to its interpreters, assumed a
different guise. Hitherto, popular culture had been defined by a
process of exclusion (which was never, of course, to define what
it really consisted of). In the making of this new configuration
the key figures were moved by sympathy for a way of life that,
imperiled by the pace of change, still lingered on at the margins
of society. This perception stirred Sir Walter Scott to collect and
preserve certain customs before they vanished altogether. Scott

and his contemporaries on the Continent believed that they had stumbled upon the remnants of a "rural" culture, one with roots that stretched far back in time.[5] This was a culture that sustained its songs and stories by "oral tradition," as well as one that confused "magic" with "religion."

In arriving at this representation of popular culture, the antiquarians and folklorists of the early 19th century were prisoners of their own position. They

> came from the upper classes, to whom the people were a mysterious Them, described in terms their discoverers were not (or thought they were not): the people were natural, simple, illiterate, instinctive, irrational, rooted in tradition, and in the soil of the region, lacking any sense of individuality.[6]

These same antiquarians were powerfully caught up in romantic nationalism, which stood classicism on its head by preferring the local to the universal, the heart to the head, the vernacular to the cosmopolitan. Poets were now to draw their subjects and their very language from "the people," to sing "the meal in the firkin, the milk in the pan," as Emerson would say in America, echoing Wordsworth and Coleridge. Romanticism thereby generated the concept of the "folk" as set apart and living in a special culture of their own.

This quick overview of representations of popular culture leads to several observations. I borrow one of them from Gunther Löttes, who, in calling for a more precise and detailed integration of culture and society, expresses disappointment with the vagueness of "the people" in most modern studies of popular belief. His criticism has wide application. In no theory from the past, whether Scott's or Bourne's or some medieval cleric's, was the "social localization" of belief − the phrase is Löttes' − ever made specific. Our efforts to succeed in this direction are complicated by the stock words that we inherit from old ideologies. In his essay, Roger Chartier warns against transposing terms from one context into another: "Historians, thinking that they had identified popular culture, had in fact merely described in different words the fundamental distinction that the Church had made to 'disqualify' a set of thoughts and practices."

This comment has a broader relevance. One conception of popular culture may seem to differ greatly from another, as the history of "forms of expertise" would seek to demonstrate. But

alongside change there was also continuity. Certain terms have
been handed down for centuries, to reappear in modern dress as
categories of our own interpretations. Consider, for example, the
word "illiteratus," which in the middle ages denoted the line
between the Latin culture of the clergy and the vernacular culture
of the laity. "Illiteratus" does not mean the same as illiterate, and
it has no bearing whatsoever on the concept of "oral culture."
Yet this category continues to inform the familiar and quite common pairing of oral-illiterate-lay versus print-literate-clerical.[7]
"Superstition" is yet another word that will not go away; nor
will its opposite, the "rational" or the "scientific." "Magic" and
"religion" also have long histories, and the sequence of peasant-
rural-folk extends into the present. It seems fair to say that all
these words contain misleading implications. The messages in
books were not foreclosed to the illiterate. The clergy cannot
always be distinguished from the people. Magic stubbornly resists our efforts to distinguish it from religion.[8] Worse yet, these
words enforce a separation between cultures that is surely too
extreme.

Words like "superstition" are suspect, finally, because they
arise out of the learned tradition and not from popular culture
itself. They are words that imply some deviation from a norm,
whether it be orthodox Christianity, or rationality, or cosmopolitanism. Originating with some group that wants to make
discriminations, these words impose a worldview on the people
that may never have been theirs. Supposing that a separate culture did exist, these words discredit its coherence and legitimacy.

To undertake a history of representations of popular culture
is eventually to arrive at the point of doubting whether we can
ever describe the thing in itself. The essays in *Understanding
Popular Culture* do not capitulate to such total skepticism. They
retain a confidence in the search while agreeing on the imperative,
here voiced most clearly by Hans-Ulrich Thamer, that research
on representations of popular culture must be a part of the analysis of popular culture itself.

How, then, to track our quarry? The second direction in which
these essays move is to affirm that folklore offers "empirical
data of unquestionable value." These words of Jacques Le Goff's
imply the *dubious* value of many data. But let me emphasize the
positive. Le Goff has found a major source of data in the *Motif-*

*Index* developed by the American folklorist Stith Thompson.[9] In his essay, Le Goff draws on the *Motif-Index* to distinguish between learned and folkloric elements in imaginary voyages to the otherworld. He and others, such as Jean-Claude Schmitt, move on to trace the history of the interaction of these elements and then to specify how clerical or learned culture imposed changes upon the folklore. Elsewhere in this volume, Carlo Ginzburg relies on folklore or mythology in arguing that the concept of the witches' sabbath originated "from below" as well as from the learned culture; he, like Le Goff, is concerned to uncover a "layer of popular culture" with an integrity of its own.

Is it really possible to accord such privileged status to folklore? The *Motif-Index* seems thoroughly empirical, representing, as it does, one phase of the effort to make a science out of comparative mythology and folklore. I would suggest, however, that the motifs it contains emerge from several contexts or traditions. As one example, let me cite C. Grant Loomis's *White Magic: An Introduction to the Folklore of Christian Legend*, which presents the legends of the saints as folklore. Loomis drew on literary sources that were clerical in origin or, at best, a mixture of some sort; he did not make the discriminations that Le Goff pursues so ably in his essay.[10] Incorporating in its vast sweep the stories in *White Magic*, the *Motif-Index* becomes a composite, reflecting back a "folklore" that has many different sources. We must be wary, also, of confounding the Anglo-Scandinavian inquiry into folklore with the meaning of this term to social theorists such as Gramsci, to whom it signified an autonomous, coherent system. That meaning, which informs the work of Ginzburg, is open to another set of objections, at least when it is used to interpret specific texts and situations.[11]

What qualifies as folklore may have originated in systems, sometimes learned, sometimes not, that long since disintegrated. In 19th century England, many persons became critical of beliefs concerning nature that seemed "the traditionary sympathies of a most rustic ignorance." But as Keith Thomas has recently observed, some of these beliefs were lore "derived from classical sources, like Pliny's *Natural History*, and were learned errors rather than vulgar ones." And Thomas goes on to observe that "it is often hard to tell how seriously these notions were held and how widely . . . let alone whether they fitted together into one coherent cosmology or are better regarded as isolated 'super-stitions,' long severed from their original moorings in an integrated view of the world."[12] Peter Burke has other reasons, like the role of intermediaries, for being skeptical of folklore's purity. As Burke and others note, English ballads, once thought to be the products of a self-contained oral tradition, turn out to have depended for transmission on the activity of printers.[13] When scrutinized so closely, folklore, and the folk, lose some of the innocence they were accorded in the 19th century.

Still, it may be possible to peel the onion until we reach a layer that is "of the people." This is a task or problem with every source we use. Several of the essays in *Understanding Popular Culture* are notable for using sources that have never been fully exploited. Clive Holmes, for example, examines English witchcraft through court records. He is well aware of the difficul-ties: the witchcraft records arose from a "most complex social process." The actors and informants spoke for and represented different social levels. But Holmes persists, ending with an in-ventory of beliefs he labels "popular." It requires a specialist to evaluate his list, though to my eye the affinity between women and the Devil appears as much a theme of learned as of popular belief. His essay is impressive in its cautions. To him it is clear that interchange was taking place, and he rightly adds that popular belief was not "unchanging" and "inert."

A third direction in which these essays move is to define popu-lar culture as the culture of the "subordinate classes." No one in this volume argues sharply for this point of view, though it in-forms all of these essays. It is a point of view with political as well as methodological implications. In our day, it is the historian of radical or "Left" persuasion who seems especially committed to uncovering the culture of the people. "In the past," Carlo Ginzburg remarks in his preface to *The Cheese and the Worms*,

historians could be accused of wanting to know only about "the great deeds of kings," but today this is certainly no longer true. More and more they are turning toward what their predecessors passed over in silence, discarded, or simply ignored. 'Who built Thebes of the seven gates?' Bertolt Brecht's 'literate worker' was already asking. The sources tell us nothing about these anonymous masons, but the question retains all its significance.[14]

In their different fashions, Natalie Davis and E. P. Thompson have made the same claim of significance, and there are echoes of that claim in several of the essays here. To recognize the "social creativity of the so-called inarticulate" is now almost a necessity for those who go in search of popular belief.[15] So, too, we owe to this tradition the important argument that the culture of the people had coherence and integrity; that it was not a culture lacking order or composed of fragments of "elite" belief.

In recent years, Natalie Davis has been especially insistent that the people were not passive ciphers; even if the people learned from clergy and their like, the process of consumption was a process of re-working and revision. Any theory of popular culture, Davis argues, must acknowledge the competence of the lower orders, a competence so often denied them by elite groups in the past.[16] This shift in point of view has led to the important recognition that popular culture embodies social protest. The play of carnival inverts the ordinary rules of social control; the rituals of the Corpus Christi dramas may ridicule authority.[17] The decay of these rituals, or their outright termination, may signal a new phase of efforts to control the people. The reform of popular culture has, therefore, a class dimension. Control could be so total that "popular culture" became the creation of a ruling group. Two of the essays in this volume, those by Gunther Löttes and Richard Trexler, trace the progress of such domination.

In these two essays, as in several others, the history of popular culture is joined with the history of social structure. Too often this is not the case, and especially among the literary historians who otherwise have done so much to demarcate the "popular." But in heeding social structure, we cannot use it to distinguish what was popular from what was not. Culture lived more freely than any one-to-one relationship can recognize. Another difficulty is to tell when protest was mere "play" or when it was a real instrument of transformation. Löttes echoes Peter Burke and Natalie Davis in pointing out the "ambivalent potential" of ritual play. Carnival could at once be social protest *and* social control; elites may willingly allow such play in order to release tensions that could otherwise be threatening. Ritual may enforce and not disturb the boundaries of a social order. Davis has it both ways in her celebrated study of the charivari — which leaves us still uncertain as to the means of differentiating protest from control.[18]

The argument for understanding popular culture in relation to the "dominant" and "subordinate" classes has one other limitation. It may seem to preclude sharing, compromise, and interchange. I say "seem to," since any category implicitly contains its opposite and since historians like Ginzburg have been quick to say that they acknowledge interchange. But something is at issue here; almost all these essays comment on it in giving so much emphasis to interchange. Consider the examples, both here and in other studies. The bourgeois reader bought and read the same chapbooks and almanacs as did the *menu peuple.* Everyone attended carnival. Christianity of the late middle ages incorporated many compromises, as in the overlap between the prodigy and miracle. Apparitions, relics, and the like appealed to groups throughout society. Stories and motifs could descend from learned culture or move up. The Bible, once it had been translated into the vernacular, became a book for everyone. In an essay notable for its richness of description, Mary O'Neill shows how priests in 16th century Italy were caught in an ambivalent culture, partly learned, partly folkloric.

It is instructive to read *The Cheese and the Worms* with this ambivalence in mind. Ginzburg seems to argue for the separation of elite belief and popular culture. Certainly he proposes (and here the context is in part the difficult task of authenticating folk belief) that there was an "autonomous oral tradition," a lore maintained among the peasants. But Menocchio, the miller whose unorthodox cosmogony got him into trouble with the Inquisition, was a reader of books, a circumstance that leads Ginzburg to acknowledge "a reciprocal influence between the culture of subordinate and ruling classes." Indeed, the story may be one of more indebtedness to elite culture than Ginzburg would prefer.[19] Similarly, it is instructive to reflect on Peter Burke's *Popular Culture in Early Modern Europe;* for Burke, though less committed at the outset to the notion of dominant and subordinate classes, puts increasing emphasis on the role of intermediaries and even comes to argue that the culture of the carnival and chapbooks was common to all groups. In keeping with this argument, he construes the clergy (he is speaking of the friars in particular) as ambiguously "bicultural, men of the university as well as men of the market-place."[20]

This rethinking comes to something of a climax in Roger Chartier's remarks on "Culture as Appropriation," which represents the fourth and last direction taken by these essays. The cumulative weight of doubts and difficulties leads Chartier to propose a major change in how we conceive popular culture. Any theory that assigns cultural artifacts to some specific social level, labeling one pile "popular," and another "elite," collapses in the face of the evidence. For Chartier, the immediate evidence is the *livrets bleus*, the so-called "popular books" of the 17th and 18th centuries that historians of *livre et societé* have made famous. To regard these books as "of the people" is, he argues, a mistake. They circulated among the urban bourgeoisie before they reached the peasants; in effect they drew readers from most social classes. In content, the *livrets bleus* were a composite. Chartier finds in their intellectual confusion and eclecticism another reason for rejecting the assumption that popular culture inheres in certain "sets of text, gestures, and beliefs." Generalizing from these books, he argues that popular culture and popular religion embody a "cultural complexity" that we too often simplify or overlook. The *livrets bleus* comprise a "mixed corpus, containing elements of diverse origins." So too does popular religion, which "at the same time [is] both acculturated and acculturating." His conclusion is emphatic: "We must replace the study of cultural sets that were considered as socially pure with another point of view that recognizes each cultural form as a mixture, whose constituent elements meld together indissolubly."

From this recognition flows the argument for "culture as appropriation." Since the meaning of "popular" does not automatically reside in certain texts and practices, the historian must turn to studying the uses (the patterns of consumption) that were made of artifacts or practices accessible to many. The act of reading will vary from one milieu to the next; and in these patterns lie the basis for a new history of popular culture. This is a history that makes much of sharing, compromise, and interchange. But it is also a history of ordinary people and their powers to adapt, trespass, and subvert whatever is directed at them.

Chartier's is an important position. Our sources may not always permit a history of "appropriation," and some may still insist that certain themes or practices were unequivocally popular. It may be, also, that books are singularly well served by this interpretation; few artifacts are so multiple in their signification or so dependent on the viewpoint of the user. Yet this is true of ritual as well, and Chartier's interpretation opens out into a history of popular religion as those meanings that the people gave to certain sacraments and celebrations.[21]

I shall close by reaffirming the elusiveness of popular culture. Its boundaries shift in response to many kinds of circumstances: the changing program of elites and their zeal to reform the people; the social context, be it one of villages or cities or the rise of central states; the economic context and the types of work; the strength or weakness of alternative traditions; the possibilities for compromise and play. It takes several axes of measurement to comprehend these multiple dimensions; no one theory, no one set of terms, will do. Let me therefore summarize the major possibilities, noting that we sometimes confront contradictions.

First, culture is a repertory of languages. I mean not only the spoken and the written word, but the codes embedded in a thousand different practices – the naming of plants,[22] the characterizations of madness, the rituals of the Church, the arrangements of space, the iconography applied to gravestones. Natalie Davis has spoken of her recognition

that forms of associational life and collective behavior are cultural artifacts. ... A journeymen's initiation rite, a village festive organization, an informal gathering of women for a lying-in or of men and women for story-telling, or a street disturbance could be "read" as fruitfully as a diary, a political tract, a sermon, or a body of laws.[23]

The historian of popular culture must ceaselessly expand upon this recognition. Codes lie buried in the most unassuming of phenomena; and in the search for them we need the help of many other disciplines: folklore, literary criticism, cultural anthropology, sociology, linguistics.[24]

Second, culture contains codes that "represent" society. Social order, whether real or hoped for, is revealed in witchcraft accusations, the nomenclature for bees,[25] and rituals like the charivari. In decoding these languages, historians of popular culture work in creative tension with social historians, for they never assume that a one-to-one relationship exists between their codes and the structure of society.

Third, the languages that comprise culture are very old, persisting less as formal systems than as decayed fragments. I do not mean to deny intellectual coherence to popular culture. But I am struck by the extraordinary tenacity of certain languages or myths, and by the mingling that occurs among them.[26] Chapbooks are a case in point. Another is the world of "magic" that Keith Thomas has described. I want to reemphasize the point on which I quoted Thomas previously; everywhere we look, we find fragments of an older lore, and sometimes these are *simply* bits of decayed systems. The intellectual historian delights in recreating intellectual order. But the logic of popular culture is not so neat and tidy. How could it be, when things are so pell-mell?

It is not easy to reconcile the tenacity of these codes with their role in "representing" social structure. Both are true, though contradictory.

Fourth, the languages that make up culture are always in motion. They invade books and go wherever books are carried; they circulate as stories handed down for generations; they disappear down some back road, then suddenly return to the main highway — I think here of prophecy and visions of the coming kingdom.[27] To map these routes is an exacting task, for we really do not know how culture is communicated or where it runs into firm boundaries. Do some codes circulate among the people but not elsewhere? At issue here is the purity of folklore, of oral tradition, and even, for that matter, of "learned" culture. Again we face a contradiction: languages, like water, seem to seep through every barrier, yet still we want to emphasize their separation and autonomy.

Fifth, it is always in the interest of some group to place limits on the range of languages, to set up fences, guards, and priests who control sacred symbols. The history of popular culture becomes, of necessity, a history of all such efforts to control or reform the culture of the people. Sometimes, as with the rise of Methodism, a new style or language escapes from its creators and becomes a language of the people. Yet we must also recognize that reform movements often failed; reform is not, therefore, identical with domination. The groups so often charged with seeking domination, the clergy, the bourgeoisie, the learned, often faced in two directions, like the priests described by O'Neill.

We must not simplify their own confusion, as if they knew exactly how to line up culture and society.

Sixth, languages are playful. To the structuralist, the Freudian, the symbolist, the student of folklore and mythology, culture is protean. Historians of popular culture may not agree with any of the theories that lead up to this conclusion, but their subject matter forces them to recognize a "logic of ambivalence" in much of their materials. Money, sex, medicine, ritual, proverbs, prophecy, how marvelously ambivalent these all turn out to be, and how interlaced with one another! Let us leave to learned culture, and to its historians, a clarity of meaning and a crisp set of boundaries, enforced through categories such as "Calvinism" and "The Enlightenment." For us there is the play of culture, the priest who heals by using "superstitious" remedies, the carnival and its inversions, the almanac with its predictions (themselves a form of play), and the "man of signs" descended from astrology. Meanings are prolific.

But let this not discourage. Culture, as a saying goes, is what your butcher would have if he were your surgeon. United in opposing such sharp distinctions, united in their sympathy for those who in the past were people without history, the historians of popular culture whose essays follow are equally united in their recognition of compromise, fluidity, and interchange, and from this recognition draw their several versions of the past.

I am grateful to Steven Kaplan for his advice and criticism.

## NOTES

1. The phrase is Peter Burke's, in *Popular Culture in Early Modern Europe* (New York: 1978), chap. 3.
2. Arnaldo Momigliano, "Popular Religious Belief and the Late Roman Historians," in G. J. Cuming and Derek Baker, eds., *Popular Belief and Practice*, Studies in Church History, VIII (Cambridge: 1972), p. 8.
3. Richard Dorson, *The British Folklorists* (London: 1968), p. 12.
4. The English situation is described in John Redwood, *Reason, Ridicule and Religion: The Age of Enlightenment in England* (London: 1976), and in Keith Thomas, *Religion and the Decline of Magic* (London: 1971).
5. David Vincent, "The Decline of the Oral Tradition," in Robert Storch, ed., *Popular Culture in Nineteenth Century Britain* (London: 1982).

6. Burke, *Popular Culture in Early Modern Europe*, p. 9.
7. M. T. Clanchy, *From Memory to Written Record: England 1066–1307* (Cambridge, Mass.: 1979), pp. 177–82.
8. Jean-Claude Schmitt, "Les traditions folkloriques dans la culture medievale," *Archives de Sciences Sociales des Religions* 52 (1981), pp. 5–20; Natalie Z. Davis, "Some Themes and Tasks in the Study of Popular Religion," in Charles Trinkaus with Heiko A. Oberman, eds., *The Pursuit of Holiness in Late Medieval and Renaissance Religion,* Studies in Medieval and Reformation Thought, X (Leiden: 1974), pp. 307–10, 336.
9. *Motif-Index of Folk-Literature*, 6 vols. (Bloomington, Ind.: 1955).
10. C. Grant Loomis, *White Magic: An Introduction to the Folklore of Christian Legend* (Cambridge, Mass.: 1948). Criticism of Loomis is noted in Richard Kieckhefer, *European Witch Trials: Their Foundations in Popular and Learned Culture, 1300–1500* (Berkeley and Los Angeles: 1976), p. 154.
11. Cf. Valerio Valieri's review of *The Cheese and the Worms* in *Journal of Modern History* 54 (1982), pp. 139–43.
12. Keith Thomas, *Man and the Natural World* (London: 1983), pp. 76–77. The initial quotation is Wordsworth, as cited in Thomas.
13. Burke, *Popular Culture in Early Modern Europe*, chap. 3; Robert S. Thomson, "The Development of the Broadside Ballad Trade and Its Influence upon the Transmission of English Folksongs" (Ph.D. diss., Cambridge, 1974), a citation I owe to David Vincent.
14. Carlo Ginzburg, *The Cheese and the Worms*, trans. John and Anne Tedeschi (Harmondsworth, U.K.: 1982), p. xiii.
15. Natalie Z. Davis, *Society and Culture in Early Modern France* (Stanford, Calif.: 1975), p. 122.
16. Davis, "Some Themes and Tasks," pp. 308, 313.
17. Davis, *Society and Culture in Early Modern France*, chap. 4; Mervyn James, "Ritual, Drama and Social Body in the Late Medieval English Town," *Past and Present* 98 (1983), pp. 3–29.
18. Burke, *Popular Culture in Early Modern Europe*, pp. 199–204.
19. Ginzburg, *The Cheese and the Worms*, pp. 154–55.
20. Burke, *Popular Culture in Early Modern Europe*, p. 70.
21. John Bossy, "Blood and Baptism: Kinship, Community, and Christianity in Western Europe from the Fourteenth to the Seventeenth Centuries," in Derek Baker, ed., *Sanctity and Secularity: The Church and the World*, Studies in Church History, X (Oxford: 1973), pp. 129–44.
22. Thomas, *Man and the Natural World*, pp. 72ff.
23. Davis, *Society and Culture in Early Modern France*, pp. xvi-xvii.
24. "Language" may seem too ideal, too remote from "behavior," as a term to encompass all that must pass as popular culture. But I want to insist that language is merely a word for patterned meanings, and these meanings may be found – are found – in the chests carved by folk artisans, in ritual play; in short, in every sort of behavior and material artifacts.
25. Thomas, *Man and the Natural World*, p. 62.
26. Demonstrations of this point include R. W. Scribner, *For the Sake of*

*Simple Folk: Popular Propaganda for the German Reformation* (Cambridge: 1981), especially pp. 126ff.

27. J. F. C. Harrison, *The Second Coming: Popular Millenarianism 1780–1850* (London: 1979).

# The Learned and Popular Dimensions
# of Journeys in the Otherworld
# in the Middle Ages

JACQUES LE GOFF

For the past twenty years or so, historians of European culture
from antiquity to the Industrial Revolution (from the 4th to the
19th centuries) have interested themselves in what they call
"popular" culture. They have oscillated between two methods of
interpreting the corpus they happen to be considering, whether
it be made up of texts, rituals, or gestures.[1] One method emphasizes the cultural object by demanding that the corpus itself
explicate the nature and meaning of its culture, whether through
structural analysis or content analysis, or both simultaneously.
Since a culture almost never makes itself known in a raw or
pure form, this attitude to cultural objects precipitates a hierarchic-
ally organized opposition between "learned" culture and "popular" culture, "high" culture and "popular" culture, "dominant"
culture and "dominated" culture, the culture of the "elite" and
that of "subordinate classes" or "subcultures," and so on. The
second method of interpretation, meanwhile, concentrates on
the actors, seeking its definition of what was popular in attitudes
vis-à-vis cultural objects, in the way cultural products were con-
sumed in a given period and by a particular group of actors.
   It is appropriate and even easy to criticize the first model
when its exponents start out by postulating the existence of a
"popular" culture for which proof remains to be given. But their
method does furnish solid points of departure in two systems of

reference whose empirical value is beyond question. The first such system is that of "genres" of "texts," texts that may be written, oral, or composed of physical gestures.[2] Despite their unavoidably uncertain boundaries, the fabliau, the vision, the exemplum, the tale, the song, the oath, the carnival, the charivari, the *sotie*, all provide safe bases for analysis. The second system is that which folklorists have been working on since the 19th century. They have compiled inventories that, despite some questionable classifications, permit us to identify in more or less "objective" fashion the materials on which we can base an analysis of the "popular."[3] Two obvious examples are *The Types of the Folktale* by Aarne and Thompson, and Stith Thompson's *Motif-Index of Folk-Literature.*[4]

However, this second strategy seems to present at least two sets of serious difficulties. The first concerns the near-impossibility of transferring to the study of the past those methods of observation, interrogation, and quantification that sociologists of contemporary society use. How does one identify the "social groups" whose behavior one wants to study? The second derives from the fundamentally questionable character of the conceptual tools involved. Is it not dangerous to isolate the "channels of reproduction, reception, and communication" from the conditions that produce cultural objects?[5] It is the entire process that is important; even though the social milieux of production are in general easier to locate and define, those of consumption also demand investigation. The division of society into categories of analysis is a delicate matter in the case of contemporary societies; in the case of the societies of the past, the anachronistic transfer of modern concepts — especially that of class structure — and the confusion of the conceptual classifications of past actor and modern analyst set innumerable traps for the unwary.[6]

I note without completely endorsing the critical views of Pierre Bourdieu. "There are those who believe in the existence of a 'popular' culture," he writes. "The very phrase is an alliance of words through which one imposes, like it or not, the dominant definition of a culture. Such observers must not expect to find any more than scattered fragments of some more or less ancient learned culture (such as medical knowledge). These fragments are obviously selected and reinterpreted according to the fundamental principles of the class habitus, and are integrated into the holistic vision of the world it engenders. Observers must not expect to find the 'counter-culture' to which they refer, for no culture is *deliberately* erected to oppose the dominant culture, or consciously held as a counter-code or as a way of professing a separate way of life."[7]

If this criticism is appropriate, it applies especially to the working-class culture to which Bourdieu refers. It is quite obvious that the expression "popular culture" is related to "the dominant definition of culture," as is the term "superstitious" – indeed, that last term is even more deeply marked by the ideological imprint of learned culture. Yet the very historical context that shapes us, and from which we have not yet extricated ourselves, obliges us to begin with this vocabulary. Though it may be true that "popular culture" carries the burden of numerous "scattered fragments of learned culture," it cannot be reduced to a mere inventory of these shards. I stress that popular culture manifests its originality in what it does with the fragments concerned. If "learned" culture manipulates "popular" culture, then "popular" culture picks and chooses from "learned" culture at will. Thus what the historian attempts to identify, and what he or she actually identifies, is not simply some "counter-culture." Rather, it is a different *kind* of culture, which often stems from historical situations where defense against "learned" culture was in many ways essential. If I had an epistemological principle to offer, it would be the specificity of the historical context.

But to approach the "popular" by studying cultural channels has one great advantage: it captures the history of the culture as it moves and changes, as it functions. In so doing we discover history.

To oppose the two cultures one against the other tends to reduce "popular" culture to one that "superior" culture essentially dominates, manipulates, and uses. From this perspective learned culture destroys, deforms, or obliterates popular culture. It shapes popular culture from above whether "above" is the church, the aristocracy, or, later, the bourgeoisie. Under these circumstances the historian can only recover popular culture when it has been esthetically tamed, when it retains merely "the beauty of the dead."[8]

The study of the cultural behavior of ordinary people, on the other hand, often reveals "a relationship of defiance and of

defense regarding the dominant messages."[9] It is certainly hard
to come to terms with the existence, the true nature, and the
significance of "popular" cultural behavior in past times – difficult for the 19th century, it is ever more arduous before the
16th century as history's silences progressively muffle our understanding. Nevertheless, if one can identify a domain of "popular"
culture (mixed with and shaped by learned culture though it may
be) it becomes possible to evaluate its role as a producer as well as
a consumer of culture.

In this article I attempt to merge the methods of the two
approaches outlined above in order to define the interactions of
learned and popular culture. My field is the global society of the
Occident in the Middle Ages, my concentration a literary genre:
medieval accounts of journeys in the otherworld.

## 1. THE GENRE AND THE CORPUS.

The corpus is made up of a selection of narrative accounts of
journeys in the otherworld, from the 7th century to the early
14th century. This is the list:

1.  *Vision of Barontus*, a monk from the monastery of Longore-
    tus (Saint Cyran, near Bourges), written shortly after the
    vision in 678 or 679 (*MGH, Scriptores Rerum Merovingi-
    carum*, 5:377–94).
2.  *Vision of Bonellus*, a monk whose account was narrated by
    the Spanish abbot Valerius. Valerius died in the last decade
    of the 7th century (*PL*, 87, cols. 433–35).
3.  *Vision of the monk of Wenloch* (ca. 717), narrated by Saint
    Boniface (*MGH Epistolae*, 3:252–57).
4.  *Visions of Saint Fursey* and of the pious layman *Drythelm*,
    described by Bede in the *Historia ecclesiastica gentis Anglo-
    rum*, completed in 731 (3:19 and 5:12).
5.  *Vision of Wettinus*, a monk who died at Reichenau in 824,
    written by the abbot Hetto (*PL*, 105, cols. 771–780, and
    *MGH, Poetae latini aevi carolini*, vol. 2).
6.  *Vision of Charles the Fat*, of the last decade of the 9th
    century. It was recorded by Hariulf, around 1100, in his
    *Chronique de l'Abbaye de Saint-Riquier* (ed. F. Lot, Paris:

1894, pp. 144–48); by William of Malmesbury in the 12th century in his *De gestis regum Anglorum* (ed. W. Stubbs, 1:112–16); and by Vincent of Beauvais in his *Speculum* in the 13th century.

7. *The vision of the Mother of Guibert of Nogent*, in the *De Vita Sua*, at the beginning of the 12th century (ed. E. R. Labande, Paris: 1981, pp. 148–58).

8. *The vision of the monk of Monte Cassino, Alberic of Settefrati*, written down around 1130 with the help of Peter the Deacon (ed. Mauro Inguanez, in *Miscellanea Cassinese*, 11 (1932), pp. 83–103).

9. The *Vision of Tnugdal*, an Irish knight, related by a monastic writer in 1149.[10]

10. The *Purgatorium Sancti Patricii*, written down between 1180 and 1220 and probably closer to 1180, by an English Cistercian, H. of Saltrey.[11]

11. *The Vision of Turchill* (1206), probably the work of the Cistercian Ralph of Cogeshall. It was taken up again by the Benedictines of Saint Albans Roger of Wendover (died in 1236) in his *Flores historiarum*, and Matthew Paris (died in 1259) in his *Chronica majora*.[12]

12. *La Divina Commedia* by Dante (early 14th century).

In general terms, each of these accounts relates a *vision*. They belong, therefore, to a genre that thrived during the Middle Ages, especially in the monastic environment.[13] Together, they constitute a particularly important variety of these visions: narrative accounts of journeys in the otherworld. These accounts develop from three traditions. The first is an antique tradition of tales of descent into the netherworld. The tradition is bounded on the one hand by tales of the judgment of an Egyptian hero by the King of the Underworld, Nergal, and especially the journeys through hell of Assyro-Babylonian heroes, Our-Nammou, prince of Our, and Enkidou in the *Epic of Gilgamesh*; and on the other hand by the famous descent of Eneas into Hades in the 6th book of Vergil's *Aeneid*.[14] The second is accounts of journeys in the otherworld from the Judeo-Christian apocalyptic tradition, between the 2nd century B. C. and the 3rd century A. D. This tradition was extended by Greek and Latin versions of Hebrew, Syriac, Coptic, Ethiopian, and Arabic text.[15] The third is "barbarian" accounts — especially Celtic, and more particularly Irish — of journeys to the otherworld.[16]

The two latter traditions are not merely precedents for the medieval visions but are genuine sources for them. More accurately, the visions of the Middle Ages extend the traditions, often by blending the two types of sources; moreover, the third, "barbarian" tradition is known to us only through medieval versions, the anterior pagan or semipagan versions having belonged to an oral tradition.

In most cases, the hero, who may be a monk or a layman (a great character as, in another vision, Charlemagne and, in our corpus, Charles the Fat; a knight like the Irishmen Tnugdal and Owen in *Saint Patrick's Purgatory*; or a peasant like Drythelm or Turchill), is transported during his sleep to the otherworld where he is guided by a saint (often Paul or Peter) or an angel (most often an archangel, Gabriel or Raphael). He visits first the premises of hell, where he is terrified by the cold and the heat, by dreadful mountains and valleys, by rivers of fire and lakes of molten metal populated by monsters, snakes, and dragons, and where he witnesses the awful torments inflicted by monstrous beasts and loathsome demons upon the dead (souls endowed with the appearance of a body sensitive to tortures). Then he experiences the places of paradise, where he admires fragrant, blossoming meadows, houses built with gold, silver, and precious stones, and troups of luminous deceased singing marvelous songs among angels shining with beauty. This image of the otherworld is comprised of several places, several "receptacles of souls," according to a more or less disordered configuration. The infernal part is often subdivided into an upper gehenna through which the visionary travels and a lower gehenna of which the traveler only sees the opening, the terrifying mouth of the pit. The paradisiac part is often divided into regions — sometimes separated by walls — progressively more luminous and fragrant. At the end of the 12th century, with the *Purgatorium Sancti Patricii,* the space of the otherworld becomes organized with an intermediary region between Hell and Paradise, the Purgatory from which the souls, purified by trial and torment, gain access to Paradise.

I have completed this corpus with several texts of a somewhat different nature. Some that belong to the Celtic tradition remain close to the pre-Christian models that surface in them. They describe voyages in which the successive sojourns differ from those carried out in the Christian Hell and Paradise. Islands populated with supernatural beings, awesome or enchanting, with frightening or seductive wonders are separated by seas filled with monsters and ordeals. In this realm of the dead, nonetheless, joy and delight often outweigh fear or evil: the *Voyage of Bran* and the *Navigation of Saint Brendan*[17] and, in particular, a vision of a journey to Paradise that I will discuss further on.

I have also added to the corpus the first version of a theme that will become very successful at the end of the Middle Ages and during the Renaissance, the Land of Cokaygne.[18] Indeed, it also concerns a journey through an imaginary world filled with marvels, a world of plenty, of idleness – a world turned upside down.

## 2. THE SYSTEM OF INTERACTION BETWEEN THE LEARNED AND THE POPULAR.

The learned character of the texts making up this corpus is obvious. Their authors were clerics, their language is Latin, and most of them are crammed with bookish reminiscences and quotations drawn particularly from Judeo-Christian apocalyptic literature. Emerging from a monastic environment, they were at first destined for that specific setting.

But they are also close to popular culture, as the presence of important elements of these texts in the catalogues and repertories of folklore demonstrates. Thus, the themes of these narrative accounts can be found in Stith Thompson's *Motif-Index of Folk-Literature*, where the motif of "other world journeys" inaugurates the chapter on Marvels and covers its first two hundred entries: F0-F199. The essential characteristics and many secondary themes of our accounts correspond to themes recorded in the *Motif-Index*: F.1 (journey to otherworld as dream or vision), F.5 (journey to otherworld as penance), F.7 (journey to otherworld with angel), F.10 (journey to upper world). F.11 (journey to heaven – upper-world paradise), F.52 (ladder to upper world – this is the theme of Jacob's ladder), F.80 (journey to lower world), F.81 (descent to lower world of dead – Hell, Hades), F.92 (pit entrance to lower world), F.92.4 (entrance to lower world through mountain), F.93.0.2.1 (well entrance to lower world), F.95 (path to lower world), F.101.4 (escape from lower world by magic), F.102 (accidental arrival in lower world).

Accounts such as the *Voyage of Bran*, the *Navigation of Saint Brendan*, or the *Land of Cokaygne* refer to other motifs of the *Motif-Index*: F.110 (journey to terrestrial otherworlds), F.111 (journey to earthly paradise), F.111.1 (journey to Isle of Laughter), F.116.1 (voyage to the Land of Youth), F.123 (journey to land of little men – pygmies).

The localization of the other world (F.130 location of otherworld) involves either categories of places defined by physical geography (F.131 otherworld in hollow mountain, F.132.1 earthly paradise on mountain) or countries richly endowed with the geographic supernatural, such as Ireland (F.130.3 Ancient Ireland as location of otherworld).[19]

Access to the otherworld (F.150 access to otherworld) also reveals traits common to both the world of folklore and our medieval corpus: F.150.1 (entrance to otherworld guarded by monsters or animals), F.151.1 (perilous path to otherworld), and especially the theme of the bridge (F.152 bridge to otherworld).[20]

The nature and the activities of the otherworld are divided, in folklore as well as in the medieval texts, between the vision of a universe filled with happiness and satiety (F.162.2.2 rivers of wine in otherworld, F.162.2.3 rivers of honey in otherworld, F.169.8 abundance in otherworld, F.169.9 pleasant fragrance in otherworld, F.173 otherworld land of happiness, F.173.1 otherworld land of pleasure) and that of a world filled with dread and ordeals (F.171.2 broad and narrow road in otherworld, F.171.6 mysterious punishments in otherworld).

Finally – and we shall see the problems this raised for medieval authors of journeys to the beyond – the otherworld is a universe outside of time and removed from the reaches of death (F.172. no time, no birth, no death in otherworld).

One could find the same community of motifs regarding the journey to the otherworld in the case of demons (F.400–F.499 spirits and demons) and of fire (*Motif-Index* 6:286–89).

Likewise, most of these medieval accounts resemble the tale-types in Aarne and Thompson's classification. For example T. 301 The three stolen princesses includes a section (II) entitled a "descent into the lower world"; T. 460A and T. 461A are voyages to discover the secrets of the beyond (The journey to God to receive reward; The journey to the deity for advice or repayment). The journey to the otherworld is at the heart of the tale of the two friends "in life and death," in which the survivor follows the one who died into the otherworld (T. 470 Friends in life and death). The bridge to the beyond is the object of T. 471 (The bridge to the other world). The *Land of Cokaygne* has become T. 1930 (*Schlaraffenland – Land of Cokaygne*).

While these correspondences are interesting, what matters is to identify, analyze, and interpret the relationships between learned and popular culture in these accounts.

Jean-Claude Schmitt has given an interesting schema of such relations in the matter of a journey to Paradise recently studied by the Italian ethnologist Giuseppe Gatto.[21] It concerns a 13th century text that is doubtless the most ancient version of Aarne and Thompson's T. 470. A young lord invites a friend to his wedding, an old man (an angel) dressed in white and riding a white mule who, in return, invites him to a feast to take place three days after the young man's wedding. Passing through a narrow strait, the bridegroom reaches a vast plateau covered with flowers, with fruit trees stocked with innumerable birds, where his host and a following of youths all dressed in white greet him. After he has gone through three "abodes," they welcome him to a fourth where he knows an ineffable happiness that lasts three hundred years. This period of time seems to him to have lasted no longer than three hours or, at most, a day's length. But when he returns home, his castle has been turned into a monastery, his wife and his parents are long dead, and when the prince "who once had been lost" brings to his mouth a piece of bread, he becomes an old man and dies.

Most extraordinary and highly interesting is that the anonymous author of this text, about whom we are told only that he is attached to a monastery in northern Italy, relates how he came to know this story. The cleric states precisely that he has only "written this story down," that he is not its "source" (*fons ejus*), but just the "channel" (*canalis*) by which it is transmitted. The one who had related it to him was an "*illiteratus*" who had not himself, "as the vulgar say, sucked it from his finger" (*nec ipse, ut vulgo dicirur, ex suo digito suxit*), that is, invented it; he had heard it from a "*litteratus*," retaining only what was in the vernacular and forgetting what was said in the "other language," probably meaning in Latin (*sed a literato remudiens materne lingue verba retinuit, alterius lingue vocabula retinere non potuit*). The scribe judged the story worthy of being written down but, all the while denying having altered anything in it, he is describing the double process of Christianization and of learned formalization to which he has submitted this folkloric account: "I have added to it nothing more than what writers are allowed to do; if I have ordered the events into sequences, if I have aptly mixed old things with new ones, if I have added the wood of Moses, the salt of Elisha, and finally the wine of Christ made from water, I have done so not to deceive but to enhance the elegance of the account."[22]

This admission concerning sources allows us to identify a schema of transmission in four phases. The first three phases remain in the oral realm, whereas the fourth passes into a written relation. First, there is the oral folk tradition, then a "*litteratus*," a learned cleric, then an "*illiteratus*," and, finally, a "writer," an anonymous "*scriptor*" of the second half of the 13th century.

We do not know how the man of "popular" culture altered the learned cleric's account, except that he did not retain that which in the story was probably said in Latin. Concerning the scholarly scribe's transformation of the "*illiteratus*" account, we know it consists of a "literary" and "logical" formalization, a "modernization," and a "Christianization." Regarding the last point, one can identify three probable modifications: the transformation of the psychopomp old man into an angel, the assimilation of the otherworld to the place where "reside Enoch and Elijah," that is, the earthly Paradise, and the conversion of the hero's castle into a monastery.

Two remarks seem in order. First, one suspects that a sizable part of the process described in this text must be applicable to several of the visions belonging to our corpus. Indeed, we are told that the visionary monk related his vision and that it was up to a learned cleric, often the monastery's abbot, to set it down in writing, either dictating it or writing it out himself. From a more or less "illiterate" monk, representing "popular" culture, the account of the journey passed, through the mediation of the "scholarly" writer, to the world of learned culture. We possess a few details of this transition in the case of one of the strangest visions, that of Alberic of Settefrati. Alberic, born around 1100, experienced his vision during an illness when he was ten years of age (he is thus twice "illiterate": he belongs to the simple folk and he is a child). Having entered the monastery of Monte Cassino during the tenure of abbot Gerard (1111–1123), he related his vision to a monk named Guido who transcribed it. But in being passed from hand to hand and from mouth to ear, his account was altered and abbot Senioretto (1127–1137) advised Alberic to rewrite it (that is, to dictate it again) with the help of Peter the Deacon. It is this last version that survives. Here it is clear how the account of a half-educated monk has reached us through several rearrangements, all marked with the learned clerical stamp but borrowing both oral and written forms of transmission. Indeed, one must not forget, regarding this complex process of acculturation during medieval times, that the cultural history of the period was seldom that of a clearcut opposition between popular and learned or between oral and written (these two oppositions are not, of course, one and the same thing). Rather, it took the form of interactions between more or less learned and more or less popular cultural acts and actors.[23]

The second remark concerns the "space" of this acculturation. The tavern and, in particular, the public square have been cited as places of social and cultural exchange during the Middle Ages.[24] One should also stress the role played by monasteries. The intercourse between the "educated" monks and the "uneducated" members of the monastic *familia*, including the equally "rustic" guests of the monastery, as well as the relationships between the monastic "elite" who belonged socially and culturally to the dominant strata of society (and exercised authority in the monastic setting) and "simple," semiliterate monks, must have provided an exceptionally favorable breeding-ground for these forms of acculturation.

I must stress how difficult it is to establish, for these remote periods, the ways in which the folklorization of learned culture took place (contrary to the case at the end of the Middle Ages, when some "popular" works of art facilitate the study of acceptances of, resistance to, and adaptations toward the "learned" models). One can only formulate a few hypotheses.

First, let us try to reconstruct, *backwards*, the text of the 13th century vision of paradise mentioned earlier. It can be safely assumed, for instance, that the psychopomp old man designated

as an angel belongs to folk culture, since angels are generally
presented as "ageless" beings but of a "youthful" countenance.
One cannot forget, however, the tendency of the monastic environment to assimilate the image of the monk and especially the
hermit to that of the angel; the stereotype of the monk is, rather,
that of an old man. This decoding of a cultural palimpsest must,
therefore, be performed prudently.

Second, taking up more recent examples (Carlo Ginzburg's
miller Menocchio, the novels of the *Bibliothèque bleue*), Roger
Chartier has identified the operation of agents of "popular"
culture that I believe are present in the filigree of my medieval
narratives of journeys in the otherworld: "the segmentation of
the text into autonomous units that stand meaningfully by themselves, the decentering of motives, the radicalization of significa-
tions, the analogical treatment of fragments which would have
been deemed unrelated from a more learned point of view, the
literal reading of metaphors,"[25] and, furthermore, "the repetitions
and recalls, the organization [of the text] according to a restricted
number of narrative schemes, the constant revamping of a text
that is never settled."[26] Nevertheless, one should not assume the
existence of a "popular" reading and a "learned" reading, both
unchangeable or almost so, throughout history. From the early
Middle Ages to the Renaissance, the cultural habits of the various
sociocultural categories kept changing and, above all, their inter-
relationships kept modifying themselves. As propounded by Keith
Thomas, the most enduring characteristic of the Middle Ages is a
certain "common mentality" in the domain of culture as well as
of religion.[27] This set of common cultural and mental attitudes
was shared by both the "literate" and the "illiterate," notwithstanding the difference – actually quite important – between the
bilingual clerics, who were conversant in both Latin and the
vernacular, and the monolingual "common people."

Third, Piero Camporesi has eloquently insisted that "the culture
of poverty (and thus almost the entirety of folk-culture) can only
represent the world under the form its epistemological apparatus
made available to it" and that its "cognitive statutes" are different
from those of the intellectual elites "even though the areas of
contamination, the suggestions, the interferences between the
two cultures can be manifold."[28] Thus, if "the *image of the world*
elaborated by the popular mental representations of the prein-

dustrial epoch differs from the classical model utilized by the clerics and the scholars," the same is true for the *image of the otherworld.*[29] Camporesi mentions "the popular optic of the distorted, the inordinate, the hyperbolic (or the miniature), the monstrous, the excessive, the amorphous," an optic in which "the chaotic prevails over a rational design that presupposes a center ... where the relationships between time and space can reverse themselves." Time after time one finds "the compensatory dream projected by the popular utopia conquering an ever-increasing territory from which superior rationality is banned."[30]

Camporesi rightly insists on the specificity of this "oneiric universe." I would emphasize that, even though the dream had become by the Middle Ages a *topos* backed by a long learned tradition, recourse to the dream or the vision opens wide the gates to the flood of the popular imagination. Monastic phantasms are situated at the crossroads of this popular oneirism and the visionary apocalyptic tradition. Dreams, which can hardly be controlled by the Church, unfold freely in the imaginary universe of the beyond.[31] One recognizes in them the compensatory imagination so violently expressed during the Middle Ages (abundancy and sloth as in the Land of Cokaygne, ardent sexual phantasms especially in the *Vision of Wettinus*, the breaking loose of the marvelous as opposed to the miraculous).

What is easier to grasp is how learned culture tends to manipulate folklore, that is, the objects of popular culture. Its action can be briefly characterized in regard to otherworld journeys (provided one can actually discern the "popular" datum under its learned or half-learned disguise).

The essential process is that of *Christianization.* It manifests itself primarily by substituting Christian motifs for pagan elements and conceptions. Though psychopomp beasts are sometimes retained, the guides and the auxiliaries of the journeying hero are transformed into saints and angels. The object or the gesture or the magical word that grants safekeeping in the course of the journey is specifically Christian (the sign of the cross, the name of Jesus). Above all, the places of the beyond have become Christian spaces and the "receptacles" of souls are reduced to three in number: Hell, Heaven, and Purgatory. Occasionally a fourth is added, the Earthly Paradise, and sometimes a fifth or sixth with the limbos (the limbo of the unbaptized, the limbo of the patriarchs).

More importantly, a profound transformation is performed, even more upon fundamental *structures* than on contents. It affects the spatial and temporal framework, the nature of the beyond, and the style of the narrative.

The space of the otherworld is organized and rationalized. The multiplicity of traditional sites, the variety of the "receptacles," their more or less anarchic succession in the course of a rather erratic itinerary (still very much in evidence in the confused structure that the otherworld possesses in the *Vision of Tnugdal*, of the middle of the 12th century), give way to a space divided into the three major areas: Hell and Paradise, plus an intermediate site, Purgatory, each in turn subdivided according to a scholastic partitioning that culminates in the circles and cornices of the *Divine Comedy*. This effort at organizing the space of the otherworld is notable for being exerted at the boundaries: in Saint Patrick's Purgatory, in which the intermediate site is in the process of being constructed, the successive fields through which the traveler in the otherworld passes lack visible limits, extending beyond sight. Even more fundamentally, it is the very process of the *spatialization* of the otherworld, specifically that of Purgatory, which incarnates a spiritual transformation (a purification rather than a situational state), that is worrisome to the learned culture and to ecclesiastical orthodoxy. From Augustine through Thomas Aquinas to the fathers of the Council of Trent, the learned circles of theologians do their best to keep in check this "popular" need to spatialize spiritual life and to localize beliefs.

This effort on the part of learned culture is oriented toward the elimination of the ambiguity or rather the ambivalence characteristic of "popular" culture. As Schmitt correctly noted, scholastic theology refuses to recognize a beyond that would be Purgatory, Heaven, and Hell all at once. The bipartite Hell, consisting of a superior gehenna from which one could ascend and an inferior gehenna into which one could fall forever, and the Celtic otherworld of King Arthur, a composite of exquisite pleasures and trying ordeals, are replaced by eternal sites — Hell and Paradise — separated until Judgment Day by Purgatory, the antechamber to Paradise.

Learned labor to transform the notion of time is particularly intense and significant. Time spent in Purgatory is divided into an objective and a subjective temporality. Objective time can be measured, segmented, manipulated in the fashion of the time that rules the earth; it is a time largely dependent, according to Euclidean principles of "proportionality," on the quantity and the quality of the sins of the deceased, and on the supplications of the survivors. Subjective time is popular time in reverse. Whereas the folkloric traveler experiences a very short period of time in the otherworld, the guest of Purgatory imagines having endured a period of time ten or one hundred times longer.[32]

The difficulty encountered by the clerics of Christianity in allowing an *intermediary* otherworld, for logical as well as ideological reasons, led the Church to a quasi-identification between Hell and Purgatory, to an "infernalization" of Purgatory (as Arturo Graf showed long ago).[33]

Finally, one must not omit the basic manipulation exerted by the style of the learned report upon the radically different esthetic of the folk narrative. The author of the vision examined by Gatto declared that he wished only "to enhance the elegance of the account." But this concern for form on the part of the learned clerics is more than a mere esthetic fancy, more than purely a matter of "literary" taste. It profoundly marks the passage from one world of sensibility and culture to another. One *notices* the learned writer, such as the editor of the vision of Turchill who confers on his otherworld the aspect of a stage-set and transforms his travelers into spectators at the theatre.[34] One may wonder whether this is not at one and the same time a radical rationalization of popular space and an advanced effort to domesticate the narrative ramblings of the folkloric account by way of theatrical confinement.

### 3. OUTLINE OF A SOCIOCULTURAL HISTORY OF JOURNEYS IN THE OTHERWORLD DURING THE MIDDLE AGES.

I shall only sketch a periodization of journeys in the otherworld; a complete periodization would be grounded in a systematic inventory and analysis of all existing texts. As a working hypothesis, the four periods may be characterized in these terms.

1. Before the 7th century, the Church's determination to destroy or occlude folkloric culture, which it assimilated under the label of paganism, has practically wiped out all accounts of journeys to the beyond. A few shreds of the otherworld find their way into certain *Dialogues* of Gregory the Great.
2. The 7th to the 10th centuries are the great era of visions of the beyond. It corresponds to the rapid growth of monasticism and to monastic culture's filtering of resurgent popular elements.
3. During the 11th and 12th centuries, especially during the latter, folklore spreads the visions widely. This is connected with an improved status for the laity.
4. Learned culture's counter-attack unfolds on two levels at once: it rationalizes the beyond and it infernalizes the subterranean otherworld.

Translated by Victor Aboulaffia

NOTES

1. The three main theoretical texts are Peter Burke, "Oblique Approaches to the History of Popular Culture," in C. Bigsby, ed., *Approaches to Popular Culture* (London: 1976), pp. 69–84; Roger Chartier, "La culture populaire en question," in *H. Histoire* no. 8 (1981), pp. 85–96; and Jean-Claude Schmitt, "Les traditions folkloriques dans la culture médiévale: Quelques réflexions de méthode," in *Archives des Sciences Sociales de Religions* no. 52/1 (1981), pp. 5–20. The essential bibliography on the topic can be found in these articles, particularly in Schmitt's.
2. I recognize that one can criticize with cause the notion of *genre* or of literary *form*. For instance, the use made of André Jolles's 1929 work, *Einfache Formen: Legende/Sage/Mythe/Rätsel/Spruch/Kasus/Memorabile/Märchen/Witz* (Darmstadt: 1958), has been disappointing. The blame, however, does not lie in the historically defined forms studied by Jolles, but in the weakness of his use of the concept of "simplicity."
3. One can criticize specifically the notions of *tale-type*, of *motif*, of Proppian *function*, without denying the value of the works of A. Aarne, Stith Thompson, and V. Propp as reference tools.
4. A. Aarne, *Verzeichnis der Märchentypen* (1920, 1928), translated and revised by Stith Thompson (1961, 1964, *FFC* no. 184). The use of the *Index exemplorum: A Handbook of Medieval Religious Tales*, by F. C. Tubach (*FFC* no. 204, Helsinki: 1969), is a more delicate matter, given

the shortcomings of the work (cf. Cl. Brémond, J. Le Goff, and J.-Cl. Schmitt, "L'exemplum," in *Typologie des sources du moyen-âge occidental* [Turnhout: 1982]). Stith Thompson, *Motif-Index of Folk-Literature: A Classification of Narrative Elements in Folktales, Ballads, Myths, Fables and Local Legends*, 6 vols. (Copenhagen: 1955–1958).

5. H. R. Jauss, quoted by Jean Starobinski in his preface to a collection of articles by Jauss, published in French under the title *Pour une esthétique de la réception* (Paris: 1978).

6. On the aporias of naive sociological methods applied to the fabliaux, see M. Th. Lorcin, *Façons de sentir et de penser: Les fabliaux français* (Paris: 1979). However, the sociological perspectives on medieval literature of Erich Kohler remain very suggestive; see especially his "Observations historiques et sociologiques sur la poésie des troubadours," *Cahiers de civilisation médiévale*, 1964, pp. 27–51.

7. Bourdieu, *La distinction: Critique sociale du jugement* (Paris: 1979), p. 459.

8. See the brilliant essay by M. de Certeau, D. Julia, and J. Revel, "La beauté du mort: le concept de culture populaire," *Politique aujourd'hui* (12/1970), pp. 3–23.

9. These expressions belong to Chartier, "La culture populaire," p. 94, addressing the sociologist Richard Hoggart's *La culture du pauvre: Etude sur la style de vie des classes populaires en Angleterre* (Paris: 1970). It concerns England in the 1950s.

10. *Visio Tnugdali*, ed. A. Wagner (Erlangen: 1882). There are many medieval translations into vernaculars, including Icelandic, Russian, and Serbo-Croatian. Cf. Nigel Palmer, *The German and Dutch Translations of the "Visio Tundali"* (Munich: 1975).

11. For the editions of the *Purgatorium Sancti Patricii*, cf. J. Le Goff, *La naissance du Purgatoire*, p. 259, n. 1.

12. *Visio Thurkilli*, ed. P. G. Schmidt, Bibliotheca Teubneriana (Leipzig: 1978). "Chronica Rogeri de Wendover," in *Flores Historiarum* (London: 1887), 2:16–35; and Matthew Paris, *Chronica Majora* (London, 1874), 2:497–511.

13. On the topic of medieval visions, cf. P. Dinzelbacher, *Vision und Visionsliteratur im Mittelalter* (Stuttgart: 1981), and, by the same author, "Die Visionen des Mittelalters, Ein geschichtlicher Umriss," *Zeitschrift für Religions- und Geistesgeschichte* 30 (1978), pp. 116–28, and "Klassen und Hierarchien im Jenseits in Soziale Ordnungen im Selbstverstandnis des Mittelalters," in *Miscellanea Mediaevalia* 12/1 (Berlin and New York: 1979), pp. 20–40. Also, C. J. Holdsworth, "Visions and Visionaries in the Middle Ages," in *History* no. 48 (1963), pp. 141–53; M. Aubrun, "Caractère et portée religieuse et sociale des 'Visiones' en Occident du VIᵉ au XIᵉ siècle," *Cahiers de Civilisation Médiévale* (1980), pp. 109–30. Claude Carozzi is preparing a thesis on the visions of the early Middle Ages; see the overview in "La géographie de l'au-delà et sa signification pendant le haut Moyen-Age," in *Popoli e paesi nella cultura altomedievale*, XXIX Settimana del Centro Italiano di Studi sull'Alto Medioevo (Spoleto: 4/1981, in press).

14. J. Kroll, *Gott und Höll: Der Mythos vom Descensus Kampfe* (Leipzig and Berlin: 1932); F. Bar, *Les routes de l'autre-monde: descente aux enfers et voyages dans l'au-delà* (Paris: 1946).
15. H. H. Rowley, *The Relevance of Apocalyptic: A Study of Jewish and Christian Apocalypses from Daniel to the Revelation* (New York: 1963). The apocalyptic vision that had the greatest influence on medieval visions is the Apocalypse of Paul. Consult particularly Th. Silverstein, *Visio sancti Pauli: The History of the Apocalypse in Latin, Together with Nine Texts* (London: 1935).
16. H. R. Patch, *The Other World, According to Descriptions in Medieval Literature* (Cambridge, Mass.: 1950), and John D. Seymour, *Irish Visions of the Other World* (London: 1930).
17. Kuno Meyer, *The Voyage of Bran, Son of Febal, to the Land of the Living: An Old Irish Saga* (London: 1895), with an appendix including Alfred Nutt, *The Happy Otherworld in the Mythico-romantic Literature of the Irish: The Celtic Doctrine of Re-birth*. See also Antonietta Grignani, *Navigatio Sancti Brendani, La navigazione di San Brandano* (Milan: 1975).
18. *Le fabliau de Cocagne*, of the middle of the 13th century, was edited by V. Väänänen in *Neuphilologische Mitteilungen*, bulletin of the Neophilological Society of Helsinki (1947), pp. 20–32; and reprinted with an Italian translation in Gian Carlo Belle, ed., *Fabliaux: Racconti comici medievali* (Ivrea: 1982), pp. 94–105. Cf. G. Cocchiara, *Il paese di Cuccagna e altri studi di folclore* (Turin, 1980), and *Il mundo a rovescia* (Turin: 1963); C. Hill, *The World Turned Upside Down* (London: 1972); J. Delumeau, *La mort des Pays de Cocagne* (Paris: 1976); R. Chartier and D. Julia, "Le monde à l'envers," *L'Arc* no. 65 (1976), pp. 43–53.
19. Sicily should be added since it refers to F.131 (otherworld in hollow mountain). Cf. Le Goff, *La naissance du Purgatoire*, chap. 6: "Le Purgatoire entre la Sicile et l'Irlande," pp. 241–81.
20. P. Dinzelbacher, "Die Jenseitsbrücke im Mittelalter," Diss., Universität Wien, 104 (Vienna: 1973).
21. Schmitt, *Les traditions folkloriques*, pp. 11–14; G. Gatto, "Le voyage au paradis: la christianisation des traditions folkloriques au Moyen Age," *Annales E. S. C.* (1979), pp. 929–42. The 13th century text was published by J. Schwarzer, "Visionslegende," *Zeitschrift für deutsche Philologie* 13 (1882), pp. 338–51.
22. Schmitt, *Les traditions folkloriques*, pp. 12–13.
23. Cf. Franz H. Bäuml, "Varieties and Consequences of Medieval Literacy and Illiteracy," *Speculum* (1980), pp. 237–65. On yet another cultural intermediary, the curate, cf. L. Allegra, "Il parocco: un mediatore fra alta e bassa cultura in Storia d'Italia," *Annali 4. Intellettuali e potere* (Turin: 1981), pp. 897–947. Allegra starts with the 16th century.
24. I am thinking specifically of Mikhail Bakhtin, *Rabelais and His World* (Cambridge, Mass.: 1968).
25. Chartier, "La culture populaire," p. 92.
26. Ibid., p. 93.

27. K. Thomas, *Religion and the Decline of Magic* (New York: 1971).
28. P. Camporesi, *Il pane selvaggio* (Bologna: 1980); in French, *La pain sauvage: L'imaginaire de la faim de la Renaissance au XVIII$^e$ siècle* (Paris: 1981), p. 87.
29. Ibid., p. 87.
30. Ibid., p. 88. On medieval utopias, see F. Graus, "Social Utopias in the Middle Ages," *Past and Present* 38 (1967), pp. 3−19.
31. J. Le Goff, "Les rêves dans la culture et la psychologie collective de l'Occident médiéval," *Scolies* 1 (1971), pp. 123−30, reprinted in *Pour un autre Moyen Age* (Paris: 1977), pp. 299−306. Also consult V. Lanternari, "Sogno-Visione," *Enciclopedia Einaudi* 13 (Turin: 1981), pp. 94−126.
32. J.-Cl. Schmitt's talk on this theme at the CNRS colloquium on "Christian Time, 3rd-13th Centuries," is to be published.
33. A. Graf, "Artù nell'Etna," in *Leggende, miti e superstizioni del Medio Evo* (Turin: 1925).
34. Henri Rey-Flaud, *Pour une dramaturgie du Moyen Age* (Paris: 1980), pp. 82−83, has compared the Vision of Thurchill to the theatre of the beginning of the 13th century, specifically relating it to the *Jeu de Saint Nicolas* of Jean Bodel of Arras.

# The Witches' Sabbat:
# Popular Cult
# or Inquisitorial Stereotype?

CARLO GINZBURG

In the last fifteen years the study of witchcraft has become a flourishing academic industry. However, we still know much more about the attitudes of the judges and the patterns of persecution in different parts of Europe than we know about witches and witchcraft. The ideological bias that underlies this choice has occasionally been betrayed, as in Hugh Trevor-Roper's contemptuous remarks about "the mental rubbish of peasant credulity and feminine hysteria."[1] More often it has remained implicit. Nevertheless, it must be said that the reconstruction of popular notions of witchcraft, beyond the learned stereotypes described by demonologists and imposed by judges (lay and clerical) through physical and psychological pressure, is a difficult task. It is not always easy to say where methodological difficulties end and criteria of ideologically determined relevance take over.

In the particular case of the witches' sabbat the distinction seems justified. Margaret Murray suggested sixty years ago that the witches' sabbats were gatherings of people who performed rituals connected to a pre-Christian fertility cult;[2] nowadays serious historians reject this interpretation. Norman Cohn's book *Europe's Inner Demons* (1975) authoritatively states the new orthodoxy: the sabbat was the last revival of an ancient negative stereotype that had been projected serially on Jews, early Christians, and medieval heretics. All these sects or groups had been accused of meeting in secret places, mostly during the night, to perform sexual orgies (including incest) and ritual anthropophagy. Inquisitors and demonologists concocted an image of the sabbat that was, from this perspective, only the last link of a chain that started at the very beginning of the Christian era. But does this mean that the witches' sabbat was totally foreign to popular culture?

Murray's interpretation of *all* witches' confessions about the sabbat as descriptions of physical events was certainly absurd – and based on a misreading of the evidence. (For instance, as Cohn has conclusively shown, Murray as she quoted from witches' confessions systematically suppressed all references to nocturnal flights and metamorphoses into animals, incidents that would have made her interpretation rather puzzling.)[3] Ignoring the problem of the physical reality of the witches' sabbat, I shall limit myself to a discussion of its cultural meaning. In other words, I shall try to explore not the *ritual* but the *mythical* dimension of the sabbat image. Maybe the ritual existed only in the inquisitors' minds; but even if that were the case it would be wrong to conclude that the whole sabbat myth was a learned artifact. A confusion of these two levels – mythical and ritual – has prevented a full discussion of the witches' sabbat, insofar as historians have been satisfied with the mere refutation of the so-called "Murray thesis." I think, on the contrary, that many questions about the witches' sabbat are still to be asked even if we provisionally agree that a full-fledged sect of witches never existed.

In a forthcoming book I shall try to show that the witches' sabbat was neither a learned myth (as Cohn argued) nor a popular myth, but a compromise formation – a cultural, not a psychological, compromise. We can distinguish in the sabbat stereotype elements coming from above and elements coming from below. The emergence of this compromise forms a good example of the interrelations between learned and popular culture in preindustrial Europe.

Everyone knows what the sabbat stereotype was. It would be possible to inventory its elements: ointments, metamorphosis into animals, nocturnal flights, gatherings in faraway places, sexual orgies, banquets, homage to the Devil, debasement of the Cross, and so on. It would also be possible to try to reconstruct the cultural origin of each element, but such an approach would be too abstract. After all, the sabbat myth was not a sudden invention but the coherent result of a slow process. The real problem is to reconstruct how the fusion of the stereotype's various elements became possible.

I shall analyze first the inquisitorial image of the sabbat. Cohn's argument that it came from a very old tradition is too internalist and, in fact, begs several questions. First, his stereotype's historical coherence is only apparent: it implies a wide chronological gap and a discontinuity in its content. In the matter of chronology, between the accusations charging the early Christians with performing sexual orgies and ritual anthropophagy and the same accusations against the medieval heretical sects, many centuries passed during which the stereotype was silent. The only exception appears in a sermon against the sect of the Paulicians written by the head of the Armenian church, John of Ojun, at the beginning of the 8th century.[4] Much later, it was echoed in the dialogue *On the Operations of the Demons,* until very recently ascribed to the Byzantine writer Michael Psellos, where the standard accusation is leveled against the Thrakian Bogomiles.[5] The passage is especially important because it included an element that would become part of the Western stereotype — almost the same words were used against various heretical sects, including the Cathars. Those heretics were still accused of practicing anthropophagy; but they were now said to eat the ashes of babies born from sexual intercourse, often of an incestuous nature, that the sect performed in their nocturnal gatherings.[6]

The stereotype was certainly negative, but not aggressive. Medieval heretics were represented as dreadful people, secluded from society, ignoring the basic laws of human life — practicing incest, devouring their own babies — but not, as witches would later be, a physical threat to society as a whole. I do not deny, of course, that certain elements of the sabbat stereotype had previously been imputed to heretics: above all, the homage to the Devil, the abjuration of the Christian faith, and the debasement of the Cross. In order to understand the emergence of the notion of an all-powerful sect of witches threatening society, however, we have to look elsewhere.

My evidence, therefore, will differ from Cohn's. I shall start with the famous lepers' conspiracy discovered in France in 1321.[7]

A rumor suddenly spread in various parts of France that the lepers had attempted to poison wells, fountains, and rivers. Incensed groups of people tried to burn lepers alive. A series of trials began and, jailed and tortured, the lepers confessed their crime.

But the lepers were not alone. Various versions of the conspiracy circulated. It was the lepers; it was lepers stirred up by Jews; it was lepers stirred up by Jews stirred up by Moslem kings. The directors of the leper hospitals confessed that they had gathered many times to plan the conspiracy and had distributed to lepers poisons made of such dreadful things as toads, lizards, and human blood. The purpose of the conspiracy was to spread leprosy and to kill sane people, in order to overturn society: the directors of leper hospitals were dreaming of becoming king of France, duke of Burgundy, and so on. Other evidence emerged: in a letter found in Anjou a Jew wrote to the Moslem king of Jerusalem offering to exchange the kingship over Paris, France, and all Christendom for the Holy Land, which was to revert to the Jewish people. Letters from the Moslem kings of Granada and Tunis stirring up the lepers' and Jews' conspiracy were found in Mâcon and duly authenticated by local notaries.[8] The king of France, Philip the Tall, confiscated all properties owned by leprosaries and ordered all lepers found guilty to be burned; innocent lepers had to live henceforth a life of strict segregation in closed institutions. In different parts of France there were mass murders of Jews. By paying a large ransom to the royal treasury Jews obtained permission to remain in the country for one more year, but in 1323 they were expelled from France.[9]

There is no doubt that a conspiracy was organized in 1321. There were two conspiracies, in fact: the first against the lepers, the second against the Jews. The evidence of these conspiracies lies in fake letters, fake confessions wrung by torture in Inquisitorial trials, and so on. It is worthwhile remembering that Michelet doubted the lepers' guilt (and rejected the accusations against the Jews as fake). During the time of the Dreyfus affair a Catholic scholar, J. M. Vidal, who discovered an extraordinary trial against the director of Pamiers hospital, Guillaume Agassa, emphasized the reality (as well as the ineffectiveness) of the lepers' conspiracy and implied that the Jews could have had a part in it. Some years ago the first editor of the Agassa trial, J. Duvernoy, tried to whitewash the judges (among them Jacques Fournier,

bishop of Pamiers), saying that they had extorted absurd confessions from the defendant in order to rescue him from being
lynched by the crowd.[10] In some ways the conspiracy is still
a burning issue, but detailed analysis of the surviving evidence
shows that in 1321 religious and political authorities deliberately
faked evidence to reinforce a growing hostility from below against
lepers and Jews.

Many links connect the 1321 conspiracy to the emergence
of the inquisitorial image of the witches' sabbat. Lepers and Jews
were accused of placing not only poisons but also charms in wells,
fountains, and rivers; lepers confessed that Jews asked them to
renounce the Christian faith and to debase the Cross; lepers'
gatherings foreshadowed in some ways the witches' nocturnal
gatherings. But the main link is provided by the conspiracy itself —
or by its myth.[11] In an age of crisis (demographic, economic,
political, and religious) marginal groups such as lepers and Jews,
who had been associated in many ways in the public's perception,
were physically segregated or ejected.[12] For the first time in
European history, the chain provided by the conspiracy myth
(devil-Moslem kings-Jews-lepers) connected internal and external
enemies, giving political and religious authorities the opportunity
to purge society on a mass scale. In that chain, witches were still
absent — but not for long.

The second chapter of my story is also famous (or infamous).
In 1348, the start of the Black Death again provoked accusations
that wells and fountains were being poisoned. This time, however,
there was only one target, the classic one: the Jews. The lepers
had disappeared (leprosy was at the time receding throughout
Europe). This new conspiracy had been discovered by the lord
of Chillon, a small town on Lake Geneva. A group of Jews, men
and women who lived in towns and villages around the lake
(Montreux, Evian, Villeneuve), made confessions under torture,
and these confessions all follow the same pattern: the defendants
admitted having received letters and poison from abroad, usually
from Toledo. The alleged criminals were put to death. The lord
of Chillon sent a summary of the trials to the political authorities
in Basel, Strasbourg, Bern, and elsewhere, urging them to punish
their own prisoners. Not everybody agreed with this Jewish conspiracy theory: Chonrad von Winterthur, for instance, wrote a
letter to Strasbourg saying that he had found the Jews to be

totally innocent. He urged, notwithstanding the popular pressure against the Jews, that the Black Death had to be recognized as a scourge of God, not as a product of human malevolence. But in other places new evidence was found against the Jews: the Schlett-stadt town councilors wrote a letter to their counterparts in Strasbourg informing them that a Jew had confessed to having put poison in some wells. So the persecution of the Jews went on.[13]

The most relevant aspect in these events is not the content of the confessions (in which there was no novelty) but their geographical location. Fifty years later, in 1409, Ponce Fougey-ron, Inquisitor General over a large region that included Geneva and its environs, Dauphiné, and so on, received a letter from Pope Alexander V. The pope expressed his grief that in Fougey-ron's region Christians and Jews had together built "new sects and new rituals hostile to both faiths" (*novas sectas et novos ritus eidem fidei repugnantes*).[14] What were these "*new* sects and *new* rituals?" It is impossible to identify them with the old, traditional magic because in the same letter the pope also con-demned Christians and Jews who practiced "sorcery, divination, demons' invocation," and so on. I suggest the reference to "new sects and new rituals" is an allusion to the witches' sabbat, pro-viding the missing link in the region between the accusation against the Jews as poisoners and the new image of witches as a threatening sect.

Historians usually date the first recorded trials in which the sabbat played a major role to the Valais in 1428 — that is, nearly twenty years after the pope's letter to the Inquisitor who was in charge of the trials in the same region. But in Johannes Nider's *Formicarius*, a dialogue written during the Basel council in 1435—1437, there is a long passage on a new kind of witchcraft that began (Nider says) *sixty years before*; that is, around 1375.[15] Nider's informants were a secular judge from Bern, Peter von Greyerz, who had sent many witches to the stake, and the In-quisitor of Evian (where Jews had confessed to using poison in 1348). The image of witchcraft emerging from the evidence recorded by Nider was new. The old stereotype of sexual orgies and ritual anthropophagy of babies born within the sect, assigned in the past to various heresies (Paulicians, Euchitians, Cathars, and others), was linked to witches, male and female. Moreover, these witches were supposed to attack not only their own children but also other parents' babies in their cradles.[16] The fearful image of the witches' sect − much more dreadful than isolated sorcerers and magicians − was taking form at the same time on both sides of the Alps. The Inquisitor Bernardo da Como wrote at the beginning of the 16th century that the trials preserved in the archives of the local Inquisition indicated that a new kind of witchcraft, centered on the sabbat, had begun nearly one hundred fifty years earlier − that is, around 1350.[17]

In Nider's passage on the "new witches" we find many elements of the sabbat image: orgies, anthropophagy, renunciation of the Christian faith, homage to the Devil. Two elements, however, are conspicuously lacking: metamorphosis into animals and the magic flight. They appear for the first time in the Valais trials conducted in 1428. The judicial records are, unfortunately, lost: the only evidence is provided by a local chronicle, written ten years later. The trials lasted eighteen months; the defendants confessed only after having been tortured. They said that their sect (*"gesellschaft"*) had seven hundred members and was fifty years old: had it lasted one more year, they would have become the lords of the land.[18] This detail looks bizarre but it fits perfectly in the sequence I have suggested − the same accusation had been launched against the lepers in 1321. More than a century later, a full image of the sabbat had at last come to the surface.

I suggested earlier that the final image of the sabbat was a compromise between learned (mainly inquisitorial) and popular elements. In fact, it is possible to argue that the sabbat image had such lasting success because it embodied in a perverted form the structure of an ancient myth, deeply rooted in the folklore of various parts of Europe.

The Valais witches confessed that coming back from their gatherings they drank wine from the cellars. The same detail can be found in the confessions of the Friulian *benandanti* in 1575 and in the confessions of Arnaud Gélis from Haute Ariège in 1319.[19] This wide divergence in absolute chronology is irrelevant: from the point of view of relative chronology, all three documents come from the same layer of popular culture. At this level we must forget the tight, unilinear chronology and the close geographical sequence that I tried to reconstruct in the first part of this article. On the contrary, we must suggest the

existence of a plural, flexible time, full of flashbacks and stag-
nations as well as the possibility of a meaningful convergence of
data in a widely scattered space.[20] To analyze the mythical
content of the sabbat, utterly ignored by those historians of
witchcraft who despised the "mental rubbish of peasant credulity
and feminine hysteria," we must use the intellectual tools provided by symbolic anthropology and the history of religions.
Above all we need a broad, comparative approach.

   The detail about people drinking wine in the cellars is truly
mythical; it is connected with the dead. The *armier* Arnaud Gélis
"went with the dead"; so did the *benandanti* in Friuli, the *kerstniki* in the Balkan peninsula, the *kallikantzaroi* in Greece, the
*calusarii* in Rumania, the *táltos* in Hungary, the Ossetic *Burkudzäutä* in the Caucasus, and the Lapp and Siberian shamans.[21]
Rather than demonstrate analytically the deep, structural unity
underlying these cultural phenomena, as well as describing their
specific symbolic richness, I shall confine myself to some basic
conclusions. In a very wide cultural area we find the belief that
certain people, men or women, could communicate with the
world of the dead. Their role, duly recognized by the community,
was linked to specific physical features (being born with the caul,
as the *benandanti,* or with teeth, as the *táltos*), calendar circumstances (being born in the Twelve Days, as the *kallikantzaroi*),
or psychological attitudes (as the case of the Lapp or Siberian
shamans). Their journey to the world of the dead was usually
preceded by an ecstatic sleep, during which the soul left the
body as though dead. This ecstasy could be self-induced or aided
by narcotic drugs – fly agaric in the case of Lapp or Siberian
shamans, ergot (I suspect) in many European contexts. But drugs
obviously cannot explain the mythical content of this journey
into the beyond. Communication with the dead or battles with
evil spirits to ensure the crops' fertility, performed by the chosen
people, expressed in mythical form basic emotional needs in the
life of the community.

   It is difficult to say how old this myth is. The answer will
probably be provided by its puzzling geographical distribution.
Maybe it is Indo-European, possibly even older. Its central role
in fairy tales (as demonstrated by Propp[22]) is probably a clue to
remote antiquity. More subtle but sounder research tools will

eventually allow us to date more precisely this deep cultural layer.

I suggest therefore that the fundamental contribution of popular culture to the image of witches' sabbat — that is, animal metamorphosis and magic flight — is connected with the mythical journey into the beyond.[23] In other words, the image of the sabbat took its full form when and where the stereotype of a group threatening society as a whole mingled with a deep layer of beliefs related to the possibility of communicating with the world of the dead. It could be objected that the geographical area where this myth spread did not coincide with the diffusion area of the belief related to the witches' sabbat. But we know that Inquisitors and lay judges extorted, with the aid of torture, confessions about the sabbat from nothing — that is, from people totally foreign to this deep layer of popular culture (the case of the Arras Vauderie in 1460 is a good example). The spread of the sabbat image must be distinguished from the form in which it coalesced for the first time. This happened, as we have seen, in the Western Alps around 1350. In the folklore of that region themes like the Wild Hunt (that is, the procession of dead souls) and werewolves were conspicuous. Nider in his *Formicarius* compared the "new witches" to wolves; the Vaudois witches confessed in 1428 that with the aid of the Devil, they could transform themselves into wolves. Now, the werewolf belief was recorded as early as in Herodotus and is certainly related to ritual death, followed by a mythical journey into the world of the dead.[24]

In conclusion, in the sabbat image we can detect deep roots in popular culture. But how did those Alpine peasants and shepherds accept the distortion of their myths that the Inquisitors suggested? How did those benevolent figures, magical protectors of the community, become malignant witches, enemies of men's, women's, cattle's, and crops' fertility? Obviously, physical and psychological pressures must have played a major role. This is an easy guess, but the earliest trials centered on the sabbat are lost. A more analytic (albeit analogical) answer is provided by the extraordinary evidence I discovered twenty years ago in the Eastern Alps. There, as though in slow motion, we can see how, between 1575 and 1650, the *benandanti*, urged by the Inquisitors, lost their original character as protectors of crops against the witches to become themselves diabolical witches going to the sabbat. It is probable that in the same way the image of the sabbat was diffused in other parts of Europe. We can certainly speak, in this case, of cultural violence but it is a violence that followed, as I have demonstrated, a cultural compromise. Relations between learned and popular culture are rarely a one-way process.

## NOTES

1. H. R. Trevor-Roper, *The European Witch-Craze of the 16th and 17th Centuries* (London: 1969), p. 41.
2. M. Murray, *The Witch-Cult in Western Europe* (1921; Oxford: 1962).
3. N. Cohn, *Europe's Inner Demons: An Enquiry Inspired by the Great Witch-hunt* (London: 1975), pp. 111−15.
4. Cf. Cohn, *Europe's*, pp. 18 ff. The accusation of sexual orgies (includ-ing incest) recurs several times in hostile sources on the Paulicians: cf. Ch. Astruc et al., eds., *Les sources grècques pour l'histoire des Pauliciens d'Asie Mineure*, in *Travaux et Memoires du Centre de Recherche d'Histoire et Civilisation Byzantine*, 4 (1970), pp. 92, 131, 201, 205 (section edited by J. Gouillard; I am grateful to Evelyne Patlagean for this reference, as well as for other useful suggestions). In all these pas-sages, however, anthropophagy is conspicuously absent: there is only a vague reference to "ashes of babies' umbilical cords mixed with food for ceremonial purposes" in a well-known formula of anathema, ascribed either to the 9th or to the middle 10th century (ibid., pp. 188−89, 201). Both themes (incest and anthropophagy) can be found in John of Ojun's sermon: cf. *Domini Johannis Philosophi Ozniensis Armeniorum Catholici Opera*, ed. by G. B. Aucher (Venice: 1834), pp. 85 ff. See also N. G. Gar-soïan, *The Paulician Heresy* (The Hague and Paris: 1967), pp. 94−95.
5. See P. Gautier, "Le *De daemonibus* du Pseudo-Gellos," *Revue des études byzantines* 38 (1980), pp. 105−94. For the passage on orgies, see pp. 140−41. The author suggests, tentatively, that the dialogue could have been written after 1250 or even later (p. 131).
6. See for instance Biondo's well-known passage on the Fraticelli; having described their orgies he went on to say "sive vero ex huiusmodi coitu conceperit mulier, infans genitus ad conventiculum illud in speluncam delatus per singulorum manus traditum tamdiu totiensque baiulandus quousque animam exhalaverit. Isque in cuius manibus infans expiraverit maximus pontifex divino ut aiunt spiritu creatus habetur . . . " (F. Bion-do, *Italia illustrata* [Verona: 1482], cc. E r-v). The last detail is a precise echo of John of Ojun's text: "Similiter et primum parientis foeminae puerum de manu in manum inter eos invicem projectum, quum pessima morte occiderint, illum, in cujus manu exspiravit puer, ad primam sectae dignitatem provectum venerantur" (*Opera*, p. 87; quotation from J. B. Aucher's Latin translation of the Armenian original).

7. There is still no full study of it. Among local studies see L. Guibert, "Les lépreux et les léproseries de Limoges," *Bulletin de la société archéologique et historique du Limousin,* 4 (1905), pp. 5–146; Vincent, "Le complot de 1320 contre les lépreux et ses repercussions en Poitou," *Bulletin de la Société des Antiquaires de l'Ouest,* 3d series, 7 (1927), pp. 325–44; G. Lavergne, "La persecution et spoliation des lépreux à Perigueux en 1321," *Recueil de travaux offert à M. Clovis Brunel . . .* (Paris: 1955), 2: 107–13. For more comprehensive reconstructions, see H. Chrétien, *Le prétendu complot des Juifs et lépreux en 1321* (Châteauroux: 1887); J. M. Vidal, "La poursuite des lépreux en 1321 d'après des documents nouveaux," *Annales de Saint-Louis-des-Français,* 4 (1900), pp. 419–78; R. Anchel, *Les Juifs en France* (Paris: 1946), pp. 79–91; V. R. Rivière-Chalan, *La marque infâme des lépreux et de christians sous l'Ancien Régime* (Paris: 1978). See the accurate study by M. Barber, "The Plot to Overthrow Christendom in 1321," *History* 66 (February 1981), pp. 1–17, who denies the existence of a conspiracy from above. On this point, I follow the reconstruction suggested in Rivière-Chalan's essay, which Barber seems to have missed.

8. The relevant chronicles are listed in Vidal, "La poursuite." The letter found in Anjou, sent by Philip, count of Anjou, to Pope John XXII, is printed in G. D. Mansi, *Sacrorum Conciliorum nova, et amplissima collectio* (Venice: 1782), 25, coll. 569–572: it was accepted as a trustworthy document by the antisemite writer L. Rupert, *L'Eglise et la synagogue* (Paris: 1859), pp. 172 ff., and rejected as an example of false accusations concocted against the Jews (with an obvious link to the Dreyfus affair) by Chrétien, *Le prétendu,* p. 17; rather surprisingly, subsequent literature on the subject has ignored it. The two letters to the Moslem kings, already mentioned as fake by H. Sauval, *Histoire et recherches des antiquités de la ville de Paris* (Paris: 1724), 2: 517–18, were also printed by Chrétien and then, as unpublished, by Vidal, "La poursuite," pp. 459–61.

9. Cf. Anchel, *Les Juifs,* pp. 86 ff., and B. Blumenkranz, "A propos des Juifs en France sous Charles IV le Bel," *Archives juives,* 6 (1969–70), pp. 36–38, who corrects the usually accepted date (1322) for the expulsion.

10. Cf. J. Michelet, *Histoire de France (livres V–IX),* ed. by P. Viallaneix *Oeuvres complètes,* V (Paris: 1975), pp. 155–57; Vidal, "La poursuite"; J. Duvernoy, *Le registre d'Inquisition de Jacques Fournier (1318–1325)* (Paris: 1965), 2: 135–47, especially p. 135 fn. For a different interpretation of the Agassa trial see E. Le Roy Ladurie, *Montailloux, village occitan de 1294 à 1324* (Paris: 1975), pp. 17, 583 fn. 1.

11. In a forthcoming book I will explore the connection between the 1321 conspiracy and some events that in different ways prepared for it (the trials against the Templars; the alleged attempt made by Hugues Géraud, bishop of Cahors, to kill Pope John XXII; the Pastoureaux crusade).

12. Cf. U. Robert, *Les signes d'infamie au Moyen Age* (Paris: 1889), pp. 11, 90–91, 148; J.-C. Schmitt, "L'histoire des marginaux," in *La Nouvelle histoire,* ed. by J. Le Goff (Paris: 1978), p. 355.

50 *Carlo Ginzburg*

13. Cf. J. von Königshoven, *Die alteste Teutsche so wol Allgemeine als insonderheit Elsassische und Strassburgische Chronicke* . . . (Strasbourg: 1698), pp. 1029–1048; *Urkundenbuch der Stadt Strassburg*, V, ed. by H. Witte and G. Wolfram (Strasbourg: 1896), pp. 162–79. For a general summary, see *The Jewish Encyclopedia*, s.v. "Black Death." For more detailed accounts see, among others, R. Hoeniger, *Der schwarze Tod in Deutschland* (Berlin: 1882); A. Lopez de Meneses, "Una consequencia de la Peste Negra en Cataluña: el pogrom de 1348," *Sefarad*, 19 (1975), pp. 92–131, 321–64; J. Schatzmiller, "Les Juifs de Provence pendant la Peste Noire," *Revue des études juives*, 133 (1974), pp. 457–80. For the cultural background of the persecution, see S. Guerchberg, "La controverse sur les prétendus semeurs de la Peste Noire d'après les traités de peste de l'époque," *Revue des études juives*, 108 (1948), pp. 3–40.

14. Cf. L. Wadding, *Annales Minorum*, IX (Rome: 1734), pp. 327–29.

15. Cf. J. Nider, *Formicarius*, book 5, chap. 4. It seems that this section of the dialogue was written in 1437: cf. K. Schieler, *Magister Johannes Nider aus dem Orden der Prediger-Brüder. Ein Beitrag zur Kirchengeschichte des fünfzehnten Jahrhunderts* (Mainz: 1885), p. 379 fn. 5.

16. On Peter von Greyerz see J. Hansen, *Quellen und Untersuchungen zur Geschichte des Hexenwahns und der Hexenverfolgung im Mittelalters* (Bonn: 1901), p. 91 fn. 2. For the passages on witches devouring babies see *Formicarius*, book 5, chap. 3.

17. Cf. Cohn, *Europe's*, pp. 145–46, who, however, dismisses this authority on the ground that "no later writer has found any trace of the documents in question, though the archives of Como have been searched by historians who had these matters in mind." It must be emphasized that no scholar (including Cantù, quoted by Cohn) ever had access to the ecclesiastical archives of Como, where the inquisitorial records might be preserved – if they had survived wars, fires, and pillage across the centuries. (My own attempts to enter this archive have been wholly unsuccessful.) On the other hand, in his discussion of Nider's treatise (*Europe's*, pp. 204–5) Cohn does not take account of the very precise chronological statement that follows the description of the anthropophagous witches: "Praeterea quemadmodum a supradicto Petro iudice audivi in territorio Bernensium et in locis eidem adiacentibus a sexaginta circiter annis superfata malefitia a multis practicata sunt." The remarkable convergence between Nider's and Bernardo da Como's chronologies makes the latter altogether convincing.

18. Cf. Th. von Liebenau, ed., "Von den Hexen, so in Wallis verbrannt wurdent in den Tagen, do Cristofel von Silinen herr und richter was," *Anzeiger für schweizerische Geschichte*, n.s. 9 (1902–1905), pp. 135–38; J. B. Bertrand, "Notes sur les procès d'hérésie et de sorcellerie en Valais," *Annales Valaisannes*, 3 (August 1921), pp. 166–67, 173 ff.

19. Cf. C. Ginzburg, *I benandanti* (Turin: 1972), pp. 7, 63–64; J. Duvernoy, *Le registre*, 1: 139; Le Roy Ladurie, *Montaillou*, pp. 592 ff.

20. Cf. J. Le Goff, *Pour un autre Moyen Age* (Paris: 1978), p. 314 fn. 12.

21. On the *kerstniki* cf. M. Boškovič-Stulli, "Kresnik-Krsnik, ein Wesen aus der kroatischen und slovenischen Volksüberlieferung," *Fabula*, 3 (1959–60) pp. 275–98. On the *kallikantzaroi*, J. C. Lawson, *Modern Greek Folklore and Ancient Greek Religion* (1910; New York: 1964, with an introduction by A. N. Oikonomides), pp. 190 ff.; P. P. Argenti and H. J. Rose, *The Folk-Lore of Chios* (Cambridge: 1949), pp. 21 ff., 242 ff. On the *calusarii*, O. Buhociu, "Le folklore roumain de printemps," thesis (University of Paris: 1957); Gail Kligman, *Calus: Symbolic Transformation in Romanian Rituals* (Chicago: 1981). On the *táltos*, see the excellent essay by G. Klaniczay, "Benandante–kresnik–zduhač–táltos," *Ethnographia* 84 (1983), pp. 116–33 (which I was able to read in an English translation kindly prepared by the author.). On the *Burkudzäutä,* G. Dumézil, *Le problème des Centaures* (Paris: 1929), pp. 91–93; for an earlier report see J. Klaproth, *Voyage au Mont Caucase et en Georgie* (Paris: 1823), 2: 255. The connection between *táltos* and shamans has been repeatedly discussed: see for instance V. Dioszegi, ed., *Glaubenswelt und Folklore der Sibirischen Volker* (Budapest: 1963); on *benandanti* and shamans, the hypothesis suggested in Ginzburg, *Benandanti,* p. 3, has been confirmed by M. Eliade, "Some Observations on European Witchcraft," *History of Religions,* 14 (1975), pp. 153–58.

22. See V. Propp, *Le radici storiche dei racconti di fate* (1946; Turin: 1949). Propp's analysis of the mythical content of fairy tales is very convincing; much more debatable is his attempt to decipher in them the traces of specific rites: see M. Eliade, *Aspects du mythe* (Paris: 1963), pp. 235–36. It must be emphasized that, notwithstanding the debts paid to Stalinist orthodoxy, Propp's book remains an outstanding contribution.

23. This hypothesis was advanced, on the basis of much more circumscribed evidence, in my book on *Benandanti* (see particularly pp. 30–35). I did not notice that a similar interpretation had been already suggested, albeit with a question mark, by J. Grimm, *Deutsche Mythologie,* 4th ed., edited by E. H. Meyer (Berlin: 1876), 2: 906 (*Teutonic Mythology* [London: 1883], 2: 1082).

24. Cf. Nider, *Formicarius,* book 5, chap. 3: "idem inquisitor [of Evian] et dominus Petrus [of Bern] mihi retulerunt et fama communis habet circa districtum Bernensis dominii quidam malefici utriusque sexus qui contra humane nature inclinacionem ymo adversus condiciones spetierum omnium bestiarum lupina specie excepta tantummodo proprie spetiei infantes vorant et comedere solent"; "Von den Hexen," p. 136. See also J. Sprenger and H. Institoris, *Malleus maleficarum,* in *Malleorum quorundum maleficarum, tam veterum quam recentium authorum, tomi duo* (Frankfurt: 1582), p. 13: "moderni malefici saepius opere daemonum transformantur in lupos et alias bestias. . . ." On the interpretation of belief in werewolves, still fundamental is W. H. Roscher, "Das von der 'Kynanthropie' handelnde Fragment des Marcellus von Side," *Abhandlungen der philologisch-historischen Classe der königlich Sächsischen Gesellschaft der Wissenschaften,* 17 (1897).

# *Sacerdote ovvero strione:*
# Ecclesiastical and Superstitious Remedies in 16th Century Italy

MARY R. O'NEIL

Both Catholic and Protestant orthodoxies of the 16th century responded to the "ignorance and superstition" of the European people with a mixture of catechesis and repression. Preachers, schoolmasters, and church courts all participated in an intensive effort to raise the religious and moral level of society by enforcing stricter standards of belief and behavior. But despite similarities in learned laments and in the apparatus of indoctrination, important differences existed between Protestant and Catholic approaches to this "reform of popular culture," differences that are clearly visible in their programs for the suppression of magical beliefs and practices.[1]

The Protestant Reformation eliminated ecclesiastically sanctioned remedies against misfortunes of both natural and supernatural origin, urging reliance on prayer and trust in divine providence as the correct approach to adversity. By contrast, active mediation with supernatural forces for human benefit remained basic to the sacramental and ceremonial core of Catholicism. The Roman Church did, however, wish to redirect popular attempts at independent access to the supernatural into orthodox channels, thus consolidating its monopoly on dealing with positive and negative supernatural forces alike.[2] Magical self-help was to be combatted not with Protestant stoicism but through the liberal provision of authorized, clerically administered relief.

A clear statement of orthodox responsibility for combatting the effects commonly attributed to negative supernatural forces (*maleficium*[3] and possession) is presented in Fra Girolamo Menghi's *Compendio dell'arte essorcista* of 1576. Citing a range of evidence including Scripture, canon law, and the "testimony of the common people of practically every nation who suffer in great numbers from various maleficial infirmities," Menghi defended the reality of diabolical harm against the skeptics who wished to trace such injuries to natural (if hidden) causes.[4] The recapitulation of traditional demonology and witch lore in Books I and II of the *Compendio* served as background to the central purpose of the treatise, the discussion of orthodox remedies against such dangers.

It would be a shameful and indecent thing for an expert physician to describe in his writings the symptoms of various illnesses, unless he also knew the preventative and curative remedies that applied in each case. In order that no one should judge this modest effort of ours to be curious, vain, superfluous and composed to no purpose, we wish, like an expert physician who first diagnoses the sickness and then applies the appropriate remedies, to speak in this third book of the protective and curative remedies which correspond to the infirmities discussed above, so that with these remedies each person can defend himself against the assaults of demons and witches.[5]

The remedies to which Menghi counseled recourse were "exorcisms and other forces of ecclesiastical medicine," among which he included pilgrimages, confession, and the sign of the cross. Although he took no overt stand against witch hunting, that option is conspicuously absent. For Menghi, the *medicine ecclesiastiche* are sufficient to thwart or reverse the actions of demons and witches alike. An experienced Franciscan exorcist, Menghi gave particular emphasis to the broadly remedial functions of exorcism, which could be used to undo the effects of *maleficia* as well as possession.[6]

The *Compendio*'s assertion of the efficacy of traditional ecclesiastical remedies was aimed at several different groups. The most sophisticated consisted of those "elevated intellects" who denied the utility of exorcism along with the reality of possession and *maleficia*. Mistaking demonic presence for madness or disease, they discouraged people from calling in exorcists and thus served as tools of a carefully planned diabolical ploy to achieve the unilateral disarmament of the human race.[7] At the other end of the cultural spectrum were those who firmly believed in the necessity for protection against *maleficia* but who turned to magical and superstitious remedies rather than to those approved by the Church. Somewhere between these extremes lay the central audience for Menghi's manual, the clerics and exorcists whose task it was to dispense the various *medicine ecclesiastiche* in an orthodox manner.[8]

In both timing and content, Menghi's work forms part of the post-Tridentine effort to reform various aspects of popular belief and behavior, an effort that involved clergy of all levels in the struggle against popular error. The regional offices of the Roman Inquisition stepped up prosecution of superstitious offenses in the period after 1570, leading to a marked increase in trials against lay persons involved in magical healing, divination, and love magic.[9] The parallel task of preventing recourse to magical remedies was delegated to the local representatives of orthodoxy, the parish clergy and the friars. The quasi-ethnographic character of the campaign to detect and catalogue the possible forms of superstitious error can be seen in the recommendation made in 1577 to the curates of Bologna by the annual congregation of parish priests meeting under episcopal auspices.

They should seek to collect all the superstitions, incantations and *brevi da portar adosso* [handwritten prayers or charms, worn or carried on one's person] containing superstitious words, unapproved names and similar abuses. Even if they do not appear to be evil, they should be collected and notice given of them, for it is planned that a small book warning of these matters should be compiled.[10]

Inquisitorial edicts required preachers to use sermons as an occasion for exhortations against magical remedies and gave detailed instructions on the precise types of possible offenses. Absolution in confession was made contingent on denunciation not just of one's own failings in this regard but of the observed lapses of neighbors and relatives as well.[11] Such decrees were aimed in particular at the illiterate and uneducated, the *pusillis et rudibus Christifidelibus,* and the clergymen who read the edicts constituted, in the Tridentine model, the front line of defense against such rustic errors.[12]

As a program for the elimination of superstition, this model required that clerics themselves be of certified orthodoxy so that in the most remote village there would be at least one person qualified to tell a legitimate prayer from a superstitious charm, a natural remedy from a magical cure. The trials that the Inquisition conducted against clerics and exorcists for superstitious offenses in the late 16th century therefore indicate both a flaw in the model and a determination to remedy that flaw. Out of sixty-four trials held in Modena between 1580 and 1600 on charges of superstition, twelve, or close to 20 percent, were directed against clerics, four of whom were exorcists.[13] Thus the specialists in orthodox alternatives to superstitious remedies were repeatedly found guilty of complicity in the very errors they were charged to eradicate.

Drawing on Inquisition records from Modena, Bologna, and Venice in the late 16th century, this essay examines the exercise of the remedial function by the lower clergy.[14] Recruited from among artisans or peasants, this group occupied a crucial position as mediators between the cultural levels of early modern society. They acted as the local representatives of orthodoxy but nonetheless they often shared both milieu and *mentalité* with their parishioners. The trials of ordinary clerics for superstitious offenses reflect ambiguities that stemmed from their incomplete personal transitions between *culture folklorique* and *culture cléricale,* as well as from their role as administrators of one of a set of parallel and competing remedies for maleficial injuries.[15] This essay considers the church's concern for detecting clerical complicity in popular errors, the laity's expectations from clerically administered remedies, and the predicaments of individual clerics as they attempted to respond to often-conflicting demands.

Given the sacramental and teaching functions entrusted to the lowliest priest, clerical superstition was inherently far more dangerous to orthodoxy than the lay variety. The lengthy and probing interrogations to which clerics were subjected when arrested reveal the hierarchy's concern for assuring that its own delegates, at least, acted only within authorized channels. The laymen and women tried by the Inquisition in the late 16th century were more frequently involved in the actual practice of magical remedies; but clerical trials provide more information about the development and application of the orthodox category of "superstition" itself. For although lay persons were asked whether they knew a given procedure to be forbidden, only clerics were questioned in any depth about the *assumptions* underlying their suspect actions or about their understanding of *why* a given action might be considered superstitious. This difference in style of interrogation of lay and clerical defendants can be illustrated by comparing the trial of an uneducated, sixty-year-old Modenese with that of a literate Franciscan in Venice.

The Modenese Inquisition found Antonio de Correggi guilty in 1595 of the superstitious offenses of "vain observance of times and abuse of the Gospel" in connection with his technique of curing fevers by reciting the opening verses of Saint John's Gospel over the sick person on a hilltop at sunrise, on Good Friday, or on the feast of Saint John the Baptist. The court's sentence indicated that his error was essentially a jurisdictional one, that of believing the "holy words, the most holy gospel and holy days ... can be used for ends other than those instituted by the Holy Church."[16]

Antonio's replies show, however, that he did not categorize his admitted actions in the court's terms. He had heard the "priest say many times, both at the altar and in confession, that one should not practice superstitious customs." But when pressed on what this meant, Antonio replied, "by superstitious things, I mean doing harm to one's neighbor, taking another person's goods and so forth." The numerous edicts against superstition read in church and aimed at the illiterate had succeeded only partially in Antonio's case. He knew that superstition was "wrong" but it remained simply a synonym for a generic concept of sin as doing harm to others.[17] Significantly the Inquisitor made no comment on Antonio's lack of understanding of the concept, and hence of the charges against him, but moved to the next on a list of prepared questions. If the trial did not expand Antonio's theological understanding, it did alert him to the fact that his sunrise healing, effective though it might have been, had to be discontinued. Such reliance on the coercive setting of the trial and the lack of any attempt to convey just what made a given action "superstitious" is typical of Inquisitorial procedure against the uneducated laity.

By contrast a Franciscan in Venice, also charged with superstitious healing, faced more intensive and doctrinally revealing interrogations in his 1590 trial. As a cure for fevers, Fra Geremia da Udine dispensed pieces of paper (*bollettini* or *polizze*) on each of which he had written the name of one of the twelve

Apostles. The sick person was to open one of these folded papers
each day, burning it if the fever persisted; but if the fever
abated, he should vow to fast on the vigil of the Apostle named
for that day and should not burn the paper. Fra Geremia's open
distribution of this charm from the *scuola* of the Franciscan
convent constituted an informal imprimatur that caused the
Inquisition to regard his case with particular seriousness.

Since he did not simply offer this to people, but they came to ask for the
cure even without his knowing them, this is a clear sign that it was public
knowledge in Venice that he dispensed this medication. . . . This *dottrina*
or *secreta* of his was notorious and the people flocked to him to get these
*bollettini.*[18]

Directed insistently at the defendant's grasp of the concept of
superstition, the interrogation of Fra Geremia was undertaken
to educate as well as to convict. It goes well beyond the coercive
scope of Antonio's trial and attempts to isolate precisely the
error in Geremia's healing procedure.

I: If it seemed to him that this was licit, knowing it rather to be pure and
simple superstition, and furthermore irreverence towards the name of the
Apostle which was to be burned.
R: It seems bad to me, but I did it for the benefit of those persons, and
I never received anything for it.
I: If it seems just to him to do evil for the benefit of others.
R: It no longer seems just, no. I knew that I was doing wrong, but I did it
to heal them of that sickness.[19]

Although it is not specified that the fevers cured by Fra Geremia's procedure were of maleficial origin, a standard issue in
the literature on the prevention and cure of witchcraft was
"whether it is permissible to do harm in order to do good." The
debate centered on the legitimacy of dissolving *maleficia* by
means of further *maleficia*; supporters of strictly orthodox remedies like Girolamo Menghi argued that death should be preferred to a maleficial cure.[20] Fra Geremia's good intentions and
his desire to respond to people's needs by any available means
are thus dismissed as irrelevant for only the character of the
means employed was at issue, not the worthiness of the goal.

Seeking to "clarify in what way it seemed to him that he
had done wrong," the court asked

whether he saw it as the act of a faithful Christian to burn the paper with the name of an Apostle on it when the fever persisted, as if in scorn and resentment for not having been granted this favor (*gratia*).[21]

Fra Geremia explained that the *bollettino* was to be burned without being opened, implying that if one did not know the name of the Apostle no disrespect could be construed. The judges were unimpressed, noting that "this amounts to the same thing, for it is the act of throwing it on the fire that creates the superstition and shows neglect of that Apostle."[22]

Nowhere does this interrogation hint that this cure is superstitious because it does not work; together with Geremia and his Venetian following the court accepts, or at least does not contest, the efficacy of the charm. Rather, the cure was judged superstitious precisely because of the manner in which it *did* work – through an inappropriate method of appeal to the Apostles.[23] Responding to his explanation that the *bollettino* was to be burned so that it would take on the sickness, the court noted that "from this reply of his, it seems that he wanted to force the Apostles. If they wanted to free themselves, they must heal the sick person in order not to be burned at the end of the day."[24] The cure, then, went beyond simple irreverence to active coercion of the Apostles through a classic combination of bribery and threats. A tacit acceptance of the magical principle that the written name represents the Apostle, so that burning the name is tantamount to an assault on the Apostle himself, underlies the court's concern for this aspect of the cure.[25] While less attention is given to the reward held out to the cooperative saint, the assumption that the cure was indeed effected through Apostolic agency may explain the absence in this trial of the standard charge of implicit diabolism.

Although often accepted by the Inquisition in cases of lay superstition, Fra Geremia's last line of defense, "I did this out of simplicity and not out of disrespect towards any saint," was rejected out of hand: "since he is a religious and lettered, his claim of simplicity is not credible."[26] Holding clerics to stricter standards than the laity is consonant with the Church's definition of their role in society. Yet the frequency of clerical activity judged superstitious by the Church indicates that the actual position of clerics vis-à-vis the beliefs and practices of the *pusillis et rudibus* was less distant than hoped.

Considered in this light, Fra Geremia's defense of *semplicità* emerges as more than a last-ditch effort to exculpate himself. It was also a description of his own participation in a milieu and a set of beliefs that he had learned to perceive as characteristic of simple, uneducated people.[27] His explanation that "I learned this thing at Udine when I was a boy, but I never taught it to anyone," reflects a division in his own experience that was both geographic and ideological: a childhood in Friuli, about which we know only that he learned this cure, and a clerical adulthood in Venice, where his provincial lore, though well received by the people "who flocked to him to get these *bollettini*," was readily discerned as superstitious by the enforcers of public orthodoxy and, after some coerced reflection, by Fra Geremia himself.[28]

However, not all clerical remedies were unorthodox. The legitimate healing activities of clerics included simple blessings, reading prayers, and dispensing handwritten *brevi* containing orthodox texts. Mothers frequently brought their sick children to priests to have them blessed with the sign of the cross (*segnati*) or to have prayers read over them (*legere sopra*); these routine, noncontroversial matters are encountered throughout the trial records. The Bolognese plan of 1577 to collect even those *brevi* that "do not appear to be evil" reflects the suspicions aroused by the circulation of unapproved formulae. Yet if the words they contained could be shown to be orthodox, the wearing or carrying of such brevi was permissible, even advisable.[29] All of these less formal measures could be appropriately invoked to mitigate any illness, including those of natural origin, but the more potent clerical remedies of conjuration (*scongiurare*) and exorcism (*esorcizzare*) were reserved for maleficial conditions of negative supernatural origin.

Although Italian exorcist literature does describe public dispossessions similar to the famous episodes of post-Reformation France, the exorcist activity that Inquisition trials describe was of a far less spectacular variety. It focused on undoing the effects of *maleficia* rather than on direct encounters with possessing demons.[30] The concentration on curing disease placed exorcists squarely in the ranks of the healers; to their public they represented a source of concrete aid, an alternative to either medical advice or the local village healer.

Since an exorcist could not deal effectively with diseases of natural origin, his first order of business was discerning *maleficia*, a task complicated by the fact that the same disease could arise from either natural or maleficial causes. Exorcist manuals attempted to introduce some rigor into this inherently difficult process by spelling out criteria for distinguishing the different sources of identical symptoms.[31] In practice, however, adherence to such guidelines was lax; Girolamo Menghi inveighed at length against exorcists' ignorance of "the knowledge required for the exercise of this art," and cited examples from his own experience.

In a certain city of Lombardy, I saw one of these [exorcists] with my own eyes, who had never had a book of this art in his hands, and nevertheless promised that he could recognize and cure all the *maleficati* that he saw, and they flocked to his hands. So widely had his reputation spread that people came to him from all parts of Italy to have their ailments cured. He maintained that he discerned and cured them by certain powders and waters which he offered to them. He went to such lengths in this that although he might be at a great distance from the sick person, he declared that he could nonetheless recognize illnesses, often divining symptoms as well at a distance.[32]

The manuals did not provide for detecting *maleficia* in the absence of the victim; to Menghi, such abilities implied either fraud or divination.

Although this function was officially within the competence of the exorcist alone, in practice the relatives and neighbors of a sick person often made initial diagnoses of *maleficium* before calling in an expert. Testifying in the 1582 trial of Don Teofilo Zani, official exorcist of the Cathedral Church in Modena, Francesca dei Vincenzi described the exorcism of her nephew.

Thomaso, the little son of my brother, was sick. He was so distressed and screamed so loudly that he was judged by various people to be *maleficato*. So it was suggested by his grandmother that we call in Don Teofilo to exorcize Thomaso.[33]

Though presumably he could have made an independent diagnosis, reversing or confirming the untutored perceptions of the family, Don Teofilo seems to have felt no need for a conclusive verdict on the origin of Thomaso's illness; he went ahead with his standard procedure as the family wished.

Twice I signed and exorcized a child suspected of being *maleficato*; this I did at the request of the mother of Madonna Francheschina who came in person to ask me, and also had her *capellano*, Don Sebastian Sassolo, ask me. . . . But to tell the truth, I had little desire to do so.[34]

Familial pressure overcame Zani's professional doubts but his reservations about the efficacy of exorcism in this case were shared by Francesca, who witnessed the procedure.

[Zani] tried all the remedies customarily used on the *maleficati*; I was present at the beginning, but seeing those ointments of his it appeared to me that Thomaso continued to scream and cry, so I doubted it was having any effect.[35]

In her opinion, the boy had always been and still was sickly (*mal conditionato*); he had not been exorcized since. Like the original diagnosis, the decision to abandon exorcism was not made by the clerical expert but by the family, which seems to have retreated to a naturalistic explanation.

It was at this crucial point – deciding whether and where to seek relief – that many lay persons fell into error. The alternatives open to them were posed with particular clarity during the interrogation of a woman whose *maleficato* child had been cured by Don Teofilo Zani in 1578. A pious widow, Gasparina Ballotta, testified to the Inquisition that she was regularly visited by an apparition that took the form of various deceased relatives. She was accustomed to consult with her *cosa spirituale* on issues of importance, such as that under urgent consideration by the Livizzano family, to which she was related by marriage.[36] Their daughter Laura was *fatturata* (bewitched) and her mother Margarita wished to know "whether there is a remedy to the sickness of Madonna Laura, whether of witches or of priests – *sia di strione hover di sacerdote*."

Gasparina's vision assured her that they "didn't want any witches involved, but only ministers of Christ," and approved the choice of Zani as exorcist on the condition that he would do this "as a work of charity."[37] The reply served the cause of orthodoxy but the initial question illustrates the options that the worried family considered. Clearly, the remedial powers of the *sacerdote* were perceived as parallel to those of other local healers of *maleficia,* here classified as *strioni.*

Laura's mother was willing to follow the recommendation to seek out an exorcist rather than a witch but she felt the need to know more than just how to remove the *fattura*. Gasparina was thus instructed to question her vision on a further point.

Madonna Margarita wanted to know if she had been harmed (*guasta*) by her husband's mother or by her brother-in-law, and whether her children too had been harmed by them, as she assumed to be the case.[38]

Her acceptance of the orthodox remedy notwithstanding, Margarita suspected that the root cause of the problem lay in the hostility of her husband's family and wanted this confirmed. Later witnesses would testify that Gasparina's vision had indeed "caused discord and dissension between many people by saying this person had bewitched (*maleficavit*) this or that one."[39] But Gasparina's own version of the apparition's response to Margarita — "My child, let Jesus Christ look to souls and sins" — piously deflected concern away from identifying the agents of the *maleficium* (the essential impulse behind witch hunting) and toward the remedial approach of undoing their effects through orthodox means.[40]

In fact, not everyone who perceived an act of *maleficium* sought to identify the perpetrator. But such an approach is certainly underrepresented in the sources since it produced no charges and no trial records. The stoic response is however occasionally visible, as in the testimony of a reluctant witness, Isabella, called in 1579 during Maria de Mariani's trial on charges of *maleficium*. In answer to the court's questioning about Maria's reputation in the rural Villa di Fre, she replied:

I know of not a single *malefica*. Although six of my little children have been *guasti* and all of them died, from the first to the last, I never wanted to find out who had undone them.[41]

Since the desire to identify the source of such injuries had more drastic consequences than this silent endurance, it is the various methods by which such identification took place that have become the focus of historical interest.

In the case of Gasparina and her vision, the stoic response was accompanied by recourse to the ecclesiastical remedy of exorcism, thus lending support to Keith Thomas's argument that there was an inverse correlation between witch hunting and the availability of orthodox remedies for maleficial conditions in the post-Reformation period.[42] However, the concept of *maleficium* re-

mained incomplete without its perpetrator for it was only through
the identification of someone who wished the victim harm that
suffering became meaningful.[43] The idea tends strongly toward
the naming of a culprit, whether or not that person is punished,
and despite their role as custodians of the *medicine ecclesiastiche*
clerics were no more immune than their parishioners to such
culturally grounded thought processes. Indeed, if Gasparina's
edifying account of her role in urging Margarita to let higher
powers settle the accounts is a reliable one, she was being far
more careful than her clerical advisor.

For, once having accepted the invitation to exorcize Madonna
Laura, Don Teofilo Zani displayed an unseemly interest in the
circumstances and authors of her maleficial condition. As Margarita Livizzano explained,

he said it had been necessary to recite a Gospel at Santa Chiara, and that
all the evildoers who had bewitched (*fatturato*) the girl had gone one by
one to that church while he recited the Gospel. After this he had a Vesper
said in San Domenico . . . saying this was necessary for the health of the girl,
because another Vesper had been said in that church in *maleficio* against
her.[44]

In the opinion of the official exorcist of the Modenese *Duomo* it
was thus possible to use a liturgical ceremony both to cast a
maleficial spell and to undo one, and to use the Mass as a charm
to ferret out the agents of such a *maleficium*. To Gasparina, he
disclosed exactly who they were.

While he sang the Gospel, he saw them going back and forth past the doors
of the Church, and he said there was Madonna Orsolina, the mother of
Augusto Livizzano, and Giovanni Maria, her son.[45]

Questioned by the Inquisition on these points, Zani denied none
of Margarita's allegations.

I: Whether he had held it opportune to recite a Gospel in the Church of
Santa Chiara to which whose who had harmed (*maleficavit*) the oppressed
girl had gone?
R: It is true that I sang a Passion during Holy Week in that church, and that
I told them I had seen those enemies whom they [Laura's family] blamed
for making her sick and causing her *fattura*.
I: Whether he had a Vesper said in the Church of San Domenico saying it
was necessary to heal the above mentioned sick person because a Vesper had
been celebrated in that church in order to cause her *maleficium*?
R: It is true.[46]

Unfortunately, the surviving records of Zani's trial lack both a final summary of charges and a sentence. Although there is thus no clear statement by the court about exactly where his errors lay, it is clear that the exorcist's zeal for combatting *maleficia* had extended far beyond the limits of orthodox relief. Whether fraudulent or sincere in motive, his confirmation of Margarita's suspicions about the link between familial hostilities and Laura's condition, as well as the strict parallelism of his undoing the *maleficium* by the same means used to cause it, could readily be classified as superstitious misuses of liturgical ceremonies.

So even if one chose the *sacerdote* over the *strione*, there was no guarantee that the choice would result in an orthodox cure. The functional equivalence of orthodox and superstitious remedies asserted in Gasparina's formula indicates that people went to priests with many of the same expectations that they brought to magical healers, creating pressures that these men were often ill-equipped to resist. Moreover, the Church's identification of clerics as an authorized source of relief itself contributed to the demands made upon them. The resulting tensions often led them to expand their healing activities well beyond orthodox boundaries.

While the Church expected clerics to perceive clearly and to enforce the jurisdictional line separating superstitious from religiously acceptable techniques, other forces diluted this capacity. Even if a cleric had a fairly solid grasp of the limits of assistance he could legitimately offer, an insistent parishioner could confuse the issues in his mind. Thus Madonna Margarita Simonini of Modena approached her parish priest, Don Camillo Malpiglia, for aid in writing the names of Christ and the twelve Apostles on thirteen almonds; she wished to give them to her son as a cure for fever. Rebuffed by Don Camillo on the grounds that he was too busy, rather than on any stated objection to the procedure, Margarita then turned to Don Teofilo Zani. As he testified, the procedure was a familiar one.

Many times I have heard it said in Modena that the sick person was to eat each day, at random, one of those thirteen almonds on which the names were written. When he ate that bearing the name of Christ, the fever would immediately leave.[47]

This cure is closely related to the apostolic lottery of Fra Geremia da Udine, though here the role of the Apostles is subordinated to that of Christ and the retribution for nonperformance is eliminated. Whether Margarita's request stemmed from an inability to write these words herself or whether the power of priestly script was an element in the efficacy of the charm is not clear.

Zani indignantly denied having consecrated Mass over these almonds, although he did admit to having written the holy names on them. Asked "whether or not he believed in this sort of superstition," Zani explained that he had attempted to keep his distance and had initially refused Margarita's request. But in a striking reversal of the prescribed direction of the lay-clerical relationship, she was able to convince him of the devout and religious content of her healing method.

No, Father, I did not believe in it, nor do I believe it now. On the contrary, I resisted this woman's demands, saying I didn't want to write those names. But when she said that she did this for the devotion she bore to the name of Jesus Christ, I let myself be worn down (*mi lasciai ridur*) and so I wrote those names on the almonds to give her satisfaction. . . . This custom is used by many people, and for these reasons I wrote those names on the almonds, thinking it was a matter of devotion.[48]

As further evidence that it had indeed been a "matter of devotion," Zani cited Margarita's request that he say the Mass of the Centurion for her son; she had offered the *elemosina* of one *canalotto* for this service. There was clearly no question in Margarita's mind that this combination of a devout healing charm and a Mass was appropriate, and the strength of her understanding of what belonged in the sphere of religion was instrumental in overcoming Zani's hesitation. But other statements made by Zani — "so it is said in Modena . . . this custom is used by many people" — indicate that the noncontroversial nature of such methods in the community at large was also at work, eating away at the cleric's ability to categorize such procedure in a correct, orthodox manner.

The indelible mark of Holy Orders and the Church's efforts to hold the clergy to stricter standards notwithstanding, individual priests came from and often continued to participate actively in the popular milieux where superstitious remedies were sought after and highly valued. Moreover, the cleric's access to such liturgical apparatus as holy oils, together with his linguistic and ceremonial knowledge, made his cooperation crucial to various magical procedures. The pressures that could be brought to bear on clerics by their unabashed parishioners again emerge in the 1585 trial of Don Gian Battista, a priest in the Cathedral Church of Modena. Asked by a noblewoman to baptize a piece of magnet (*calamita*) for her use as a love charm, he resisted at first, well aware that this was a sacrilegious misuse of the baptismal ceremony. "But although I had refused her more than ten times, in the end I was obliged by the many importunities of the Signora, and I promised to serve her in this matter."[49] The language of service in which his acquiescence is couched and the social importance of the Signora Costanza, wife of Signor Camillo Superechio, *cittadino modenese,* suggest that Don Gian Battista found it difficult to resist a social superior.

While this case illustrates pressures from above, the expectations of social equals and especially of relatives could prove even more compelling. For, unlike Fra Geremia, not all clerics left their provincial birthplace; village priests often continued to function as members of a kinship group even when the demands such a role placed upon them conflicted directly with their role as representatives of orthodoxy.[50] Don Camillo Forbicino, curate of the Church of San Matteo in Villa Nova, a rural community in Modenese territory, was called before the Inquisitor in 1594 for having requested a local seer to perform a magical procedure aimed at finding a relative's stolen property. He described a situation in which his familial position forced him to prove his innocence of theft by consenting to superstition. A store of sausage had been stolen from Don Camillo's aunt:

since I took care of my aunt's affairs, she told several people, in the presence of my mother, that no one was familiar with her house except me, so that suspicions focused on me. When she told me that she wanted to draw lots (*tirar le sorte*) to identify the thief, I put up some resistance, reminding her that it was a sin. Still I could not really oppose her, lest she then become certain that I had stolen these things.[51]

This priest's close involvement with his female relatives implicated him in a traditional method of detecting theft; despite his show of resistance, their sense of how to proceed overrode his mild clerical scruples.

Alert to his predicament, the court displayed a certain protectiveness for this cleric caught in a web of rustic female error, asking solicitously whether "the above named women forced him into doing this through sorcery?" To his credit, Don Camillo did not avail himself of this classic opportunity to transfer blame. Though finding him guilty, the court noted that his error derived "not from lack of faith, but from the requests of others and for your own honor."[52] The close ties between the village priest and the people were thus recognized, though certainly not approved, by the 16th century enforcers of orthodoxy.

While Don Gian Battista and Don Camillo were aware of being drawn into explicitly superstitious remedies (love magic and divination), the cases of Fra Geremia and Don Teofilo Zani suggest that clerics' own sense of the limits of orthodox assistance was often unsure and conflicted with other assumptions operative in their environment. If the laity viewed the functions of the *sacerdote* as continuous with those of the *strione*, so did some clerics. An extreme case of the functional equivalence of orthodox and magical remedies is found in the trial of a Franciscan Tertiary in Modena in 1599. Fra Girolamo Azzolini, "who makes a profession of exorcizing and of telling who had been bewitched," was commonly consulted for information about whether a given sickness was of maleficial origin and victims of *maleficium* were brought to him to be blessed (*segnati*). The court's summary of his trial focused on his reply to a woman who brought her sick child (*creatura guasta*) to him for this purpose.

'My lady, this child of yours is bewitched (*striata*) and I cannot heal her. If you want her cured you must take her to a witch (*strega*) so that she can look at her and free her.' When the woman replied that she didn't know any witches, Fra Azzolini added, 'Go to Villa Franca, to such and such a person, and tell her on my behalf that she should cure this child of yours, and she will do it.'[53]

Thus the central accusation against Fra Azzolini was that of "having commerce with a witch" by referring a trusting Christian soul to an implicitly diabolical source of relief. Aware of the limits of his own healing powers, he acknowledged the superior abilities of a local healer (here called *strega*) and sent serious cases to her.

Though Fra Azzolini admitted having given this advice, he was reticent about the circumstances in which he had made his acquaintance with this *strega*. Not until his third interrogation did he explain that his relatives had sent for the "old woman who *may have been* a witch" during his own recent illness (italics added).

But when she arrived and learned for what purpose she had been called, she refused to heal him, saying that her confessor no longer wanted to absolve her when she did such things. To which you [Fra Azzolini] replied that since she had performed this remedy before, and had been absolved, you could assure her that she would be absolved again. Encouraged by your words, she signed you with her superstitious remedy.[54]

After his recovery, Fra Azzolini had taken to sending people with an illness similar to his to this woman, although "being a religious, I was ashamed to have done this." All the parties to this procedure were thus aware that it was forbidden "to call for witches in one's own infirmity and to make use of their superstitious secrets and remedies."[55] But under the duress of illness such recourse remained a culturally valid option, even when the Church's prohibitions were fully understood.

Fra Azzolini's case was treated with severity by the court, both because of the "seriousness of the crimes to which you have confessed and especially because of the quality of your person and of the office of exorcist exercised by you." For a specialist in ecclesiastical medicine to send his clients to a *strega*, acknowledging the relative deficiency of his own powers, constituted propaganda in favor of the opposition and clear evidence of his unworthiness to hold the office. Fra Azzolini was duly condemned to exile from the city of Modena and ordered "under pain of *ipso facto* suspension from holy orders, that you should never again exercise the office of exorcist."[56]

While reciprocity between lay and clerical healers was possible, competition between them was more common and certainly more orthodox. In 1600, Gasparino da Carpo called on a Modenese Dominican, Fra Benedetto, because he suspected that his wife Madalena had been *affatturata*. The friar, "having seen and blessed (*segnata*) Madalena three times, confirmed that she was *guasta* and *amaliata*." This recourse to ecclesiastical healing power angered a local woman who had often boasted of knowing various secret remedies of her own.

Having learned that my wife had come to have herself signed by Fra Benedetto, Hippolita arrived at our house and said these or similar words to my
wife: 'Why have you not allowed me to heal? Didn't you think I could heal
you without going to the friar of San Domenico?'[57]

Protecting her territory and her healing function from the in-
trusion of an orthodox clerical healer, Hippolita was seen by
Gasparino as practically announcing herself as the cause of his
wife's illness. For on the principle that *qui scit sanare, scit damnare,* healers were commonly suspected of inducing the very
symptoms they offered to cure.[58] Hippolita was in fact denounced
to the Inquisition as a *malefica* on the basis of this incident.

The perception that the power to heal implied its opposite
has been noted in various areas of Europe in this period; in the
Modenese trials it is first invoked by witnesses testifying against
healers and may therefore be of popular origin.[59] In the 1579
trial of Maria de Mariani, various former clients cited her healing
abilities as evidence against her. Asked *an cognoscat aliquam
maleficam?* one witness replied carefully:

Father, I don't know any *malefica* or *stria*, but I do know well a woman
named Maria de Mariani, a widow who lives in the Villa di Fre and is held
to be a *stria* though she denies it. I have heard Maria say that she has healed
and restored more children than she has hairs on her head, and it is commonly said that those who know how to heal know how to harm. . . . *si dice
communemente che quelli che li sano conzare li sano anco guastare.*[60]

Presented here as everyday common knowledge, the principle
was also incorporated into learned analyses of the same phenomenon. The theological category used to describe superstitious lay
healing – *maleficia ad sananda* – succinctly expresses this ambivalence.[61] Learned discussions of the legitimacy of lay healing
were thus included in the question of "whether it is permissible
to remove a *maleficium* by means of another *maleficium*" for,
though such healing was prohibited as implicitly diabolical, its
efficacy was nonetheless recognized.[62]

The pressures that these alternative remedies created led to
clerical toleration of their use in certain instances, despite their
illicit nature. But unlike the situation described by Delcambre
in Lorraine, where recourse to a priest annulled the therapeutic
powers of the *malefica*, drastic mutual exclusiveness of lay and
clerical healing is not present in the Modenese setting.[63] The
dominant tone is rather one of competitive antagonism like that

present in the case of Thomaso Salani, who called in Don Giacomo Bernardo Lamburano to deal with his violent illness.

When Ludovica Guardasone learned that the priest had come to conjure
(*scongiurare*) me, she went to his house, bringing him a garland of onions,
entreating him to do no more for me. She also confessed that she had bewitched me . . . but that little by little she should heal me. The Reverend
Father answered that she should heal me, otherwise he would find another
remedy.[64]

In fact Ludovica's visit may have been as much defensive as
competitive in tone, for the vaguely menacing tone of Don Giacomo's reply indicates his intention to have her denounced to the
Inquisition — as he later did.

Although the Church's delegation of powers against *maleficia*
to clerics gave priestly healing a solid orthodox basis, certain
accusations against exorcists bear a striking resemblance to those
arising from the ambivalence of lay healing powers. Testimony
against Don Teofilo Zani included allegations of causing the
death of an elderly patient by administering hellebore and unconsecrated hosts during a sick-bed exorcism.[65] Since this was
done against medical advice the physician in the case, named
Arlotto, attempted to have Zani tried by the Bishop of Reggio,
where the patient, Alessandro Pattacio, had been a prominent
citizen. Though Zani was able to justify his intervention to the
Bishop, suspicions about him continued to mount within the
family. The original idea that Zani had inadvertently provoked
Pattacio's death began to shift to the more sinister interpretation
that he had caused the death by occult means. When the physician
Arlotto himself became sick shortly thereafter, the cause was
clear to him. His widow later testified that "her husband had
been *guasto* by Don Teofilo, and on these charges he denounced
him to the Bishopric" before his own death, which resulted
from his maleficial condition.[66]

A fundamental ambivalence thus adhered to the perception
of the exorcist and underlay his transition from a healer of *maleficia* to a suspected perpetrator. Charges against Fra Girolamo
Azzolini in 1599 included similar allegations that he had *guastato*
a young girl whom he was later called to heal.[67] Why were exorcists so easily suspect of causing the conditions they should have
cured? The trial of Fra Basileo da Parma in 1584 is illuminating.
Formerly prior of the Carmelite convent in Sabbioneta, Fra

Basileo had been banned by city officials from exorcizing in
Venice. Relicensed by his superiors in Bologna, he continued
to exorcize until his ill-advised boasting about his prowess with
women resulted in his denunciation to the Inquisition. His accuser,
a scandalized Capuchin, testified:

> He told me that when he was in Parma hardly a day passed that he did not
> commit some sin with a woman, and that this did not at all prevent his
> exorcizing, *since he knew secrets through which the spirits had of necessity
> to obey him.*[68]

The idea that the moral state of the practitioner might limit his
ability to deal with demons was not Donatist in its implications,
for exorcism was not a sacrament and did not achieve its effects
*ex opere operato.* Relating its efficacy to the exorcist's personal
morality was therefore theologically justified and reformers
like Menghi placed great emphasis on this point.[69]

The Capuchin's fear that it was through "some superstition
that these marvels were done" was echoed by Basileo's superior
in the Carmelite convent in Bologna, Aurelio da Crema:

> I know that he is famous for expelling spirits, but what seems amazing to
> myself and to others in our convent is that this Fra Basileo is ignorant and
> leads a rather low life. Nonetheless wherever he goes, though there may
> have been no rumor of spirits, as soon as he shows up, cities and villages
> begin to move, and many possessed persons (*spiritati*) are discovered. At
> times it has been wondered if he has some Key of Solomon or pact with
> the demon or some other special secret for discovering spirits. . . . especially
> since he himself has said . . . that with a word spoken in the ear of the *spirita-
> ti*, he can uncover spirits. This generates a certain suspicion of evil.[70]

Aurelio's doubts express the recurrent suspicion that such famous
and successful exorcists were in league with the very demons
they purported to expel, inducing them to enter a person so
profits and reputation could be generated through their expulsion. If the specialists in controlling the demonic should be suspect
of complicity with the enemy, the central orthodox remedy
against negative supernatural forces would be severely undermined.

Accusations and implications of this sort reflect the deep
mistrust aroused by the exorcists' close contact with demons
and by their control over demons in the exorcist ritual. The
close parallel with the common charge of witchcraft against lay

healers shows that the principle of *qui scit sanare, scit damnare* could be easily extended to clerics. Contact with the supernatural, even when specifically remedial in intent, was, perforce, dangerous to orthodox and independent practitioners alike.

To avoid such damaging suspicions, exorcist manuals such as those by Girolamo Menghi, the prolific Franciscan expert, established guidelines for interacting with demons and above all warned against even the appearance of "familiarity or fraternization" with them.[71] For abuses of exorcism like those of Fra Basileo created opposition and even calls for its suppression by critics and skeptics, the "enemies of adjuration." But discerning observers like Menghi understood that the source of such a suggestion, as of the abuses themselves, lay in the demons' fear of exorcism, which led them to devote much of their energy to combatting this potent ecclesiastical remedy.

Through the services of his assistants, who unfairly and impiously usurp the name of exorcist, instigated to do that which no other Christian would agree to do, the Demon manages to disgrace and tries to destroy the practice of adjuration itself.[72]

The implication that many exorcists are indeed servants of the demon, if not demons in disguise, is striking in a militant defender of exorcism; but the clear message is that this demonic ploy must be thwarted by carrying on with the task, as Menghi himself did during his long exorcist career.[73]

The protection of orthodox remedies therefore demanded the reform of exorcism, carried out through trials against abusive and superstitious exorcists, on the one hand, and through better preparation and stricter licensing of the average exorcist, on the other. All exorcists were to be approved by the episcopal authorities of the area in which they operated; a rigorously reforming prelate like Cardinal Federigo Borromeo granted exorcist authorization to no more than "four or six men of conspicuous piety and learning" for the whole large diocese of Milan.[74] The various exorcist manuals written by Menghi between 1555 and 1595, from the vernacular *Compendio dell'arte essorcista* through the *Flagellum Daemonum, Fustis Daemonum*, and *Fuga Daemonum*, were directed specifically at practitioners in the field and against the errors and abuses associated with exorcism.[75]

Evidence that Menghi's manuals reached the marginally educated exorcists for whom they were intended is provided by the Inquisition's trials against exorcists. When called before the court, the exorcist could use the basic defense that he had only acted, as Fra Basileo da Parma testified, "according to the rules set forth in the printed books of this art."[76] And in every such case, the books cited by exorcists on trial were those of Girolamo Menghi; many of the accused arrived in court with the *Flagellum* in hand, hoping that this would suffice to convince the judges of their orthodoxy.

In some cases it did. Don Bartolomeo, a Celestine friar and formerly a licensed exorcist, was able to defend the orthodoxy of the *brevi* that he had dispensed to heal victims of maleficial illness by explaining that he had "taken them from this book which I have brought with me to show Your Reverences."[77] The court duly noted that the title of the book in question was the *Flagellum Daemonum*, bound in the same volume as the *Fustis Daemonum*. A search of the friar's room turned up a copy of the Italian *Compendio*, which he had left behind when called to Modena, thus giving indirect testimony to his perception of the superior authority of the Latin version.

Similarly, Don Teofilo Zani defended his practice of administering both hellebore and unconsecrated hosts during routine exorcisms of the sick by citing not only Menghi but personal Inquisitorial approval of his use of Menghi's works.

I did not consecrate those hosts which I customarily gave to the sick who were in my care, but rather I blessed the hosts in the manner taught in the book *Flagellum Daemonum*, the book from which I learned the art of exorcizing. I showed this book to the Inquisitor of Ferrara; His Reverence approved it as good and gave me permission to keep it. . . . I neither add nor delete in the office of exorcizing from that which the books teach.[78]

Accused of deviating from normal exorcist procedures, Zani simply cited the authorized text and asserted the identity of the ritual as prescribed and as performed, extending the authoritative repeatability of the printed work from the page to the realm of action.[79] However, the other charges against Zani, which included sexual misconduct, performing an exorcism while dressed in Carneval costume (as a gypsy), and causing the death of Alessandro Pattacio by acting against medical advice, provide a textbook case of the pattern of abuses that Menghi denounced.

Finding his books in the hands of exorcists whose unorthodox practices and immoral lives were similar to those he had denounced is certainly an ambiguous compliment to Menghi's work. But despite the many examples of superstitious and charlatan exorcists presented in his last work, the *Fuga Daemonum* of 1595, Menghi remained optimistic that the trend of events favored the enforcement of orthodoxy.

In these days, there are few superstitious exorcists to be found, for by the grace of God and through the vigilance of pastors and Inquisitors, they have no place except in the galleys or in perpetual prison.[80]

Menghi's self-satisfied judgment was somewhat premature, for problems in the practice of exorcism and trials for superstition against exorcists continued throughout the 17th century. In 1636, for example, the Sacred Congregation at Rome instructed local Inquisitors to issue edicts directed against the "many disorders that continually arise in exorcisms, which many perform with little knowledge and less prudence."[81]

What do these Inquisitorial records contribute to a study of popular culture in the 16th century? The existence of parallel and competing remedies to fundamental problems of everyday life is one indication of the tensions between cultural levels in early modern society. At the same time, the identity of purpose and the structural similarities shared by orthodox and superstitious remedies indicate that these alternatives existed within the same universe rather than deriving from fundamentally antagonistic world views.

These trials demonstrate the pivotal position of the lower clergy in mediating between popular demands and the requirements of orthodoxy. As the local representatives of the Roman Church, the clergy should have constituted the primary barrier against rustic error. But the line between orthodox and popular cultures, if such a line can be drawn, cut through the biographies, personalities, and experience of these men. Their individual transitions between *culture folklorique* and *culture cléricale* led them inevitably to improvisations and compromises that, creative though they may have been, were unacceptable to the Church. No reform of popular culture was therefore possible without a corresponding reform of the clergy in general and of exorcists in particular.[82]

The efforts of the Tridentine Church to erect secure boundaries between clergy and laity, or between religion and superstition, aimed to define and control an often resistant social reality. But the complexity and multiplicity of that reality meant that these ultimately jurisdictional efforts resulted not in achieved cultural facts but in an ongoing historical process to which the records of these trials bear witness.

## NOTES

1. The pejorative orthodox categories of "ignorance and superstition" were used on both sides of the 16th century schism with social as well as doctrinal connotations. For the Protestant version, see Jean Delumeau, "Les réformateurs et la superstition," in *Actes du colloque l'Admiral de Coligny et son temps,* Société de l'Histoire du Protestantisme Français (Paris: 1972), pp. 451–87.

   More neutral language to describe this campaign is proposed by Peter Burke, *Popular Culture in Early Modern Europe* (New York: 1978), pp. 207–43; his phrase, the "reform of popular culture," remains useful despite the ambiguities of each of its terms. Discussing similar difficulties inherent in the phrase "popular religion," J.-C. Schmitt has urged that historians avoid such ambiguities by enumerating "in every case the social categories of which [they] speak and the precise nature of the "cultural levels" by historians is based on the recognition that the distinctions to be made are multiple and contextually varied. This paper, Assumptions that cultural influences proceed unidirectionally or that the "people" represent a unified social or cultural entity are to be avoided; these points are stressed by Carlo Ginzburg in his introduction to *Le religioni delle classi popolari,* a special edition of *Quaderni storici,* An. XIV, No. 41 (1979), pp. 393–97. The increasing use of the plural "cultural levels" by historians is based on the recognition that the distinctions to be made are multiple and contextually varied. This paper, which examines the ambiguous position of the lower clergy in the reform of popular beliefs, is intended as a contribution to this ongoing discussion.

2. The Protestant rejection of the "magic of the medieval Church" is a central theme of Keith Thomas, *Religion and the Decline of Magic* (New York: 1971). The problems encountered by Lutheran reformers in their efforts to suppress magical beliefs are discussed by Gerald Strauss in "Success and Failure in the German Reformation," *Past and Present* 67 (1975), pp. 30–63, and in *Luther's House of Learning: Indoctrination of the Young in the German Reformation* (Baltimore: 1978). Analogous Catholic efforts in the period following the Council of Trent are

described as a program of "Christianization" by Jean Delumeau, *Le Catholicisme entre Luther et Voltaire* (Paris: 1971). The Catholic definition of superstition at the Council of Malines in 1607 reflects the desire to achieve an ecclesiastical monopoly on supernatural effects: "It is superstitious to expect any effect from anything when such an effect cannot be produced by natural causes, by divine institution, or by the ordination and approval of the Church." Quoted by Thomas, *Religion*, p. 49, from Jean-Baptist Thiers, *Traité des Superstitions qui regàrdent les Sacramens* (1679) 5th ed. (Paris: 1741), Vol. 2, p. i. ˙

3. *Maleficium* refers to any harm done by occult means; it is the basic Latin term used throughout Europe for describing the effects of witchcraft. For a discussion of this concept in the middle ages see Norman Cohn, *Europe's Inner Demons: An Enquiry Inspired by the Great Witch Hunt* (New York: 1975), pp. 147–63. A *malefica* is a female perpetrator of maleficial deeds (a witch).

4. Girolamo Menghi, O.F.M., *Compendio dell'arte essorcista e possibilità delle mirabili e stupende operationi delli demoni e dei malefici con i rimedii opportuni all'infirmità maleficiali* (Bologna: 1578). For the skeptics, see below, note 7.

5. Menghi, *Compendio*, p. 225. For a review of the medieval polemic against *curiositas*, the vice of intellectuals, see Christian K. Zacher, *Curiosity and Pilgrimage: The Literature of Discovery in Fourteenth Century England* (Baltimore: 1976), pp. 18–41.

6. For biographical information on Menghi, see the *Dictionnaire de Théologie Catholique*, Vol. 10, pt. 1 (Paris: 1928), pp. 550–51, which cites the various Franciscan sources. Born in 1529, Menghi entered the Franciscan order in 1550, published his first exorcist work in 1555, practiced his art in Venice, Bologna, and Lombardy, and died in his home town of Viadana in 1609. The inscription on his tombstone there relates the "joy of the infernal hosts" at the death of their "most rigorous assailant" and describes him as the greatest exorcist of his century. The text is given in full by Melchiorri de Cerreto, O.F.M., *Annales Minorum seu Trium Ordinum a S. Francisco Institutorum*, vol. 24: *1601–1611* (Florence: 1934), pp. 304–5.

7. It is not clear exactly who the "*curiosi et elevanti intelletti*" are, but the arguments attributed to them are similar to those of Pomponazzi in *De naturalium effectuum causis sive de Incantationibus*. Although manuscript copies circulated in Italy from the 1520s on, this work was only published in Basel in 1556 under Protestant auspices. It is, however, possible that Menghi was aware of Pomponazzi's attack on traditional demonology.

8. For Menghi's list of the *medicine ecclesiastiche*, see *Compendio*, p. 253.

9. On these trials, see my "Discerning Superstition: Popular Errors and Orthodox Response in Late Sixteenth Century Italy" (Ph.D. diss., Stanford University, 1982). For an examination of similar offenses earlier in the century, see Albano Biondi, "Streghe ed eretici nei domini estensi all'epoca dell'Ariosto," in *Il Rinascimento nelle corti padane* (Bari: 1977), pp. 165–98.

10. Canon 12 of *Alcune cose per memoria dei Reverendi Curati di Bologna, tratte nelle Congregazione fatta in Vescovado alli 24 d'ottobre 1577*, in *Stabilimenti e Dichiarazione delli Congregationi annuali dei R. R. Arcipreti, Pievani e Vicari Foranei* (Bologna: 1577), quoted in Cleto Corrain and Pier-Luigi Zampini, *Documenti etnografici e folkloristici nei sinodi diocesani italiani* (Bologna: 1970), p. 36.

11. The requirement of reporting on superstitious or magical activity is outlined in a Bolognese Inquisitorial Edict of 1636, which states: "Si raccorda a tutti li fedeli l'obligo che hanno sotto pena di scommunica riservata, di revelare e notificare giuridicamente al S. Officio (e non con bollettini, o lettere senza nomi) tutti quelli che sanno, hanno saputo, conoscono o hanno conosciuto o conosceranno, che siano heretici, o sospetti d'heresia, negromantia, che faccino o habbino fatti incanti, stregarie, maleficii, sortilegi e sperimenti magicio negromantia, come di tirar fave, far martelli con allume di rocco, sale, piombo, e pignattini con cuori d'animali nel fuoco, misurare o spannare il braccio, tirar le sorti, et altre simili, specialmente con l'invocazione de Demoni esplicitamente o implicitamente" (Aviso della Santa Inquisizione de Bologna, 4 March 1636, Biblioteca Communale di Bologna [BCB], ms B1891, f. 119). It is clear from trial testimony referring to similar edicts that they were issued from at least the 1580s on.

12. The phrase *"pusillis et rudibus"* recurs in official documents referring to the uneducated lower orders of society. See for instance the papal bull of 1571 on the reform of the Office of the Blessed Virgin, "Officii B. Mariae nuper reformati," Pius V, An. VI, *Magnum Bullarium Romanum* 4, pt. 3 (Austria: 1965), p. 153.

13. These figures are based on the trials preserved in the Fondo dell'Inquisizione, Archivio di Stato di Modena (ASM). This fondo was renumbered in 1983; references given here use the new numbering system.

14. The surviving but fragmentary records of the Bolognese Holy Office are preserved in the manuscript collection of the Biblioteca Communale di Bologna (BCB). The intact Venetian Inquisition records are in the Archivio di Stato di Venezia (ASV), Fondo del Sant'Uffizio.

15. These categories have been elaborated by Jacques Le Goff in "Culture cléricale et traditions folkloriques dans la civilisation merovingienne," *Annales: E.S.C.* (1967), pp. 780–91, and in "Culture ecclesiastique et culture folklorique au Moyen Age: Saint Marcel de Paris et le Dragon," in *Ricerche storiche ed economiche in memoria di Corrado Barbagallo*, ed. L. De Rosa, vol. 2 (Naples: 1970), pp. 51–90. Both are now available in J. Le Goff, *Time, Work and Culture in the Middle Ages*, trans. Arthur Goldhammer (Chicago: 1980). An argument supporting the use of these categories is made by Schmitt, " 'Religion populaire' et culture folklorique," pp. 941–53.

16. Trial of Antonio de Correggi, ASM, Inquisizione, b. 9, f.i, 1595.

17. For a similar concept of sin in 14th century France, see Emmanuel Le Roy Ladurie, *Montaillou: The Promised Land of Error* (New York: 1978), pp. 327ff.

18. Trial of Fra Geremia da Udine, ASV, Sant'Uffizio, b. 66, 1590. Choosing among various saints by lot was traditional in Western Europe; it was not necessarily an unorthodox procedure, for when performed with proper reverence it represented an appeal to divine judgment. For its use in Spain, see William A. Christian Jr., *Local Religion in Sixteenth Century Spain* (Princeton: 1981), pp. 47–53; for similar practices in medieval England, see Ronald Finucane, *Miracles and Pilgrims: Popular Beliefs in Medieval England* (London: 1977), pp. 63–85.

19. Trial of Fra Geremia da Udine, ASV, Sant'Uffizio, b. 66, 1590.

20. Opinion was surprisingly divided on this issue; witch hunters, in their zeal to ferret out witches, tolerated a wide array of superstitious remedies most of which were mechanisms for detecting witches and forcing them to undo their spells; for a discussion of the permissible range of "Methods of Curing and Destroying Witchcraft," see Part II, Question 2 of Heinrich Kramer and James Sprenger, *Malleus Maleficarum*, English translation by Montague Summers (New York, 1971), pp. 155–64. Menghi's *Compendio* discusses the same issue in Book III, chap. 2, "Of remedies in general: that is, how one can undo and dissolve *maleficia*, and whether it is permitted to true Christians to destroy them by means of further *maleficia*," pp. 236ff., where he takes a much harder line against superstitious remedies. This opposition is, of course, motivated by the assumption that all nonecclesiastical remedies are implicitly diabolical.

21. Trial of Fra Geremia da Udine, ASV, Sant'Uffizio, b. 66, 1590.

22. Ibid.

23. A systematic survey of the evolution of the category of superstition in medieval theological and canon law literature has been undertaken by Dieter Harmening, *Superstitio: Überlieferungs- und theoriegeschichtliche Untersuchungen zur kirchlich-theologischen Aberglaubensliteratur des Mittelalters* (Berlin: 1979). For discussions of the modern meaning of the term, see Giuseppe Cochiara, *Sul concetto della superstitione* (Palermo: 1940), and Gustav Jahoda, *The Psychology of Superstition* (London: 1969).

24. Trial of Fra Geremia da Udine, ASV, Sant'Uffizio, b. 66, 1590.

25. On the principles underlying magical actions, see Marcel Mauss, *A General Theory of Magic* (New York: 1972).

26. Trial of Fra Geremia da Udine, ASV, Sant'Uffizio, b. 66, 1590.

27. The popular beliefs systems of Friuli, the province of Fra Geremia's origin, are depicted in the works of Carlo Ginzburg, *I benandanti: Stregoneria e culti agrari tra Cinquecento e Seicento* (Turin: 1966) and *Il formaggio ed i vermi: Il cosmo di un mugnaio del Cinquecento* (Turin: 1976).

28. Trial of Fra Geremia da Udine, ASV, Sant'Uffizio, b. 66, 1590. His sentence of 17 October required him to fast and recite psalms on feast days for a year and to perform private penances, including *la disciplina*. His trial is particularly interesting for the information it provides, not so much on the abstract content of the category "superstition" but

about the *process* by which superstition was detected and defined in a specific case.

29. Indeed, the charges against Antonio de Correggi included "lack of reverence for the holy things," including *brevi*, contained in a small sack which he removed from the neck of a sick child during his healing procedure: ASM, Inquisizione, b. 9, f. i, 1595. A case in which a cleric was able to demonstrate the orthodoxy of the *brevi* he dispensed is discussed below, note 77.

30. On exorcism as Counter-Reformation propaganda in 16th century France, see D. P. Walker, *Unclean Spirits: Possession and Exorcism in France and England in the Late Sixteenth and Early Seventeenth Centuries* (Philadelphia: 1981).

31. Among Menghi's requirements for the office of exorcist was the ability to tell natural from maleficial symptoms. The techniques are described in his *Fuga Daemonum* (Venice: 1596), Cap. XII, "De modo quo infirmitates maleficiales cognoscuntur et signis ad hoc pertinentibus," p. 59r.

32. Ibid., p. 49v.

33. Trial of Don Teofilo Zani, ASM, Inquisizione, b. 8, f.i, testimony of 21 May 1582, f. 21r.

34. Ibid., testimony of 1 June 1582, f. 24r-v.

35. Ibid., testimony of 23 May 1582, f. 21r.

36. It should be noted that the family in question was representative of the upper levels of Modenese society. The Livizzano were wealthy bankers and merchants whose members occupied important local positions in both secular and ecclesiastical life throughout the 16th century. See Susanna Peyronel Rambaldi, *Speranze e crisi nel cinquecento modenese: Tensioni religiose e vita cittadina ai tempi di Giovanni Morone* (Milan: 1979), pp. 102, 162.

37. Trial of Don Teofilo Zani, ASM, Inquisizione, b. 8, f.i, testimony of Gasparina Ballotta, 16 October 1582, f. 14r: "Mi apparve un'altra volta con gran splendore in effigie di sua Madre, cioè di Madonna Caterina, et mi disse, 'Che vuoi tu da me, che cosa domandi?' 'Vorei sapere se gli è rimedio all'infirmita 'di Madonna Laura, sia di strione hover di sacerdote, et questo m'a detto Madonna Zia che io vi adimandi.' Mi ripose lei che non gli voleva strioni ma ministri di Christo. Et essendo proposto un Don Teofilo dal Padre Desiderio a mia Zia, lei mi disse ch'io dovessi interrogar la vision se era al proposito, et mi rispose che si, se lui faceva l'opra per charità."

38. Ibid., testimony of Gasparina Ballotta, 16 October 1582, f. 15r.

39. Ibid., testimony of Don Teofilo Zani, 8 September 1582, f. 31r.

40. Ibid., testimony of Gasparina Ballotta, 16 October 1582, f. 15r: "Madonna Margarita una volta mi disse che io gli adimandasse se lei era stata guasta da sua Madonna o da suoi cugnati, et ancora da loro sera stato guaste le sue figliole come lei prosupponeva che fusse vero, et apparendomi [la visione] mi disse, 'Che cosa vuoi? Mia figliola, e sulle anime e sul far de peccati, che attendi Iesu Christo.'"

41. Trial of Maria de Mariani, ASM, Inquisizione, b. 7, f.i, 1579.

42. On the inverse correlation between witch hunting and exorcism, see Thomas, *Religion and the Decline of Magic*, pp. 70–77 and 493–501. The question of the validity of this correlation in Catholic countries, where exorcism and witch hunting coexisted, emerged during a round-table discussion held at Vicenza in 1976 on the theme of "Religione e religiosità popolare," the proceedings of which are collected in *Ricerche di storia sociale e religiosa*, n.s., 6, no. 11 (January – June 1977), pp. 5–205. Carlo Ginzburg, though doubtful of the applicability of Thomas's formula outside England, stressed the need for comparative studies to deal with this issue (p. 175). It would be possible to argue that the relative infrequency of witch trials in Italy, as compared with the con-temporary "witch panic" in northern Europe, is related to the reinforce-ment of exorcism as an orthodox remedy.

43. Lucy Mair's account of the general structure of witch beliefs and their function as an explanation for misfortune sees the need to identify a known person as basic to African witch beliefs; see Mair, *Witchcraft* (New York: 1970).

44. Trial of Don Teofilo Zani, ASM, Inquisizione, b. 8, f.i, testimony of Margarita Livizzano, 29 June 1581, f. 7r. There is confirming testimony about these events by Gasparina on 16 October 1582, f. 16r.

45. Ibid., testimony of Gasparina, 16 October 1582, f. 16r.

46. Ibid., testimony of Don Teofilo Zani, 18 October 1582, f. 18r.

47. Ibid., testimony of Don Teofilo Zani, 28 April 1582, f. 14r.

48. Ibid., testimony of 29 April 1582, f. 11r.

49. Trial of Don Gian Battista, ASM, Inquisizione, b. 8, f.i, 1585. The use of the *calamita baptizata*, as of other love charms, was most often as-sociated with prostitutes; Don Gian Battista was won over in part by the Signora's assurance that she only wanted the magnet to shore up the marital bond, rather than for any illicit purposes. This case is discussed by Luciano Allegra, in "Il parroco: un mediatore fra alta e bassa cul-tura," *Storia d'Italia Einaudi, Annali*, Vol. 4 (Turin, 1981), pp. 899–900, an important article which came to my attention only after the present paper had been written.

50. The now classic figure of the village priest as head of a kinship network is Pierre Clergue of Montaillou, as portrayed by Le Roy Ladurie, *Mon-taillou*, pp. 53ff and passim.

51. Trial of Don Camillo Forbicino, ASM, Inquisizione, b. 8, f.ii, 1594, testimony of 6 May 1594.

52. Ibid. Found to be "sospetto leggiermente d'apostasia da Dio al Diavolo" for his participation in this superstition, Don Camillo's sentence required recitation of litanies and psalms each month for a year, and of a Rosary each Friday for the same year. He was also suspended *a divinis* for one month and required to pay all the expenses of his trial (Sentence dated 18 June 1594).

53. Trial of Fra Girolamo Azzolini, ASM, Inquisizione, b. 8, testimony of Madonna Genevra Buoncuggino, 25 August 1599 (in court's sum-mary).

54. Ibid., summary of trial included with sentence of 9 March 1600.
55. Ibid.
56. Ibid., sentence of 9 May 1600; a note appended to the trial records dated 17 December 1604 indicates that Fra Girolamo Azzolini was granted permission to return to Modena after five years in exile.
57. Trial of Hippolita de Figarolo and Bernardina de Forli, 1600, ASM, Inquisizione, b. 11.
58. Such a principle had long been recognized in Modena; one of the earliest surviving trials of 1499 includes an identical statement, *qui scit sanare, scit destruere*, made by a witness in a case of *maleficium*. This case is discussed by Ginzburg, *I benandanti*, pp. 116–17; he notes similar principles in trials from Lucca.
59. In his study of Jura witch beliefs, E. William Monter has stressed this point, placing the initiative for the equation of healing and harming with the peasantry and arguing that the demonologists learned it from them: Monter, *Witchcraft in France and Switzerland: The Borderlands during the Reformation* (Ithaca: 1976), p. 179.
60. Trial of Maria de Mariani, ASM, Inquisizione, b. 7 f.i, 1579, testimony of Andreas di Saviolis.
61. One example of the usage of this term in the 17th century by the Inquisition: "Di piu avvertano i Giudici, che quantunque alcuna donna resti convinta o confessa d'haver fatta incanti ... o vero ad sananda maleficia o a qual si voglia altro effetto, non segue pero necessariamente che ella sia strega formale, potendo il sortilegio farsi senza formale apostasi al Demonio"; in Eliseo Masini, *Sacro Arsenale, overo Prattica dell'Officio della S. Inquisitione ampliata* (Rome: 1639), p. 178.
62. For discussion of this issue by Kramer and Sprenger and by Menghi, see above, note 20.
63. "Cette même vertu thérapeutique était en outre suspendue ... si le malade avait reçu la visite du prêtre ou du médecin ou avait été administré," Étienne Delcambre, *Les Devins-guérisseurs*, Vol. 3 of *Le concept de la sorcellerie dans le Duché de Lorraine au XVI et au XVII siècle* (Nancy: 1951) p. 207.
64. Trial of Ludovica Guardasone, ASM, Inquisizione, b. 8, f.i, 1589.
65. Hellebore was the name given to a group of plants considered medically effective both for mental disease and for maleficial conditions.
66. These allegations are included in the trial of Don Teofilo Zani, ASM, Inquisizione, b. 8, f.i, testimony of Beatrice Pattacio and Cambius Cambiator, May 1582.
67. Trial of Fra Girolamo Azzolini, ASM, Inquisizione, b. 9, 1599, testimony of Genevra Buoncuggino, 25 August 1599.
68. Trial of Fra Basileo da Parma, BCB, ms B1877, processo 6, 1584, testimony of Fra Angelo da Bologna. Italics in original.
69. The "first condition" listed by Menghi for an exorcist's efficacy is "goodness of life, that is that he not be in a state of mortal sin." The full twelve conditions are described in *Fuga Daemonum*, Cap. V, pp. 18r–23r.

70. Trial of Fra Basileo da Parma, BCB, ms B1877, processo 6, 1584, testimony of R. M. Aurelio da Crema.

71. Menghi, *Compendio dell'arte essorcista*, p. 20.

72. Menghi, *Fuga Daemonum*, p. 47v.

73. For biographical information on Menghi, see above, note 6.

74. The conditions required for lawful exercise of the exorcist office are summarized by Menghi, *Fuga Daemonum*, Cap. V, pp. 18ff. On Borromeo, see Cesare Carena, *Tractatus de Officio Sanctissimae Inquisitione, et modo procedendi in causis fidei* (Cremona: 1636), p. 494.

75. For a brief survey of the Italian exorcist literature, see Massimo Petrocchi, *Esorcismi e magia nell'Italia del Cinquecento e del Seicento* (Naples: 1951). The various works of Menghi are also outlined by Lynn Thorndike, *History of Magic and Experimental Science*, vol. 6 (New York: 1941), pp. 556–59.

76. Trial of Basileo da Parma, BCB, ms B1877, processo 6, 1584.

77. Trial of Don Bartolomeo, Fratre Celestini, ASM, Inquisizione, b. 9, testimony of 20 February 1599.

78. Trial of Don Teofilo Zani, ASM, Inquisizione, b. 8, f.i, testimony of 28 August 1582, ff. 26v–27r.

79. Despite his protestations of fidelity to Menghi, Zani clearly missed some points, especially those warning exorcists against practicing medicine or interfering with physicians. Given the difficulty of finding evidence on how books were read and perceived, the appeal to Menghi by exorcists on trial is important evidence of the ways in which a practical manual was actually used. Some of the problems associated with how books were read are considered by Carlo Ginzburg, *Il formaggio ed i vermi*, pp. 33–61.

80. Menghi, *Fuga Daemonum*, p. 53r. Besides being overly optimistic, this conclusion is exaggerated; the most serious penalty imposed in any of these trials was that against Fra Azzolini, exiled from Modena and stripped of the order of exorcist. Fra Basileo's trial records unfortunately contain no sentence; he was subjected to extensive torture because of the "lack of verisimilitude" in much of his defense.

81. Form letter to the vicars of the Modenese Inquisition, 1636; ASM, Inquisizione, b. 277–78, Miscellanea.

82. The Tridentine model of a reformed clergy is outlined by G. G. Meersseman, O.P., "Il tipo ideale di parroco secondo la riforma tridentina nelle sue fonti letterarie," *Il concilio di Trento e la riforma tridentina*, vol. 1 (Rome: 1965), pp. 27–44; for the decrees concerning the reform, see H. J. Schroeder, *Canons and Decrees of the Council of Trent* (St. Louis: 1951).

# Popular Culture?
# Witches, Magistrates, and Divines
# in Early Modern England

CLIVE HOLMES

A decade ago the publication of two works fundamentally re-oriented the study of witchcraft in early modern England.[1] Alan Macfarlane and Keith Thomas rescued a subject that had been treated at best as a branch of old-style intellectual history, revealing the progressive triumph of liberal rationalism over gross superstition. Macfarlane and Thomas sought to locate the phenomenon in its social context. They argued, both from the chronology of prosecution and from detailed analysis of the trials, that witchcraft accusations were a response to the disruption of the traditional communal values of village societies by the rapid social changes that wracked early modern England.[2] Witchcraft was central to social experience; it could no longer be dismissed as a peripheral aberration. Macfarlane and Thomas's innovatory studies were greeted with deserved enthusiasm but there were some friendly critics. The misgivings expressed in reviews of Thomas's work by two of the latter, Hildred Geertz and E. P. Thompson, raise the issue of the interrelationship of popular and elite culture.[3]

Thomas, both critics argued, had produced a simplified, re-ductionist account of popular culture. He had chosen to treat popular beliefs and practices in general, and thus witchcraft in particular, as "specific, incoherent, and primarily oriented to-wards practical solutions to immediate problems." Thomas had not considered that popular culture might be as coherent and comprehensive as that of the elite: an independent *system* of belief, entailing "a consistent structure of feeling, a whole way of apprehending the world."[4] Geertz was content to postulate the existence of two alternative but equally coherent "cognitive maps" and to demand equal time for the popular cosmology. The historian, she argued, must seek to comprehend the "un-articulated view of reality," the "hidden conceptual foundation" that made sense of the various epiphenomena – "diagnoses, prescriptions, recipes" – that Thomas had studied as isolated and fragmentary. Thompson insisted additionally on the need to in-troduce a class dimension, to see popular beliefs as an "anti-culture" forged in deliberate opposition to the ideology of the elite, thus raising the problem of the relationship between the two systems.[5]

These, then, were the challenges posed by Thomas's most acute critics: to excavate the mental structures that underlie the fragmentary manifestations of popular culture and to analyze the interaction between popular and elite belief. They drive us back to the sources upon which our knowledge of English witch-craft depends: to the records of the judicial system and pamphlets generated by the trials, to the tracts of the theologians and the polemics of the controversialists. Historians of witchcraft in continental Europe and Scotland, wrestling with the difficulties of their own sources, have wistfully remarked that the English materials seemed peculiarly suited to such inquiry.[6] But I find their judgment sanguine; there are Herculean methodological and conceptual difficulties.

Richard Kieckhefer, in his pioneering study of medieval Eu-ropean witchcraft, has proposed a system of source criticism designed to disentangle the popular and elite beliefs conjoined in the trial records.[7] His model, in which the two elements are treated as essentially inert, simply juxtaposed in a static system, may work for medieval Europe but it does not sit well with the situation in early modern England. It neglects two interrelated phenomena. The first is the social complexity of the administra-tion of the criminal law in England. The second is the vigorous attempt by some of the Protestant clergy not merely to police but to transform popular belief and action.

## 1. WITCHCRAFT AND THE LEGAL SYSTEM

To the chagrin of many divines the penal statutes never thoroughly incorporated the theological definition, common to
both Catholic and Protestant Europe, of witchcraft as heresy.
The Elizabethan statute (1563) made the conjuration of evil
spirits and killing by witchcraft capital offenses; a year's im-
prisonment, with four appearances in the pillory, was the punishment for harm to the person or damage to property by witchcraft
and for a number of techniques associated with the white witches.
Such leniency troubled the clergy. All witchcraft entailed a
league with the devil, they argued, and therefore all witches
should die. "It were to be wished," wrote Gifford, "that the law
were more perfect in that respect." In 1604 Parliament recon-
sidered the issue and revised the legislation "for the better re-
strayninge the saide Offenses, and more severe punishinge the
same." Harm to the person was made capital; the penalty against
invocation was extended to any who "shall consult, covenant
with, entertaine, employ, feede or rewarde any evil spirit"; a
new felony, necromancy, was created. Yet the legislators still
failed to acknowledge the divines' insistent contention that
diabolic compact was the central element in all witchcraft, and
harm to property and white witchcraft remained subordinate
offenses.[8] Further clerical protests were unavailing, and in the
late Jacobean and Caroline periods even the 1604 extensions
of the 1563 statute were whittled down by judicial interpretation. The judges rejected indictments for witchcraft unless
the accused "be charged with the murdering of some person."[9]

It is the reluctance of the legal and political establishment
to accede to clerical persuasion, and the consequent concern
of the courts with harm rather than heresy, that has led some
commentators to suppose that the records of the English system
would embody popular rather than elite concerns. But analysis
of the trials demonstrates that this assumption is suspect. Before
the clerk of assizes could scrawl his cold "Po. se. cul. ca. null.
Judm." at the foot of the formal indictment, a complex series
of transactions between various elite and popular elements had
occurred.[10]

This point can be demonstrated at every stage of the judicial
process. In accusations the bulk of the charges were rooted in

popular suspicions. The only significant exception is provided by certain cases of diabolic possession that involved a witch as intermediary.[11] Yet even in this particular class of allegations most of the victims, usually adolescents of bourgeois or gentry families, fastened upon those who were popularly reputed to be witches. So the Fairfax girls first accused Margaret Waite, "of evil report for witchcraft," and widow Fletcher, the daughter of "a woman notoriously famed for a witch."[12] The imposters of the period, those who pretended possession, also tailored their accusations to fit prevailing local sentiment; like William Perry, they charged those who were already "ill thought of and suspected of such like things."[13] Yet, if popular fears generated most accusations, these latter cases should remind us that on many occasions suspicions only surfaced formally as a consequence of some external catalyst. The prosecution of a witch was a troublesome and expensive process; if it failed the accusers might become targets of the witch's malice.[14] In consequence, some stimulus was often required to transmute longstanding fears into prosecution. The inhabitants of Knaresborough Forest lived uneasily with the notorious witch clans of the areas until the mysterious illness of Helen Fairfax activated the local magistracy. For at least a decade the villagers of Walton in Essex had feared Joan Robinson. If they offended her they found that their beasts died or aborted, that their horses refused to pull, or their geese to hatch their eggs. In 1582 they brought charges. Undoubtedly they were encouraged to vent their fears by the contemporary witch-hunt in nearby St. Osyths, orchestrated by the zealous magistrate Brian Darcy.[15] Thus although the process by which suspicions became formalized is largely invisible, in a significant number of cases it is clear that the popular concerns upon which the action was founded were voiced only after some interaction with the elite.

The dialogue between popular and elite beliefs is also clear in the concluding stage of criminal process, the deliberation and verdict of the petty jury. Lord Chief Justice North's rueful comment, that "the countrymen, the triers" were not easily cowed by the authority of the judges in witchcraft cases, should disabuse us of any notion that the jury's verdict simply echoed judicial sentiment. The jury at Lancaster Assizes in 1612 released some of the accused who, in the opinion of the presiding judge, were "as deepe in this action as any of them that are condemned to die." A century later the jury at Hertford condemned Jane Wenham despite Justice Powell's derisive demolition of the prosecutor's case.[16] The jury's continued performance of its traditional role, as the embodiment of local sentiment and knowledge rather than as a neutral evaluator of evidence under the direction of the judge, may be attributed to two factors. First, pretrial publicity attended a witchcraft accusation. "I have heard already, perhaps, as much as I shall at the time of the tryal," says the man summoned to serve on a jury in Hutchinson's imaginary dialogue. Edward Fairfax permitted a local freeholder to try a number of experiments on his "possessed" daughters because "he used to serve upon juries at the assizes . . . and therefore might perhaps be one upon [the witches'] . . . trial." Second, as North suggests, the clamor and excitement at the trial itself could sway the jury. The crowd was an important actor in the denouement of the drama: at the trial of Ann Bodenham at Salisbury Assizes in 1653, "the crowd of spectators made such a noise that the judge could not heere the prisoner, nor the prisoner the judge; but the words were handed from one to the other . . . and sometimes not truly reported."[17]

Popular sentiment, in a complex dialogue with the concerns of the elite, informed the inception and conclusion of criminal proceedings against a witch, and it could be active in the intermediate stages. Prisons where the accused were held prior to trial became places of pilgrimage. Villagers visited the gaol to "see the witches"; to jostle, jeer at, and bait them; but also to seek explanations of mysterious events and resolutions of inchoate tensions that troubled their own communities. Such cathartic rituals might also act as a catalyst, transforming village suspicions into formal accusation.[18]

Popular beliefs and concerns are omnipresent throughout the trial procedures. But they set in motion, and were subsequently expressed through, a complex machinery staffed by members of the elite who might shape those concerns in the light of their own attitudes. Those attitudes might differ markedly from the norms and values not only of the populace but those expressed in the legislation they were supposedly enforcing.

Throughout the period some magistrates were skeptical of witchcraft accusations. Both the leading 16th century intellectuals upon the agnostic side, Reginald Scot and Samuel Harsnett, record incidents that demonstrate that some justices of the peace shared their ideas. Reginald Scot's kinsman, Sir Thomas, had "manie poore old women convented before [him] . . . for working of miracles," yet none of these accusations proceeded to trial. Scot also records with satisfaction another Kentish case in which the skillful examination conducted by two J.Ps., "men of great worship and credit," revealed the fraud of the accuser. Harsnett reports with malicious delight how John Darrell's spectacular career as an exorcist nearly foundered early on the hostility of the Derbyshire magistrate Godfrey Foljambe.[19] Some royal judges were equally suspicious of witchcraft accusations. Sir John Holt, Lord Chief Justice between 1689 and 1701, who, as an observer wrote, "seem'd . . . to believe nothing of witchery at all," secured the acquittal of all the eleven persons known to have been tried before him. The prosecutors of Jane Wenham in 1712, lashed by Sir John Powell's sardonic comments at the trial, wrote mournfully of "the incredulity of the judge."[20] These skeptics had their counterparts in the early 17th century: Williams at the Abingdon Assizes in 1605, the judges at the Yorkshire Assizes in 1622, those at Lancaster in 1634.[21]

Other functionaries of the legal system were zealous in hounding witchcraft. Most adhered firmly to the arguments of the divines that witchcraft was necessarily a product of diabolic compact. The Essex J.P. Brian Darcy affirmed that witches "have sworn allegiance" to Satan and that in consequence hanging was too light a penalty. He orchestrated the 1582 St. Osyths witch-hunt. Magistrates of like attitude and enthusiasm were Roger Nowell, responsible for the 1612 purge of Pendle forest, and Robert Hunt, who would have ferreted out "a whole clan of these Hellish Confederates" from eastern Somerset in 1665 had his efforts not been thwarted by the "great opposition" of "some then in authority."[22] In each of these cases the enthusiasm of a local magistrate transformed an initial accusation into a pogrom; the pattern is apparent in the records from St. Osyths. Brian Darcy, to whom the initial accusation was made, proved to be an enthusiastic and talented inquisitor, eliciting damning evidence from the accuseds' children and inducing confession by a mixture of formidable threats and promises of reprieve: "They which doe confesse the truth of their doeings, they shall have much favour:

but the other they shall be burnt and hanged." In the course of four separate interrogations Ursley Kemp's initial admission, that she employed a few herbal remedies, was transformed into a confession of her murderous proclivities, her imps, and her accomplices, who were then subjected to Darcy's inquisitorial techniques, so broadening the web of accusation.

These attitudes were found not only among local magistrates but among some of the "oracles of the law," the assize judges. In 1602 Lord Chief Justice Anderson, having contemptuously dismissed the suggestion that the alleged possession of the witch's "victim" was a mental illness, assured the London jury that "the land is full of witches, they abound in all places. I have hanged five or six and twenty of them. . . . They have forsaken God, renounced their baptisme and vowed their service to the divill." Lesser functionaries of the judicial system might also hold such opinions: the keeper of Lancaster gaol in 1617 blended interrogation and exhortation to extract one of the accused's confession of his compact with Satan.[23]

Between the zealot and the agnostic lies the bulk of those members of the elite involved in the operation of the legal system. Very occasionally can we examine their actions, even more rarely the concerns that led them to investigate deeply, simply to proceed with, or to quash, any particular accusation. A unique correspondence provides a cameo of the deliberations of the Malmesbury magistrates in 1672. Their determination to proceed with the cases of only three of fourteen suspects named in a witch-scare in the town represented a nice balance between local fears and a sense that they might be thought overcredulous at the assizes by "the Reverend Judges, the learned counsayle there, the persons Ecclesiastique, and the gentry of the body of the county."[24] Similar decisions were made in every other case but they are invisible to the historian.

English judicial procedures involved a series of formal and informal transactions between the populace and the court machinery. Those who staffed that machinery subscribed to no monolithic perception of the intrinsic nature of the offense. This complexity of the English judicial system suggests that Kieckhefer's model, designed to distinguish the popular from the elite elements in witch trials, could not easily be applied in the English context. The surviving records, in their illusory uniformity, are the product of a most complex process. The argument that "English trials closely reflected village belief" is therefore highly dubious.[25]


## 2. 'THE PREACHING OF THE WORD'

The medievalist assumes an isolated popular culture, barely touched by the clerical elite's arcane theological concerns; but the post-Reformation period rejects the assumption. In the 16th century many of the parish clergy, Catholic and Protestant, sought to transform popular belief, not merely to monitor it. Throughout Europe the clerical argument of witchcraft-as-heresy was actively disseminated and in some regions – Scotland, the Jura – it was in some measure absorbed by the populace.[26]

The English clergy, as against their Scottish and continental counterparts, labored under a considerable disadvantage: the law never explicitly embodied a thoroughgoing theological definition of witchcraft. Yet this did not stop them from vigorously asserting their view that the "maine ground of witchcraft" was "that reall covenant that is between Satan and the witch" and that it was this blasphemous compact, rather than the mischief that the witch subsequently wrought, which merited death. Sickened by the gross delusions that flourished among the "ignorant and superstitious people," the clergy's interest lay less in the arcane questions of academic debate than in the transformation of popular opinion. George Gifford, after publishing a treatise, recast his arguments in the form of a dialogue, hoping that this would prove "fitter for the capacity of the simpler sort." Perkin's influential *Discourse* was first "framed and delivered . . . in his ordinarie course of preaching"; Bernard directed his tract to the yeomen and lesser gentry who served on juries at the assizes.[27]

The divines did not limit their educational efforts to preaching and writing. They also sought to employ the public forum provided by the judicial machinery to their own purposes. Their role enabled them to interfere at any and every stage of the process. The minister might encourage the prosecutors, advise the examining magistrates, participate in the trial, and exhort the convicted to confession and repentance.[28] These interventions were not disinterested; the clergy sought to confirm and disseminate their understanding of the essential nature of witchcraft. This is apparent in published accounts of confessions, like those of Mary Smith of King's Lynn (1616) and Elizabeth Sawyer of Edmonton (1621). The trials revealed a typical pattern of local tension: two sharp-tongued women, whose frequent quarrels with their neighbors had unfortunate consequences for the latter. Suspicion was confirmed (to the intense embarrassment of the clerical reporters) by the traditional means: consultation with a cunning-man; scratching the witch; burning the thatch of her house. After the women's convictions on these grounds the ministers took over. Both women confessed their compact with the devil. Henry Goodcole, who secured Sawyer's confession, reported that "with great labour it was extorted from her." A team of "reverend and learned" Norfolk divines worked on Smith, who resisted their attentions "in this holy service" for some time before surrendering the required information. The ministers offered a stay of execution "upon hope that more might have been acknowledged" but Smith, no doubt exhausted by their importunities, "in no wise would condescend" that her execution should be deferred.[29]

The divines were not without lay assistance in their missionary endeavors. Educated laymen, some magistrates or lesser functionaries of the legal system, wrote accounts of investigations or trials that echoed the ministers' theological concerns.[30] Dramatists and ballad-makers were also allies, if less welcome. The minister Henry Goodcole was shocked by the "most base and false ballets ... fitter for an ale-bench" that were sung about Elizabeth Sawyer, but their "ridiculous fictions" were combined with a very proper theological emphasis upon the witch's dealings with Satan.[31]

My investigation was sparked by the challenge to display the "unarticulated view of reality" of popular culture in early modern England, insofar as it might emerge in beliefs surrounding witchcraft. Ideally, this would entail developing a source criticism designed to distinguish the elements of popular and elite belief conjoined in the records. This task, as I have argued, is peculiarly difficult. The records are products of a most complex social process, involving individuals from every plane of society — actors, moreover, whose perceptions were neither uniform nor consistent

Nor can the historian assume an unchanging, inert body of popular belief for the early modern period, given the new techniques for disseminating novel ideas and, more important, the sustained missionary endeavors among the populace of elements of the clerical elite.

Yet, for all their difficulties, the records do permit some tentative conclusions about popular belief. Following the suggestions of Ginzburg and Monter, we have to concentrate on dissonances, aspects of the interrogations, depositions, and commentaries that are not entirely congruent with the legal or theological definitions of the crime.[32] Equally, a sensitive reading of these sources suggests the degree to which popular culture was molded by the concerns of the elite. It is also apparent that the traffic was not entirely in one direction.

Of elements of English popular belief, three emerge with some clarity. The ability to manipulate malignant powers inheres chiefly in women. Power descends through matrilineal ties of kinship. Finally, the witch's power is in part a function of her ability to coopt the forces of the animal world.

That witchcraft was sex-linked is no revelation. However, it is worthwhile to reexamine some of the explanations that have been offered in the light of my previous discussion of sources. Monter has argued that "the roots of the stereotype seem simple and obvious," a conjunction of the "broad misogynistic streak in European letters which flourished during the Renaissance" with the "misogynistic elements embedded in some parts of the Christian tradition . . . re-emphasized during the . . . Reformation."[33] The latter point is certainly apparent in the treaties of the English divines. Perkins is succinct: women "beeing the weaker sexe, is sooner entangled by the devill's illusions" – this backed by the obvious reference to Eve. The theme is embroidered by his followers into a litany of misogynistic tenets. Women are "by nature" more ignorant, more credulous, more obstinate, more impressionable, more proud, more malicious, more ambitious – "the latter because they are bound to subiection."[34] But to emphasize this element is to miss the tone of the English discussion. The divines developed their arguments in opposition to those skeptics who emphasized the incongruity of the devil's seduction of "poore doating old women." John Wagstaffe's heavy irony underscored the point: the Bible's witches were "the wise men of this world," rulers, priests, philosophers; by contrast, their modern counterparts are "poor silly contemptible people, for instead of such as King Manasses and Queen Jezebel we now hear talk of this old Gammer and that old Goodwife. It seems the kingdom of darkness is quite altered in its Politicks."[35] Challenged, the divines were obliged to provide almost apologetic rationalizations of a phenomenon, the preponderance of female witches, that made little theological sense but that "from experience . . . is found to be true."[36] In producing biblical and philosophical justifications no doubt they reinforced existing expectations; but they did not create the sexual attribution. The maleficent powers that witches deployed were traditionally associated with women.[37]

This simple conclusion raises some doubts concerning other recent explanations of the sexual dimension of witchcraft. Thomas's argument, which subordinates sexual to social status, is clearly inadequate. The preponderance of accusations against women is a product of traditional assumptions about witchcraft; it is not a function of women's greater dependence (an unproved assumption) in early modern England, and thus the greater likelihood that a woman's request for neighborly charity would spark the conflict of communitarian and individualistic values — the idea on which Thomas's hypothesis centers.[38] Also suspect is the argument that the persecution of witches was a forcible attempt to compel women to accept the subordinate, limited role of a revised gender ideology. Individual cases undoubtedly illuminate contemporary assumptions about behavioral norms and deviance. Accusations might be leveled against insubordinate wives like Sarah Moordike or Jane Wenham, whose husband had the Hertford bellman publicly "cry down" his wife, "lest any person should trust her to his damage."[39] Undutiful daughters were another target; so were women of aggressive sexuality like Mary Sutton of Milton, the mother of three bastard children, whose promiscuity figured in the fantasies of her "possessed" accuser.[40] Thus, while witchcraft accusations might be employed to uphold the values of patriarchal society in early modern England, the fundamental sex-linkage, which attributed dangerous powers predominately to women, was not an invention of the 16th century. It was a perdurable component of popular belief.

The second element of English popular belief is to be found in the assumption that kinship ties often existed among witches. The divines who wrote on witchcraft explained such ties in terms of simple propinquity. Witchcraft, wrote Perkins, was "an art that may be learned" and therefore those close to a convicted witch – servants, neighbors, and friends – might also have been seduced.[41] The popular belief was of blood relationship, of lineage. In 1626 the spirits that possessed Edward Dinham denounced Edward Bull and Joan Greedy; they were witches "by discent . . . from the grandmother to the mother, and from the mother to the children." A similar attitude informs the sad confession of Alexander Sussums of Melford in 1645. His mother and aunt had been hung, and his grandmother burned, as witches: "he said he could not help it, for that all his kindred were naught." In 1699 the minister of Coggeshall had to comfort a distraught parishioner; she was the "next relation" of a notorious witch, recently dead, and she was in "terrible fear" that her relative's powers would devolve upon her.[42]

The idea that witchcraft was in the blood may be related to a popular remedial measure: the victim would gain some relief by scratching the witch until the blood ran. The practice is found in 13th century England and survived into the 19th, despite the objections of Puritan divines ("a means which hath no warrant or power thereunto, either by the word of God or from nature") and the readiness of some magistrates to give damages for assault to those who had been scratched.[43] Yet some members of the clerical and magisterial elite continued to sanction the practice, a fact that may explain its continued popular vitality. Confronted by the mysterious and excruciating afflictions of family members, neighbors, or parishioners, individuals might find any possible remedy, however philosophically dubious, appropriate and even justify it casuistically.[44]

An appreciation of the belief that witchcraft was an inherited characteristic may enable us to penetrate a neglected aspect of prosecution: the selectivity of accusation. Obviously not all poor old women who depended upon the occasional charity of their neighbors were hounded. Appearance ("did you ever see . . . one more like a witch than she is") and certain patterns of behavior may have encouraged denunciations; but blood relationship to a witch aroused fears that might jell into prosecution. Some individuals successfully traded upon their family's evil reputation to extort tribute from their uneasy neighbors, as did the witches of Fewston in Knaresborough Forest. The head of one of these clans "had so powerful hand over the wealthiest neighbours about her, that none of them refused to do anything she required; yea unbesought they provided her with fire, and meat from their own tables and did what else they thought would please her."[45]

The third element of popular belief is that the power of the witch was thought to be a function of her ability to harness the mysterious forces of the animal world. Familiars, the creatures kept by the witch (Ursley Kemp lodged her two cats, a lamb and a toad, in a large wool-lined pot, providing them with a diet of beer, cake, and white bread) and employed to execute her designs, are a phenomenon virtually unique to the English form of witchcraft. Popular belief attributed to them an importance that skeptics ridiculed and that embarrassed zealots.[46] Satan was the efficient cause of the witch's maleficence; Satan and his minions were described in scripture "to be mightie terrible spirits, full of power, rage and cruelties"; why, then, were they masquerading as "such paltrie vermin, as cats, mise, toads and weasils"?

Doe you think Satan lodgeth in an hollow tree? is hee become so lazie and idle? hath he left off to be as a roaring lion, seeking whom he may devour? hath he put off the bloodie and cruell nature of the firie dragon, so that hee mindeth no harme, but when an angrie woman intreate him to goe kill a cow or a horse?

George Gifford, who posed the question in this form, provides an answer: "it is even of subtiltie." The devils seek to persuade men that they "be but meane fellows," engaged in paltry actions, to hide "their mightinesse and effectual working, which they exercise in the dark hearts of men." Thus men turn to trivial and delusory remedies to drive away Satan's power and "are farre from knowing the spirituall battell in which we are to warre under the banner of Christ against the divell." Most commentators repeat this argument; some speculate more widely. Bernard suggests that Satan is socially discriminating: to the rich and educated he appears in human guise, to the "base, sordid, filthy and blockish ... hee cometh in the baser formes." Glanville argues that, while we know little of the hierarchy of the dark kingdom, it is probable that animal familiars are lower-echelon devils – "servile kinds of spirits." But in all the writings concerning familiars is an uneasy defensive sense that these are, in Glanville's troubled phrase, "odd performances."[47]

The popular belief in animal familiars who attended and assisted the witch, however theologically disquieting, was ultimately incorporated by the divines. The familiar, they came to argue, was given to the witch by the devil upon the conclusion of their compact; Satan's purpose in this was to nourish the delusion that his fearsome power is trivial, "limited by that creature." This composite belief has an interesting side-effect, twisting English practices with respect to evidence away from continental norms.

Sixteenth century European commentators, particularly Protestants, laid considerable stress on the devil's mark. The witch, clawed or branded by Satan, retained an insensible scar as the tangible symbol of the compact. The discovery of such stigmata became a crucial proof of guilt; they were a sine qua non for conviction in Geneva by 1600.[48] English divines followed their continental (and Scottish) counterparts in describing the anaesthetic mark, yet it scarcely figures in English investigations and trials — the Scots witch-pricker hired by the corporation of Newcastle in 1650 remains an alien figure.[49] In England the diabolic mark was transformed from an anaesthetic brand into a sore or teat from which the familiar sucked the witch's blood.

The belief that the witch's animal companions were rewarded with her blood seems to have been a traditional element of popular belief. It appears in a developed form in the earliest trials, those of 1566. Mother Waterhouse, having employed her cat to kill a hog,

gave him for his labour a chicken, which he fyrste required of her and a drop of her blod. And thys she gave him at all times when he dyd anythinge for her, by pricking her hand or face and putting the bloud to hys mouth whyche he sucked.[50]

The first example of a continental examination of the suspect's body, but in the context of the popular belief of the witch's feeding her familiar, occurs in 1579. The Southampton magistrates summoned a jury of women to search for "eny bludie marke . . . which is a comon token to know all witches by"; three years later Brian Darcy employed the technique in the St. Osyths investigation. The 1604 statute, which made it a felony to "feede or rewarde any evill and wicked spirit," ensured that the search for "marks or paps" would become a feature of most 17th century investigations. Although the suspicions harbored by some physicians concerning the reliability of the test were amply confirmed during the great Lancashire trial of 1634, the searches did not halt. They were systematically employed by Matthew Hopkins, the witch-finder, and his associates during their peregrinations through East Anglia in the mid 1640s, when suspects were examined by "a dozen . . . ancient skilful matrons and midwives."[51]

The English searches owed much in their detail to continental procedures: the emphasis upon the genitals, for example, very obvious by 1634, seems to be a direct import. The theological framework is the same in both cases: devil worship. The continental stigmata are the tangible symbol of the compact. In England, the familiar's sucking from the witch's teat is a "diabolical sacrament and ceremony to confirm the hellish covenant," an inverted communion and a parody by which the witch is reminded of the original compact when Satan had drawn her blood to sign that document.[52] Yet the basic notion of the animal companion rewarded with blood is of popular origin. And, by incorporating this aspect of local "experience," English intellectuals were obliged to explain what was, on the face of it, "so strange an action."[53]

Maleficent power as a feminine attribute, associated with matriarchal lineage, and the witch's familiarity with and employment of the forces of the animal world – these are elements of the traditional concept of witchcraft that predate the elite's new interest in the subject in early modern England. Consideration of the evidence for these ideas enables us to comment on our second theme, the interaction of popular belief with the concerns of divines and lawyers in the 16th and 17th centuries. Clearly the English elite modified the European intellectual paradigm as they incorporated aspects of local "experience" within it. Theological and philosophical arguments could be adjusted with only a modicum of rationalization to the sex-linkage and kinship aspect of popular belief. But the creatures associated with the witch in the traditional account enforced a more substantial, and ultimately troubling, addition to the theoretical model.

While the elite modified their intellectual scheme to accommodate some longstanding elements of popular belief, an inverse process, the absorption into popular culture of ideas generated by the elite, is also apparent. This cannot be regarded as a simple imposition upon a plastic medium, however. E. P. Thompson has reminded us that official doctrine was often translated by the lower orders "into a symbolism more appropriate to their own life experience."[54] His conclusion is reinforced by consideration of the varying degrees to which elite ideas concerning witchcraft were incorporated into popular belief. I examine three such ideas of elite origin: the diabolic compact, hostility to white witchcraft, and the water ordeal.

The first is the compact or covenant. The dissemination of the theory that the diabolic compact was "the maine ground of witchcraft" seems, at first glance, to approximate to a simple model of cultural transformation. It was imposed, temporarily and superficially, by the clerical elite. "Not until the seventeenth century did the diabolic compact figure very prominently in the witch trials."[55] It emerges then, I would argue, because it had been accepted into popular culture.

This was not the case in the 16th century. Four tracts were published in the Elizabethan period (in 1566, 1579, 1582, 1589) that give details of twenty-five cases from Essex. Each of the tracts commences with a preface or dedication in which the editor emphasizes the satanic origin of witchcraft.[56] Yet the doctrine makes at most a peripheral appearance in the cases, and then in only five of them. Furthermore, in these five the idea is entwined with the popular tradition of the witch's familiar. The Hatfield Peveril witches gave blood and promised their souls to "Satan"; but Satan was a "whyte spotted cat," the familiar they shared. Joan Curry of Stisted promised her soul to her two black frogs, "Jack and Jyll." Joan Prentice of Sible Hedingham was accosted by the devil "in the shape and proportion of a dunnish culloured ferrit having fiery eyes." The devil-ferret's greeting was awesome: "Joan Prentice, give me thy soule . . . I am Satan, feare me not; my comming unto thee is to doe thee no hurt, but to obtaine thy soule, which I must and wil have before I departe." Yet when Prentice replied that her soul was Christ's, the ferret simply asked for a drop of blood, promised to do her will, and reidentified himself as "Bidd."[57]

By the mid 17th century such a conflation of the roles of Satan and the familiar is far less evident. In the examinations made as a consequence of Hopkins's mission the devil appears in human guise, he contracts directly with his follower, discusses her domestic problems, has "the carnall knowledge of her as a man." This large group of confessions no doubt owes much to Hopkins's acquaintance with continental practices, his prurient imagination, and the efficacy of the fourth-degree methods he employed against suspects. Yet contemporary confessions, from old and new England, contain similar details.[58] And many of the confessions that Hopkins extracted are far from stereotyped: they suggest that the idea of a direct relationship with the devil as the foundation of the witch's power had become generally understood at the popular level.[59]

This is a tribute to the propaganda of the divines: they had molded popular conceptions of witchcraft to square with their own intellectual constructs. Their treatises, sermons, and editions of depositions and confessions had borne fruit. These efforts to instill a recognition of the centrality of the satanic contract were seconded by writers whose works were more obviously popular, the authors of broadsides and ballads. The message was also emphasized in public spectacles, not only the theater of court and gallows but in cases of diabolic possession and exorcism, which were invariably well attended and well publicized.[60] These cases, which in England usually involved the agency of a witch, clearly emphasized the satanic origins of the witch's maleficent powers. The first English confession of a direct contract with the devil occurs in the 1612 trial in Lancashire: the idea may have become rooted in the popular imagination during the wave of exorcisms in the county by competing Puritan and Roman Catholic factions at the end of Elizabeth's reign.[61]

By the mid 17th century the propaganda barrage had affected popular concepts of witchcraft. But a belief in the satanic compact was neither universally held nor deeply imbedded. There seems to have been a total gulf of understanding between Jane Wenham and her clerical interrogators in 1711; "she was particularly asked in what manner she made a contract with the Devil. But we could make nothing of her answer, save that an old man did spit upon her."[62] When the clerical and magisterial elite abandoned belief in witchcraft their theological addendum faded from popular consciousness. The folklorists seldom discovered it: so Couch found that in Cornwall belief in the power of witches "holds its ground very firmly," but not "the notion that

mysterious compacts are formed between evil spirits and men."[63]
The success that the divines enjoyed in promulgating their theological argument concerning the compact should not lead us to
general conclusions about the elite's ability to colonize or to the
passivity of popular culture, however. Other elements of the divines' theoretical model, for which they contended as fiercely,
were effectively rejected by the populace.

The second elite idea is hostility to white witchcraft.[64] "All
witches," wrote Bernard, "in truth are bad witches and none
good, but thus we distinguish them after the vulgar speech." The
"good" witches, engaged in healing and divination ("blessers,"
"white witches," and "cunningfolk"), were anathema to the
zealots. Their powers, like those of the maleficent witch, were of
satanic origin — "one artificer hath devised them all." Indeed, the
white witches were more pernicious than their overtly evil counterparts because, while the latter were feared, "the silly people
. . . sought unto and honoured" the former "ministers of Satan"
for the various useful services they performed. Thus were people
seduced "from the light of the gospel and such holy meanes as
are offered for their relief" and entangled in "the bands of error,
ignorance and false faith." And, like the "Goodwife R" of Gifford'd *Dialogue*, people might shun a powerful ministry, preferring the immediate, tangible remedies for afflictions that the
blesser provided. "The good woman . . . doth more good in one
year then all these scripture men will do as long as they live."[65]

The divines in their efforts to counter these seductive dangers
were not content to assert that the division of witchcraft into
good and bad was theologically invalid. Where possible they emphasized that operationally it was meaningless, rejoicing when a
supposed white witch was brought to confess employing his or her
power for malign purposes.[66] And in this respect the ministers'
arguments were congruent with an element of popular belief. At
the village level suspicions of maleficent witchcraft might well fix
upon those who claimed limited powers for good, women who
could mumble a few old charms for healing or divination like Ursley
Kemp or "Old Chattox."[67]

Yet despite their vigorous propagation of ideas that were congruent with a stratum of popular belief, the divines' insistence
upon the diabolic origins of beneficent witchcraft never took root
except among a small cadre of godly laymen. The latter, when

afflicted, would ostentatiously reject suggestions that they secure
the aid of cunningfolk and might act upon the contention that
supposedly "good" witches were perfectly capable of surrepti-
tiously working evil by virtue of their satanic compact.[68] But
these were a small minority: in general, the divines' insistent arguments went unheard.

Why was this so? Thomas is no doubt correct to insist primarily
upon the functional utility of the cunningfolk.[69] Yet cultural
values and expectations were also involved. The elite did not sub-
scribe uniformly to the arguments of the divines, whose failure to
secure a revision of the laws, to make white witchcraft a capital
offense, testifies to the point. That the cunningfolk enjoyed the
extensive patronage of members of the elite must have weakened
the effect of the divines' arguments at the popular level. So too
must the ability of the white witches to manipulate elite cultural
symbols — complex rituals, arcane language and learning — in their
practices.[70] In both respects there was no easy or categorical distinction to be made between the cunningfolk and the "legitimate"
practitioners of medicine or divinity: Redman of Amersham,
"whom some say is a conjurer, others say he is an honest and able
physician, and doth abundance of good," was a typical figure.[71]
But the zealots' ability to proselytize was not only weakened by
the confusion introduced by contradictory elite norms. More
fundamentally, their argument that apparent good might be done
by a satanic agency ran counter to ingrained belief. Ministers like
John Gaule of Great Staughton, who fulminated against "the
vulger conceit" of good witchcraft, might find the scriptures
deployed against them by their parishioners — specifically
Matthew 12:26 ("And if Satan cast out Satan, he is divided against
himself; how shall then his kingdom stand?'). But this is a legitimation of an older ethical perspective, which Gifford parodied in
the robust common sense of his "Goodwife R." The "good
woman" did *good.* Her power, consequently, must be a divine
gift: "I thinke the Holy Spirit of God doth teach her." The 1621
testimonial from the villagers of South Perrot insists upon the
same point: Joan Guppy was no witch, "contrariwise she hath
done much good to many people . . . and . . . in drenchinge of
cattell."[72]

The general rejection of the divines' antipathy to white witchcraft suggests that popular culture was not the passive, malleable

entity that some historians describe. The active filtering, and ultimate transformation, of elite concerns emerges equally from
considerations of the water ordeal. English intellectuals of the late
16th century knew of the practice of "swimming" a suspected
witch. Scot mentions it and Perkins reviews its merits; but for
both men it is a foreign practice. "In other countries," wrote
Perkins, "they have a further proofe justified by some that be
learned."[73] James VI of Scotland, who recommended the technique in his *Daemonologie* (1597), explained its rationale: water,
as the element of baptism, would reject those who had renounced
that sacrament by swearing allegiance to the devil. Perkins rejected
these arguments despite their royal provenance, and his denial of
the validity of the ordeal was followed by his clerical acolytes and
by Dr. John Cotta.

While divines debated its merits, the ordeal began to be employed in England. The first two recorded cases date from 1612 and
1613. It was used in Northamptonshire by the order of the local
magistrates. The three accused floated and "the suspition that was
before not well grounded was now confirmed." The contemporary Bedfordshire case had no such official sanction. Master Enger,
a wealthy miller, had experienced a number of misfortunes – the
death of his son, losses to property, the madness of a servant. He
suspected Mother Sutton and her daughter Mary, and a friend
advised recourse to the water-ordeal: "I have seene it often tried in
the north countrey." Enger and his servants thereupon seized
Mary Sutton, beat her "until she was scarce able to stire," and
threw her into his mill pond where she "floated upon the water
like a planke."[74] The peak of English use of the water-ordeal with
the approval of the local magistracy occurred during the Civil War.
However, the lavish use of the technique in the investigations
conducted by Hopkins and Stearne hardened the objections of
clerical intellectuals. Judge Godbolt, backed by "the opinion of
the unlawfulnesse thereof" of a number of "able Divines whom I
reverence" (Hopkins's own pious phrase), ordered its abandon-
ment.[75]

Yet the example provided by officially sanctioned ordeals in the
three decades before 1645 proved infectious and the swimming of
a suspected witch became a vigorous aspect of popular culture. It
flourished into the late 19th century despite the opposition of the
elite (a mix of scorn, sermons, and occasional prosecutions of the

principals for assault or murder).[76] The survival of swimming can be explained in functional terms. It served as a public test, resolving village tensions generated by proliferating suspicions of witchcraft; as such it was often sought by those who were the objects of suspicion, like the poor woman of Mears Ashby who, in 1785, "voluntarily offered herself for trial. . . . This poor woman being thrown into a pond, sank instantly and was with difficulty saved. On which the cry was 'No witch! No witch!' "[77] Equally, the ordeal could become a punishment, a popular replacement for the official sanction formally abandoned in 1736. In 1751 Thomas Colley was hung for murder after the death of an accused witch in a "swimming." "Many thousands" stood some distance from the scaffold, "grumbling and muttering that it was a hard case to hang a man for destroying an old wicked woman who had done so much mischief by her witchcraft."[78] The swimming ordeal was functional but, equally, it was deeply rooted in the symbolic world of popular culture. The ducking of those who challenged the values of the local community, notably scolds, was a long-established practice.

What conclusions can be drawn from the records of the witchcraft cases concerning popular belief? First, we must repeat the obvious caveat: the judicial records are the product of a complex interweaving of the concerns of the elite and those of the populace. Yet, by isolating those elements that, though peripheral or anomalous in terms of elite perceptions, regularly emerge in the documents, we can draw some conclusions concerning traditional ideas. Witchcraft is sex-linked; it is an inherited power; it entails the manipulation of the forces of the animal world. The records also permit some discussion of the interactions between popular and elite concerns. This was a symbiotic relationship. The elite felt obliged to incorporate "experience," manifestations of traditional folklore, into their intellectual system. The latter modified popular belief — although the process was not one of passive acquiescence in the values of the dominant classes. Generally, acceptance of the cultural products of the elite depended less upon the vigor of the missionary efforts of divines and lawyers than upon the fit between their concerns and the needs, aspirations, and intellectual expectations of the populace.

## NOTES

The author wishes to thank Susan Amussen, Stuart Clark, and Felicity Heal, who read and criticized earlier drafts of this paper; the staff of the Cornell University Rare Book Room, where a splendid collection of witchcraft materials is housed; and his students, particularly Sara B. Johnson, in those of his classes that have focused upon witchcraft in 16th- and 17th-century England.

1. Alan Macfarlane, *Witchcraft in Tudor and Stuart England* (London: 1970); Keith Thomas, *Religion and the Decline of Magic* (London: 1971), especially chaps. 14–18.
2. Macfarlane has since abandoned this interpretation; see his *The Origins of English Individualism* (Oxford: 1978), pp. 1–2, 59.
3. H. Geertz, "An Anthropology of Religion and Magic," *Journal of Interdisciplinary History*, 6 (Summer 1975), pp. 71–89; E. P. Thompson, "Anthropology and the Discipline of Historical Context," *Midland History* 1 (Spring 1972), pp. 41–55.
4. Thompson, "Discipline of Historical Context," p. 54; Geertz, "Anthropology of Religion and Magic," pp. 72, 74–75.
5. Geertz, "Anthropology of Religion and Magic," pp. 83, 84; Thompson, "Discipline of Historical Context," pp. 51–52.
6. Norman Cohn, *Europe's Inner Demons* (New York: 1975), p. 239; Christina Larner, *Enemies of God* (Baltimore, Md.: 1981), pp. 15, 136–37.
7. Richard Kieckhefer, *European Witch-Trials: Their Foundation in Popular and Learned Culture* (Berkeley: 1976); especially pp. 27- 29, 44- 45.
8. The statutes are conveniently available in C. L'Estrange Ewen, *Witch Hunting and Witch Trials* (London: 1929), pp. 15--21. For clerical criticism of the Elizabethan statute, see George Gifford, *A Dialogue Concerning Witches* (1593; reprinted by the Percy Society, 1842), p. 96; William Perkins, *A Discourse of the Damned Art of Witchcraft* (Cambridge: 1608), pp. 255–57; of its Jacobean successor, Richard Bernard, *A Guide to Grand Jury Men* (London: 1627), pp. 242, 250, 253- 54.
9. Sir Edward Filmer, writing in 1653, first notes the "favorable" judicial interpretation of the statute (*An Advertisement to the Jury-men of England Touching Witches* [London: 1653], p. 2); I infer that it had been developed two or three decades earlier from Coke's insistence that each of the statute's clauses was to be understood as establishing a particular felony (Sir Edward Coke, *The Third Part of the Institutes of the Laws of England* [London: 1644], p. 45).
10. The abbreviated Latin indicates that the accused pleaded not guilty; that the jury found her guilty; that she had no goods or chattels for forfeiture to the Crown; and that the judgment was executed. See Ewen, *Witch Hunting*, pp. 80, 93--97.

11. For examples, see British Library, Sloane Ms 831 f. 129, and *The Most Strange Discoverie of the Three Witches of Warboys* (London: 1593), sig. A3v.
12. Edward Fairfax, *Daemonologia*, ed. W. Grainge (Harrowgate: 1882), pp. 33—35.
13. Richard Baddeley, *The Boy of Bilson* (London: 1622), p. 70. For examples see the two tracts by Samuel Harsnett, *A Discoverie of the Fraudulent Practices* (London: 1599), pp. 101—2, and *A Declaration of Egregious Popish Impostures* (London: 1605), p. 224; see also *Calendar of State Papers: Domestic Series, 1634—1635,* pp. 152—53.
14. Both points — expense and danger — appear in the letter of an anonymous Wiltshire magistrate printed in *The Gentleman's Magazine* 102 (1832, part 1), p. 492. On expense, see Richard Baxter, *The Certainty of the World of Spirits* (London: 1691), p. 46; Francis Bragge, *A Full and Impartial Account* (London: 1712), p. 28.
15. Fairfax, *Daemonologia*, pp. 33--35; W. W., *A True and Iust Recorde* (London: 1582), sig. F4—F5v.
16. Roger North, *The Lives of the Norths* (London: 1826), I, 266—71; Thomas Potts, *A Wonderfull Discoverie of Witches* (London: 1613), sig. V4v; Bragge, *Full and Impartial Account*, pp. 24—28. For another account of a jury employing its local knowledge, see *The Doctrine of Devils* (London: 1676), p. 60.
17. Francis Hutchinson, *An Historical Essay Concerning Witchcraft* (London: 1720), p. 2; Fairfax, *Daemonologia*, p. 80; John Aubrey, *Remaines of Gentilisme and Judaisme*, ed. James Britten (London: 1881), p. 261.
18. W. W., *True and Iust Recorde*, sig. D5; Edmond Bower, *Dr. Lamb Revived* (London: 1653), pp. 15—30; *A True and Impartial Relation of the Informations against Three Witches* (London: 1682), p. 24.
19. Reginald Scot, *The Discoverie of Witchcraft* (London: 1584), sig. (A vi), pp. 127--31; Harsnett, *Discoverie*, pp. 304, 310—11.
20. Hutchinson, *Historical Essay*, pp. 58—61; *Notes and Queries*, 1st series, 11 (London, 1855), p. 499; Francis Bragge, *Witchcraft Further Display'd* (London: 1712), intro.
21. London, Public Record Office, Star Chamber Documents, 8/4/10, especially ff. 18--18v; Fairfax, *Daemonologia*, pp. 122—23, 126--27; John Webster, *The Displaying of Supposed Witchcraft* (London: 1677), p. 277.
22. For Darcy, see W. W., *True and Iust Recorde*, especially the dedication; for Nowell, see Potts, *Wonderfull Discoverie*, especially sig. B2, C3, D3; for Hunt, Joseph Glanville, *Sadducismus Triumphatus* (London: 1682) part 2, pp. 118—65.
23. British Library, Sloane Ms 831 f. 38; Potts, *Wonderfull Discoverie*, sig. I4v.
24. *The Gentleman's Magazine*, 102 (1832, part 1), pp. 405—10, 489—92.
25. Larner, *Enemies of God*, p. 136.
26. Larner, *Enemies of God*, pp. 112, 133—45; E. William Monter, *Witchcraft in France and Switzerland* (Ithaca, N. Y., 1976), pp. 142—66.
27. Gifford, *Dialogue*, p. v. Gifford's treatise was published six years earlier:

George Gifford, *A Discourse of the Subtill Practices of Devilles* (London: 1587); Perkins, *Discourse,* title page; Bernard, *Guide,* title page.

28. George More, *A True Discourse Concerning the Certaine Possession* (London: 1600), pp. 18–19; John Davenport, *The Witches of Huntingdon* (London: 1646), dedication; Bernard, *Guide,* sig. A3–A4; Bower, *Dr. Lamb,* p. 33; C. L'Estrange Ewen, *Witchcraft and Demonianism* (London: 1933), pp. 369–72.

29. Alexander Roberts, *A Treatise of Witchcraft* (London: 1616), sig. A3, pp. 46–47, 52, 58; Henry Goodcole, *The Wonderfull Discoverie of Elizabeth Sawyer* (London: 1621), sig. A4, B3, C–Dv.

30. Internal evidence suggests that "W. W.," the author of the account of the St Osyths trials, was Brian Darcy, the investigating magistrate; Thomas Potts, clerk of the assizes, wrote the account of the 1612 Lancashire trials at the request of the judges (Potts, *Wonderful Discoverie,* title page); the account of the Suffolk witches tried by Sir Matthew Hale in 1665 (*A Tryal of Witches* [London: 1682]) was written by Hale's marshall (*A Collection of Modern Relations . . . Concerning Witches,* Part I [London: 1693], preface).

31. Goodcole, *Wonderfull Discoverie,* preface. The ballads Goodcole criticizes have not survived but elements from them may be incorporated in Thomas Dekker's play, *The Witch of Edmonton* (see *Dramatic Works,* ed. Fredson Bowers, vol. 3 [Cambridge: 1958], pp. 505–14, 551–56). For a ballad account of witchcraft that embodies the satanic covenant, see *Damnable Practices of Three Lincoln-shire Witches* (1619), in H. E. Rollins, *A Pepysian Garland* (Cambridge: 1922), p. 99.

32. Carlo Ginzburg, *The Cheese and the Worms* (Baltimore, Md.: 1980), p. 6; Monter, *Witchcraft in France,* p. 144.

33. Monter, *Witchcraft in France,* p. 123; see, in general, pp. 115–24.

34. Perkins, *Discourse,* pp. 168, 169; Bernard, *Guide,* pp. 91–93; Cooper, *Mystery,* p. 206; Roberts, *Treatise,* pp. 4–12, 40–44.

35. John Wagstaffe, *The Question of Witchcraft Debated,* 2d ed. (London: 1671), pp. 78, 95. As early as 1590 Henry Holland was overtly seeking to answer the skeptics on this point; see his *A Treatise Against Witchcraft* (Cambridge: 1590), sig. El.

36. Bernard, *Guide,* p. 91; see also Roberts, *Treatise,* p. 5.

37. Norman Cohn (*Europe's Inner Demons,* p. 251) reaches a similar conclusion with respect to the medieval evidence.

38. Thomas, *Religion,* p. 568.

39. For Moordike, see *A Full and True Account of the Apprehending of Mrs. Sarah Moordike* (London: 1702); for Wenham, see Bragge, *Full and Impartial Account,* pp. 13–14, 33.

40. *Witches of Warboys,* sig. F4; *Witches Apprehended, Examined and Executed* (London: 1613), sig. B, B3v.

41. Perkins, *Discourse,* p. 202: see also Bernard, *Guide,* pp. 210–11.

42. Thomas Wright, *Narratives of Sorcery and Magic* (London: 1851) II, p. 140; John Stearne, *A Confirmation and Discovery of Witchcraft* (London: 1648), p. 36; J. Boys, *The Case of Witchcraft at Coggeshall* (London: 1901), p. 22.

43. Perkins, *Discourse,* pp. 152, 206–7: for a history of scratching, see Ewen, *Witch Hunting,* pp. 28, 106–7, 191, 201, 362; for a 19th-century example, *The Gentleman's Magazine,* 100 (1830, part 1), p. 107.
44. A leading London magistrate, Sir Thomas Lane, sanctioned a scratching in 1700; the vicar of Coggeshall provided a qualified justification in the previous year. *A Complete Collection of State Trials,* ed. T. B. Howell (London: 1816), XIV, cols. 643, 660, 685; Boys, *Witchcraft at Coggeshall,* p. 19.
45. Fairfax, *Daemonologia,* pp. 33–34.
46. Thomas Ady, *A Candle in the Dark* (London: 1655), pp. 36–37; Hutchinson, *Historical Essay,* p. 77.
47. Gifford, *Dialogue,* pp. 22–29, 89; Cooper, *Mystery,* pp. 79–81; Bernard, *Guide,* pp. 107–8; Glanville, *Sadducismus,* part 1, pp. 17–21; Bragge, *Witchcraft Further Display'd,* p. 32.
48. Monter, *Witchcraft in France,* pp. 157–66; Larner, *Enemies of God,* pp. 110–12; Perkins, *Discourse,* p. 203; Cooper, *Mystery,* p. 88.
49. Ralph Gardiner, *England's Grievance Discovered in Relation to the Coal Trade* (London: 1655), pp. 107–9. Ewen (*Witchcraft,* pp. 322, 345, 455) notes some other cases involving the search for the insensible mark.
50. Ewen, *Witchcraft,* pp. 72–76; Ewen, *Witch Hunting,* p. 319.
51. Ewen, *Witchcraft,* pp. 74, 246–47; W. W., *True and Iust Recorde,* sig. D4, E5v; Wallace Notestein, *A History of Witchcraft in England* (New York: 1968), pp. 151, 154–55. For medical doubts about the reliability of the test, see John Cotta, *The Triall of Witchcraft* (London: 1616), p. 123.
52. Matthew Hopkins, *The Discovery of Witches* (London: 1647), p. 3.
53. Glanville, *Sadducismus,* part 1, p. 17; Hopkins, *Discovery,* pp. 2–5.
54. Thompson, "Discipline of Historical Context," p. 52.
55. Thomas, *Religion,* p. 444.
56. *The Examination and Confession of Certaine Wytches,* ed. H. Beigel (Miscellanies of the Philobiblion Society, 8 [1863–4]), pp. 17–19. (This rare tract was published in 1566: reference to the text will be to Ewen's transcription [*Witch Hunting,* pp. 317–24], but this omits the preface.) *A Detection of Damnable Driftes, Practized by Three Witches* (London: 1579), title page, sig. A2–A2v; W. W. *True and Iust Recorde,* dedication; *The Apprehension and Confession of Three Notorious Witches* (London: 1589), sig. A2.
57. Ewen, *Witch Hunting,* pp. 317–24; *Apprehension and Confession,* sig. A3, B.
58. Intercourse with the devil was confessed in trials in Kent, Northumberland, and Connecticut in the 1650s: *A Prodigious and Tragical History of the . . . Condemnation of Six Witches* (London: 1652), p. 3; Mary Moore, *Wonderfull News from the North* (London: 1650), p. 24; Lyle Koehler, *A Search for Power* (Urbana, Ill.: 1980), pp. 241–42.
59. For confessions that do not suggest stereotyping, see those of Elizabeth Clarke concerning her sexual relations with the devil and those of the two Dunwich women concerning their discussions with Satan on econo-

mic and family problems: Stearne, *Confirmation*, p. 15; *A True and Exact Relation of the Severall Informations* (London: 1645), pp. 2–3, 6; Ewen, *Witch Hunting*, pp. 298–99.

60. *The Triall of Maist. Dorell* (London: 1599), p. 94; Baddeley, *Boy of Bilson*, pp. 65–66; *The Most Wonderfull and True Storie, of a Certain Witch Named Alse Gooderige* (London: 1597), pp. 4, 12.

61. Potts, *Wonderfull Discoverie*, sig. B2v; for exorcism in Lancashire, see John Darrell, *A True Narrative* (London: 1600), pp. 7–13; More, *True Discourse*, pp. 12–13, 50–81; *Historical Manuscripts Commission: Calendar of the Manuscripts of the . . . Marquis of Salisbury*, 8 (London: 1899), pp. 213–14.

62. Bragge, *Full and Impartial Account*, p. 21.

63. *Notes and Queries*, 1st series, 11 (1855), p. 497.

64. Thomas (*Religion*, pp. 177–279) provides a superb general account of white witchcraft.

65. Gifford, *Discourse*, sig. B2, C4, H, I; Gifford, *Dialogue*, pp. 9, 44, 47, 48, 70, 71, 116; Holland, *Treatise*, sig. B1, F4–G2v; Perkins, *Discourse*, pp. 174–77; Roberts, *Treatise*, p. 2; Cooper, *Mystery*, pp. 19, 200, 232; Bernard, *Guide*, sig. A5v–A6, pp. 126–29, 155.

66. Cooper, *Mystery*, p. 225; More, *True Discourse*, p. 22.

67. W. W., *True and Iust Recorde*, sig. A1–A2v, A7; Potts, *Wonderfull Discoverie*, sig. E2v–E3. The two Newcastle women prosecuted in 1660–1 are in the same class: *Depositions from the Castle of York*, ed. James Raine (Surtees Society, 40 [1861]), pp. 82, 92–93. In none of these cases is there any obvious interposition of the *clergy's* conflation of good and bad witchcraft.

68. *Wonderfull and True Storie*, pp. 18, 22, 23; British Library, Sloane Ms. 831 f. 7v; [Moore,] *Wonderfull News*, pp. 7, 10.

69. Thomas, *Religion*, p. 278.

70. In his unpublished tract "The Winnowing of White Witchcraft," the physician Edward Poeton emphasized both the status of the white witches' clientele and their manipulation of orthodox religious and medical symbols (British Library, Sloane Ms 1954 ff. 165–67).

71. William Drage, *Daimonomageia* (London: 1665), pp. 39–40.

72. British Library, Sloane Ms 1954 f. 171v; John Gaule, *Select Cases of Conscience Touching Witchcraft* (London: 1646), p. 32; Gifford, *Dialogue*, pp. 116–18; London, Public Record Office, Exchequer 163 17/5.

73. Perkins, *Discourse*, pp. 206–7; for the whole question of the water ordeal and a substantial bibliography, see G. L. Kittredge, *Witchcraft in Old and New England* (New York: 1956), pp. 235–38, 539–44.

74. *Witches of Northamptonshire*, sig. C2; *Witches Apprehended, Examined and Executed* (London: 1613), sig. C2v, C3.

75. Hopkins, *Discovery*, pp. 6–7; Stearne, *Confirmation*, pp. 18–19. The test was employed by magistrates elsewhere – see [Robert Greenstreet,] *The Examination, Confession, Triall and Execution of Joane Williford* (London: 1645), pp. 2, 4.

76. For sermons, see Joseph Juxon, *A Sermon Upon Witchcraft Occasion'd by a Late Illegal Attempt to Discover Witches by Swimming* (London: 1736); Isaac Nicholson, *A Sermon Against Witchcraft* (London: 1808), p. viii. For prosecutions, see *The Gentleman's Magazine*, 1 (London: 1731), p. 30; 21 (1751), pp.186, 198, 375, 378; 30 (1760), p. 346; 32 (1762), p. 596; 39 (1769), pp. 411, 506.

77. *The Gentleman's Magazine*, 55 (1785, part 2), p. 658. For other examples, see Bragge, *Full and Impartial Account*, p. 10; "Diary of the Rev. Humphrey Michel," ed. J. H. Hill, in *Transactions of the Leicestershire Archeological and Historical Society*, 1 (1866), p. 378.

78. *The Gentleman's Magazine*, 21 (1751), p. 378.

# Sin, Melancholy, Obsession: Insanity and Culture in 16th Century Germany

## H. C. ERIK MIDELFORT

Like sharp stones in a rushing stream, the words we use can be worn smooth and indistinct in the rush of argument and communication. It does not take much reflection to see that the "popularity" of "popular culture" depends necessarily upon what we mean by the people. Shall we mean the illiterate in contrast to the literate, the unlearned, the folk, the poor, the laity, the rural, the commoners, the powerless, the participants in the little tradition, the subordinate classes, or the transmitters of oral tradition? Each of these definitions has inspired a body of scholarship that seems to mark off one group of persons as "the people" in contrast to the learned, powerful, elite cultivators of the great tradition. And yet these terms do not cut clearly. The laity were not all unlearned; the literate were not all wealthy and powerful; many participants in oral tradition were equally enthusiastic participants in the written tradition. Peter Burke has argued that popular festivals in 16th century Europe were popular in the sense that everyone, from all cultural strata, took part.[1] In this usage, then, "the people" includes everyone and the term loses its analytic edge; it has been rubbed smooth. The same linguistic entropy threatens "culture" as well. It is relatively well-defined in anthropology but historians are creating a term that is well on its way to anarchy.[2]

Hunger, for example, is not usually seen as a cultural artifact, but the ways in which we learn to express, appreciate, experience, and evaluate our hunger are clearly cultural. I assume that even in its origins madness is (and has been) partly cultural, that it too depends on acquired (learned) behavior and ideas to some extent and is not simply determined by genetics or chemicals. But I shall also argue that, being cultural, madness can change. I see no point in trying to reduce the variety of mental disorders from other ages and cultures to the system currently fashionable in the West. The modern psychiatric consulting room or hospital is no adequate sample of human abnormality; elsewhere, and in other times, mental afflictions have been different.

Rather than add to the futility of reworking such round, smooth terms, I prefer to proceed as if we know what these concepts mean even if we cannot agree on exact definitions. Theologians, after all, can worship together even if they disagree bitterly in the lecture halls. And in my investigations into the history of madness in Germany it is important to be able to distinguish the attitudes and opinions of people who had little or no contact with the written word, especially in ancient languages, from the attitudes and opinions of the learned participants in academic tradition. I do not mean to imply that there was a constant and unbridgeable gulf between the popular and the elite. In fact, part of my argument depends on the difference between religious and medical traditions in the 16th century, one eager to instruct the multitudes while the other strove to restrict its learning. Culture I will apply with extreme generality to all acquired (learned) behavior and ideas that are not purely instinctive, genetically determined, or the result of physical and chemical causes.

These apparently bland affirmations are far from being generally accepted. Scholars dealing with the 16th century, for example, have been eager to diagnose the ailments of that society and of its members in modern terms; they have, in consequence, ignored at least two historical developments of some importance.[3] On the one hand it seems clear that although melancholy declined as a theme for painters, it was becoming increasingly common in literature and in life toward the end of the 16th century. I shall argue that the medical condition of melancholy was actually on the rise and that we have here a real change in the way certain people regarded their world and themselves, not just a shift of labels attached to some unchanging fundament. On the other hand, there can be little doubt that demon possession also became much more common in the second half of the 16th century. Again, I shall argue that this represents a real shift of mental behavior, not just a rearrangement of labels. The explanation of these two developments has implications for our understanding of "popular culture."

Perhaps it is our familiarity with Albrecht Dürer's *Melencolia I* that has blinded us to the fact that as a medical diagnosis melancholy was not prominent in early 16th-century Germany.[4] But then psychiatry, if we may use such a term, was itself poorly represented among the medical arts and was not yet part of the rigorous academic tradition. By this I mean that when German physicians expressed themselves on questions of mental disorder, their thoughts had a popular tone and a naive substance that would seem distinctly superstitious and incoherent by the standard of just seventy-five years later. Elite, academic culture was blended with popular culture and in the first half of the 16th century physicians often ran the risk of drifting away from the medical teachings of the ancients into theology or empirical (rather than academic) herbalism. If even the physicians were little concerned with melancholy, can it surprise us to find very little melancholy among the madnesses of the early 1500s? I shall illustrate what I mean from several medical writings.

Walter Ryff was a famous medical popularizer, whose numerous works often rashly and radically reduced all illnesses, including madness, to pharmacological problems best treated with fruits, herbs, flowers, wine, and sugar.[5] Although reviled by Vesalius as a plagiarizer, Ryff represented well the editorial energies and philosophical naivety of the early 16th century in Germany. But some have been so offended by Ryff that his memory is controversial, so I shall examine more closely another example. In 1507 Johann Tollat published his *Margarita medicine,* in which he laid claim to the help of his adviser, "the most experienced physician, Dr. Schrick," and of the "world famous University of Vienna."[6] His short treatise is actually another list of herbal remedies for a chaotic hodge-podge of human ills and diseases; it lacks even the normal anatomical order, from the ills of the head to those of the foot. Tollat affirmed that anyone desiring the gift of chastity (celibacy?) should inscribe the paternoster on a sheet of paper and carry it with him: "It takes away evil desires and makes one chaste." But if that proved ineffective, "boxwood drives out the devil too, so that he can have no place in the house, and therefore

Platearius says one should bless [the house] on Palm Sunday." So useful was boxwood that one could use it for illnesses of the brain as well, if one ground up the leaves and mixed them with lavender water.[7] There were other herbs to use against demons. Carrying *berivica jugrien* on one's person deprived the devil of all his power; and hanging it over one's door prevented all evil magic. If witches should enter a house so protected, they would complain at once that they had been betrayed and flee. "So with this herb one can gauge which people have the evil spirit in them."[8] So, too, carrying *gagatis* rendered the devil powerless "so that he cannot do what he gladly would. . . . And thus Magister Enax says that it is good against diabolical melancholy."[9] It is not especially surprising to find these sorts of gross confusion between pharmacy and demonology, but it is striking that Tollat appeals to learned authorities in order to construct his argument.

In a little book by Johann Schöner of Karlstadt (1477–1547) we again find brief, vague assertions and a remarkable naivety with respect to mental disorders. Trained as a theologian, mathematician, and astrologer, Schöner did not flinch from the duty he felt to publish the diverse recipes and cures he had assembled. From the outset he stressed that one had to match the cure to the time of year and to the twelve signs of the zodiac and the twenty-eight mansions of the moon. But Schöner proceeded to ignore his own injunction and descended to the rank empiricism of a herbalist. "When someone goes mad he should be often treated with Meister-wurtz and the 'herb'; soak a cloth in the cooked herb and bind it to the head, and he will come to his senses. Or give him gentian and rue seed in vinegar to drink. Or give him swallow's heart in honey to eat."[10] That was his prescription for mental disorders, and it is little wonder that academic physicians preferred a less popular and more theoretical approach.

We find a more refined analysis in the works of Lorenz Fries (1490? –1531), a physician from Colmar who defended Arab medicine against its contemporary detractors. In Fries we find none of the confusion between matter and spirits of Tollat, none of the desultory herbalism of Schöner, but instead a resolute effort to interpret all human ills in physical terms. Even Aristotle had misled many, "not only by slandering the divine art [of medicine] but also by turning many of his disciples from the true path."[11] To recover the respect of jurists, philosophers, and poets for the practice of medicine, Fries insisted that it was much more than the oft-ridiculed analysis of urine. It was properly a holy art requiring exact knowledge of human nature (e.g., the seven naturals, three counter-naturals, and six non-naturals). In practice Fries recommended a humoral and herbal therapy that counteracted disease by increasing or decreasing the qualities of hotness, coldness, wetness, and dryness, in the manner precisely familiar to us from countless other Renaissance medical treatises. As an intellectual construct this sort of medicine marked a real advance beyond the chaos of Tollat and the empiricism of Schöner. On mental disorder, for example, the physician's main task was to discover the source of the illness, from which one could usually deduce a remedy. If a patient suffered headaches from too much black bile, for example, he would very likely be unable to sleep, be full of fears, and show a leaden or pale face, a slow, small pulse, and clear urine. "Treat him by giving him a good routine and see to it that he is not sad." Every morning he was to receive four half-ounces of *oximellis* mixed in the water of oxtongue.[12] It is noteworthy that Fries also gave melancholy extremely short shrift even though, within a few decades, it was to become the premier disease of the 16th century, encouraging (and responding to) the growth of a dense literature.[13]

Fries considered mania a more complex disease. It had a wide variety of causes ranging from too much wine, the bite of a rabid dog, and poisonous air, to highly seasoned food. Any of the four humors could be corrupted to produce mania as well. If the patient had too much blood, he might "talk constantly, dance, hop about, sing, and be gay, desiring to hear harp music all the time. His pulse is fast and hard, his urine red and thick, and his age eighteen to twenty. His complexion is warm and moist, and the season is also warm and moist."[14] On other occasions it is corrupt choler that causes mania — complaining, screaming, murderous drives. At still other times, phlegm was at fault, producing the delusion that one was surrounded by water or a continuous sleep. And finally, of course, black bile or melancholy could induce a mania that was characterized by constant sadness and fearfulness, the sense of being "among dead and monstrous things" and the "constant worry that someone would catch him."[15] With all the confidence of a systematician, Fries provided humoral and herbal prescriptions for all of these serious disorders. Even when dealing with

sexual complaints, Fries scrupulously avoided moralizing comment
and contented himself with adjusting the patient's bodily fluids.[16]
In so doing he was practicing the physician's discretion, that traditional attitude of somatic reductionism by which medical doctors
set themselves off from their philosophical, theological, and juridical colleagues.

When Philip Melanchthon undertook to describe the soul and its
ills, both physical and spiritual, he seems to have followed Fries's
exposition rather closely.[17] Inevitably this caused Melanchthon
some trouble, for somatic reductionism could not well be brought
to agree with man's nature as a moral agent. Sin had to originate in
the free will of man and of the devil.[18] Without freedom man
would be no more than a cow, Melanchthon thought, incapable of
sin and beyond all punishment.[19] And so the theologian had to
part company from his medical model in order to avoid serious
theological trouble. For most theologians, as indeed for most
persons, man had to be more than his humors.

But for the medical academic the charms of somatic reduction
were precisely that it excluded extraneous concerns and allowed a
retreat from (or advance beyond) the dolors of common sense. It
does, in fact, seem that one of the tacitly accepted features of any
profession or discipline is a sturdy aversion to what I shall simply
call "common sense." As Renaissance German physicians recoiled
from the popular culture of vulgar empiricism, they came to
appreciate more fully the theoretical mysteries of Galenism.
Academic psychiatry in Germany became not less but *more* Gale-
nist in the second half of the 16th century, despite the legendary
discoveries of Vesalius and others.

In psychiatric subjects what mattered most was getting the
theory straight, and theory was nowhere clearer than in the formal
academic disputation. Academic disputations and the inaugural
dissertation provided a parade ground for academic discipline, the
display of learned commentary on ancient Greek medical sources
in an environment inured to the siren songs of theology, jurispru-
dence, philosophy, and folk wisdom. I do not mean to imply that
academic medicine was a preserve of autistic nonsense, but only
that it sustained its proud autonomy and its professional status by
maintaining a vigil over its chosen sources and by excluding popular notions and the dogmas of the other professions.

Increasingly in the 16th century, medical professionals in Germany distinguished themselves from popularizing dabblers by resolutely holding that all phenomena (and especially all diseases) were physical in origin. Such an attitude meant rejecting all popular and learned attempts to link disease with sin or immorality, or with demons, or with God himself. The somatic approach to all human ills spelled a sharp foreshortening of the human horizon, it seems, but it also shielded medicine from the vulgar intrusions of those who were not trained to appreciate the charms of the somatic dispensation.[20]

One reason for this rise of a specifically academic psychiatry was the growing prominence of classical topics after 1550. Printed dissertations became common after 1570 and they reveal a new fascination surely inspired in part by the fact that Galen and Hippocrates had themselves lavished substantial attention on mental disorders; from these sources Renaissance physicians had both an ancient tradition and an esoteric language on which to draw. Thus, as psychiatric topics entered the medical elite mainstream in Germany, the influence of Galen actually rose. Of the 241 disputations registered by Oskar Diethelm for the period 1550–1650, fully 138 dealt with just four classical disorders: melancholy, hypochondriasis (and hypochondriacal melancholy), mania, and phrenesis. After 1600 theses on hysteria, another classical topic, became increasingly common as well.[21] To gauge the extent of the shift from the earlier part of the 16th century, I shall examine briefly a few of the disputations held at the University of Tübingen.

The earliest of the Tübingen disputations was the 1580 *Disputatio medica de capite et cerebro hominis* proposed by Andreas Planer, with Helias Waldner of Memmingen as respondent.[22] It was an extraordinary analysis, not so much because of the wide variety of diseases it had to consider (for that was common enough) as because of an obsessive emphasis on the hair. The chief problem in studying the brain, of course, was that physicians in the 16th century had no way of observing a living brain directly. They had to infer everything from easily visible signs; and Galen provided the structure of inference. There were, he had thought, two kinds of sign, innate and external, from which one might hope to estimate the condition of the brain. The innate signs consisted of its size and shape (thesis 3), its operations in sensation and sleep (theses 7, 8), the bodily motions prompted by the brain (thesis 9), the mental guides to the brain revealed in the *sensus communis*, phantasy, memory, and thought (theses 11, 12), and finally the process of nourishing the brain, which could be studied indirectly through cerebral excrements of various sorts (theses 14, 15). The external signs were composed of the way in which the brain responded to the six non-naturals: air, sleep, food and drink, rest and exercise, excretion and retention, and the mental affections.

Physicians could also gauge the state of the brain from the heat, toughness, and moisture of the cerebral substance. Too soft, too thick, too hot a brain — all spelled mental difficulties. How could one judge these qualities? Cerebral excrements in the eyes, ears, nose, and mouth could all be observed but excrement could also flood the lungs, nerves, throat, veins, and stomach, producing an amazing variety of physical ills (theses 32—42). Faced with this bewildering catalog of cerebral symptoms, the physician might turn with some relief to a consideration of the hair, as discussed by the ancients. At first this bizarre suggestion might seem arbitrary but on reflection the emphasis on hair is a perfect example of the medical retreat from common sense into a system of judgment that could only be based on the secret wisdom of the academy. Since hair sprouted almost from the brain itself, its growth, color, strength, and texture revealed something of the brain itself (theses 46—51). A dry brain, for example, produced curly, strong, fast-growing hair, but also baldness. Such persons could be unusually wise. A humid head, on the other hand, resulted in straight hair and no baldness. Such persons were often dull, stupid, and somnolent (theses 68—72). Without the structure of inference provided by Galen, where would this dissertation have been? Without the search for secret coherence, indeed, where would any science be?

A very different disputation was that of Daniel Moegling of Tübingen, held at Heidelberg in 1584 with Johann Kuhn (Cuno) as respondent.[23] Beginning with the theological proposition that man was made in God's image, having the use of reason, the formal *quaestio* asked how it was that phrenesis, or brain fever, could push man so far from reason that he became like the wild beasts. Although this opening statement seemed to invite theological commentary on the human nature of the mad, the dissertation quickly entered calmer medical waters by asserting that the cause and cure of such metamorphoses were matters for the physician. Revealing a keen grasp of philosophical complexities, however, Moegling and Kuhn noted that, strictly speaking, the human mind was not liable to death or disease; but so long as it was trapped in this prison of a body (*in hoc ergastulo*), it had to abandon its integrity and attach itself to the inferior faculties of the soul and use the ministry of the interior and exterior senses. Being in this way a composite construction, it became capable of suffering (thesis 1). Here then is a disputation in which major theological and philosophical issues do break the surface but only in such a way as to justify the medical concern with physical things.

Phrenesis was defined as inflammation of the brain with acute fever and delirium (thesis 4). After distinguishing various sorts of phrenesis, Moegling and Kuhn turned to a detailed consideration of its etiology, symptomatology, and prognosis. Since cure was exceedingly difficult, they noted that the prudent physician would rather avoid the disease altogether (thesis 38). Still, a cure could be effected if the matter of the disease (i.e., the corrupt phlegm) were destroyed or if the source of the corruption itself were corrected. All of these procedures required the use of purges "with a skilled moderation" (*docta moderatione*) (theses 38, 43, 46), or diet, or venesection, or baths (theses 46, 47, 52, 54, 55, 57). Only when the crisis was past and the disease was in retreat did Moegling and Kuhn concede the utility of applying to a feverish head such ancient remedies as split chickens, capons, piglets, and dogs (all alive but with their spines cut), or the fresh lung of a ram, or warm woman's milk (thesis 60). Since it seems unlikely that Moegling actually held these steps to be effective, it is noteworthy that he relegated this advice to the stage when the patient was already on the mend. Ultimately, diet and soothing surroundings were of prime importance in helping the patient. Friends too could help to calm and flatter him. But if these measures failed to cool the rage, the patient might need chains to confine him. Even so, it was not for the physician to take this last step but for the sick man himself and the attending officials "to make sure that all is done in right order" (thesis 64). This last statement seems to reveal an awareness of the ethical issues involved in the incarceration or involuntary coercion of the mad. Physicians were to have no part in such decisions. Medicine was not yet an arm of the state.

In 1588 the Tübingen professor Georg Hamberger presided at another disputation on phrenesis with Balthasar Bruno (Braun) as respondent.[24] Although the dissertation follows the same explanatory scheme as that of Moegling and Kuhn four years earlier, it is striking how much room there was for shifts in emphasis. Hamberger began, for example, by stressing the divergent views of the ancient *prisci medici* (*quaestio*). Instead of worrying about corrupt phlegm reaching the head, this disputation concentrated on the dangers of overly thin blood shooting up to the brain and, finding its return blocked, causing inflammation. Brain fever could also be caused by an excess of bright bile (choler), which could turn men into animals requiring chains. Hamberger was not bothered by the question of who should make such decisions.

In 1602 yet another Tübingen professor, Sebastian Bloss, undertook a discussion of phrenesis with Matthaeus Müller as respondent.[25] Unlike the disputations considered so far, this one cited a fair amount of recent literature instead of commenting exclusively on Galen and Hippocrates. In addition, it showed a lively interest in the effects of brain fever on each of the three internal senses: phantasy, memory, and the common sense (theses 12–20). After agreeing that phrenesis was so dangerous that most patients died, the disputation turned nonetheless to cures; here, amid the common recommendations of blood-letting and purging, was an unusual emphasis on cooling off the patient with special drinks and drugs. Among the prescriptions for oil of roses and violets, for lettuce water and the like, the modern reader may be amused to discover recipes for a medicinal blend of the juice of oranges or lemons and sugar: lemonade? These were truly exotic prescriptions in the 16th and early 17th centuries, for both sugar and citrous fruits were very likely hard to find except in a well-stocked pharmacy. With this emphasis on drinks and drugs, however, Bloss and Müller were clearly defending an approach to phrenesis that differed from that of their Tübingen predecessors. The Galenic system was a house of many mansions.

Some of the other Tübingen dissertations showed a similarly creative approach to their topics. We cannot say that they were aimed at producing original conclusions; in fact, the basic assumption in most cases was probably that originality was no virtue. And yet the spread of printed disputations probably encouraged an elite taste for novelty, creativity, or even originality. So long as disputation of Andreas Planer with Johann Fabri (Schmidt?) as content himself by answering timeless questions with timeless answers. But as professors and respondents began to publish these questions and answers, an unspoken urge may have shaped the old materials into new forms, probing and testing the old conclusions. Although this urge did not send physicians rushing to their laboratories for new evidence and controlled experiments, pages as dusty and neglected as these medical dissertations evince an effort to arrive at new conclusions or at least to apply the old wisdom to more recent topics.

A good example of this tendency may be found in the 1593 disputation of Andreas Planer with Johann Fabri (Schmidt? ) as respondent.[26] Entitled *De morbo Saturnino seu melancholia,* the dissertation was not content with the ancients but pushed on to consider whether witches were really only melancholy. "The demon can make one melancholic. Melancholy persons possessed by the devil are healed not by use of drugs but by prayers. The melancholy are authors of their own death, not all of the things of hell. Old women with melancholy tend to become witches." These assertions betray a feeble attempt to keep medicine and theology separate, especially in the claim that the possessed need prayer rather than medical care. But in the last claim, the authors seemed to agree with Johann Weyer and his disciples that witches were mainly melancholy, a controversial claim usually taken to imply that their confessions were the worthless products of hallucination. If so, we have here another case of medical reduction, the invasion of medical thinking into the domain of law and theology. We do not know what was actually said at this point of the disputation; as it stands the utterance is a gnomic reminder of how little we know of the past.

In addition to these extraordinary extensions, this disputation also revealed an unusual interest in man as the microcosm, as comprehending, reflecting, and participating in all of the parts and processes of the cosmos. Although the theme was a commonplace among neo-Platonic thinkers, medical writers often paid it no mind. Here, however, Fabri's dedicatory epistle to Duke Ludwig of Württemberg contended that human diseases were strictly analogous to earthly disturbances. Just as the sun is sometimes eclipsed by the moon, so too the brain is sometimes darkened by phrenesis, delirium, mania, dizziness, suffusions, and cataracts.[27]

Melancholy was analogically distinct: it corresponded rather to the windy, cold, dry season of autumn, a time of sad storms. The forging of this neo-Platonic link between melancholy and the cosmos made this disputation unusual and it is not surprising that it also referred to the pseudo-Aristotelian claim that melancholy predisposed one to genius.[28] This medical dissertation approached philosophy and theology so closely that it ran the risk of overstepping the professional boundaries that ensured physicians an autonomous existence as a separate discipline.

That danger did not exist for the authors of a 1586 dissertation on diseases of the temperament.[29] Andreas Planer presided with Thomas Schlaier of Tübingen as respondent. Together they analyzed the ways that heat, cold, moisture, and dryness could become unbalanced and produce a host of psychosomatic disorders. The disputants allowed no moral, ethical, or theological issues to interfere with a strictly medical approach.

These examples from the University of Tübingen do not prove my argument but they should suffice to indicate that the disputations produced by the academic medical establishment were not the monophonic chorus that some historians have supposed. But it is also true that we do not find here the adumbration of modern psychiatry. Rather, they lift the veil from a learned, elite culture that was often content to comment self-indulgently on its Greek founders. Even unadventurous writers on psychiatric topics were able to forge a variety of responses to the classical questions. There was no orthodoxy except with respect to the language and the language-game within which an answer had to be given. The language of Galen encouraged academic physicians to abandon the popular or vulgar herbalism and "superstition" that was sometimes to be found in German medicine before about 1550. The theoretical search that Galen inspired supported an academic method of inquiry that allowed psychiatry to transform itself from within. The 17th century produced a number of physicians who unconsciously affirmed Galen's method even as they rejected his conclusions. But it must also be said that the Galenic system blunted the use of case histories, of detailed clinical reporting, and of categories of disease drawn from philosophy and theology – notably disorders brought on by guilt and demon possession.

This academic retreat from the world of theology and folklore also meant that physicians did not proselytize the folk, baptizing

them in the name of Galen or preaching the word of humoral
therapy. We find here a clear and early effect of what Peter Burke
suggestively described as the separation of high culture from popular culture.[30] In any event academic physicians were too thinly
spread and too dependent on clients who could pay their fees to
have had a genuinely popular audience before the rise of health
insurance and socialized medicine.[31]

Academically trained physicians did, however, make demonstra-
ble inroads on the understanding of their wealthy client-patients.
If one surveys the peculiar subgroup of mad princes in 16th-century
Germany, for example, one notes humoral therapy replacing the
common practice around 1500 of simply locking or chaining an
offensive prince in some (preferably remote) castle, where he
could no longer waste the substance of his territory, shoot ran-
domly at his neighbors, or threaten his attendants. When relatives
decided that it was time to take forceful steps against Count Heinrich of Württemberg (in 1490), Margrave Friedrich the Elder of
Ansbach and Bayreuth (in 1515), and Margrave Christoph I of
Baden (in 1518), medical care was the least of their concerns; the
princes were treated as indifferently as the more famous case of
Juana la Loca of Spain, the mother of Charles V.[32] This subject
merits detailed investigation but it seems clear that, by the late
16th century, princes were regularly subjected to humoral treatment (purging, bleeding, change of diet) and were expected to
improve. Albrecht Friedrich, Duke of Prussia, for example, was
given the best, up-to-date care by learned physicians.[33] Under the
care of an English physician, mad Duke Johann Wilhelm of Jülich-
Cleves improved so dramatically in the 1590s that he was released
from confinement and allowed to remarry.[34] Such cases, common
by the late 16th century, were virtually unimaginable in Germany
two or three generations earlier. Princes had come to think in
Galenic, humoral, and that is to say therapeutic, terms. Such
changes in attitude and in therapy do not, of course, imply that
the mental disorders of princes had actually changed as well; but
that is a strong possibility that warrants close scrutiny.

When poor people got sick, they were smitten with different
ills. When they went mad, they went mad with a difference.[35]
Hospital records from the 16th century rarely tell us anything
about the symptoms of their patient-residents but a cache of
*Rezeptionsreskripte* from Hesse suggests that the key characteris-

tics of the poor mad were "nonsense" and "silliness," an inability to work, and regression both socially and legally to the status of children. These documents were petitions requesting entry into the newly founded hospitals of Haina (for men) and Merxhausen (for women); and they form a source unparalleled (at least in Germany) for the study of mental disorders among the poor. Of the 183 persons for whom a petition survives for the period 1550–1622, 39 were retarded, brain-damaged, or mentally ill. In some cases the petition simply remarks, as with Catrin Koch in 1577, that she was now "thoroughly and completely bereft of her senses and reason, and there is no hope of improvement."[36] Or the document might describe a girl admitted to Merxhausen in 1612 as simply "crazy and mute."[37] But the descriptions could be much richer.

If we try to construct rough categories for these afflicted persons, we confront at once the often impossibly vague language regarding the poor. The petitioners had no real interest in or familiarity with medical diagnosis; they intended simply to demonstrate that a person needed care and no fancy Latin description was necessary for that. Therefore, in several cases the writers referred to persons who were "bereft of reason," "senseless," "silly," or "nonsensical." When such a person was a child one can, perhaps, conclude that he or she was retarded but that is not clear in every case. When the person was aged, forgetful, and "crazy," one suspects senility but again it is a guessing game. I have constructed a table of such guesswork, however, with the hope that it is not thoroughly arbitrary.

Table I: Frequency of Brain Damage, Retardation, and Mental Illness among Applicants to Haina and Merxhausen

| Probable Classification | Number of Cases |
| --- | --- |
| Retarded or brain damaged at birth | 11 |
| Brain damaged in accident | 2 |
| Mentally ill, "mad" | 16 |
| Senile | 1 |
| "Foolishness" produced by epilepsy | 1 |
| Indistinct cases | 8 |
| Total | 39 |

Although many of these diagnoses remain questionable, several cases shine a bright light into some dark corners of social behavior. Take the case of Steffan Mauschnud, whose four daughters pleaded with Landgrave Phillip late in 1560 to take their father into Haina. He had entered Haina originally as a brother early in 1560 but, after fighting there, he had been expelled. The four daughters were trying to care for him but he fought and argued with them too, demanding food and drink at all times and flying into rages in which he "strikes and tries to strangle us." In addition, in this "staggeringly expensive time," the daughters claimed that they could not afford to keep him. To strengthen their petition they reminded the Landgrave that God would surely reward his charity if he would readmit their father.

On 18 July 1587 a widow asked Landgrave Wilhelm to take pity on her. When her husband had died three years earlier, she had been left with six small children, one of whom was "bereft of his senses." He was now fifteen and "so lacking in reason that he is a great domestic affliction and a heavy burden." If pious neighbors had not taken care of him, he would already have drowned or harmed himself with fire. And now with prices so high, she could not earn enough to support him. The boy was ordered admitted to Haina on 10 October 1587.

These cases suggest that family members and neighbors were expected to care for their own and were to seek aid from the territorial prince only when a person became unmanageable. This was clearly the case with Heinrich Senger of Homberg, who fell into a more and more serious madness. The local pastor, Caspar Arcularius, explained that "some years ago Senger had behaved strangely both in words and in deeds, as if he was a madman." The neighbors had tried to practice "Christian love, patience, and sympathy" in tolerating him, but matters grew worse. Now, in 1593, his reason and human understanding were totally deranged and he was too much for his wife, "who up to now has cared for him not only with great trouble and effort, but also in danger of life and limb." The neighborhood could "no longer stand to see this miserable specimen, nor could they trust this irrational and senseless person, who might at any hour or moment either kill himself (as he doubtless would have long ago if his wife and neighbors had not kept watch over him) or wound others by hitting, stabbing, burning, etc., and thus produce irreparable damage." Arcularius concluded

that Senger must be admitted to Haina "in order that greater misfortune be avoided and that the poor man be helped." The pastor
did not neglect to say that God would richly reward such charity
"both here temporally and then eternally, in body and soul."
Senger was, of course, admitted to the stout cells of Haina.

In 1581 a widow burdened with four deformed, retarded, mute
children petitioned for relief, saying that their monstrous form
and foolish behavior made them useless for work and incapable of
learning. Landgrave Wilhelm noted in his order that he had seen
these sorry creatures himself and that two of the four should be
taken from her and sent to Haina.

Another example of gradually strained neighborhood tolerance
was the case of Daniel Hoffmann of Stauffenberg. In this case, in
March 1590 the Burghermaster and Council of Stauffenberg wrote
to the Captain of Giessen, Rudolf Wilhelm Raw, ten kilometers
distant, to inform him that Hoffmann was acting as if possessed.
He had been found in his barn with a loaded gun and a handful of
flax tow (used for starting fires) under his coat. On other occasions
he had thrown knives and other weapons at his wife and children
and had tried to stab them; he had beaten his wife with his fists
and had tried to strangle her. The officials of Stauffenberg noted
that he needed to be restrained in a "blockhouse" or with chains
while further advice in the matter was being sought. Two weeks
after this letter was sent, Hoffmann was ordered confined at Haina
where he would stay until God might send him a recovery.

In 1596 a father in Schmalkalden appealed to Landgrave Moritz
that his son be admitted to Haina. For three years the boy had
been a singer in church and school but now he was so "disabled
and crazy" that he "cannot well be tolerated here because of the
danger." He should be admitted to Haina "until he improves." The
Superintendent, Johann Clauer, agreed and ordered the boy confined "until Almighty God sends him some improvement."

In mid-July of 1587, Barba, wife of Jost Bucking from Alsfeld,
appealed for the confinement of her husband because he was
bereft of his senses. The treasurer of Alsfeld confirmed that Bucking had been mad for four years, when he had begun irritating
several citizens with "unnecessary wrangling and hatred, which no
one had previously noticed in him since he had been zealous in
obeying the church and God's Word, and had always seemed reasonable and beyond reproach." But complaints about him began

to accumulate. "He began to fantasize, which from day to day got so much worse that at last he went completely out of his mind and in the past had to be kept in chains at great expense and danger. Several times he worked himself free from them, and if dear God had not especially prevented it, he would have done horrible damage with fire or murder." Bucking had been a wool-weaver and had eight children, some of them still small. Although he had been "rather lively" while working, ever since he was chained and prevented from working he "seems all used up." In an earlier letter Bucking's wife noted that her husband used to beat her whenever he was displeased; and he was wont to go into the barn and stables carrying fire. Thus he clearly endangered not only her but the children and neighbors. Since chaining him, they had all been reduced to poverty. He tore all his clothes and any bedding given to him. There seemed no hope that he would, without God's special mercy, ever recover his reason. On 29 August he was ordered to be admitted to Haina.

Let us look at one more example of Hessian madness among the folk. In 1579 the neighbors of widow Aldehens complained that they were strained beyond endurance. The widow "had become completely mentally disabled in the past year, and we had to care for her for a time." But then God sent her some improvement and the local community hoped that they were free of their great burden. Now she was much worse "and is once again completely disabled and senseless, and she smears herself with excrement so gruesomely and so horribly that no one really wants or dares to stay with her." So the neighbor women made a special chest for her where they kept her day and night. This expedient was expensive, however, and the petitioners claimed that they had neither the incomes nor the husbands to keep up this system much longer. Widow Aldehens was sent to Merxhausen with her children, where she was to stay until God sent some improvement.

A number of things are striking in these cases from village society. First, the petitioners and the Hessian officials often assumed that mental condition could improve, although in every case the cure was ascribed to God alone. Second, there are surprisingly few instances in which a mad person was thought to be demonically possessed. In these documents only Daniel Hoffmann came close, and no-one seems to have treated him differently just because he acted "as if possessed." It is hard to say whether this lack of concern about demonic possession was a result of Protestant skepticism about possession and exorcism, or whether such ideas had never been current among the Hessians. We do know that Landgrave Ludwig in 1575 advised that a woman thought by some to be possessed was "more likely suffering from weakness in her head and silly melancholy thoughts." (It is noteworthy that this suggestion of melancholy came from a prince, not a villager.) He urged that she be cared for and comforted with God's Word "so that she may be discretely diverted from such heavy thoughts." The landgrave had heard that an exorcist named Homberger, from Weidenhaussen, had made bold to drive the evil spirit from her. In future the landgrave commanded that such efforts be severely punished; and two Marburg preachers were to talk to Homberger and warn him to give up his own "phantasei."[38]

The third noteworthy fact about all 39 cases of mental disability in these Hessian hospital records is that the local community was obviously supposed to exhaust its own resources before turning to the territorial administration. Even when spouse and neighbors had been driven to despair, however, they did not apparently attack, punish, ridicule, or demean the afflicted. They may have chained or confined such people but only as a last resort and to prevent self-inflicted injury as well as harm to others. It would be going too far to claim that such communities were "in dialogue" with the mad, that they deeply respected or were in awe of lunatics and the feeble-minded. But they did continue to practice what they saw as Christian patience and charity.

These case histories are one way of observing the Haina and Merxhausen hospitals for the poor at work. Some simple statistics, extracted from the same *Rezeptionsreskripte,* provide a more general view. I have grouped the 183 cases between ca. 1550 and 1622 into decades and into four broad categories of basic disability (and five categories of combined disabilities) (see Table II.) The largest group of residents at Haina and Merxhausen was composed of men and women often described simply as "old, lame and disabled." This group also includes those persons suffering from leprosy, physical deformity, deaf-mutism, epilepsy, and desperate poverty. The second broad category includes orphans and disabled, deformed, and crippled children. The third category contains cases of mental disability, retardation, madness, and brain damage. And finally, a fourth category singles out the blind, who made up a

Table II: Residents Admitted to Haina (H) and Merxhausen (M): ca. 1550–1622

| | I | | II | | III | | IV | | I & IV | | II & IV | | I & II | | II & III | | I & III | | | |
|---|---|---|---|---|---|---|---|---|---|---|---|---|---|---|---|---|---|---|---|---|
| | H | M | H | M | H | M | H | M | H | M | H | M | H | M | H | M | H | M | H | M |
| 1550–60 | 3 | 0 | 3 | 0 | 1 | 0 | 0 | 0 | 0 | 0 | 0 | 0 | 0 | 0 | 0 | 0 | 1 | 0 | 8 | 0 |
| 61–70 | 25 | 0 | 2 | 1 | 3 | 0 | 0 | 0 | 1 | 0 | 1 | 0 | 0 | 0 | 0 | 0 | 1 | 0 | 33 | 1 |
| 71–80 | 12 | 2 | 4 | 2 | 1 | 0 | 1 | 0 | 0 | 0 | 0 | 1 | 0 | 0 | 1 | 1+ | 0 | 0 | 19 | 6+ |
| 81–90 | 16 | 1 | 1 | 0 | 8 | 0 | 1 | 0 | 0 | 0 | 1 | 0 | 2 | 0 | 1 | 0 | 0 | 0 | 30 | 1 |
| 91–1600 | 9 | 0 | 7 | 0 | 3 | 0 | 0 | 0 | 1 | 0 | 0 | 0 | 0 | 0 | 2 | 0 | 1 | 0 | 23 | 0 |
| 1601–10 | 5 | 1 | 2 | 2 | 1 | 1* | 1 | 0 | 0 | 0 | 0 | 0 | 0 | 0 | 2 | 0 | 0 | 0 | 11 | 3** |
| 1611–22 | 11 | 11 | 1 | 1 | 4 | 6 | 0 | 2 | 0 | 2 | 1 | 0 | 0 | 0 | 0 | 0 | 0 | 0 | 17 | 22 |
| (indistinct 16th c.) | 3 | 0 | 1 | 2 | 2 | 1 | 0 | 0 | 0 | 0 | 0 | 0 | 0 | 1 | 0 | 0 | 0 | 0 | 5 | 3 |
| Totals | 84 | 15 | 21 | 8 | 22 | 6 (+1) | 3 | 2 | 2 | 2 | 3 | 1 | 2 | 1 | 6 | 1+ | 3 | 0 | 146 | 36+ (+1) |

Key: I = Old, disabled, crippled
II = Orphans, deformed children
III = Mentally disabled: retarded, mentally ill, brain damaged
IV = Blind

\* one woman remanded to Hofheim instead of to Merxhausen
\*\* excludes the one sent to Hofheim
Haina mentally disabled = 31; percentage = 31/146 = 21.2%
Merxhausen mentally disabled = 7; percentage = 7/36+ = 19.4%
Total mentally disabled = 39; percentage = 39/183+ = 21.3%

small but sorry minority in the Hessian hospitals. The five combi-
nations of these categories have been kept to simple pairs of equally debilitating afflictions (a sixth possible pair, combining blind-
ness with mental disability, does not occur in these records).

If one examines how the hospitals' residents changed during the
period under consideration, one can see the contours of the future
mental hospital emerging from the more broadly oriented original
hospital. By dividing the period ca. 1550–1622 into three roughly
equal periods, one observes a marked rise in the proportion of
mentally disabled residents (see Table III).

The reasons for this slight but noticeable shift in emphasis at
Haina and Merxhausen are far from clear. Perhaps it took forty or
fifty years for communities to discover that the hospitals could
relieve them of problems that were not, strictly speaking, poverty
and starvation. Perhaps the admissions process was relaxed more
frequently for the urban mad as time went by. One cannot use-
fully speculate much further until other hospitals have been studied in similar detail.

But this much is clear: the Hessian hospital system from its very
beginnings housed more than a few mentally disabled residents
and by 1600 mental patients were common. One can surmise that
they were, with the exception of those who were forcibly detained,
as happy as the other residents to find a refuge from the world of
high prices, poverty, and starvation.

Although food was plentiful, medical care was usually nonexist-
ent at such hospitals for the poor. In fact the general assumption
in the Hessian hospital system was that one did not even qualify
for admission if one had a curable condition. Unlike the madnesses
of the wealthy, the maladies of the poor were a fact of life to be
borne with whatever grace one could muster. The only regular
therapy available was religious, for hospitals employed full-time
pastors who maintained a lively schedule of services and instruction, much of it aimed at warding off the despair of the terminally
disabled. Melancholy, with its attendant therapy, was for the rich.
The poor received what an eminent historian of medicine has called
"the therapy of the word."[39] Their madness may not have been
thought of as a medical condition at all, but as a spiritual condition whose cornerstone was not physiology but mental behavior of
a radically offensive sort.

Table III: Mentally Disabled as a Proportion of All Hospital Residents, in Three Periods ca. 1550–1622

| | Haina | Merxhausen | Hofheim | Total Patients | Mental Patients as percentage of total |
|---|---|---|---|---|---|
| ca. 1550–1580 | 8 | 1 | 0 | 67 | 13.4 % |
| 1581–1600 | 15 | 0 | 0 | 54 | 27.7 % |
| 1601–1622 | 7 | 6 | 1 | 54 | 25.9 % |
| | 30 | 7 | 1 | 175 | |

n = 175. 8 undated cases from the 16th century have been excluded from consideration in this table.

For centuries religious thinkers had used the language of madness to describe the condition of sin. Insanity was thought to be a punishment for sin while at the same time providing an emblem of crazed self-disregard, of blind, wanton, uncontrolled, sinful willfulness.[40] As 16th-century thinkers strove to intensify men's sense of sin, they dramatically adapted the language of madness and demonic possession for their purposes. Martin Luther, for example, had insisted that all men were generally sinful, but resolute sinners were rabid, furious, raging, fuming, demon-possessed, insane, lunatic; they were fools, idiots, imbeciles; mad, crazy, disturbed, cracked, nuts. (Interestingly enough, Luther did not use the word "melancholy" to describe them. The few times he used the word, he applied it to the saints.) With this flood of opprobrium Luther did not merely intend to heap scorn on his (and God's) opponents but also to explain, at least to himself, why reasonable arguments made no noticeable impact on them. As the level of theological argument rose in the 16th century, so did the apparent level of religious madness and of demonic possession — that is, of resolute and stubborn error. I think it noteworthy that a thinker as different from Luther as Paracelsus found the equation of sin with madness and possession a fruitful and arresting image of man's deep alienation from his truest self and from God.[41]

This theological concern did not remain a matter for erudite speculation alone. One of the major institutional differences between the clergy and the physicians has been the clergy's desire to instruct the folk. Certainly in Germany during the 16th century a flood of translations of ancient sources testifies to the hope of religious thinkers that common people could share in the authentic roots of religion. Unlike physicians, theologians did not retreat into an esoteric language. Rather, they succeeded in fair measure in making their voices heard before crowds of parishioners. This is certainly not to say that common folk believed or even fully understood what their priests and pastors said but it does mean that the basic language for dealing with the devil and Christ, with sin and madness, became familiar.

This theological success is essential for understanding the rise of demonic possession in the late 16th century. Some of the folk seem to have learned a new language of mental rebellion, a newly legitimate form of madness. And the advantage of demon possession was that one could even claim that one's words were no longer one's own, that one was not even remotely responsible for the terrible things that the devil might say or do.

Most of our information regarding demon possession comes from tracts written (usually in the vernacular) to prove a number of possible points: that the devil was everywhere, that Catholic exorcism was an effective antidote, that Catholic exorcism was a sham and a fraud. This polemical literature has been best studied for England and France but it was abundant in Germany as well, where it provides us with instances of popular religious expression and of communal therapy.[42] Of course, the modern reader must read between the lines. In 1583, for example, Georg Scherer, S. J., preached a sermon concerning a poor maid, Anna Schultterbawr, who was possessed by 12,652 devils. The ever-loquacious father of lies cursed the bishop of Vienna, the Jesuits, and all Catholics, while claiming that all Jews, Turks, heathens, and Lutherans were among the saved.[43] But ultimately Catholic prayer, holy water, and exorcism drove out all the demons. In a doctrinal appendix, Scherer admitted that the ability to cast out demons was no sure guarantee that the exorcist was godly since it was a *donum gratis datum* and not a *donum gratum faciens* (using language familiar from disputes over grace and justification). Even so it seemed significant to Scherer that the Lutherans did not even claim the ability to cast out demons.[44]

In other cases of exorcism the learned investigators tested the demon and the possessed by developing controlled experiments, perhaps the first methodical efforts to falsify the hypothesis that a person was indeed demon-possessed.[45] Even if these "experiments" were not conducted in good faith, they were represented as reliable and objective. In these efforts the demonologists were far in advance of their medical colleagues. They recognized the need for case histories and empirical tests not because they were brighter than their medical colleagues, nor because they had been vouchsafed a glimpse of the truth, but because their polemical position required them to address audiences who did not share their assumptions. Unlike physicians of the academy, the demonologists were writing for the general public – and it made a difference. To take a couple of examples, let us first examine another Austrian case, reported by Sebastian Khueller in 1574. Another maid, Veronica Steiner, was possessed so that she spoke not only with her own tender, maidenly, reasonable and Christian voice but also with a coarse, manly, blasphemous voice that sang unchaste songs and perverted psalms.[46] Although she suffered strange swellings on her face, neck, and breasts, a little holy water made the swellings go down. Indeed, she could not be fed unless some holy water were mixed with her food. When the gospel of John was read to her in Latin (a language women were assumed not to know), she fell unconscious precisely at the words, "Verbum caro factum est." None of these experiments was fully controlled but the lord in whose castle she worked, Philipp von Taxis, tried sewing a bit of the true cross into his clothing. When he approached she accused him at once of being a magical thief: "What do you want to do with that magical thing?" She was further tested and it was found that she could locate hidden objects and discover secrets.[47] After terrible tortures the ceremony of exorcism forced more than thirty demons to leave her. When she was fully recovered, she renounced her Lutheran faith and gladly accepted Roman Catholicism, to all of which reliable, honorable, and noble witnesses firmly attested. The concern to provide trustworthy, tested empirical evidence could hardly have been more explicit.

In 1582 another Protestant, this time a married woman, was rescued from the clutches of the Evil One. Before the Catholic priest accepted the fact that this was a true demon possession, he tested the spirit by hiding next to his body a piece of the true cross, a piece of the post on which Jesus had been flogged, an agnus dei, and a piece of white wax blessed by the pope. Sure enough, the demon reviled him for his deception. When he secretly placed the relics on the woman's head, she fell into great shrieks, shaking her chains and biting at the priest. "O Pastor, O Pastor, take that thing off my head or I'll bite you to pieces."[48] The experiment proceeded with holy water. When she refused baptismal water, she was offered water from a spring that was blessed every year. Although she was told that it was mere water, Satan answered that they all knew it was more than that.[49] After a long and fierce struggle, described in full detail, the devil was finally forced to leave.

Such tales of Catholic victory could be multiplied but the basic picture is surely clear.[50] Protestants all over Europe had reason to worry about these dramatic successes. In regions where the Reform tradition was strong, an eschatology developed in which it could be claimed that although Christ and the apostles had cast out demons, the age of such miracles was now over. Calvinists regularly suspected that demon possessions were fraudulent and that the exorcisms were illusory.[51] But in Lutheran lands God's plan ran in different channels. Most Lutherans agreed that they were living at the very end of time and that the devil had indeed been allowed to rage as never before.[52] Therefore the reported cases of demon possession were often all too true, increasing the pressure on Lutherans to find a response to their Catholic rivals. In the process a dense apologetic literature sprang up, much of it going back to a story told by Johann Bugenhagen, the reformer of North Germany.[53] He said that in 1530 he went to Lübeck to see an eighteen-year-old maiden who was demon-possessed. Although he could not avail himself of exorcism, Bugenhagen found that reading the German Bible aloud helped a good deal and that sincere prayer finally drove out the demon.

In an interesting case from 1536 we learn that sixteen-year-old Gertrud Fischer in Frankfurt on the Oder fell ill and became weak-headed. Although some unspecified treatment seemed to help, she next fell into a Satanic possession in which she found and swallowed coins and needles and spoke an Upper German dialect apparently unknown to her. The Protestant clergy were bewildered by this "money devil," as they called it, and, so new was the problem of possession, wrote to Martin Luther for advice. In the meanwhile a Catholic priest intervened and tried exorcism for six days, but all to no avail (as the pastors pointed out exultantly). Luther recommended bringing the girl to divine services and praying for her improvement; and after several noisy performances in church she did improve, remembering nothing of her previous possession.[54] In this case it seems plausible to suggest that coin-eating constituted a gross image of greed and a moral indictment of a sinful society. Gertrud's madness, if we can call it that, had a transparent meaning she could never have conveyed through normal channels.

In other cases Protestants had to admit to edifying failure. A report from 1562 told the story of a man from Thuringia, thirty years old and of scrupulously upright character, who was obsessed and finally possessed by the devil, beaten, choked, bound with the veils and braids of women and girls, and subjected to visions. Although held fast by strong men, he often escaped and no prayers seemed to be effective. The anonymous author contented himself with the thought that the poor man was a mirror to his fellow Germans of God's terrible wrath and of the coming punishment for Germany's lack of faith.[55]

Later Lutheran cases came to rival Catholic descriptions in detail but a special feature of this kind of mental deviation was the appearance of godly visions as well as demonic delusions. By the 1620s and 1630s visions had become common. As a consequence, Lutheran writers had to confront a more complex set of possibilities: mental aberrations might be natural or angelic in inspiration and, if angelic, they might be godly or demonic. Usually the spirits were tested by a simple resort to Scripture. Lutherans were willing to grant the possibility of godly visions so long as they did not contradict the sovereign Word of God. Thus, when another eighteen-year-old maiden fell into fits and a trance in 1560, learned observers concluded that it was a godly call to repentance since she said nothing that went beyond Scripture.[56] Certainly this visionary role as public accuser provided the girl with an opportunity for public attention and acclaim that her church otherwise would never have granted her. Similarly, when Martha Creützer died three days after giving birth to twins in 1569, she departed only to return from death after twelve hours full of warnings to the sinful world. Her visions of God's judgment were orthodox and therefore angelic, if not indeed inspired by the Holy Ghost itself.[57] Surely it is not going very far to see in such visions the results of an increasingly successful campaign by pastors to convict the world of sin. Popular culture was responding to the learned onslaught.

On the other hand heretical utterances could be quickly labeled demonic dreams, as in the striking case of the enthusiastic followers of Ezechiel Meth in 1614. His autotheistic claim to be the Grand-Prince Michael, the embodiment of God's Word, and his assertion that he and his disciples fulfilled the law and were now immortal, were proof enough that he had suffered "devilish dreams."[58] From his point of view, however, his religious dissatisfaction found expression in a powerful mental disorder that now we should be reluctant to describe as an illness.

Although Lutheran theology did not permit exorcism except at baptism, Lutherans went to some lengths to show that Catholics' pretended ceremonies were nothing less than diabolical magic.[59] These negative attacks were never so inspiring as Lutheran success stories, however, and such episodes were recounted in at least as much detail as the Catholic accounts. In 1605, for example, a twelve-year-old girl was dreadfully possessed in the Lutheran town of Löwenberg, in Silesia. The extraordinary account of her illness and liberation included long theological discussions with the devil speaking through the girl's mouth. Indeed, the amount of theological information conveyed by the devil is so extensive that we may suspect the accuracy of the report. Even if we cannot accept all of the details, however, the account probably had at its basis another religiously inspired girl on whom the pastors had had only too vivid an impact. In the end, a regime of communal prayer and fasting finally succeeded in driving out the Evil One; but not before he admitted that he preferred to afflict Lutherans since the Turks, the works-righteous (i.e., the Catholics), and the Calvinists were already safely in his clutches.[60] It is worth noting that in this instance (as in other Lutheran cases) the devil was taken to be speaking the truth.

The stories recounted so far may give the impression that the possessed were mainly young girls. From other sources, however, it seems that older women were equally likely to become tormented by the devil. If we tabulate the stories of demonic possession in Martin Delrio's famous book on magic, the *Disquisitionum Magicarum Libri Sex* (1599–1600), we obtain the following picture of "modern" (i.e., 16th-century) possessions:

Table IV

| | Male | Female | Groups: | Male | Female | Mixed |
|---|---|---|---|---|---|---|
| Adults | 4 | 13 | | 0 | 1 | 1 |
| Youth | 2 | 2 | | 1 | 1 | 0 |
| Children | 1 | 0 | | 0 | 0 | 0 |
| Unspecified | 0 | 1 | | 0 | 0 | 0 |
| Totals | 7 | 16 | | 1 | 2 | 1 |

Clearly Delrio's stories of modern possession support the view that mature women were more susceptible to the assaults of the devil than other age or sex groups.[61]

If we perform the same sort of tabulation with the equally famous Protestant attack on witchcraft beliefs, the *De Praestigiis Daemonum* (1583) of Johann Weyer, we obtain this table.

## Table V

| | Male | Female | Groups: | Male | Female | Mixed |
|---|---|---|---|---|---|---|
| Adults | 4 | 9 | | 2 | 7 | 0 |
| Youth | 2 | 10 | | 0 | 4 | 0 |
| Children | 1 | 1 | | 0 | 0 | 2 |
| Unspecified | 0 | 0 | | 0 | 0 | 1 |
| Totals | 7 | 20 | | 2 | 11 | 3 |

In Weyer's case I have listed only those cases he claimed to have investigated himself.[62] Perhaps this gives his reports greater authority but it should also be said that his Protestant bias led him to emphasize the widespread hold that the devil had established in female religious communities. Certainly tales of possessed convents became common throughout Europe by the early 17th century; they made exciting reading. More importantly, convents may actually have suffered more assaults than any other social group. If that is the case, I cannot avoid the conclusion that religious instruction must have been unusually successful in prompting the religious fears and needs of unmarried girls and women, and that this instruction must have been increasingly successful in the late 16th century.

In sum, I have tried to suggest that as academically trained physicians came to emphasize an exclusively humoral and Galenic approach to mental disorders, one kind of patient came increasingly to be treated for melancholy and to exhibit the symptoms of humoral disorder. Although I do not pretend that I have proved this case, it seems significant that mentally irresponsible princes received little or no therapy at the beginning of the century while obtaining full care by the end of the century. As in learned literature, so too in the life of the learned, melancholy was reaching epidemic proportions by 1600.[63] But because physicians kept their doctrines to themselves and their immediate clients, it also seems that the poor did not obtain the benefits, such as they were, of the Galenic dispensation. Care for them remained an eclectic mixture of herbal formulas, forcible restraint, and the various therapies of the word: pastoral consolation, confession, prayer, and, increasingly, exorcism. Although Protestant territories might show no upsurge of demonism, as the Hessian hospital records seem to show, demonic possession in Catholic territories became dramatically more common by the end of the 16th century, providing a painful avenue, especially for women, to express mad thoughts and lewd, disorderly, disobedient gestures. The increase in demonic possession, like the increase in melancholy, was partly a suffering response to the doctrines of the learned, for learned theologians and pastors (both Catholic and Protestant) spent their renewed energies in the 16th century convicting the world of sin and persuading their listeners that the devil went abroad like a lion, seeking whom he might devour. It is important in this respect that even opponents of witchcraft trials, such as Johann Weyer, were sure that demonic possession was real and that it was on the rise.

It is surely not difficult to accept the idea that basic or modal personality types have in the past varied from the psychic norms of today. Furthermore, historians are just beginning to unravel differences among specific social strata and social groups. Therefore, to the extent that mental disorder is a cultural artifact it should not surprise us to find an equal flexibility in the experience and definition of madness. I have argued that elite culture listened to the learned physicians and developed a peculiarly medical understanding of madness, one in which anxiety was often channeled painfully into the experience of melancholy. Popular culture, meanwhile, was not isolated from all strands of elite culture but seems to have received few impulses from learned medical men. Not only did physicians try to seal off their wisdom from the vulgar by explaining themselves mainly in Latin, but they mainly sought out patients who could pay their fees; such physicians were not usually set in charge of hospitals for the poor. Unlike medical learning, religious instruction had a truly popular impact that reformulated madness in terms of sin and demonic possession. To some extent, of course, the popular understanding of madness remained both unmedical and untheological, concerned rather with nonsense, violence, and self-control. But the 16th century also saw changes in the popular experience of madness, most notably in the expansion of demonic possession. It would be wrongheaded to conclude that the mental disorders of common people merely suffered a redefinition or reclassification at the hands of the learned. It would be equally rash to argue that commoners fraudulently "performed" as if demonically possessed. It seems more plausible to conclude that even mental suffering demands legitimacy in order to be accepted by the world, and that the

channeling of experience into sin, obsession, and demonic possession provided a painful legitimacy even if onlookers could not
fully understand the tortured utterances of the possessed.

Changes in the expression and experience of madness, therefore,
point to important changes in the relations between popular and
elite culture as well as to changes within elite culture itself. Learned culture provided articulate medical and religious models of
madness in melancholy and in demonic possession. It enables us to
observe part of the social and mental process by which the two
cultures became more separate, as specific social strata gravitated
toward these newly legitimate disorders.

## NOTES

1. Peter Burke, *Popular Culture in Early Modern Europe* (New York: 1978),
   pp. 24—29, 58—64.
2. A. L. Kroeber and C. Kluckhohn, *Culture: A Critical Review of Concepts
   and Definitions* (New York: 1963); Raymond Williams, *Keywords: A
   Vocabulary of Culture and Society* (New York: 1976).
3. I have reviewed much of this literature in "Madness and Civilization in
   Early Modern Europe: A Reappraisal of Michel Foucault," in Barbara
   Malament, ed., *After the Reformation. Essays in Honor of J. H. Hexter*
   (Philadelphia: 1980), pp. 247—65.
4. See Raymond Klibansky, Erwin Panofsky, and Fritz Saxl, *Saturn and
   Melancholy* (London: 1964), and the lengthy critique by Noel L. Brann,
   "The Renaissance Passion of Melancholy: The Paradox of Its Cultivation
   and Resistance" (Ph. D. diss., Stanford University, 1965).
5. Walter H. Ryff, *Warhafftige künstliche und gerechte underweisung und
   anzeygung, Alle Latwegen, Confect, Conserven, eynbeytzungen und
   einmachungen . . . wie solche in den Apotheken gemacht* (Strasbourg:
   1540). See the extremely hostile remarks of Lynn Thorndike, *A History
   of Magic and Experimental Science*, vol. 5: *The Sixteenth Century* (New
   York: 1941), pp. 442—43.
6. Johann Tollat, *Margarita medicine, ein meisterlichs usserlesens biechlin
   der artzny für mancherley kranckheit und siechtagen der menschen*
   (Strasbourg: 1507), title page.
7. Ibid., fol. 10 v.
8. Ibid., fol. 11 v.
9. Ibid., fol. 22 r.
10. Johann Schöner von Karlstadt, *Ein nutzlichs büchlein viler bewerter
    Ertzney, lang zeyt versamlet und züsammen pracht* (Nuremberg: [1528]),
    fol. E4 r-v.

11. Laurentius Fries, *Spiegel der Artzny* (Strasbourg: 1519), fol. 1 v. I have also used the expanded edition by Otto Brunfels (Strasbourg: 1532).

12. Ibid., fol. 96 r.

13. See Brann, "Renaissance Passion of Melancholy."

14. Fries, *Spiegel,* fol. 101 v.

15. Ibid., fol. 101 v.

16. Ibid., fols. 157 v, 160 v — 162 r, 172 v.

17. Melanchthon, *Commentarius de Anima* (Wittenberg: 1548), fols. 76r — 77r.

18. Ibid., fol. 141 v.

19. Ibid., fol. 142 v. This was a theological commonplace; see Johannes Altenstaig, *Vocabularius Theologiae* (Hagenau: 1517), fol. 184 r, *s.v.* peccatum.

20. Oswei Temkin is one of the few to consider this important problem in historical perspective. See especially "Medicine and the Problem of Moral Responsibility," in his *The Double Face of Janus and Other Essays in the History of Medicine* (Baltimore: 1977), pp. 50–67.

21. Based on an examination of the list provided in Oskar Diethelm, *Medical Dissertations of Psychiatric Interest Printed before 1750* (Basel: 1971).

22. Tübingen: 1580.

23. *Theses de Phrenetide* (Heidelberg: 1584).

24. *Disputatio de Phrenetide* (Tübingen: 1588).

25. *PERI TES PHRENITIDE. De Phrenetide Assertiones Medicae* (Tübingen: 1602).

26. Tübingen: 1593.

27. Ibid., fol. A2 v.

28. Ibid., fol. Cl v.

29. *Disputatio Medica de Morbis Temperamenti* (Tübingen: 1586).

30. Burke, *Popular Culture,* pp. 270–91.

31. I know of no German physician whose career even roughly paralleled that of the extraordinary Richard Napier, whose 17th-century English patients included hundreds of common folk. See Michael MacDonald, *Mystical Bedlam. Madness, Anxiety and Healing in Seventeenth-Century England* (Cambridge: 1981).

32. Careful studies are lacking for some of these figures, but see the entries for each of them in the *Allgemeine Deutsche Biographie;* H. H. Beek, *Waanzin in de middeleeuwen. Beeld van de gestoorde en bemoeienis met de zieke* (Nijkerk: 1969), pp. 47–51; Christian Friedrich Sattler, *Geschichte des Herzogthums Würtenberg unter der Regierung der Graven,* Vierter Teil, 2. Auflage (Tübingen: 1777), pp. 8–9; Christoph Friedrich von Stälin, *Wirtembergische Geschichte* (Stuttgart: 1856), III, p. 601; Albert Moll, "Die Krankheits- und Todesfälle im württembergischen Regentenhause," *Medicinisches Correspondenz-Blatt* 30 (1860), pp. 281–87; K. W. Bouterwek, "Wesel huldigt dem Herzog Johann Wilhelm, am 26. Juni 1598," *Zeitschrift des Bergischen Geschichtsvereins* 2 (1865), pp. 151–96, 201–11; W. Crecelius, "Urkundliche Beiträge zur Krankheitsgeschicht der Herzöge Wilhelm und Johann Wilhelm von Jülich, Cleve

und Berg," in ibid. 23 (1887), pp. 1–29; E. Pauls, "Zur Geschichte der Krankheit des Herzogs Johann Wilhelm von Jülich-Cleve-Berg," in ibid. 33 (1897), pp. 7–48; E. Pauls, "Geisteskrankheit, Ableben und Beerdigung Johann Wilhelms, des letzten Herzogs von Jülich-Kleve-Berg," in Alfred Herrmann, ed., *Beiträge zur Geschichte des Herzogtums Kleve* (Cologne: 1909), pp. 257–75; Karl Faber, "Tagebuch über Albrecht Friedrichs Gemüths-Krankheit. Nach einem im geheimen Archiv befindlichen Manuscript des Lukas David," *Preussisches Archiv* 2 (1810), pp. 127–78; J. Voigt, "Über die Erziehung und die Krankheit des Herzogs Albrecht Friedrich von Preussen," *Neue Preussische Provinzial-Blätter*, Third series, 8 (1861), pp. 33–48, 93–106; Ivan Bloch, "Der rheinische Arzt Solenander und die Geisteskrankheit des Herzogs Albrecht Friedrich von Preussen," *Klinische Therapeutische Wochenschrift*, 1922, nos. 17/18.

33. See Bloch, "Solenander."
34. See Crecelius, "Urkundliche Beiträge," and Pauls, "Zur Geschichte der Krankheit."
35. MacDonald, *Mystical Bedlam*, pp. 150–54, also argues that aristocrats were demonstrably more often melancholy than Napier's average clients. Almost two-thirds of all of Napier's aristocratic patients complained of black bile (40 out of 62), while only 16.5 % of patients with no title came to him with that complaint (271 out of 1643).
36. Hospitalsarchiv Haina (Hessen), Rezeptionsreskripte, Landgraf Wilhelm to Johann Clauer, 30 April 1577.
37. Hospitalsarchiv Haina (Hessen), Rezeptionsreskripte, Landgraf Moritz to Georg Milchlingen, 26 June 1612.
38. The episode is described in Hugo Brunner, "Behandlung einer Geisteskranken im Jahre 1575," *Zeitschrift des Vereins für hessische Geschichte und Landeskunde* N. F. 24 (1901), pp. 403–4.
39. Pedro Lain Entralgo, *The Therapy of the Word in Classical Antiquity* (New Haven: 1970).
40. Penelope B. R. Doob, *Nebuchadnezzar's Children* (New Haven: 1974).
41. Ernst W. Kämmerer, "Mensch und Krankheit bei Paracelsus," in Sepp Domandl, ed., *Paracelsus. Werke und Wirkung. Festgabe für Kurt Goldammer* (Vienna: 1975), pp. 119–24; and my essay, "The Anthropological Roots of Paracelsus' Psychiatry," *Medizinhistorisches Journal* 16 (1981), pp. 67–77.
42. The two best recent studies are Cecile Ernst, *Teufelaustreibungen. Die Praxis der katholischen Kirche im 16. und 17. Jahrhundert* (Bern: 1972), and D. P. Walker, *Unclean Spirits: Possession and Exorcism in France and England in the Late Sixteenth and Early Seventeenth Centuries* (Philadelphia: 1981).
43. Georg Scherer, *Christliche Erinnerung bey der Historien von jüngst beschehener Erledigung einer Junckfrawen* (Ingolstadt: 1584), pp. 28–29.
44. Ibid., pp. 43, 56–62.
45. See Johann Weyer, *De Praestigiis Daemonum* (Basel: 1583), Book 5,

chap. 35, on "Certain and Approved Cures for Pretended Demon Possession." See also Irving Kirsch, "Demonology and the Rise of Science: An
Example of the Misperception of Historical Data," *Journal of the History
of the Behavioral Sciences* 14 (1978), pp. 149–57, and "Demonology
and Science during the Scientific Revolution," ibid. 16 (1980), pp.
359–68.

46. Sebastian Khueller, *Kurtze unnd warhafftige Historia von einer Junckfrawen, wölche mit etlich unnd dreissig bösen Geistern leibhafftig besessen* (Munich: 1574), fol. A2 r.

47. Ibid., fols. A2 v – A3 r.

48. Sixtus Agricola and Georg Witmer, *Erschröckliche gantz warhafftige
Geschicht welche sich mit Apolonia, Hannsen Geisslbrechts Burgers zu
Spalt inn dem Eystätter Bistumb Haussfrawen . . . von dem bösen Feind
besessen . . . verlauffen hat* (Ingolstadt: 1584), p. 9.

49. Ibid., p. 10.

50. See especially Ernst, *Teufelaustreibungen.*

51. Keith Thomas, *Religion and the Decline of Magic* (London: 1971), pp.
477–92; Walker, *Unclean Spirits.*

52. On this large subject see Robin B. Barnes, "Prophecy and the Eschaton
in Lutheran Germany, 1530–1630" (Ph. D. diss., University of Virginia,
1980).

53. Johann Bugenhagen and Philipp Melanchthon, *Zwo wunderbarlich
Hystorien zu bestettigung der lere des Evangelii* (n.p.: 1531).

54. Andreas Ebert, *Wundere zeitung von einem Geld teuffel* (Frankfurt a. O.:
1538).

55. *Newe Zeytunge. Von einem Manne Hans Vader genannt* (Augsburg:
1562). Weyer reported exultantly that Vader (Vatter) finally admitted
that he had fraudulently put on his own fetters, *De Praestigiis Daemonum*, cols. 478–80.

56. *Newe Zeytung. Von einem Megdlein das entzuckt ist gewest* (Nuremberg:
1560).

57. *Wundergeschicht, Offenbarung und Geschichte einer entzuckten Kind-
betterin* (Augsburg: 1569 [?]).

58. *Zwölff Teufelische Träum, Einbildungen oder Speculationes* (n.p.:
1614).

59. See, e.g., Johann Marbach, *Von Mirackeln und Wunderzeichen* (Augsburg
[?]: 1571).

60. Tobias Seiler, *Daemonomania. Uberaus schreckliche Historia von einem
zwelffjährigen Jungfräwlein* (Löwenberg: 1605), fol. C2 r.

61. Information extracted from Edda Fischer, "Die 'Disquisitionum Magicarum Libri Sex' von Martin Delrio als gegenreformatorische Exempel-
Quelle" (Ph.D. diss., Frankfurt a. M. 1975).

62. Weyer took extraordinary pains to substantiate his stories and always
indicated his own involvement in the cases that he knew personally.

# Popular Culture and the Early Modern State in 16th Century Germany

GÜNTHER LOTTES

The long 16th century marks a watershed in the social, econom-ic, cultural, and political formation of Europe.[1] Rapid popula-tion growth, structural changes in the agrarian economy, the ex-tension of the proto-industrial sector within the preindustrial eco-nomy, and, finally, the emergence of a new political order trans-formed European society and deeply affected daily life. These changes initiated processes of social differentiation that brought about differentiations in cultural norms and habits. The former have for some time received the attention of social and economic historians; the latter, however, and in particular the culture of what Gramsci called the subordinate classes, are only beginning to be investigated.[2] Popular culture has become a major research interest during the last few years: English, French, and American scholars have paved the way while German historians and anthro-pologists are only beginning to catch up.[3] Yet the concept, if not the term itself, has been and is being used in different ways. Some of the difficulties in dealing with popular culture can be outlined by a brief discussion of the meanings of "popular" and "culture." Peter Burke, at the very beginning of his important work on *Pop-ular Culture in Early Modern Europe,* defined "popular culture" in a negative way as "unofficial culture, the culture of the non-elite, the 'subordinate classes' as Gramsci has called them."[4] He contin-ues: "In the case of early modern Europe, the non-elite were a whole host of more or less definite social groups of whom the most prominent were craftsmen and peasants. Hence I use the

phrase 'craftsmen and peasants' (or 'ordinary people') as convenient pieces of shorthand for the whole non-elite, including
women, children, shepherds, sailors, beggars, and the rest."[5]

However vague this definition, it seems difficult to improve on
it. Neither Edward Thompson nor Natalie Davis, for instance,
offers a more precise social location for the "plebeian" in plebeian
culture or for the "popular" in popular culture.[6] This lack of
precision becomes embarrassing if culture is understood in a less
restricted way, for there may not exist such a clear-cut division
between an elite and a popular culture as the two-culture model
suggests. There may be, for example, a common ground, a lay
culture in which social divisions are reflected not by differences in
cultural substance but in different modes of participation. The
complex role of carnival in early modern popular culture is a case
in point.[7] There may also exist, particularly in cities, a distinctive
middle-class culture that is neither elite nor popular.[8] Moreover,
when the two-culture model is seen in terms of sociocultural confrontation between the elite and the subordinate classes, as often
is the case, it suggests a homogeneity and a unity in popular culture that tend to obscure the incidence of social tension and social
conflict within the sphere noted as popular.[9] In other words, the
social boundaries of popular culture have to be drawn in each
particular case.[10] Here my social reference unit for popular culture
will be the German village community of the 16th century.

The term "culture" poses even greater problems, which we cannot discuss here at length because of the many and complex theoretical and methodological points involved.[11] It is sufficient to distinguish two basic usages: the narrow one as exemplified by Peter
Burke and the wider, anthropological one that over the last few
years has come to dominate Anglo-American and some German
social history. While Burke writes cultural history in the traditional
sense, except that he chooses the "little tradition" for his subject
matter[12] and only occasionally widens his perspective toward a
more anthropological concept of culture,[13] the culturally orien-
tated new social history sees culture as an entire way of life. It
concentrates, however, on forms of protest, systems of belief,
feasts, and diverse aspects of everyday life. One of its trademarks
has been a great interest in ritual and symbolic action, which
sometimes appears a little exaggerated but has greatly improved
our understanding of early modern social life. Traditional studies

of folklore still provide much of our knowledge about early modern popular culture. Such studies, whether English, French, or German in origin, have shown a tendency to rely on a purely positivist manner and to disregard social, economic, or political setting. They have sometimes ignored even the copious information about the agrarian constitution or the agrarian economy that the older social and economic history had to offer.[14] The introduction of anthropological categories into the study of folklore and social historians' invasion of the field have changed it to some extent. In the works of Edward Thompson (on England), Natalie Davis (on France), and Robert Scribner (on Germany) — to mention several representatives of the Anglo-American brand of the new social history who have greatly influenced German social historians — the level of sophistication in interpreting early modern popular culture has been pushed to new heights. But the gap between the cultural domain and its social, economic, and political environment has seldom been satisfactorily bridged. For this reason the new social history has been accused of "culturalism," that is, of an overemphasis on culture and a reduced conception of the economic as well as of the political.[15] Insofar as it is aimed at Thompson this criticism does not seem justified.[16] But it does point to a danger inherent in the recent fusion of anthropology and history. For anthropological patterns of explanation do not encourage the investigation of either the economic or the political framework within which a given popular culture exists. And it is easy to forget that Thompson's rebellious plebeian culture of the 18th century, which has acquired something of a paradigmatic quality, has its own historical location and is explicable as a result of the relative weakness of the state in postrevolutionary England.[17] No understanding of popular culture can do without similar reference to the political macrostructure of the social unit under consideration and this is particularly true for the study of various repertoires of popular protest. It would, of course, be unfair to assert that the many studies of popular protest in recent years have ignored the point. Yet, while the abundant historiography on the German Peasants' War of 1525 has never lost sight of the major role played by the formation of the early modern state,[18] it tends in general to be more concerned with the rituals and the symbolism of protest than with its political context. As a result, the conception of the political itself has become somewhat elusive. For instance, the distinction between ritualization as a means of neutralizing the practical effect of action and ritualization as a strategy to enhance the importance or the legitimacy of an action has become blurred. Similarly, the notion that the law is an instrument of class domination and terror has been pushed so far as to politicize every breach of the law, to the point where the distinction between crime as social protest and crime as crime is easily lost.[19] Methodological reasons aside, this stems partly from the relative neglect of the political conditions under which popular protest has to be articulated.

Political conditions, however, are of particular importance in the case of Germany. For, whereas the popular culture of 18th and 19th century England – the only periods that have been studied closely – was decisively shaped by the early transformation of England into a market society and by a sharp containment of the powers of the central state, the relative weight of these two factors is virtually reversed in the case of Germany. No doubt there were periods of more intensive governmental action in England, just as there were regions in Germany and periods in German history in which the market played a more important role. Yet in England the lack of a bureaucracy diminished the efficacy of state intervention in the social, economic, and cultural life of the people, while the lack of an adequate system of communication and transport before the 19th century prevented the market from becoming a dominant formative force for German society and culture.

In other words, popular culture has to be seen as an integral part of a sociocultural totality – as one subsystem among others in the early modern formation, which is bound to change when other subsystems change. It follows that, whereas in England the growth of the market economy in its relation to popular culture has to be studied more thoroughly, the role of the state is of prime importance if we are investigating the development of popular culture in Germany. (This raises an interesting theoretical point. Many Anglo-American historians tend to view popular culture as somehow autochthonous, as a genuine and independent, if submerged, expression of the people's mind, which they oppose to the cultural hegemony of the ruling class. The German case shows to what extent popular culture can be manipulated.)

It is for these reasons that I have chosen the relationship between the early modern state and popular culture in Germany as my subject, though it may strike some as outmoded or even as an attempt to cloak old-fashioned institutional history in the more fashionable dress of popular culture research. My observations concentrate on three points. First, the impact of the early modern state on the sociopolitical framework within which popular culture existed and developed: I concentrate in particular on its effect on the structure of popular political participation and popular protest. Second, I examine one specific function of the early modern state, namely the regulation of consumption, as it affected popular culture. Third, I offer some observations on the authorities' attempt to impress the new values of Protestantism or post-Tridentine Catholicism on the popular mind.

In the course of the 15th and 16th centuries the agrarian constitutions of Eastern and Western Germany developed along different lines.[20] In the West the old manorial system had dissolved into a system of farming by tenant-proprietors with considerable freedom of movement in economic, social, and even political terms. Even if their legal titles to their land were weak and their personal legal status bad, they were secured by the absence of large-scale demesne farming against the dangers of eviction or increased labor obligations under conditions of serfdom. Meanwhile, access to expanding markets brought them into a position to profit from the agrarian boom and gave their independence a sound economic base.[21] The noble landlord practically withdrew from the agrarian economic scene. The conversion of dues and services into money payments made it possible for him to content himself with the role of rent-collector (*Rentengrundherrschaft*).[22] As such he might try to gain a higher income by digging up old or by inventing new claims, but he saw no need to increase domination over his peasants by fusing economic and jurisdictional rights. On the contrary, manorial and jurisdictional titles fragmented, which worked in favor of the peasantry. This was in part a consequence of the fact that in the formation of villages the diverse manorial affiliations of the inhabitants were often disregarded. There were villages whose inhabitants might belong or owe dues and services to different lords. The manor's legal and institutional potential for domination had lost its grip on socio-economic reality. These conditions enhanced the importance and the self-consciousness of the village community as a formal institution of economic and social self-government, and thereby prepared the ground for the evolution of a distinct political culture among the peasantry.[23]

Meanwhile the East moved in the opposite direction. The landholding territorial nobility beyond the Elbe, the *Junkers,* took to running their estates as agrarian entrepreneurs, producing wheat for the expanding markets of Western Europe.[24] They incorporated waste farms into their demesnes and further enlarged them by buying out or evicting their peasants. The labor problem was solved by imposing serfdom on the remaining peasants and exploiting to the full their obligation to perform compulsory labor on the demesne. The result was the *Gutswirtschaft,* that peculiar feudo-capitalist institution that was to play an eminent role in German social and political history well into the 20th century.[25]

Among the many factors responsible for this development, the different degrees of political organization in Western and Eastern Germany deserve special attention. In the South and West the territorial princes had succeeded in building up a monopoly of legitimate power, which they wielded through a rudimentary but by no means negligible, and sometimes remarkably rationally organized, bureaucracy. Although they too had to make concessions to their nobles and could neither wholly deprive them of official functions nor disregard their voice in the estates, they tended to see the peasants as the immediate subjects of the territorial state and, if necessary, actively protected them against attempts of the nobility to encroach on their lands in order to weaken the latter's socio-economic power base.[26] One powerful motive for this policy was the fear that the tax-paying capacity of the territory would be eroded gradually if peasant land became noble and thus exempt from all taxes.[27] The peasants profited, therefore, from the power struggle between the territorial princes and their nobility, which went hand in hand with the formation of the early modern state.

The territorial princes in the Eastern parts of Germany shared these views but they lacked the financial means as well as the institutional prerequisites to put them into practice. On the contrary, they had no choice but to cooperate with the Junkers, who had effectively organized themselves on the local, the regional, and the territorial levels.[28] Always in debt, the princes were repeatedly driven to sell out their sovereign rights in return for money grants from the estates. This led to a fragmentation of public authority that in practice made the Junkers the territorial lords of their peasants.[29] It is true that the *Kammergericht* in Berlin tried to counterbalance the growth of Junker power by upholding the peasants' position when they took legal steps against the increase of labor obligations or against the commutation of quit-rents into services.[30] Yet in the event the margrave yielded to the political pressure of his nobles and sanctioned the introduction of unlimited services as well as the gradual imposition of serfdom. By the end of the 16th century the territorial princes and the peasantry had lost the battle. The Junkers had acquired far-reaching jurisdictional powers over their peasants (*Patrimonialgerichtsbarkeit*) and took pains to discourage them from litigation in the territorial courts.[31] In short, the virtual absence of a centralized modern state in the East permitted the total subjugation of the peasantry and promoted the erosion of their institutions and traditions of self-government. Significantly, the *Gemeinde* developed into a seigneurial institution in the East and into the organizational backbone of a peasant political culture in the West.[32]

These conditions shaped the configuration of the political in the popular culture of the different regions of Germany. East of the Elbe the dominant position of the Junker, armed with the weapon of patrimonial justice, drove the peasants to submerged forms of popular protest, which, due to the archival situation, have mostly been studied by Marxist historians of the German Democratic Republic.[33] Although much research remains to be done, particularly in the 15th and 16th centuries, there appear to have been three basic types of action, which GDR historians classify as "the lower forms of the class struggle."

The first and most widespread form of resistance was unpunctuality and a deliberately low standard of performance when working on the demesne. The peasants, indeed, showed great ingenuity when it came to evading or reducing the value of their service obligations. They might bring the most worn-out and unsuitable farm tools to work or send the least capable of their servants. In Holstein special horses were kept for work on the demesne; they never saw a stable and had to find their own fodder.[34] And there was unending controversy about whether the time needed to go to work and back home should be counted as part of the working hours due.[35] Time and again the estate owners tried to remedy the evil. They employed overseers and issued a long string of detailed regulations, which resemble those used in the early factories.[36] Yet as the unceasing complaints about the peasants' low morale show, such measures brought next to nothing. In the very long run the peasants' "productivity strike" proved an efficient form of resistance since an increasing number of Junkers convinced themselves toward the end of the 18th century that the only way to raise the productivity of labor on their estates was to employ paid labor. Before this point, however, the productivity strike did little more than increase tensions on the estate and served mainly as a means of self-defense and ritual assurance of peasant solidarity in the face of the estate owner and his officials.

The second type of action was an open refusal to work when the estate owner increased the workload. If the peasants openly refused to work while taking legal steps in some territorial court, they endangered any chance they might have had to win their suit. In the end, moreover, every refusal to work or service riot only led to severe retaliations and a confirmation of the Junker's power, who, in such cases, could count on state help.[37]

Much more promising was the third type of action, the anonymous threat of violence and the simple expedient of running away, because an estate owner would carefully weigh the risk of an attack on his person or property, or of losing valuable manpower, through extreme oppressiveness or an inordinate increase in labor obligations. Yet, on the other hand, he would be well aware that only extreme provocation would drive the peasants to violence of this kind or to run away; which, apart from being dangerous,[38] meant, after all, the loss of a farmstead that might have been in the family for generations and an uncertain future. Besides, running away did not benefit the individual who resorted to this desperate form of protest.

A fourth type of protest was the lawsuit, a form of peasant resistance that can hardly be termed "subpolitical."[39] But it did not stand a good chance of success in the East and was difficult to start, since the estate owners held jurisdictional powers to counter such measures. Moreover, they had taken care to protect themselves against the litigiousness of their peasants. In 1540 the margrave had to concede that if someone complained wantonly to the *Kammergericht,* he should be put in the dungeon.[40] An equally effective deterrent must have been the fact that any lawsuit meant a step into an unknown and presumably hostile world of written records and opaque procedures, which only a very courageous peasant community with some tradition of self-government would dare to take.

These types of resistance were not confined to the East.[41] We find them in the South and West when a manorial lord tries to raise his income either by inventing new or by digging up old claims. The popular saying *"mager wie ein Zinshan"* (meager as a cock due to the lord) well illustrates the mentality of peasants who gave all the more grudgingly as they realized that the lord no longer fulfilled his boasted function of protecting the community and had become an expensive do-nothing.[42] In this respect, the growth of the early modern state with its monopoly of legitimate power and its, on the whole, effective guarantee of the peace undermined the legitimation of the lesser nobility as a functionally necessary warrior elite. It increased the class tension between them and their peasants.

Where in the East the peasants had no other but subpolitical means of protest at their disposal, the peasants in the West were developing a well organized and articulate political culture of their own. Its institutional base was the *Gemeinde*, which had taken shape as an institution of rural self-government during the long centuries of the manorial system's decline. It owed its singular position to the fact that the complexity of the agricultural economy was growing and the density of population increasing while manorial control slackened or even disappeared. The most vigorous and longstanding institution of popular self-government in Old Europe had its roots in the need to coordinate productive effort in an agricultural system based on individuals' farming in an open-field system that obstructed individual economic decisions.[43]

As a political institution the *Gemeinde* was composed of all the householding peasants in the village regardless of the legal title they held to their land, regardless of their personal legal status, and even regardless of the size of their property and their manorial affiliations (*Haushäbirkeit*).[44] Those who had no house of their own, whether they were sons or farm servants, were excluded. The constitutive principles of the *Gemeinde* thus reflected the organizational rationale of agrarian society itself, which transcended the legal, institutional, and political superstructure imposed on it by a noble warrior elite. This rationale also becomes apparent in the attitude toward the nonpeasant members of the village community. While representatives of a manorial lord, the village priest, the less respectable village functionaries such as the bath-keeper, and, of course, the diverse groups at the fringe of rural society (Jews, gypsies) were excluded, the blacksmith, as someone whose economic function was indispensable, was generally admitted.[45] Women, on the other hand, were strictly forbidden to attend even as deputies for their husbands, who were liable to be fined if they dared send their wives.[46] The *Gemeinde* was thus an assembly of village oikos despots, one expression among many of the familial division of labor in Old European society.

During the later Middle Ages the *Gemeinde* slowly attained a position of almost equal partnership with the manorial lords, regulating most aspects of village life, from the beginning of the harvest to fire protection, through its powers of economic and social management. One source as to its activity are the *Dorfweistumer,* the codifications of (usually selected) customs governing the life of a village and defining relations between the village and its manorial lord or lords.[47] Even if they were written down at the latter's insistence and, therefore, under the latter's influence, they still suggest a remarkably high standing for the top village officials and for the *Gemeinde* as a whole.[48]

Let us look a little more closely into the *Gemeinde*'s potential for organization, communication, and political consciousness before we deal with the changes wrought by the emergence of the early modern state. The *Gemeinde* had a democratic surface structure, because it included all householders regardless of the size of their property, but an oligarchic deep structure, because the posts to be filled were presumably given to the wealthier section of the community.[49] In any case, the *Gemeinde* was firmly in control of those protected by what E. P. Thompson has called the "grid of inheritance."[50] The growing social differentiation in German agrarian society at the end of the 15th and during the 16th century reinforced these tendencies and sharpened social divisions and tension within the village.[51]

The formation of a village power elite had, however, two sides to it. If it split the village and gave rise to some hostility toward the village patricians, the *Dorfehrbarkeit* (village honorables) as they were called,[52] it also gave the peasantry an experienced and self-conscious leadership. For the responsibilities of the village officials were manifold and required a sound knowledge of agriculture for all economic decisions, the experience, tact, and (practical) sociology of a modern social worker when settling quarrels between neighbors as well as a knowledge of the law and a grasp of politics when dealing with a manorial lord or the officials of the territorial state. The continual observance of these duties brought forth a peasant political elite capable of formulating a political and social program whose failure in the Peasants' War of 1525 should not be taken as a measure of its realism. It is interesting to note that the village elites were not devastated by the defeat and managed to salvage, at least for some time, some political independence and self-consciousness out of the general wreckage of 1525.[53]

Even if the *Gemeinde* was dominated by a village power elite, its educational effect reached further. For example, it had strict rules as to attendance and punctuality. Those who stayed away or sent an unsuitable deputy were fined.[54] Punctuality was, of course, difficult to enforce in a world where practically no one owned a watch. In Franconia, first the bells of the village church were rung, which in itself was highly meaningful.[55] As soon as eight people had assembled, the mayor of the village (*Dorfmeister, Bauernmeister,* and later *Bürgermeister*) had to walk to a distant farmstead and back again. Whoever had not arrived by then had to pay a penalty. The session itself took place in the village square, in the village pub, or in the village hall if the village was rich enough to have one.[56] It seems to have been a very common practice to form a circle and vote by show of hand.[57] Decisions needed the approval of a majority, at least in many places.[58] Often ceremonious oaths were taken. Whoever broke the peace of the meeting by either word or deed was fined or excluded.[59] If he did so after the session, when the assembly was celebrating, as it often did extensively and very willingly, he could be condemned to pay the whole bill.[60]

The *Gemeinde* held virtually a monopoly of political organization in the village. Those who were unable to operate through its channels had practically no chance to articulate their interests openly. In this respect, the density of domination was higher within the village than on the level of relations between the village and the lord or the officials of the territorial state. The evolving class structure among the subordinate classes clearly affected the structure of popular protest. While it was remarkably articulate, organized, and disciplined in conflicts between the village and the lord or state, it seems to have assumed a veiled and submerged form in confrontations within the village. The status of rituals and symbols differed accordingly. In the former case, they served either to raise the importance of or to confer legitimacy upon the actions of the villagers. They were a consciously used part of the political rhetoric in a still largely illiterate society.[61] In 1475, for instance, the right to ring the village bells became an issue in a quarrel between the lords of Neipperg and the village of Dielheim in the Palatinate, because it was clearly understood as a symbol of government.[62] During the Peasants' War fishing in the ponds of the lord became a symbol for the evangelical legitimacy of the protest movement.[63]

In confrontations within the village, on the other hand, ritual and symbolic action was often partly mere camouflage, partly also a genuine safety valve for tensions in the community. Protest appears to have transformed time-honored village customs into occasions for social blackmail, in order to enforce traditions of mutuality and generosity that the have-nots felt were disappearing, or into occasions for popular justice of the charivari kind, in order to accuse and punish infringements of what they held to be the norms governing the life of the village. As a case in point we can take the South German custom of knocking on doors on the three Thursday nights before Christmas (or on the nights between Christmas and Twelfthnight) in order to announce the birth of the Lord or to wish a happy New Year in return for a small donation of apples, pears, nuts, and coins.[64] From the late 15th century on the *Klöpfleinsnächte* (knocking nights) came increasingly under attack from the authorities because of the disorders to which they gave rise and because they had taken on the character of aggressive begging.[65] For example, in 1568 a police mandate of the margrave of Ansbach expressly referred to the *"bettlische Klöpfleinsnächte"* (begging nights) and forbade the practice.[66] The few court book entries which we have so far suggest that the custom was used as a cover for private vengeance and could turn into a charivari-like affair.[67] The knocking could turn into a violent attack on the house just as the well-wishing could be replaced by a malediction or, in less serious cases, by some kind of mockery. The superstitious beliefs surrounding the *Klöpfleinsnächte* and the atmosphere of fear that a dark winter night inspired increased the value of the custom as a censorial ritual. Tellingly, the knockers went in masquerade, which not only concealed their identity but greatly increased the horror they could inspire when the symbolic meaning of the mask was not tempered by benevolent words. The mask represented, so to speak, the ambivalent potential of the ritual. First, as a symbolic attack it could either be contradicted or endorsed by words or actions or both. Second, by concealing the identity of the person behind it, it suspended, for a limited period of time, the direct and indirect mechanisms of domination woven into the public sphere. The growing concern with mumming that the authorities exhibited after the end of the 15th century may point to widespread changes in the social function of customs during a period of social differentiation.[68]

As folklorists have noted, the custom of the *Klöpfleinsnächte* was increasingly mentioned in a negative context in the 16th century.[69] This may have something to do with the Reformation but, on the other hand, the accusation of popery was a shibboleth in the ideological justification of government action that should not be taken too seriously. Besides, Catholic authorities were no less clear in their attitude toward the practice, which they condemned as devilish. They differed only in their strategy for dealing with unpopular popular customs, relying more on assimilation and revaluation in a Catholic sense than on suppression.[70] In some ways, this was the more promising policy but the more severe course of suppression, which the Protestant authorities followed, was also to some extent successful. For, from the 16th century on, the custom was increasingly associated with children instead of adults, lessening its danger as a ritual of threat and censure.[71] Moreover, we must keep in mind that the *Klöpfleinsnächte* was only one ritual among others of the sort that seem to have undergone similar changes of function.[72]

Against this background it would be easy to overestimate the political potential of the *Gemeinde*. It was no embryonic 18th century political society buzzing with political discussion or speculation. The agenda of the village meetings was dominated by the manifold problems of everyday life. It gave the peasant community a sense of corporate identity beyond the manorial context, the experience of self-government, and an organizational base that could serve different uses if need be. The politics of the ruling elite, on the other hand, seemed remote and opaque from the village perspective and if it affected the life of the village at all, did so in an intrinsically uncontrollable and catastrophic manner, as in the case of feud or war. If politics was talked about at all – and it sometimes was in the late medieval climate of upheaval and growing disorientation – it was in the village pub after a newssinger had unloaded his habitual mixture of miracles, half-truths, and genuine information. Yet these talks bore no resemblance either in form or in content to 18th century coffeehouse conversations.[73] The politicization of the peasantry had other roots and went in other directions.

It was the emergence of the early modern state that activated the dormant political potential of the *Gemeinde,* because it linked the "big politics" of the ruling elite and the "little politics" of the village through its massive intervention into social and economic life. Thus it was the politicization of everyday life that made the *Gemeinde* the focus of a distinct peasant political culture and, eventually, led the peasants to demand a revaluation of their position in the late medieval social and political order.[74] The rural uprisings of the 15th and 16th centuries reflect the peasantry's growing political awareness.

The intervention of the early modern state was basically fiscal in character. Expenses for the court and for military activities rose so rapidly that the prince was forced to exploit to the full such traditional sources of income as the dominial lands and various use-rights reserved to him. The only way to do this was to improve administration, which, in turn, cost money. In the course of the 16th century it became clear that additional means of finance had to be sought. The result was an ever-increasing tax load. In short, the emergence of the early modern state meant a significant redistribution of the gross national product of a territorial unit, to the disadvantage of the peasants. It could take direct and indirect forms and was clearly recognized, as the grievances and demands of the peasantry show. I single out three aspects of this process.

One was the growing appetite of the territorial state for the woods and pastures of the village common. Wood was an important raw material while pastures were needed for sheep-breeding (which promised to be a good investment in a period of rising demand for textile products).[75] This challenge was to be of particular importance because it unified the village against a common enemy. The haves had long protected the village common against the have-nots; they could not but resent the allout attack on what they regarded as their property. The have-nots; on the other hand, had for so long tried to force their way through the grid of inheritance in claiming use-rights on the commons that they, too, felt deprived and saw their hopes for social integration vanish.[76]

A second aspect was the ever-increasing tax load. Its extent and composition varied by territory and are only beginning to be studied in detail. The territorial state proved extremely inventive in introducing new and often vexatious taxes.[77] As Endres has shown for the archbishopric of Bamberg, the tax load could be particularly high in spiritual territories when several vacancies occurred in succession and occasioned the levy of consecration taxes.[78] In a thorough analysis of the territorial finances of Hessia under Philipp the Magnanimous, Kruger has shown that the total revenue of the territory rose from 32,559 fl. in 1500–09 to 163,188 fl. in 1560–68. The income from taxes alone rose from 2,838 fl. to 62,459 fl., that is, from under 10 percent at the beginning to 38 percent around the middle of the century.[79] The financial structure of the margravates of Ansbach and Bayreuth in Franconia was similar.[80] In Bavaria territorial taxes rose by 2200 percent between 1480 and 1660.[81] To these were added imperial taxes, which amounted to 73.5 Römermonate between 1519 and 1555 and to 409 Römermonate between 1556 and 1606.[82]

A third catalyst in politicizing the peasantry was the intensification of governmental pressure in general. The attempt to broaden the fiscal base of the early modern state led to a hitherto-unknown interference with the institutions and traditions of rural government, and threatened many of the peasants' inherited forms of life. A few examples of what was happening must suffice. The *Weistümer,* the customary local by-laws of the village, began to be replaced by uniform territorial village ordinances that interfered with many old and introduced many new practices. The powers and functions of the village assembly were being curtailed or put under the supervision of officials of the territorial state.[83] A new law with unknown legal procedures and a new legal substance made its appearance and aroused the peasants' suspicion since it not only turned against them but was practiced mainly in writing and to a much lesser extent than before under their watchful eyes.[84] And, as the peasants were quick to realize, with the officials came the fees. During the uprising known by the name of *Armer Konrad* the peasants complained "that the old customs and habits in towns and villages have been much battered by the doctors to the disadvantage and the damage of the common man. If this was not remedied," they continued, "two doctors would, in time, have to be sent to every village to dispense justice."[85] Moreover, as village ordinances and police mandates forbidding cherished local customs, regulating consumption, and interfering with many aspects of everyday life multiplied, a whole way of life seemed to be coming under attack.

At a relatively early stage the peasants offered resistance. The threat to their institutions and traditions of self-government transformed the knowledge they possessed of them through the need to describe, explain, and defend them into political consciousness and revealed the potential of the *Gemeinde* as their own political institution. Their ideological frame of reference was the Old Law, *das Alte Recht,* which was, however, ill-suited to justify anything like a revolutionary movement.[86] Customary conditions varied from region to region; the Old Law did not promote supraregional activities but tended to confirm the localism of the villages. Moreover, the very logic of an appeal to the Old Law demanded that the remembered reality be restored to its totality. The world that was thus rendered legitimate included the rightful claims of the adversary. Yet as tensions increased, to culminate in the Peasants' War of 1525, the totality of custom was broken up and segments of the peasantry began to redefine custom in a selective manner so that it contained an alternative not only to the existing social and political conditions of which they complained but to custom itself as well. They reassembled fragments of custom and "reconstructed" a customary world beyond custom.[87]

Such a radicalization of custom does not, however, alone explain the more general visionary dimension of the peasant movement in the early 16th century, which eased the way to supraregional cooperation. That derived its force from an appeal to the Bible and the egalitarian tradition in Christian thought, which provided the peasants with those arguments from the common stock of reference in 16th century political thinking that operated in their favor. For however far the interpretation of custom and the Old Law might lead, it could never completely erase the titles of legitimacy that the past conferred upon each of the contending parties. In fact, in 1525, many peasant groups were unable to conceive of a sociopolitical alternative that excluded the manorial lords, although they were experiencing self-government to a hitherto-unknown degree and could have little hope of returning to a "normal" life after the risings. In the event, a more complete break with the existing order of things could be justified only by invoking the other unquestioned authority and source of legitimacy — the Bible and the Law of God.

The time was ripe for a revitalization of the egalitarian tradition in Christianity. The gap between the ecclesiastical establishment and the mass of believers had, once again, widened and the effect of the mendicant orders had worn off. The clergy high and low were rapidly losing whatever was left of their legitimacy. The bishops and abbots — insofar as they were territorial princes — had joined the drive to intensify and increase dues and services. The lower clergy, too, did precious little, from the point of view of their flock, to earn their living as public servants of the village. *"Die pfaffen zue todt schlagen,"* even if only verbally, had become a cherished pastime in the village pub.[88] Thus, there existed fertile soil for a large-scale heretical movement as well as for spontaneous expressions of unbridled popular piety, which also exhibited the tendency to combine religious with political and social protest.[89] The so-called piper of Niklahausen in the Tauber Valley may serve as a case in point. He attracted people from all over Franconia and the neighboring regions such as Hessia, Suebia, and even Bavaria, pretending to have been commanded by the Virgin Mary to preach to the common man. What followed was a characteristic concoction of an effusive popular piety, sharp attack on the luxury and the abuses of the clergy (such as the practice in ecclesiastical courts of enforcing their basically secular decisions by spiritual penalties), and equally stringent demands for the abolition of all dues and services and the restitution of pristine equality among mankind. The piper's audience reacted in a way illustrating the social potential of religious protest: they revered him as a saint, turned away from the established spiritual authorities, and gave up their worldly goods symbolically by cutting their hair or putting aside their rich dress.[90]

Such religious explosions served to revitalize the egalitarian tradition in Christian thinking but they were not the stuff of which articulate and organized protest movements are made.

164                                                                                              *Günther Lottes*

It was the appeal to the Old Law, to concrete experience, that as a grid of interpretation prevented the appeal to the Law of God from being drowned in effusive popular piety or degenerating into sectarian utopianism. The famous saying *"Als Adam wob und Eva spann, wo war da der Edelmann?"* (When Adam wove and Eve span, where was then the gentleman?) epitomizes what was happening. Appeal to the Scriptures combined with concrete social experience.

Thus, the peasants formulated a more general conception of what the future political order ought to be. While some dreamed of a peasant empire under a peasant emperor chosen by the people at large, the more pragmatic leaders of the late medieval and early modern peasant movement aimed at representation in the estate on an equal footing with the nobility, the clergy, and the cities (which had only recently fought their way into many a territorial and even the imperial diet). In some parts of the South and West of the Empire the peasants actually won such concessions. They even managed to maintain their prizes through the dangerous waters of the 16th century reaction.

On the whole, however, that singular politicization of rural popular culture which occurred in the late 15th and the early 16th century did not survive the consolidation of the early modern state. It is true that the *Gemeinde* continued to exist and even continued, at least to some extent, to provide the experience of self-government as well as an institutional base for protest.[91] But peasant protest lost the character of an all-out challenge to the existing order. It ceased to aim at the realization of a sociopolitical alternative. Thus, it was no longer the principle of taxation or even rising taxation in itself, but the incidence of excessive demands and unfair assessment that triggered off rural resistance.[92] As Winfried Schulze has noted, this was because the early modern state did not rely exclusively on repression but offered legal channels of resistance in conflicts between the manorial lords and their peasants, channels that seem to have played an important part in the pacification of rural society in the German territories.[93] On the other hand, it must not be overlooked that this reflects a change in the way in which the ruling elites lived off the agricultural surplus. While private exploitation became more difficult, the demands of the state itself could hardly be challenged within the legal framework that it provided; the court, the administration, and military expenditure became channels of retribution.

Moreover, the village elites often made their peace with the new power structure or even welcomed it. In cases of conflict the village could split into "obedient" and "disobedient" parts that tried to capture the *Gemeinde* as an institutional base.[94] Yet, even then, the ultimate aim was to initiate and facilitate legal action, not to make the *Gemeinde* the backbone of a large-scale protest movement or the pillar of a new social order. The lines of social confrontation in this type of conflict are difficult to draw because economic and social stratification may not coincide. As claims of the manorial lords were based on the latter, substantial peasants might also stand to lose something and, therefore, be induced to support protest actions. But, as Schulze underlines, rural resistance after 1525 was often accompanied by a reversal of the social hierarchy in the village.[95] This would point to a change of function for the *Gemeinde* in the course of the 16th century, which has to be seen not only in the context of the formation of the early modern state but also against the background of class differentiation among the subordinate classes themselves.

Compared with the findings of Thompson, Davis, Le Roy Ladurie, Bercé, and others for England and France these observations allow some generalizations about the character of popular political culture in early modern Europe. It appears to have been shaped by several interlocking variables, which determined selections from the repertoire of early modern popular protest in each particular case.

The first variable is the class structure of the subordinate classes and their relationship with the ruling elite. Changes in either decidedly affected the structure of popular protest. Thus the differing forms and directions of popular protest before and after 1525 have to be seen as functions of both the changing organization of the ruling elite in its relationship with the subordinate classes and social differentiations among the subordinate classes. The switch to legal resistance after 1525 and the transformations of local customs into occasions for social blackmail or social censure are cases in point.

Second, the density of domination has to be measured at the local level as regards relations between the ruling elite and the subordinate classes as well as the incidence of domination among the subordinate classes themselves. The higher the density, the more repressed are the forms of protest. Above all, this has a bearing on the interpretation of the status of symbolic actions. Such actions may be a consciously used part of the political rhetoric in a still largely illiterate society to counter equally symbolic demonstrations of authority or to mobilize the "simple folk" by adequate means of propaganda; a consciously used but veiled form of protest, which, for instance, has to seek the protection of custom and anonymity behind masks because of a high density of domination; or a ritualization of an action that neutralizes its potential practical effect and serves as a safety valve.

The third variable is the availability of and capacity for organization. In part this is merely a function of the density of domination in a given social unit, for one feature of domination is the suppression or containment of potentially competing organizations. For example, from the late 15th century on, the authorities were increasingly concerned that village meetings should not be held without need or permission. In East Germany the Junkers used their patrimonial jurisdiction to dominate the *Gemeinde*, to the extent that it became an agency of the *Gutsherrschaft* and lost its value as an institution of the peasantry. On the other hand, the availability of organization remains an independent variable insofar as it explains why the peasants did not succeed in building a supraregional base. For the *Gemeinde* was so essentially a local organization that it obstructed supraregional cooperation, even though it provided the experience of self-government and could be thought of as the basic constitutive element of an alternative sociopolitical order. Moreover, the availability of and the capacity for organization is also determined by economic and demographic factors. Thus, the progress of market relationships on the labor market, the process of urbanization, and the increase of population would reduce the capacity for organization in England in the 18th and in Germany in the 19th century.

Fourth is the availability of a political language in which to articulate protest and to formulate a sociopolitical alternative. This is probably the vaguest of factors. But the interplay between the appeal to the Law of God and the radicalization of custom (as expressed in the appeal to the Old Law) during the Peasants' War of 1525 makes it clear how important this variable might become for popular protest. It makes the difference between popular protest as a merely reactive force, which does not question the social order as such, and popular protest as a far-reaching demand for the revision of the existing social order.

It has already been noted that the early modern state took great pains to order the everyday life of its subjects. In fact, a great deal of what we know about early modern popular culture comes either from the numerous ordinances, mandates, and edicts issued to this end or from the records that were kept when rules were infringed. This raises the question of the state's formative influence on the popular culture of early modern Germany. It is best understood if we examine in one particular instance, namely the regulation of consumption, the various motives for state intervention.

The issuing of comprehensive police ordinances or special mandates fixing, among other things, such details as the number of guests at a smallholder's or craftsman's wedding was seen as part of the duty of a Christian magistrate. He struggled against blasphemy, profanity, luxurious living, and many other abuses to protect his subjects against their own worst selves and to ensure their moral and spiritual welfare; hence the concern of the secular authorities grew when the late medieval church, through increasing negligence and aloofness, failed in its proper task of moral and spiritual control. As the prince found it necessary to make use of his *ius reformandi* to reform abuses in the church, so he gradually increased his responsibilities in that field. The culmination came with the Reformation. In Protestant territories the church became one branch of the territorial bureaucracy, while the position of the prince was decisively strengthened in Catholic principalities. Moreover, and above all in Protestant states, the interpretation of what constituted an abuse significantly widened and the understanding of what was tolerable in popular culture narrowed. And there can be no doubt that many princes and councillors were inspired in their government by the values of either Protestantism or Reformed Catholicism. To this extent the pressure on popular culture was a direct consequence of an ideological reorientation of the ruling elite. Its eventual efficacy depended on the energy with which the program of the reform of popular culture was pursued as well as on the means of discipline that the apparatus of the modern state provided. On the other hand, it is obvious that these changes in ideology were fortuitous and could be used to justify other ends. The spiritual and moral welfare of the people and, therefore, the margin of the tolerable in popular culture, was not an autonomous category but deeply embedded in the socioeconomic context. Besides, the ideological explanation does not account for the specificity of the regulations or their timing. These are much better understood if we turn to governmental motives.

The formation of the early modern state with its mounting expenditures for the court, the bureaucracy, and military affairs meant a rise in the share of public and a reduction in the share of private consumption. The instrument of redistribution was the revenue and tax system; the tax-paying capacity of the subject became a prime concern for the early modern state. The peasant had to be able to run his farm, pay regular dues to the manorial and territorial lord, and be taxed at irregular intervals. The tax load was usually high and difficult to pay out of regular income. As Kruger has shown in his excellent analysis of the finances of Hessia, a property tax of 2 percent amounted to an income tax of 40 percent that had to be paid in excess of regular payments.[96] At the same time the manorial lords, who found themselves caught between the need to defend their status by conspicuous consumption and the price revolution, also tried to raise their claims. Such sums could only be paid if the taxpayer either saved money or incurred debts that he would repay in normal years. It was, therefore, necessary for the state to ensure that peasants reduced their consumption in order to stay solvent and credit-worthy. The substantial peasants, who were profiting from rising prices for agricultural products, posed no problem. They would have enough to pay taxes and could lend money to others in the village. The smallholders, the farm servants, and the craftsmen, however, who had a hard time staying above the poverty line anyway, were another matter. With them potlatch-like celebrations, inordinate drinking, or gambling could make the difference. To keep them taxable was the underlying fiscal aim of the social discipline that the early modern state tried to implement with police ordinances and mandates.

The officials and financial experts of the early modern state were well aware of the manifold forms of overconsumption. In one way or another, however, they all had to do with the concepts of honor and status. Social relations within the village, not unlike those in the ruling elite, were determined by competitive consumption, which led to strain on the resources of the competitors.

In fixing the number of guests at life-cycle celebrations such as births, weddings, first churchings, and burials, the authorities tried to balance the resources and the consumptive behavior of a villager and to formalize the texture of status within the village. Another case was such customs as the "challenge to drink" (*Zutrinken*), which usually went on until nobody could drink any more.[97] Such drinking orgies could eventually lead to impoverishment and, of course, resulted in idleness and a loss of productivity. In short, the sumptuary legislation of the early modern state aimed at curtailing a popular culture built on unrestricted consumption and habits developed in times of comparative plenty. And this required a transformation of the prevailing rationality of social interaction in the village. It had to be adapted to the new economic and fiscal rationality of the early modern state.

No wonder the peasants saw this attempt at social discipline as an all-out attack on their whole way of life with a quite blatant fiscal motive. They suspected the regulations were meant to be broken, in order to make the ensuing fines a source of revenue. Thus the peasant subjects of Salem Abbey in the German Southwest complained "that all we have, be it great or little, bring it pleasure or pain to us, is under supervision, forbidden or fixed in order to levy fines."[98] Besides, ordinances and mandates that were making it clear that the state and its officials now took care of what had once been decided by the village community alone also demonstrated governmental presence, another vital move in the struggle for functions between the *Gemeinde* and the territorial state.

The new social policy of the early modern state had other, non-fiscal aspects. So it is suggested that sumptuary legislation represented an attempt to preserve a traditional social order that was being undermined by social differentiation. This argument is often adduced to explain dress ordinances in medieval cities where a patrician oligarchy was threatened by artisans or merchants grown rich but excluded from the inner circles and tried to hold down their consumptive challenge forcibly.[99] This explanation is valid: competitive consumption was, indeed, a disguised form of the social struggle in medieval and early modern cities. We need only be reminded of Nürnberg, where the patricians turned the *Schembartlauf,* a carnevalesque masked procession on Ash Wednesday, from a popular amusement arranged by the butchers and cutlers into a patrician display of wealth and power.[100] As regards rural regions, the same might be said for rich peasants whose conspicuous consumption diminished the social distance between them and the neighboring nobles and their officials.

On the other hand, the sumptuary legislation of the 16th century takes note of social groups that could not hope to challenge the social superiority of either the ruling elite or the wealthy in the village. If they used competitive consumption as a technique for assigning social rank in the village, the growing social differentiation among the peasantry must have made it difficult for them to play at the game of consumption as a means of class domination. Instead they were themselves on the defensive. As socioeconomic conditions undermined the traditional forms of social interaction in the village, the necessity to keep up appearances in order to veil real social decline must have made it even more difficult for them to hold on to what they had. It is interesting that the new social policy was not universally hated as unbearable harassment but actually welcomed by some. For them the coincidence of the fiscally motivated social policy of the early modern state and their own wish to preserve their property and status had, at least superficially, a beneficial effect.[101]

Finally, the regulation of consumption was a genuine reaction to the socioeconomic crisis of the 16th century. The authorities were not unaware of the fact that the increase in public expenditure and the mounting pressure on the subsistence base were dangerously lowering the margin of existence for a considerable segment of the rural population. For those who had to turn to a seller's market for their food supply the situation was critical when harvests were bad. When all resources were spent, desperation could trigger off serious disturbances of the public order.[102] Any subsistence crisis, therefore, called for state intervention. The general course was to soften the effects of market relationships by prohibiting exports, by legislating against forestallers and engrossers, by regulating market procedures, and by distributing wheat that had been stored in good years.[103] An additional expedient seemed to be the prescription of what might be called an austerity program for the common man. To some extent, at least, the sumptuary legislation of the early modern state has to be seen as an attempt to husband a region's resources. Overconsumption was reduced in order to delay a crisis of subsistence.

To sum up, the sumptuary legislation of the late 15th and the 16th centuries reflects the fact that the peasants' share of the agricultural surplus was on the decline even if individual peasants fared well. The peasantry was caught between a rising tax load (necessary to finance the formation of the early modern state) and rising food prices plus diminishing incomes (as a result of the mounting demographic pressure on the subsistence base). As the peasantry was, of course, unwilling to give up cherished cultural norms and habits adopted during a time of comparative plenty, the early modern state had to force austerity by a policy of social discipline.[104] As the underlying problem did not become manifest with equal clarity everywhere at the same time it is not surprising that there were wide variations in the implementation of this policy.

It is difficult to evaluate the success of this policy of social discipline. The common view is that police ordinances and mandates had little effect because they had to be repromulgated frequently, because enforcement standards were low, and because people saw the penalty in cases of infringement simply as an additional expense not to be spared on a great occasion. It is even suggested that the authorities acquiesced in this view for fiscal reasons.[105]

These valid arguments can easily lead us to underestimate the impact of early modern social policy. Thus, the republication of ordinances and mandates does not in itself prove that they were not heeded; there were other, equally reasonable motives. So we have to distinguish between provisions that aimed to suppress a practice and those that tried to regulate it. In the former case, republication may, indeed, often signal failure. The custom of *"Zutrinken,"* mentioned above, for instance, was difficult to eradicate. On the other hand, republication could also be a mere restatement of the law that indicated the potential for infringements, but does not justify the conclusion that it was not observed at all. Repeated prohibitions of poaching, for example, do not prove that poaching was widespread. If the aim was to control a practice, as in the case of consumption at life-cycle celebrations, it was simply necessary to state the law from time to time. Besides, while the general direction of sumptuary legislation remained the same, the details sometimes changed. Thus differing provisions as to the number of guests, the duration of the feast, and so on, may

well reflect a deterioration or an improvement of the food situation in a given region. After all, the authorities did not intend the
total abolition of life-cycle celebrations; they wanted to reduce
the expenditure on these occasions. Popular culture was to lose its
fringe of affluence.[106]

Moreover, republication could also be a form of propaganda,
either to demonstrate governmental responsibility in certain matters or to improve a common standard of obedience to the law
that, under normal circumstances, may not have been negligible at
all. Republication may, for example, be seen as a reaction to a
critical situation, as part of an administrative practice as yet in its
infancy. We have to keep in mind that ordinances were frequently
republished as a whole although some parts may already have been
outdated.

About enforcement standards we know very little. Quite often
we simply lack the necessary court or administrative records, and
the base for quantitative studies is too small. But even if it were
not, only numerous convictions would tell us something definite
while the absence of convictions could always mean either that the
ordinances were widely ignored and only negligently enforced or
that they were observed. However, we can at least be confident
that the fiscal aspect mentioned above cannot have been dominant. Even if the officials of the early modern state had strong
fiscal interests, they were no short-sighted fiscal maniacs.[107] For
instance, they attacked the custom of *Zutrinken* although they
were well aware that success would mean a loss of revenue from
the excise on beer.

There was certainly no difficulty in detecting an infringement
of the sumptuary laws since they could not and would not be
broken in secret. On the other hand, it is obvious that enforcement standards varied regionally as well as over time.[108] Some
customs were readily suppressed, others lingered on for decades or
even more than a century despite repeated prohibitions. Not surprisingly, much depended on how seriously the authorities took
the issue. Moreover, there were different ways of dealing with unwanted practices. In general, Protestant territories favored a
strategy of reform, as Peter Burke has described it,[109] while Catholic princes preferred a strategy of assimilation.

On balance, it seems that the early modern state fought a war of
attrition against overconsumption in popular culture, which

developed into a sort of crisis management when the food situation deteriorated and the public order was threatened. Compared to the naked force of actual tax exactions and of socioeconomic differentiation, the policy of social discipline had only a limited effect. But in prescribing the forms that the redistribution of the agricultural surplus away from the mass of the peasantry should take, it had a formative influence on the external appearance of popular culture. And in proscribing attitudes, values, and forms in customary popular culture, the new social policy of the early modern state drove it, at least in part, underground and transformed it from an independent counterculture into either a subculture or an assimilated culture.[110]

The early modern state was not content to suppress the political dimension and the trend toward overconsumption in popular culture in order to undermine popular resistance and to achieve that austerity in private consumption which was necessary in an age of rising public expenditure and a declining per capita surplus. The territorial princes and their officials went further. They tried to establish a far-reaching mental and spiritual control over their subjects. This control has to be seen as an end in itself and as the supporting ideology of the new policy of social discipline. The care for the spiritual welfare of subjects — the duty of a Christian prince — could be used to inculcate those virtues of obedience, industry, sobriety, and parsimony that made a good Christian, a good subject, and a good taxpayer. The secular *"policey"* was supported and supplemented by a spiritual *"policey"* that found expression in numerous church ordinances and religious mandates. Temporal and spiritual police became, in fact, so perfectly intertwined that it is difficult to separate them. Just as police ordinances included articles against blasphemy, aimed at superstitious practices in popular religion, so church ordinances contained articles against overconsumption. Many, for instance, forbade the tradition of *Kirchweihküchle;* others ordained fasts for a mixture of economic and spiritual reasons.[111]

The 16th century spiritual police stemmed from the *ius reformandi,* which the territorial princes had begun to claim during the 15th century in order to counter the dangerous decline of the established church. The Reformation vastly increased potential temporal power in the spiritual realm by closing the gap between the church and the state and by transforming the ecclesiastical

hierarchy into a branch of the territorial bureaucracy.[112] The
princes who adhered to the old faith also gained, greatly increasing
their influence over the church, although the connection with
Rome continued to exist and the powers of the ecclesiastical
courts were, in principle, upheld.[113] For the established church
had no choice but to rely on the secular powers in its counteroffensive against the Protestant challenge. The alliance of the Protestant faith with the state required, on the Catholic side, a similarly
close cooperation. So the 16th century was marked by a religious
upheaval of some magnitude, and church and state combined to
intensify governmental pressure in religious matters. The late
medieval trend toward a fragmentation of religious life reversed
itself and the individualization of religion inherent in the Protestant approach was contained at an early stage. This would profoundly affect popular culture.

The intensification of spiritual care led to a suppression or, at
best, an assimilation of many aspects of popular religion. The Reformation had made it clear to the reformers as well as to the
established church that their relative strength depended on the
number of believers they controlled: the more numerous the
flock, the stronger the shepherd. For Protestants this kind of
stock-taking was an ideological and moral as well as a tactical
requirement, whereas the Catholic tradition had previously permitted a greater tolerance toward unorthodoxies. But now, competition for souls worked against popular religion. The Catholic
church was compelled to take more rigorous measures against the
Protestant threat than it had against medieval heresies. It was no
longer enough to persecute heretics. Instead, it was necessary to
take stock of the believers and to ensure that they were not lured
away by the spiritual competitor. Tellingly, such measures of
stock-taking figure prominently in the decisions of the Council of
Trent.[114] Moreover, neither Protestant doctors nor Catholic
bishops were at ease with the gnostic threat of late medieval
popular piety.[115]

As many popular customs were intimately linked with religious
ceremonies, any change affecting the latter was bound to have
repercussions on the former and, therefore, on the whole configuration of popular culture. For example, the sequence of festivities
in town and village was geared to the religious calendar. All events
of the life cycle were accompanied by religious celebrations, if

they were not themselves rooted in religion such as baptisms, first churchings, or weddings.[116] Finally, many purely secular activities had, in time, become connected with some religious ceremony to enhance their importance. When, for instance, the *Feldgeschworenen*, the field masters of the village, made their annual round to mark the area appertaining to the village (*Untergang* or *Umgang*) in order to teach the village youth its boundaries, they were accompanied by the village priest who, on some other holiday, would make his own round praying for protection from hail and for a good harvest.[117] The new Protestant theology was unlikely to put up with such rites for doctrinal reasons and because of their intimate connection with the religion they tried to reform or replace.

There can be no doubt that the introduction of Protestantism in a given region meant a sharper break with the past than the implementation of Catholic reform. After all, such practices as the veneration of saints, the cult of the Virgin Mary, pilgrimages, and the whole complex of good works, which had been at the heart of 15th century popular piety, now ranked high on the Protestants' list of abuses, however conservative they might be in other matters. Meanwhile the established church had no difficulty in making use of them for its counteroffensive. Strictly speaking, the whole magical element in popular religion, which the late medieval church had tolerated, canalized, and sometimes encouraged for financial reasons, was coming under attack.[118]

As a popular movement, Protestantism had, at least in the beginning, the appeal of a great heresy with its mood of religious revival and its peculiar mixture of religious, social, and political protest. Moreover, there was some common ground between the new faith and popular religion. The prejudice against monks and nuns, the intense dislike of a privileged but morally lax priesthood, and the critical attitude toward institutional and liturgical peculiarities of the established church were common to both. Thus, apart from promising better pastoral care, some of the changes that the reformers demanded were certainly not unwelcome to the peasantry. They had, for instance, no reason to resent the abolition of celibacy. As the late medieval popular literature attests, the unmarried priest had always been a problem for the village. The introduction of holy communion *sub utraque specie* was readily accepted because it symbolically deprived the priest of his privileged position. Eventually, as Robert Scribner has shown in his excellent study of Reformation propaganda in Germany,[119] the reformers knew how to persuade the public. They made extensive use of the code of communication peculiar to popular culture and were masters at a selective incorporation of popular belief. Thus, Protestant propaganda could base its attack on the established church on a widespread and deeply rooted anticlericalism while its own alternative remained largely concealed. The future was, however, foreshadowed in the element of reeducation present in much Reformation propaganda, which indicates latent contradictions in the alliance between the new faith and popular religion.[120] The picture changed when the new faith had won power at the governmental level and no longer needed to mobilize a mass following. The fate of the *Schembartlauf* in Nürnberg illustrates the changing attitude of Protestantism toward popular culture in the course of the Reformation. In 1523, the *Schembartlauf* had been used to attack such abuses as indulgences. In 1539, the reformer Osiander was ridiculed during the carnival procession for his eagerness to implement Protestant reforms. Osiander reacted sharply: he complained to the city authorities and demanded a prohibition of the *Schembartlauf*. The council complied.[121]

The crucial problem in the relations between the new faith and popular religion lay in the former's determined refusal to accept the latter's magical worldview, as the established church had done and would to some extent do again. There was little common ground between the austere faith of the Protestant divines who framed religious mandates, church ordinances, and injunctions for visitations, and a popular religion that combined an effusive and spontaneous popular piety with magical beliefs pagan in character and Christian in form. There were, of course, regional variations. The electors of Brandenburg and Saxony were, for instance, more conservative than the Landgrave of Hessia or the Count Palatine. But the basic confrontation was the same everywhere. To political repression and social austerity were added religious repression and austerity.

How did popular culture react? It was definitely not reconciled to the new faith by an intensification of pastoral care. Although the Protestants were quick to occupy the higher echelons of the church establishment and effectively invaded the administration of the early modern state, it took more than a century before there existed a rank-and-file Protestant clergy capable of fulfilling the promise. Until then the village priest remained the weak link in the Protestant chain of power and a population hostile to religious interference knew how to take advantage of the fact. This is apparent in some of the theaters of the guerilla war that popular religion was waging against the new faith.

As to divine service itself, there was little room for resistance. It was largely impossible either to evade it or to influence it, since the initiative lay with the priest. He, however, might himself be no full-fledged Protestant and stick to at least some of the old rites. It was a common complaint of visitation boards to the end of the 16th century that, for instance, the elevation of the host continued to be practiced in holy communion.[122] This amounted to nothing less than a liturgical admission of transubstantiation and it is not surprising that the congregation acted accordingly.[123] Almost three generations of Protestant rule had not eradicated the traditional attitude toward the sacrament. Apparently, even the Protestant hierarchy was unsure how far they could go in this matter; they preferred to declare the practice an adiaphoron, although it was none, unless we totally dissociate liturgical symbolism and theological meaning. In Brandenburg the question was brought up several times but allowed to drop until the believers might be better instructed in the Christian faith.[124] In other words, the expectation of resistance forced a liturgical concession of some moment, albeit a very conservative one, on a Protestant church establishment. But other Protestant authorities, even Calvinist ones, displayed the same caution in lesser things.[125] No wonder, therefore, that the isolated village priest who had to live with his congregation and depended on their good will in many things was even more easily blackmailed into making concessions to popular religion. He could be forced to consecrate items, to ring the bells in order to ward off bad weather, or even to officiate at a prohibited pilgrimage.[126]

This leads us to another theater of war: the veneration of saints and the cult of the Virgin Mary. Protestant authorities were, on the whole, uncompromising in this respect. The farthest they would go was to preserve in their religious calendar the memory of certain saints whom they took to be particularly dear to the population. The day of the patron saint of a city, or a holiday with an important meaning in the rural calendar, was often retained.[127] This was done even though there could be no doubt that the congregation read something else into such celebration than the Protestant divines, who were happy to have found some theological justification at all. One has the impression of a tacit or even unconscious agreement to uphold certain religious customs in form while, at the same time, differing widely in their interpretation. Yet, notwithstanding such minor concessions, the Protestant clergy was, on balance, determined to suppress what they believed to be papist abuses detrimental to the souls entrusted to them by God. Visitation boards and superintendents never condoned them, and there was less room for maneuver for the local priest. After all, a saint or the Virgin Mary had to have altars where they could be prayed to and that could be endowed or, at least, decorated if the cult were not to lose its appeal. It was precisely this that was impossible for the local priest to concede. He might close an eye to certain liturgical deviations or officiate at some local custom, but to allow the peasants to preserve or erect an altar would get him into difficulties with his betters and draw a visit from the superintendent.

Unable to wring such concessions from the local priest or from the hierarchy in this matter, popular religion had no choice but to go underground. Thus, people continued to pray to their saints and to the Virgin Mary in private and went to hidden places of worship where they could pray and offer gifts in secrecy.[128] In some regions, the net of pilgrimage routes that had existed before the Reformation continued to be used, even if the vows were no longer made in public and some pretext had to be found to justify the journey. The situation was particularly delicate in the Upper Palatinate. Bordering on several Catholic territories it had a Lutheran population and a reformed church establishment, which meant high standards of enforcement. Nevertheless, whatever pains the Palatine's establishment took, people continued to make pilgrimages either to secret places in their own territory or to established places of worship in one of the neighboring Catholic regions. And, even more surprising, the Catholic population from the other side of the border made pilgrimages into the Upper Palatinate.[129]

The Protestant authorities soon realized that their strategy of prohibition threatened any chance of their controlling the cults they forbade. If popular religion had lost its freedom of expression, it had, at least for some time, preserved or even enlarged its freedom of interpretation. The Protestant refusal to attend to the magical needs of the people through an offer of licensed and hence controllable magic proved fertile soil for superstitious practices.[130] There appears to have been no revitalization or reinterpretation of rites and customs dating from pre-Christian times. They continued to be observed as part of the local heritage of customs but had apparently lost their religious potential.[131] Instead, recourse to magic took the form of what might be called a private appropriation of the traditional Catholic magic, which was being officially withheld. Visitation reports are full of complaints about widespread abuses practiced with consecrated wafers and consecrated water.[132] Such practices were traditionally associated with heresy, witchcraft, or devil worship. But there is no indication that the Protestant strategy of repression unduly encouraged such tendencies. The rural population in Protestant territories remained, on the whole, content with a mixture of furtive adherence to older religious forms and private appropriation of the traditional Catholic magic.

The incidence of religious resistance of this sort belonged to a period of transition. In the long run, popular religion stood no chance of surviving the war of attrition that the Protestant authorities waged against it. Just as popular culture in the narrower sense of customs and consumer habits lost its quality of counterculture under the impact of the policy of social discipline, so popular religion lost the relative independence it had possessed in the 15th century. It was reduced to a subterranean existence by the Protestant course of religious discipline. Again the interplay of elite culture and popular culture becomes apparent. For the changes in the religious culture of the ruling elite had an immediate effect on popular culture as a whole and on popular religion in particular.

In Catholic territories the break with the past was less marked. No doubt post-Tridentine Catholicism could be as innovative and repressive as the reformers when it was a question of strengthening the position of the established church vis-à-vis Protestant competition or of improving its hold on the mass of believers. The campaign against Protestantism and such measures as the implementation of the parish principle prove the point. If this meant a suppression of potentially dangerous elements in popular culture, such as the old fraternities that had contributed so much to the fragmentation of religious life in late medieval society, the church did not hesitate to take action. In enforcing the parish principle against "the internal articulations of a society in which kinship was a most important bond and feud, in however conventionalized a form, a flourishing activity,"[133] it went even further.

Reformed Catholicism, however, never relied on repression alone. In dealing with popular religion it developed a technique that exhibited a better understanding of the religious ideas and magical needs of the population than that of the Protestants. Thus, nobody objected when people gathered the twigs strewn all the way to the sanctissimum in the course of a procession, burned them, and distributed the ashes on their fields to ensure a good harvest. Nor did the Catholic priest refuse to perform such rites of protection as ringing the bells to ward off hail or other dangers to the harvest. Although it is impossible to say whether superstitious practices were more widespread in Protestant than in Catholic territories, there was less occasion to resort to them in the latter. As religious supply met religious demand, there was less room for a "black market" in religion and this, of course, strengthened the position of the priest.[134]

The Catholic church also strove successfully to incorporate late medieval popular piety into its post-Reformation religion. It built upon its forms and managed to control their contents. Where the Protestants gradually gave up their connection with popular culture, which had been so successful as a means of propaganda, and turned to more serious and austere forms of religious education, the Catholic church discovered the usefulness of popular culture. Neither pompous processions nor spiritual plays were forbidden, even though the costs were often dangerously high.[135] Instead, they were encouraged once they had been purged of their secular abuses and transformed into propaganda shows for the Catholic cause. The church even attempted to introduce new forms and practices, which always took into account the popular predilection for display, symbolism, and magic. Other local customs such as the *Klöpfleinsnächte* were given a new meaning. They became an occasion for the exchange of gifts with strong religious overtones.[136]

All this paved the way toward a better social control of individuals, groups, and organizations in the community. As popular participation in such shows always entailed some sort of status competition, the representative of the church gradually moved into a position from which he could look through the social network of the community and manipulate social relations within it. Thus, the Catholic priest was on his way toward privileged integration into the community he served, while the Protestant minister who had set out to intensify pastoral care remained somewhat out of touch with his flock. Reformed Catholicism became so much a part of popular culture that the common man was ready to defend it against the innovative spirit of the Enlightenment two centuries later, while secularization made better progress in Protestant regions. In this respect, the topography of popular culture in Germany has been, until very recently, determined by the religious decisions that the early modern territorial states made in the course of the 16th century.

## NOTES

1. For the most recent comprehensive survey in German see R. van Dülmen, *Entstehung des neuzeitlichen Europa 1550–1648* (Stuttgart: 1982).
2. A. Gramsci, "Osservazioni sul folclore," *Opere* vol. 6 (Turin: 1950), pp. 215 ff.
3. To mention only some recent publications: R. Berdahl et al., *Klassen und Kultur. Sozialanthropologische Perspektiven in der Geschichtswissenschaft* (Frankfurt: 1982); R. van Dülmen and N. Schindler, *Volkskultur* (Stuttgart: forthcoming). For some observations on the historiographical situation see also Alf Lüdtke, "Rekonstruktion von Alltagswirklichkeit – Entpolitisierung der Sozialgeschichte," in Berdahl et al., *Klassen*, pp. 321–53.
4. P. Burke, *Popular Culture in Early Modern Europe* (London: 1978), p. xi.
5. Ibid.
6. See E. P. Thompson, "The Moral Economy of the English Crowd," *Past and Present* 50 (1971), pp. 76–136, or Thompson, "Patrician Society, Plebeian Culture," *Journal of Social History* 7 (1974), pp. 382–405; also N. Davis, *Society and Culture in Early Modern France* (Stanford, Calif.: 1975).
7. For an introduction to the subject see Burke, *Popular Culture*, and Davis, *Society and Culture*, chaps. 4 & 6.
8. See, for example, M. Toch, *Die Nürnberger Mittelschichten im 15. Jahrhundert* (Nürnberg: 1978).

9.  See ibid.

10. See G. Lottes, "Popular Culture in England, 16–19. Jh. Zu neuen Wegen der englischen Sozialgeschichte," in van Dülmen and Schindler, *Volkskultur;* S. Hall, "Notes on Deconstructing the Popular" in R. Samuel, ed., *People's History and Socialist Theory* (London: 1981), pp. 227–40.

11. Cf. C. Geertz, *The Interpretation of Cultures* (New York: 1973).

12. Burke, *Popular Culture,* pp. 23 ff.; see also his "The Discovery of Popular Culture," in Samuel, *People's History,* pp. 216–26.

13. For examples in his observations on Carneval see Burke, *Popular Culture,* chap. 7.

14. This is the impression given by, for instance, the *Bayerisches Jahrbuch für Volkskunde,* a typical publication in the field.

15. See R. Johnson, "Edward Thompson, Eugene Genovese, and Socialist-Humanist History," *History Workshop* 6 (1978), pp. 90 ff.; E. Fox-Genovese and E. Genovese, "The Political Crisis of Social History: A Marxian Perspective," *Journal of Social History* 10 (1976/77), pp. 205–20. For the political implications of the debate cf. R. Johnson, "Against Absolutism," in Samuel, *People's History,* pp. 386–96; see further G. Eley and K. Neild, "Why Does Social History Ignore Politics?" *Social History* 5 (1980), pp. 249–71.

16. Cf. also Eley's view in G. Eley, "Rethinking the Political: Social History and Political Culture in 18th and 19th century Britain," *Archiv für Sozialgeschichte* 21 (1981), p. 432.

17. E. P. Thompson, "Eighteenth-century English Society: Class Struggle without Class?" *Social History* 3 (1978), pp. 133–68, esp. pp. 138 ff.

18. See G. Franz, *Der deutsche Bauernkrieg* (Darmstadt: 1975); recently underlined in the works of P. Blickle, *Die Revolution von 1925* (Munich: 1977), pp. 122ff, and W. Schulze, *Bauerlicher Widerstand und feudale Herrschaft in der frühen Neuzeit* (Stuttgart: 1980), pp. 62ff.

19. The whole approach owes, of course, much to E. Hobsbawm, *Primitive Rebels: Studies in Archaic Forms of Social Movement in the 19th and 20th Centuries* (Manchester: 1959). E. P. Thompson, *Whigs and Hunters: The Origins of the Black Art* (London: 1975) and D. Hay et al., *Albion's Fatal Tree: Crime and Society in Eighteenth-Century England* (London: 1975) have gone further in the radicalization of the category "crime." German contributions to the study of crime, which lay more stress on sociological and sociopsychological points of view, include C. Küthe, *Rauber und Gauner im Vormärz: Dar organisierte Bandenwesen im 18. und im frühen 19. Jahrhundert* (Gottingen: 1976), and D. Blasius, *Bürgerliche Gesellschaft und Kriminalität: Zur Sozialgeschichte Preussens im Vormärz* (Gottingen: 1976), esp. pp. 30ff., 46ff., 50ff.; cf. further R. Schlögl, "Mobilität am Rande der Agrargesellschaft: Vorstudien zur Lebensweise der ländlichen Unterschichten im Nürnberger Raum" (thesis, Erlangen: 1980).

20. Cf. F. Lütge, *Geschichte der deutschen Agrarverfassung vom fruhen Mittelalter bis zum 19. Jahrhundert* (Stuttgart: 1967), esp. pp. 118ff.

For a more recent general account, E. Ennen and W. Janssen, *Deutsche Agrargeschichte: Vom Neolithikum bis zur Schwelle des Industriezeitalters* (Wiesbaden: 1979), pp. 194ff.

21  Cf. Schulze, *Bäuerlicher Widerstand,* pp. 69ff.

22. Cf. Lütge, *Agrargeschichte,* pp. 83ff., esp. p. 86 and pp. 159ff.

23. For a brief and instructive sketch of the whole process see P. Blickle, *Deutsche Untertanen: Ein Widerspruch* (Munich: 1982), pp. 23ff., and Ennen, *Agrargeschichte,* pp. 178ff.

24. Lütge, *Agrargeschichte,* pp. 119ff., and Ennen, *Agrargeschichte,* pp. 196ff.

25. Cf. H. Rosenberg, "Die Pseudodemokratisierung der Rittergutsbesitzerklasse," in H. U. Wehler, ed., *Moderne deutsche Sozialgeschichte* (Cologne: 1973).

26. Lütge, *Agrargeschichte,* pp. 159ff.; Schulze, *Bauerlicher Widerstand,* pp. 62ff.

27. Lütge, *Agrargeschichte,* p. 162.

28. Cf. F. L. Carsten, *The Origins of Prussia* (Oxford: 1954), pp. 165–78.

29. Lütge, *Agrargeschichte,* pp. 136ff.; Carsten, *Origins,* p. 174.

30. Carstens, *Origins,* pp. 156f.

31. Ibid., pp. 149–64. Important regional studies are G. Aubin, *Zur Geschichte der gutsherrlich-bäuerlichen Verhältnisse in Ostpreussen von der Grundung des Ordensstaates bis zur Steinschen Reform* (Leipzig: 1910); F. Grossmann, *Uber die gutsherrlich-bäuerlichen Rechtsverhältnisse in der Mark Brandenburg* (Leipzig: 1890); F. W. Henning, *Herrschaft und Bauernuntertänigkeit: Beiträge zur Geschichte der Herrschaftsverhältnisse in den landlichen Bereichen Ostpreussens und des Fürstentums Paderborn vor 1800* (Wurzburg: 1964); W. A. Boelcke, *Bauer und Gutsherr in der Oberlausitz: Ein Beitrag zur Wirtschafts-Sozial und Rechtsgeschichte der ostelbischen Gutsherrschaft* (Bautzen: 1957); R. R. Müller, *Die Rechtsbeziehungen zwischen den Rittergutsherrn und den Bauern der Herrschaft Neuschönfels in Sachsen vom Jahre 1548 bis zur Mitte des 19. Jahrhunderts* (Leipzig: 1937); M. Reissner, "Die Gerichte in den Rittergütern des Amtes Bona im 17. und 18. Jahrhundert—ihre Sozialstruktur, ihre Organisation und Funktion im spatfeudalen Staat" (Ph.D. thesis, Leipzig: 1973). A comprehensive survey appears in J. Kuczynski, *Geschichte des deutschen Volkes* (Koln: 1980), 1: 154ff.

32. Blickle, *Untertanen,* pp. 43ff.

33. See the bibliographical note in Schulze, *Bäuerlicher Widerstand,* pp. 340ff. I would like to draw special attention to these works: H. Harnisch, "Klassenkämpfe der Bauern in der Mark Brandenburg zwischen frühbürgerlicher Revolution und Dreissigjährigem Krieg," *Jahrbuch für Regionalgeschichte* 5 (1974), pp. 142–72, and Harnisch, "Landgemeinde, feudalherrlich-bäuerliche Klassenkämpfe und Agrarverfassung im Spatfeudalismus," *Zeitschrift für Geschichtswissenschaft* 26 (1978), pp. 887–97; K. Wernicke, "Untersuchungen zu den niederen Formen des bäuerlichen Klassenkampfes im Gebiet der Gutsherrschaft 1648–1789" (Ph.D. thesis, Berlin: 1962).

34. Wernicke, "Bäuerlicher Klassenkampf," p. 33.
35. Ibid.
36. Ibid.
37. For the wider implications cf. P. Anderson, *Lineages of the Absolutist State* (London: 1974).
38. Wernicke, "Bäuerlicher Klassenkampf," pp. 101ff.
39. For the different evaluations of legal resistance see Schulze, *Bäuerlicher Widerstand*, pp. 76ff., 89ff.; Kuczynski, *Alltag*, pp. 181ff.
40. Carsten, *Origins*, p. 157.
41. Schulze, *Bäuerlicher Widerstand*, pp. 89ff.
42. Ibid., pp. 62f.
43. The classical study of the *Dorfgemeinde* is K. S. Bader, *Studien zur Rechtsgeschichte des mittelalterlichen Dorfes*, vol. 1: *Das mittelalterliche Dorf als Rechts- und Friedensbereich* (Weimar: 1957); vol. 2: *Dorfgenossenschaft und Dorfgemeinde* (Cologne and Graz: 1962).
44. R. H. Lutz, *Wer war der gemeine Mann? Der dritte Stand in der Krise des Spätmittelalters* (Munich and Vienna: 1979), pp. 87ff.
45. Ibid.
46. K.-S. Kramer, *Volksleben im Fürstentum Ansbach und seinen Nachbargebieten (1500–1800): Eine Volkskunde auf Grund archivalischer Quellen* (Wurzburg: 1961), p. 81.
47. Cf. G. Franz, *Geschichte des deutschen Bauernstandes vom frühen Mittelalter bis zum 19. Jahrhundert* (Stuttgart: 1970), pp. 57ff.; P. Blickle, ed., *Deutsche ländliche Rechtsquellen: Probleme und Wege der Weistumsforschung* (Stuttgart: 1977).
48. A. Gunther, "Sind die Weistümer genossenschaftlich entstanden oder von der Herrschaft oktroyiert?" (Ph.D. thesis, Erlangen: 1936); H. Stahleder, "Weistumer und verwandte Quellen in Franken, Bayern und Österreich," *Zeitschrift für Bayerische Landesgeschichte* 32 (1969), pp. 525–605, 850–85; cf. further the observations by U. Bentzien, *Bauernarbeit im Feudalismus: Landwirtschaftliche Arbeitsgeräte und -verfahren in Deutschland von der Mitte des ersten Jahrtausends u.Z. bis um 1800* (Berlin: 1980), pp. 94–97.
49. Cf. P. Bierbrauer, "Bäuerliche Revolten im Alten Reich: Ein Forschung bericht," in P. Blickle, ed., *Aufruhr und Emörung? Studien zum bäuerlichen Widerstand im Alten Reich* (Munich: 1980), pp. 35ff. His critical remarks do not invalidate the finding of G. Franz, "Die Führer im Bauernkrieg," in Franz, ed., *Bauernschaft und Bauernstand: 1500–1970*, Büdinger Vorträge 1971–72, pp. 1–15.
50. E. P. Thompson, "The Grid of Inheritance: A Comment," in J. Goody, J. Thirsk, and Thompson, eds., *Family and Inheritance: Rural Society in Western Europe 1200–1800* (Cambridge: 1976).
51. See, among other studies, R. Endres, "Zur wirtschaftlichen und sozialen Lage in Franken vor dem Dreissigjährigen Krieg," *Jahrbuch für Frankische Landesforschung* 28 (1968), pp. 34ff.; D. Sabean, *Landbesitz und Gesellschaft am Vorabend des Bauernkriegs* (Stuttgart: 1972).
52. Bader, *Dorf* II:280ff.; Franz, *Bauernstand*, pp. 210ff.

53. See Schulze, *Bäuerlicher Widerstand,* pp. 141ff.; Blickle, *Revolution,* pp. 217ff.; Bierbrauer, *Revolten,* pp. 48ff.
54. Bader, *Dorf* II:293.
55. Kramer, *Volksleben,* p. 81.
56. Bader, *Dorf* II:292.
57. Lutz, *Gemeiner Mann,* p. 93f.
58. Bader, *Dorf* II:294.
59. Kramer, *Volksleben,* p. 82.
60. Ibid., p. 85.
61. Cf. Lottes, "Popular Culture Forschung."
62. G. Franz, *Der deutsche Bauernkrieg: Aktenband* (Darmstadt: 1972), pp. 2ff.
63. H. Heimpel, "Fischerei und Bauernkrieg," in *Festschrift für Percy Ernst Schramm* (Wiesbaden: 1964), I:353–72.
64. H. Moser, "Zur Geschichte der Klöpfelnachtbräuche, ihrer Formen und ihrer Deutungen," *Bayerisches Jahrbuch für Volkskunde* 1951, pp. 121–40. See also J. Dunninger and H. Schopf, *Brauche und Feste im frankischen Jahreslauf* (Kulmbach: 1971), pp. 13ff. The custom was also practiced in cities; see F. Bock, *Zur Volkskunde der Reichsstadt Nürnberg: Lesefrüchte und Untersuchungen* (Wurzburg: 1959), pp. 18f.
65. See the sources quoted by Moser, "Klöpfelnachtbräuche," pp. 127f.
66. Quoted in Kramer, *Volksleben,* pp. 89f.
67. Moser, "Klöpfelnachtbräuche," pp. 127f.
68. See, for example, Kramer, *Volksleben,* pp. 103ff.
69. Moser, "Klöpfelnachtbräuche," p. 126, who sees it simply as a consequence of the Reformation.
70. Ibid., pp. 130f.
71. Ibid., p. 128. Moser simply recognizes a "younger" and an "older" layer of this customary practice, but does not go beyond the statement of the fact.
72. What has been said for the Klöpfkeinsnächte seems to apply for many other customs of "trick or treat" (Heischebräuche). For example, the authorities were as concerned with the many customary occasions on which adults or children went round the village singing for money or gifts (Umsingbräuche).
73. For the structure of the late medieval and early modern popular discourse see M. Bauer, "Die Gemain Sag im späteren Mittelalter: Studien zu einem Faktor mittelalterlicher Öffentlichkeit und seinem historischen Auskunftswert" (Ph.D. thesis, Erlangen: 1981).
74. D. Sabean, "The Communal Basis of Pre–1800 Peasant Uprisings in Western Europe," *Comparative Politics* 8 (1976), pp. 355–64; Harnisch, "Landgemeinde."
75. Cf. Blickle, *Untertanen,* pp. 37ff.
76. Bierbrauer, *Revolten,* p. 37, underlines the necessity for research into social differentiations among the peasantry but is rightly pessimistic as to the sources.
77. Cf., for example, R. Endres, "Der Bauernkrieg in Franken," *Blätter für*

*deutsche Landesgeschichte* 109 (1973), esp. pp. 42ff.; Endres, "Probleme des Bauernkriegs in Franken," in R. Wohlfeil, ed., *Der Bauernkrieg 1524–1526: Bauernkrieg und Reformation* (Munich: 1975), pp. 92ff.

78. R. Endres, "Probleme des Bauernkriegs im Hochstift Bamberg," *Jahrbuch für fränkische Landesforschung* 31 (1971), pp. 91–138.

79. K. Krüger, *Finanzstaat Hessen 1500–1567: Staatsbildung im Übergang vom Domänenstaat zum Steuerstaat* (Marburg: 1980), p. 297.

80. B. Sicken, "Landesherrliche Einnahmen und Territorialstruktur: Die Fürstentümer Ansbach und Kulmbach zu Beginn der Neuzeit," *Jahrbuch für fränkische Landesforschung* 42 (1982), pp. 153–248.

81. Schulze, *Bäuerlicher Widerstand*, p. 69.

82. Ibid., pp. 68f.

83. Franz, *Bauernstand*, p. 148; K. H. Burmeister, "Genossenschaftliche Rechtsfindung und herrschaftliche Rechtssetzung: Auf dem Weg zum Territorialstaat," in R. Blickle, ed., *Revolte und Revolution in Europa: Historische Zeitschrift Beiheft* 4 (N. F.) (Munich: 1975), pp. 171–85; Kramer, *Volksleben*, p. 135.

84. See also the interesting observations on the changing character of punishments in Kramer, *Volksleben*, pp. 152ff.

85. Franz, *Bauernkrieg*, p. 25.

86. Blickle, *Revolution*, pp. 135ff., esp. 138f.

87. D. Sabean, "Communion and Community: The Refusal to Attend the Eucharist in Sixteenth Century Wurttemberg," in *Mentalitäten und Lebensverhältnisse: Beispiele aus der Sozialgeschichte der Frühen Neuzeit. Festschrift für Rudolf Vierhaus* (Gottingen: 1982), pp. 95–107, esp. p. 106, gives another instance for the "active shaping of custom."

88. Bauer, *Gemain Sag*, pp. 60ff.

89. Cf. P. Baumgart, "Formen der Volksfrömmigkeit-Krise der alten Kirche und reformatorische Bewegung: Zur Ursachenproblematik des Bauernkrieges," in Blicke, *Revolte und Revolution*, pp. 186–204.

90. K. Arnold, *Niklashausen 1476: Quellen und Untersuchungen zur sozialreligiösen Bewegung des Hans Behem und zur Agrarstruktur eines spätnittelalterlichen Dorfes* (Baden-Baden: 1980).

91. Sabean, "Communal Base"; Harnisch, "Landgemeinde"; Bader, *Dorf* II:408.

92. Schulze, *Bäuerlicher Widerstand*, p. 98.

93. Ibid., pp. 76ff.; see also G. Heitz, "Probleme des bauerlichen Klassenkampfes im Spätfeudalismus," in G. Heitz et al., eds., *Der Bauer im Klassenkampf: Studien zur Geschichte des deutschen Bauernkrieges und der bauerlichen Klassenkampfe im Spätfeudalismus* (Berlin: 1975), pp. 531–25.

94. Schulze, *Bäuerlicher Widerstand*, pp. 92f.

95. Ibid., and note 23 on p. 154.

96. Kruger, *Finanzstaat*, pp. 246ff., esp. 260ff.

97. For a description see Kramer, *Volksleben*, pp. 272f.

98. Quoted in Franz, *Bauernkrieg*, p. 16.

99. Cf. L. C. Eisenbart, *Kleiderordnungen der deutschen Städte zwischen 1350 und 1700: Ein Beitrag zur Kulturgeschichte des deutschen Bürgertums* (Gottingen: 1962).
100. Cf. H. U. Roller, *Der Nürnberger Schembartlauf* (Tubingen: 1965); Dunninger and Schopf, *Brauche*, pp. 45ff.
101. See, for example, P. Blickle, "Bäuerliche Landschaft und Landstandschaft," in G. Franz, *Bauernstand*, p. 155.
102. R. Endres, "Wirtschaftliche und soziale Lage," pp. 32ff.; W. Abel, *Massenarmut und Hungerkrisen im vorindustriellen Europa: Versuch einer Synopsis* (Hamburg and Berlin: 1974), pp. 88ff.
103. Cf. Endres, "Wirtschaftliche und soziale Lage," for the central role of the cities in this context.
104. For the term see G. Oestreich, "Strukturprobleme des europäischen Absolutismus," in his *Geist und Gestalt des frühmodernen Staates: Ausgewählte Aufsätze* (Berlin: 1969), pp. 179–97.
105. Cf. Blickle, *Revolution*, pp. 126f.
106. See generally R. A. Dorwat, *The Prussian Welfare State before 1740* (Cambridge, Mass.: 1971), pp. 25ff.
107. See Kramer, *Volksleben*, p. 272.
108. Cf. K. S. Kramer, "Zeitliche und soziale Schichtung im Brauchtum, dargestellt am Überlieferungsgegenstand des Ansbacher Raumes," *Zeitschrift für Volkskunde* 58 (1962), p. 87.
109. Burke, *Popular Culture*, pp. 207–43.
110. It would be interesting to discuss the evidence from the perspective of the distinction between playing roles and playing at roles that Bailey has developed for the debate on 19th century respectability and working-class culture. See P. Bailey, "Will the Real Bill Banks Please Stand Up? Toward a Role Analysis of Mid-Victorian Working-Class Respectability," *Journal of Social History* 12 (1979), pp. 336ff.
111. See, for example, the *Kirchenordnung* for Hohenlohe.
112. Cf. for example for Brandenburg, R. A. Dorwat, "Church Organization in Brandenburg from the Reformation to 1740," *Harvard Theological Review* 31 (1938), pp. 275–98; for Hesse, the brief sketch in Kruger, *Finanzstaat*, pp. 65ff. For the subject in general cf. also E. W. Zeeden, "Grundlagen und Wege der Konfessionsbildung im Zeitalter der Glaubenskämpfe," in Zeeder, ed., *Gegenreformation* (Darmstadt: 1973), pp. 85–134.
113. Cf. Zeeden, "Konfessionsbildung," and G. Oswald, "Die tridentische Reform in Altbaiern," in G. Schreiber, ed., *Das Weltkonzil von Trient: Sein Werden und Wirken* (Freiburg: 1951), I:1–37.
114. J. Bossy, "The Counter-Reformation and the People of Catholic Europe," *Past and Present* 47 (1970), pp. 51–70, esp. p. 53.
115. Cf. for a still very informative and highly readable account of late medieval popular religion, W. Andreas, *Deutschland vor der Reformation: Eine Zeitenwende* (Berlin: 1972).
116. The original matrimonial ceremony in Germany was the betrothal.

117. K. S. Kramer, *Bauern und Bürgerim nachmittelalterlichen Unterfranken: Eine Volkskunde auf Grund archivalischer Quellen* (Wurzburg: 1957), pp. 115ff.
118. Cf., for the relationship between religion and magic in general, the magisterial work of K. Thomas, *Religion and the Decline of Magic* (New York: 1971).
119. R. W. Scribner, *For the Sake of Simple Folk: Popular Propaganda for the German Reformation* (Cambridge: 1981), chaps. 4 & 5. See also R. W. Scribner, "Flugblatt und Analphabetentum: Wie kam der gemeine Mann zur reformatorischen Ideen," in H. J. Köhler, ed., *Flugschriften als Massenmedium der Reformationszeit* (Stuttgart: 1981), pp. 65–76.
120. Scribner, *Simple Folk*, pp. 96ff.
121. Holler, *Schembartlauf*, pp. 140f.
122. E. W. Zeeden, *Katholische Überlieferungen in den lutherischen Kirchenordnungen des 16. Jahrhunderts* (Munster: 1959), pp. 22f.
123. Ibid., p. 24.
124. Ibid., p. 23.
125. Ibid., passim.
126. Ibid., pp. 59f.
127. Ibid., pp. 47ff.
128. Ibid., pp. 54ff.
129. J. B. Götz, *Die religiösen Wirren in der Oberpfalz von 1576–1620* (Freiburg: 1937).
130. Zeeden, *Überlieferung*, pp. 83ff.
131. Ibid.
132. Ibid., p. 82.
133. Bossy, "Counter-Reformation," p. 55.
134. A. Dorrer, "Die volkskulturellen Auswirkungen des Trienter Konzils auf die Alpenländer," in Schreiber, *Weltkonzil*, I:427–46.
135. See A. Dörrer, *Tiroler Umgangsspiele: Ordnungen und Sprechtext der Bozener Fronleichnamsspiele vom Ausgang des Mittelalters bis zum Abstieg des Aufgeklärten Absolutismus* (Innsbruck: 1957); Dorrer, "Auswirkungen," p. 432.
136. Moser, "Klöpfelnachtbräuche," pp. 130f.

# We Think, They Act:
# Clerical Readings of Missionary Theatre
# in 16th Century New Spain

RICHARD C. TREXLER

> May god . . . give you strength, so that
> you may mock your enemies.[1]
>
> To know whom they are ridiculing,
> you must know their language very
> well, both the phrases and modes of
> speaking.[2]

Perhaps as long as priests have formed a distinct division of labor, they have defended themselves in court and market by stereotypes that assign them a reflective character and everyone else a corporal one. "Popular culture" is a relatively recent term designating the customs of everyone else and, though no longer borne by a sacerdotal intelligentsia, serves similar ends for the old clergy's secular descendants: the term has retained the old stereotypes and is chary of specific material and sociological referents.[3] Thus the label is an epiphenomenon of fundamental stereotypes that, as in the old *corpus mysticum,* still give identity to the intelligentsia as the head while regulating its relations with the arm of power and the plebeian stomach. Ideology commonly passes for analysis; to study the concept of popular culture is to study the politics of marginalization passing for intellection.

Clerical marginalizing finds a particularly revealing context in 16th and early 17th century Mexico—revealing, because the idea of popular culture current in Mexico today is so evidently the product of a mestizo national state, which has succeeded in imposing at least the concept of popular unity on the plural tribal cultures of the past. In Mexico as, perhaps, elsewhere the idea of popular culture emerged as part of the politics of national centralization. The context is also revealing because the 16th century conquerors started the process of conceptual unification by calling everyone "Indian," which is to say applying to all tribes the stereotypes the Spaniards brought from Europe.[4] As in Europe, so in Mexico the clergy would in part regulate its relations to the Spanish state and to its flocks through such labels.

The clergy applied these labels in theatre, and that is essential to my story. While most intelligentsias count on their colleagues merely to accept one another's psychological characterizations of the nonreflectives, the Christian clergy of the Conquest was in a unique position. Because of the power of Spanish soldiers and administrators, the missionaries were able to choreograph the "Indian" culture they imagined and force the natives to perform that imagination. While scholars study today's theatre without reference to power and power's ability to honor and insult, the student of this past theatre easily recognizes its political nature in the thespian form I shall call "military theatre." I concentrate on this form because, as it links physical triumph and reflective imagination, it exhibits clerical marginalizing at work in a society where the militant word became theatrical flesh.[5]

I start by showing that the physical conquest of Mexico was itself a theatrical undertaking of a type. Then I examine the morphology, masks, and meanings of the military theatre as it was staged by missionaries and performed by native inhabitants from 1519 to the mid 17th century. This is what will later be called popular culture in the making. The theatre of New Spain was a crafted ethnography of manners, clothes, and other customs intended by its clerical stage managers to recall past native humiliations, to create memories of present failures, both native and Iberian, and to project future images of these colonized peoples.

One thinks of early American ethnography as Franciscan tomes and draws up images of Sahagún supervising native scribes' transcriptions of their customs in an enclosed monastic setting. In fact, such illustrious Mendicant scholars were also among the leading choreographers of the missionary theatre. As I have noted in the

European context as well, the master of ceremonies and the historian or ethnographer were once one.[6] I conclude this paper by examining the relations between the politics of the stage and of the pen. This culture of conquest casts an unusual light on how marginalizations can be enacted.


CONQUEST THROUGH THEATRE

The history of Mexican colonial theatre began in the conquest. Soldiers acted, crafting historical events for their subsequent performance by imitators. In mid-August 1519 the Spanish army was bivouacked at Zempoala, ready to begin its march against the Aztec empire. Meeting with the Mexican ambassadors, Hernán Cortés ordered them to take Moctezuma gifts of a crimson cap and a richly-carved armchair, "so that [Moctezuma] could place the cap on his head and be seated in [the chair] when he, Cortés, came to see and speak with him."[7] The conquistador thus imagined a theatrical setting for their meeting: the Spaniard Cortés would meet a "Spanish" Moctezuma who would obey the old-world diplomatic convention of the inferior host who wore threads gifted to him by a superior visitor.[8] Not surprisingly, the meeting between these two men became one of the historical events reenacted in colonial theatre.[9]

A second theatricalization of a planned event is significant because it involved the masters of the subsequent missionary theatre. When the evocatively named Twelve Apostles of the Indies arrived in Tenochtitlan in 1524 to begin the systematic evangelization of Mexico, they joined Cortés in a theatrical greeting that became the visual image par excellence of the spiritual conquest. Having first gathered all the caciques he could muster to watch the spectacle, the god-man Cortés rode out to greet the Apostles, then dismounted and fell on his knees, and proceeded in that posture to kiss the hand and hem of each of the Franciscan friars. Having thus "conquered himself," as one admirer put it, Cortés then ordered the assembled caciques to do likewise, kneeling on their rich robes to greet the friars who were dressed little better than the *macehuales*.[10] On first arriving in Mexico the Spaniards had learned that the natives did not kneel before their gods and had wondered how the devil had allowed that.[11] Now the caciques learned that one knelt before the friars just as one did before the Christian gods. Behavior was taught in historical events before those events were theatrically reenacted.

For this meeting was more than momentary pedagogy; it was an event that Cortés and the friars wanted recorded every time pueblos would greet friars in the future. Paintings of the event were hung in churches across New Spain and the different conquistadores, now landlords, taught their Indians far and wide to welcome the friars as they saw Cortés welcoming the Apostles in the pictures.[12] Future conquerors copied Cortés and ordered their subjects to greet friars even as those subjects had greeted them.[13] A modern Franciscan historian of the missionary theatre states that all theatre begins at the altar; his missionary ancestors understood that truism thoroughly.[14] In the eminently theatrical entrées of visiting Franciscan prelates into Mexican towns during subsequent decades, Cortés' painterly welcome of the friars would be endlessly repeated. All missionary theatre ended with the Indians on their knees humiliating themselves (*humillarse*). Franciscan missionary historians saw Cortés' historic act as the keystone of their order's authority over the subject natives.[15]

In this historic event, the Twelve Apostles had barely raised Cortés from his knees before they began to indoctrinate the same caciques through a third historic theatricalization. This one involved a mental image. They painted a verbal picture of the Battle of the Good Angels with the Bad Angels, compared that battle to the Spanish conquest, and announced that the coming evangelization of Mexico would be in its outcome as inexorable as Michael's victory over Lucifer. Amidst the ashes of Tenochtitlan, the supreme doctrine of the Apostles was the origins of hell, with Charles V as Michael's contemporary counterpart and the Indian gods as the friends of Lucifer.[16] The Battle of the Good and Bad Angels would also be part of the repertory of missionary theatre and the natives would doubtless understand the demons of that theatre, named or not, as the erstwhile leaders of their doomed way of life.[17]

In these three historic episodes, the Spanish conquerors acted like someone else and asked their subjects to play roles as well. The ensuing formal missionary theatre would in turn imitate those theatrical acts of conquest, and to the same imperative end: to win less the hearts and minds than the knees of the demons and Indians through a "moving" theatre. As Robert Ricard recognized, the missionary theatre would be part of a century-long spiritual conquest. The success of that conquest would be measured not by the assimilation of ideas but by the natives' physical and verbal comportment, which was called "devotion."[18]

The devil in these plays would be alive and well, and no mere actor. Even as the archbishop of Mexico, Zumárraga, launched a renewed search for Huitzilopochtli in 1539, the Tlaxcalans performed a Fall of Adam and Eve full of cosmic meaning for the Apostle Motolinia, who was probably the author of the text. At one point in the play, before Eve sinned by eating the apple, a wild ocelot broke out of its cage and raced toward the Indian Eve as if to attack her. Incredibly, the animal stopped in its tracks. As Motolinía noted, "This was before the sin. For if it had happened afterwards, she would not have been so lucky."[19]

The modes of missionary theatre were varied, yet the military theatre did not lag behind the autos (which I shall generally neglect) in the ominous quality of their immediacy. The stages for the military theatre differed in size, some being set in the relatively secure center around Tenochtitlan and Tlaxcala while others were placed in distant villages and on the frontiers where the fearsome Chichimecas threatened. But whether at the center or on the frontiers, the gods often clothed themselves in the threads of actors, to the discomfort or exaltation of audiences.

## THE THEATRE OF MILITARY TRIUMPH

The military theatre of the conquest best reflects the social goals that lay behind the missionary theatre as a whole. As Peter of Ghent recalled from his first years in Mexico, the first missionary problem was to get the natives into the great patios that served as churches. He was unsuccessful, he said, until he discovered that dances and songs *were* religion for the Indians. He incorporated them into the Christian spectacle and the natives came.[20] His explanation for his action was needlessly complex: Ghent meant that certain spectacles served to increase church attendance while editorializing that these spectacles were the sum and substance of Aztec religion. The clergy in Europe had been accusing its laity of externality and of an inability to distinguish sacred and profane activity in the same way for centuries.

The Jesuit Acosta would be more to the point. Discovering that the Indians had altars at home where they performed their rites, the missionaries, he said, developed a public spectacle of mass and dance as a way of avoiding domestic congregation around native gods.[21] The missionaries soon found that military theatre was particularly useful. It allowed for a maximum of participation, permitted the clergy to marshal so as to count the faithful and read their attitude, and diminished the danger of conspiracies.[22] By the fact that, like a procession, military theatre moved troops from one spot to another, it also created triumphal routes along which the stable autos could be performed.

The occasion for these military triumphs performed by Indians was either a memorial of a past triumph or the celebration of a new one. From the earliest years of occupation, for example, the feastdays of St. James, the captain of the Spanish armies, and of St. Hippolytus, patron of New Spain and the saint on whose day the Spaniards conquered Tenochtitlan and its empire, were celebrated by the Indians who had been the saints' victims.[23] Thus the humiliation of the indigenous peoples was one essential aspect of the festive calendar. I shall, however, concentrate on the better-documented, noncalendrical, military theatre.

Such triumphs took place on three occasions. Important events in Spanish royal history were celebrated by the Indians and Spaniards of New Spain; the news of Charles V's treaty with France, for example, provoked the military theatre in Mexico City, Tlaxcala, and Oaxaca in 1539.[24] A second occasion for such theatre was the viceregal entry, comparable to the entrée of a monarch in Europe. The third occasion, the clerical entrée, on the other hand, was unknown in Europe. The abundant records of Antonio de Ciudad Real, secretary to the Franciscan general commissioner on visit, Alonso Ponce (1585–1588), show that this prelate's progress offered the occasion for scores of military triumphs.[25] Though he was not permitted the sovereign pallium over his head, as was the viceroy, he was otherwise received "like one of the apostles," as his secretary would say.[26] These clerical entrées in fact replicated Cortés' reception of the Twelve Apostles.

Whether performed in Tenochtitlan or in a mere *visita,* military theatre in Mexico had a fundamental morphology consisting of greetings, battle, and submission. Greetings took place either at some distance from the center of the theatre, at the point the visitor first entered the theatrical space, or at the gate or entry into the theatrical center.[27] In the large cities the visitors or triumphal subjects might be imaginary or historical. A ship of fools might arrive at Rhodes (looking like the Dominicans arriving in New Spain, a witness remarked), or a general or emperor might be welcomed on assuming command of a Roman army.[28] But just as commonly, the visitor was real and became part of a historical theatre. As an example, the more rural records of Alonso Ponce's secretary show only a real personage arriving, to the exclusion of the imaginary or historical types that can presumably be found in other rural records.

The records of Antonio de Ciudad Real allow us to break down the morphology of greeting into its constituent parts. In scores of cases, village worthies rode out to meet Ponce and his retinue to the sound of churchbells and musical instruments, and with flags waving; the distance from the pueblo was a measure of the devotion of the village and of the resident clergy that organized the reception.[29] They greeted the commissioner and his party in a theatrical context, at one place giving him to understand that he should not be afraid: the riders of Tarécuato (Mich.) said they had come "to secure his passage and guard him because there are Chichimecas here."[30]

Behind these horsemen a mass of villagers almost invariably followed in procession and the Franciscan secretary recorded their sexes and ages. They commonly came with lit candles, kneeling on either side of the road as Ponce passed, begging to kiss the friar's hand and gown (*à la* Cortés) and to receive his benediction.[31] At one point flattened out by pounding with rocks in preparation for Ponce's arrival, the Spaniards' route was commonly lined with triumphal arches "like those in Spain."[32] Distributed along the sides of the route were stands (*ramadas*) made for the occasion, just as could be found in contemporary Europe. They might contain clowns, a theatrical auto, a living "statue" of St. Francis receiving the stigmata, or a child painted like Death. Often the *ramadas* contained altars, on which the villagers placed the vegetables or fruits that would be their pueblo's gift to the visitor; in other cases, the altars on these *ramadas* had

choirs about them.[33] Finally, some *ramadas* contained Chichimecas, who would soon spring into action.

These triumphal receptions might be repeated at the gate or
the wall, just as in Europe. Whether formal triumphal entry took
place at the gate usually depended on whether the Indians had
already performed a battle scene. If they had, the gate celebration
would be less imposing; but if the battle was still to come, an
elaborate gate celebration was common.

Battles seem to have accompanied almost all entrées, whether
of "apostles," soldiers, or officials, and they can be divided
between open-field warfare and sieges, both representable as
dances or as less-structured melées. Since cities had greater resources to build the festive castles, siege theatre was more usually but not exclusively found in population centers; open-field
theatre, on the other hand, graced both city and village. Of the
two documented subjects of battles, the uncommon Moors versus
Christians tended to be performed inside a population center after
the entry, while the Spanish versus Chichimecas took place both
inside and outside.

Both the Moors and the Chichimecas plays could, however, be
done as part of the same spectacle. In Mexico City in 1539, a
battle between "savage" Indians and mounted forces preceded a
Moor versus Christian battle with an old-world setting, the whole
having been staged by a Roman experienced in the art.[34] In
Tarécuato in 1586 an open-field battle between the welcoming
horsemen and footed Chichimecas from ambush came before the
same groups fought around a siege castle within the pueblo.[35]
Thus the village's inhabitants learned one lesson by watching
different types of battles, seeing first Chichimecas and then Moors
as if they were one great opponent. If they were lucky, they not
only watched but played.

The final element of the military triumph was the act of submission. It involved whole social groups and was uniformly performed at the center. Generally the submission involved the
warriors from both sides and the communities at large. In the city,
this act involved the losers doing obeisance to the victors, and then
all the native actors kneeling before the Eucharist and other
ecclesiastical authorities. The vanquished in this urban context
commonly underwent real baptism in one or more of their members, and baptism was viewed as reflecting submission.[36]

The submissions encountered in Ponce's country visits turn up no such baptisms. The father having entered the pueblo and the fixed theatrical pieces in the patios once past,[37] the warriors and other villagers made their kneeling obeisance. In some cases real Chichimecas made their appearance, Christians from the mountains who besides doing obeisance might take the occasion to ask for a missionary in their areas.[38] Everyone accomplished their acts of submission through giving gifts (usually edible), often after the visitor said mass as though in exchange, and on this occasion as throughout the scribe carefully noted the social composition of audience and actors: "Not just the principals and merchants, but also the *macehuales* (who are the common people), the old women, and the girls of the *doctrina*," he specified at Tuchpan after watching the scene at the patios just as, in the same visit, he had recorded the social status of the horsemen who had received him.[39] This theatre was not meant to conceal the group and class character of the players beneath the masks.

MASKS AND MESSAGES

Theatrical historians pay close attention to morphology and those who have studied this theatre have carefully reconstructed the European roots of the available texts.[40] Missionary historians, on the other hand, look for doctrine in these plays since, in their view, their purpose was to transmit Christian dogma. Neither group has stressed the political and cultural messages and contexts of this theatre, yet they pervade texts and descriptions. To the Spanish audience, military theatre helped prove the obedience and devotion of the natives while, to the indigenous actors and audience, the theatre demonstrated the honor of being Spanish. In battle theatre Indians exhibited their defeat — and did so inventively. Both Indians and Spaniards could be moved by the experience.[41]

The Spaniards expressed constant amazement at the Indians' ability to invent and to copy thematic materials for their representations. What did this native ability indicate? Most observers were content to say the natives were "like monkeys" and to bewonder the natural gift, but Bartolomé de Las Casas went further, saying that their mechanical works showed a mental genius and

judgment.⁴² No one got beyond psychology. But the Indians used
clothes and other props to state indigenous submission to the
conquerors; we should look carefully at how the theatrical win-
ners and losers dressed. One observation is immediate: the con-
ventional designation of these military plays as "Christians" versus
Moors or Chichimecas is wrong. It is Spaniards who engaged the
enemy in them to the almost universal exclusion of other Christians. The implications of this observation are clear when we
study the numerically preponderant theatre of the Chichimecas
as Ponce witnessed it in his progress.

The striking fact is that the Indians who rode out to greet the
prelate were dressed like Spaniards. Recall that Cortés had wanted
Moctezuma to assume Spanish accoutrements for their meeting;
that image helps explain the three different formations that
greeted Ponce. First, in cities where there were sizable numbers
of Spaniards, they rode out, richly but untheatrically, to meet
the friar, fully armed and firing their arquebuses in greeting.⁴³
In some pueblos the Indians followed the Spaniards but without
any indication that they performed the military greeting.⁴⁴ The
third and most common greeting was by Indians alone, playing
Spaniards. They uniformly imitated what real Spaniards would
have done if they had been present.

These "Spaniards" wore Spanish clothes, identified as livery
at two different points.⁴⁵ The visitors expected as much: "dressed
like Spaniards," the prelatial secretary wrote, "from whom they
were little different except that they did not carry swords."⁴⁶
At several other towns the Indian actors did bear Spanish weapons, including feigned and real daggers, swords, and (undis-
charged) arquebuses.⁴⁷ No Indian "Spaniards" greeted Ponce
with bows and arrows or other native weapons. The very fact
that the welcomers were mounted defined them as Spaniards over
and against the footed Chichimecas they would engage.⁴⁸

Next, Spanish was the language of the "Spaniards'" greeting
and, independent of the pueblos' native tongue, Nahuatl was the
language of its welcome.⁴⁹ In the one case where the war cry of
these riders is recorded, it was "Santiago!"⁵⁰ The inherent humiliation of having "Spaniards" welcome Spaniards is evident in-
dependently of whether, as the latter believed, self-respecting
Indians "loved to go dressed like Spaniards and to speak the little
Castillian they knew."⁵¹ Even as Ponce's secretary chronicled the

exotic talent of the subjects in mounting such scenes, he recorded the more fundamental reality that in what were, after all, real visits, only "Spaniards" greeted and only they fought the Chichimecas.

The Chichimecas who then ambushed these Spaniards and engaged them for the visitors' amusement on the route into town were made up to look like everything the Spaniards feared and all that the natives should reject. Commonly wearing masks with terrifying miens, they also wore wigs of long hair; the Iberians saw that fact in context.[52] As one of their first acts, missionaries forced natives to cut off their long locks because they knew that would render the braves passive and meek.[53] The festive wigs commented as much on the fallen youth who welcomed Ponce as they did on the live Chichimecas who still had the liberty to wear long hair. Besides, the towns that welcomed the friar were not always long-settled populations traditionally opposed to the mountain warriors but often peopled with those very warriors and their descendants who had been forced to live in the *encomiendas* of the conquistadores or in the *reducciónes* of the friars. Paradoxically, the Battle of the Mounted Spaniards with the Foot Chichimecas was really about the merits of the sedentary over the free life. The choice was meant to be easy: a ferocious Chichimeca captured and chained as a gift for the visiting commissioner showed up close all the "savagery" the Spaniards did and the pueblo should fear.[54]

In the light of the Christian war cries, the religious processions, the confraternal flags, and so forth, it would be hazardous to overemphasize the distinction between Spanish and Christian elements in these plays that featured a prelate's visit. Still, the distinction is worth making, for in this theatre honor and dishonor were paid peoples, not religions. For example, none of the plays showed non-Christian Chichimecas desecrating clergy or Christian objects, as they commonly did in reality. Instead the play Chichimecas ridiculed the Spanish soldiers. With fearsome cries, armed with bow and arrow and on foot, the players sometimes captured a horse or two from the "Spaniards" and then performed great feats of riding without halter or stirrups, to their enemies' embarrassment. The real Christian Chichimecas who occasionally greeted Ponce in these towns, and especially the Christian sierra tribes that actually played Chichimecas in this theatre, must have watched the Chichimeca plays and viewed them as insulting their way of life even as they challenged the Spanish one, but not have viewed them as insulting their religion.[55] Their skills and their "barbarism" were cultural in nature, and the word "savagery" came easily.

At times the battle on the way into town featured "Chichimecas" who engaged in fruit-slinging contests with one another; in Yucatan, where contests labeled with the Nahuatl word "Chichimecas" are not encountered, the normal entry battle engaged squadrons of boys armed with shields and engaged in similarly infantile warfare. Whether portraying them as childish primitives or mature "Chichimecas," this part of the play intended to show, in the secretary's words, "those with whom the Spaniards regularly fight."[56]

Thus the "triumph of the cross" that all missionary theatre was intended to vaunt sooner showed the victory and defeat of different ways of life. It was manifested not only in the many Spanish dances that accompanied this military theatre but by the fixed autos as well, which could be still more pointed in what one author calls their "calumniation of the indigenous pagan heritage."[57] An auto on Francis of Assisi showed him sending native witches and drunks to hell; both witchcraft and drunkenness were parts of the religious tradition.[58] Last Judgment plays regularly ended with condemnations of the natives, the earliest-known auto branding the wives of the native polygamous system prostitutes and consigning them to the infernal regions.[59] The auto of the Destruction of Jerusalem, a thinly veiled recounting of the siege of Tenochtitlan, makes the Eagle Warriors of the Aztec empire into the doomed troops of Pilate; it was not the only auto to ridicule the empire's formalized warfare.[60] Most tellingly, the gods of the Indians are singled out for abuse in autos that warned watchers of their seductions but insisted that the gods were in any case useless against Spanish arms. Quetzalcoatl became the Antichrist even as the better Christian devils allied themselves with the Christian god to humiliate the bad Indians. The Christian demons, in fact, are the greatest ridiculers of the natives and their divinities.[61]

In this panoply of cultural profanation, the military plays have a distinct character of insult. Different from the autos, they involved large groups of people committing themselves to their own defeat. In the countryside, the pueblo at large participated while in the city, where all could not take part, the natives watched their superiors playing the roles for them, perhaps driven to the theatre with the same whips used to bring them to church.[62] If the message for the natives was their submission, both they and the Spaniards read through the play a detailed statement of the social nature of that humiliation.

Both read beneath the masks the obeisance of the "signors and principals" of the native villages and cities. They determined which social groups did and did not greet them, and they measured the relative "devotion" of the natives in the theatrical forms. Ponce's secretary recorded when principals on horse greeted the party and when "a rich and principal Indian woman" gave them wine and cocoa along the road into town, "she herself serving and distributing it."[63] When these principals did not show up, the secretary explained that the party had arrived unannounced and that the men were already working in the fields.[64] He was also careful to note that not only the principals "but other particular groups" welcomed him, in one case noting the neighboring confraternities that came.[65] He also used measures other than the distance the natives came out to meet him. One mounted troop showed extraordinary devotion because it wanted to accompany Ponce to the next town, while in another case the secretary said the reception was more solemn than in the previous village because of the accompaniment.[66] One village received him "as if for the first visit," another reception was solemn even when Ponce was no longer commissioner.[67] But most important of all was the social status of the groups that humbled themselves before the friars, whether in the hustings or in the main cities. It was Motolinía who emphasized that the "signors and principals" of Tlaxcala played roles in the Moors and Christians celebration in 1539.[68] Tlaxcala was also the site of a moving Palm Sunday procession, recalled by Mendieta because in it the principal Indians, male and female, had thrown their rich mantles on the ground so that the triumphant Jesus *and his apostles,* all played by friars, could walk on them. "Once you have humiliated yourselves," the friars told the natives, "you will be heard by god."[69] We accept and rejoice in your culture and our defeat, the Indians seemed to tell the Spanish, who were moved by the message.

## THEATRE AS ETHNOGRAPHY

The military theatre of the missionaries aimed at driving home
messages of honor and humiliation through behavioral participation. A second element in this theatre deserves our attention,
the link between military theatre and ethnography. All students
of Mexican history know the importance of clerical scholars like
Sahagún, Motolinía, and Durán to the birth of American ethnography just as European scholars rightly emphasize the significance of Polydore Vergil and Battista Mantuanus. But the missionary theatre of Mexico *was* ethnography. An examination of
the clergy's historicizing imprint on the past, present, and futures
shown in the military theatre reveals that the missionaries formed
representational ethnographic subjects. If military theatre was
linked to insult, so was ethnography. We tap into the roots of
the moralism inherent in the scholarly creation of "popular
culture."

### (a) The Past

Scholars have been unable to find a pre-Hispanic play from the
Valley of Mexico. Through the destruction of codices and by the
exclusion of American history from their own missionary theatre,
the Spanish clergy had Indian history begin with the Conquest.
That was true whether the play was about Titus' Destruction of
Jerusalem, which in fact describes the fall of Tenochtitlan, or dealt
with the conquest directly, as did the various Dances of the
Conquest.[70] What is significant is that the missionaries instilled a
memory of those defeats by preserving their historical costumes
and customs.

The best example we possess comes from Tlaxcala's theatrical
tradition. Special among the Spanish possessions because after
its defeat in 1519 the city allied itself with Cortés and helped him
gain Tenochtitlan, Tlaxcala and its friars quickly developed
legends according to which its four kings were baptized after
Cortés' entry, so that Christian Indians led the Tlaxcalan army
that aided Cortés in the destruction of the Aztec capital.[71] In
Tlaxcala, then, theatre while inculcating the city's subject status
also intimated that its army had been as worthy an opponent in

the previous contest as it was an honorable ally in the conquest of Tenochtitlan.

It is in this light we must understand the historical theatre that López de Gómara (ca. 1550) says the Tlaxcalans soon took to performing:

> The Tlaxcalans were very proud of this [friendship with the Spaniards], as well as of the resistance and battle they had offered Cortés at Teocacingo. And so it is now that, when they celebrate a fiesta or receive a viceroy, some sixty or seventy thousand of them sally forth to stage a mock battle such as they fought [and lost] against [Cortés].[72]

The historical engagement was ideal for theatrical reproduction. It had been fought in the open where the worthy Tlaxcalans and invincible Spaniards could repeatedly demonstrate their glory, whereas the subsequent conquest of Tenochtitlan involved seamy house-to-house fighting.[73] In the center of the field there was a tower where the Spaniards had planted their royal banner and, along with some Zempoalan allies, had withstood a Tlaxcalan siege; so the theatre could perfectly represent, *mutatis mutandis,* a Chichimecan-type contest of foot against besieged but flaring horse. López de Gómara's account encourages us to hypothesize that many other theatrical battles between Spaniards and Indians recollected particular historical humiliations. There is no reason to contest the historian's statement that the Tlaxcalans were proud of the Spanish connection but it is necessary to recall that these battles at Teocacingo actually showed an invincible Iberian squad smashing great masses of Indians as Cortés, from the "Tower of Victory," called on his "lions of Castile" to defeat the devilish Indian dogs.[74]

The humiliation of Tlaxcala was thus first recalled in a military game outside the city. It also became a formal play done in the city. The surviving text of this "Colloquy of the New Conversion and Baptism of the Four Last Kings of Tlaxcala," whatever its age, certainly preserves the 16th century message.[75] In it, the news of the Spanish landing on the continent is followed by the kings' realization that their god Hongol — identified by Wasson and Ravicz as a personification of mushroom hallucination — is no match for the Christian god. Through a colloquy involving the kings, Hongol, and a Christian angel, the leaders further recognize that they have actually been under Lucifer's rule, that their city

is in fact barbaric, and that the Spaniards are children of the
sun.[76] This ridiculing of the Tlaxcalan heritage prepares the city
for the entry of Cortés.[77]

Imagine the Colloquy or its ancestor performed to this point
before the entry of a real viceroy (for we must understand that in
some Tlaxcalan ceremonial entrées of the colonial period, the
viceroy became Cortés). Alonso Ponce was present on 27 October
1585 for just such an entry. Familiar with the city, he must have
known the *casa real,* where the viceroys were formally received
after their entries, and have seen the pictures that decorated the
room. They showed "how Cortés arrived, and the things he
experienced up until his arrival at Tenochtitlan." In short, the
pictures that greeted each new viceroy on his formal entry into
Tlaxcala showed what greeted Cortés at Tlaxcala.[78]

On the arrival of the viceroy in 1585 the Tlaxcalans were
heartbroken, Ponce's secretary informs us, because a fire had
destroyed overnight the castle they had built for a play siege
with "soldiers dressed like Tlaxcalans and Spaniards under attack by other Tlaxcalans dressed like Chichimecas";[79] the secretary may not have recognized in this staging the Tower of Victory,
where Spaniards with Zempoalans had withstood the Tlaxcalans.[80]
Because of the fire this "lovely squadron of war Indians, some
[dressed] in their fashion, others like Spaniards," had nothing
to do but to assemble at the gate to help greet the viceroy.[81] On
a stand by that gate stood four old men. As the viceroy entered,
these men offered him the keys to the city on the condition that
he would protect their liberties. The reader receives an image of a
timeless European rite of capitulation imported to America.

Yet these four old men were in fact historical figures, and the
viceroy was part of the play:

The four old Indians stood on a stand at the gate, dressed as in the old days,
with royal crowns on their heads. They represented the four kings or four
regional [caciques] of that province of Tlaxcala who helped [Cortés] so
valiantly in the conquest of Mexico City, and who made themselves vassals
of the invincible emperor Charles V and of his successor kings of Spain.
These were the old men who spoke [in Castillian] the [words of welcome].[82]

In the Colloquy, after Cortés' entry, the kings of Tlaxcala
play grateful for the honor of being the first Christians. They
become pawns in the hands of Cortés and his priest, who in long

discussions decide which of the kings will receive what names in baptism.[83] Groveling on their knees so as to kiss the hand and hem of Cortés, the lords replicate what by all accounts was necessary behavior after their actual defeat.[84] Preserving elements of particular culture so as to make the humiliating past live, the plays of Tlaxcala also began and ended with a challenge to and humiliation of the devil who had been the Indians' lord.[85]

The Tlaxcalan historico-military theatre allows us to study in political context the middle history of what today might be called a "popular-festive form," some of the performers already costumed in "traditional" clothing. Yet the plays renewed a real subjection and were a real challenge in the ongoing early colonial struggle with the ever-present devils. Since the Battle of Teocacingo, the Colloquy, and Ciudad Real's description of the viceregal entry come to us as crafted historical documents, we may wrongly imagine that their writers were ivory-tower intellectuals, reconstructing the past so as to amuse the present. Another set of documents disabuses us of that notion and shows us that military theatre in this conquest was born in the moment of defeat as a test and challenge to dangerous Indians and demons in this "theatre of evil."[86]

## (b) The Present

The scene is the Chichimeca country around Durango, in the recently conquered area of the Tepeguanes, early 17th century, the frontier town of Zape. The Jesuits prepared to celebrate the feast of the Assumption, 1616, which was to feature the collocation of a new image of the Virgin in their church. The Tepeguanes revolted on that festive occasion and killed four members of the Company at Zape, two just as they arrived at the gates of the town and two others hard by the church. In the midst of repressing the revolt, the provincial governor staged an initial military theatre to commemorate the martyrdoms, returning triumphantly to his capital of Durango with the incorrupt bodies of the four "spiritual fighters." This "triumph of the governor and of those ministers of god and his gospel . . . celebrated the triumph of these valorous soldiers of Christ who fought till they died," the eye-witness Jesuit Pérez de Ribas tells us. Complete with the discharging of weapons,

Indian dances, and the submission of Spaniards and Indians to the cadavers, the celebration ended with their burial in a common grave that recorded the "day, month, and year in which they died."[87]

But the terrible insult, not just to the Jesuits but to the "rabidly violated" Virgin, had to be revenged. Pérez de Ribas tells us that this revenge was taken "one year to the day from when [the Virgin] had been defamed and on the very spots of the slaughter."[88] Thus a second triumphal theatre was prepared. A Spanish merchant who had escaped death through a vow now had Mary "renewed" in a shop in far-off Mexico City and he surrounded her image with jewels; this new image later became famous as the Virgin of the Martyrs. As Assumption 1617 approached, the Tepeguanes prepared a triumph to worship the places and images they had defiled:

With the Spaniards, [the Tepeguanes] spared no effort to adorn and celebrate this entrée of the Queen of Heaven, who returned triumphant over the devil and his [Indian] allies to her tabernacle and dwelling, from whence she had been torn with greater outrage than when she fled to Egypt because of the persecution of her son. At spaces of half a league on the road from Guanaceví to Zape, they raised a great number of triumphal arches of flowers from their mountains and fields, raising a bower adorned with flowers in the place where *they* had taken the life of the two blessed padres Fonte and Moranta when they went to celebrate the feast.[89]

There they collocated the Virgin at the beginning. . . . It appears that this lady wanted by her triumph to celebrate that [triumph] of her devout and loving [Jesuit] servants. A very singular circumstance of this feast augmented it and added to [the Spaniards'] joy, noticed at the time *and celebrated thereafter:* the sight of the fervor shown by the converted Tepeguanes toward (the feast), which amazed the Spaniards who were present. . . .[90] The Spaniards' awe was such that for almost half a league, from this station [where the Indians had killed the first two Jesuits] up to the church [next to which they had killed the other two] where the holy image was collocated, they all went on foot, [indeed] many [Spanish] persons of note went shoeless in procession, with [Indian] dances and clarinets and trumpets.[91]

For Pérez de Ribas, "the resurrection of the Christianity of the Tepeguanes" was patent in the fact that Mary soon rewarded the Iberians with the discovery of the mine of Parral, that the pieces of her old shattered self soon began to perform miracles, but especially in her anniversary revenge on the Tepeguanes:

At the time that the Virgin entered the pueblo, it seemed to [the Spaniards] that she entered triumphing over her enemies, a celestial thing which caused such respect and reverence among the [Spaniards] that they could not put their finger on it.[92]

Thus miraculously converted natives on this day did the reverse of what they had done the year before and Spanish "persons of note" were so moved that they were drawn into this play that had no script but a veristic stage and geography. By just such mechanisms did a military theatre of humiliation become established. Another contemporary of this revolt tells us that the devil "in the dress of a barbarian" had begun the revolt; *that* actor was always active. After whipping the image of the Virgin, the Tepeguanes in this account had then put a native woman on a platform and "so as to deride Christianity and its ceremonies" carried her in procession:

They converted sacred ornaments into indecent uses, even decorating their horses with them. Like other Balthazars, they used sacred chalices for their filthy drunken sprees.[93]

The anniversary theatre of the Tepeguanes returned the insult. If Indian rites could incorporate the profane, ecclesiastical ones would set the sacred right, insuring a decorous future by immediately recalling an historical insult in anniversary theatre.

The processional theatre of the converted Tepeguanes takes us back a generation to the theatre of the Chichimecas so extensively described by Antonio de Ciudad Real. We understand now why the secretary recorded such combats specifically in those areas where real Chichimecas threatened. These battles were frontier *defís* or *retos*.[94] Now we comprehend in part why in the same setting the secretary, like many an ethnographer, was fascinated by both the activeness and the depth of the natives' "*devoción extraña.*" He would note that "everyone dressed according to how they used to dress with great happiness in the time of their gentility" and then in presentist fashion would refer to feigned Chichimecas like those "with whom the Spaniards make war regularly," who act "in the manner that the real Chichimecas are accustomed to use when they seize horses from the Spaniards, going about in the same way, mocking and ridiculing them."[95] Historicized actors melded with present concerns. Describing another Chichimeca play, the secretary observed that "they say that [in fact,] it happens many times in the wars the Spaniards have with the real Chichimecas that they cannot engage them because the horses are terrified on seeing them and on hearing the yells and screams [the Chichimecas] raise"; the commissioner's party really was terrified when at one pueblo feigned Chichimecas sprang at them from ambush.[96] The old dress style is what the pueblos wore for their surrender but the plays were also a theatre about an ongoing war with the natives.

(c) *The Future*

I have argued that all military theatre conjured a world safe for Hispanicism. Yet this corpus of the theatre of humiliation contained a directly futuristic imagination as well, a type of representation that presented events in the future, which the performance was specifically intended to induce. I know only two examples of this genre but they are the two best-known military-theatrical events of the whole 16th century. To celebrate the arrival of news of a peace between France and Spain, the Aztecs of Mexico City performed a Siege of Rhodes during Carnival 1539.[97] According to the Apostle Motolinía, the Tlaxcalans waited to learn the subject of the celebration in Mexico City before choosing theirs; Motolinía himself was probably the playwright. The Tlaxcalans "decided to represent the Conquest of Jerusalem" on Corpus Christi (5 June), he wrote, and "we pray that god fulfills this prognostic during our lifetime."[98]

From the beginning of this play, when the Eucharist assumed its place of honor to watch the whole drama, until its conclusion, when Indians were actually baptized while all the native actors knelt, the Tlaxcalan Conquest was a conjurative prayer. The Tenochtitlan Siege of Rhodes seems to have been the same, for the "Cortés" who with certainty played a future Turkish sultan in the Tlaxcalan event must have been equally a future Master of Rhodes in the Tenochtitlan play.[99] In both cities, non-European armies played a role alongside "European" ones: in Tlaxcala an Army of New Spain had Indians playing Indians while in Mexico City a cavalcade of blacks apparently helped out the (native) Knights of Rhodes in their future reconquest of the island fortress.[100] In both settings, therefore, the future conquest of the Turks or Moors was seen to depend on the integration of neophytes into the imperial armies.

The basic plot of the Tlaxcalan story unfolded in the presence of the all-seeing Eucharist.[101] Three armies successively besiege

Turkish and Jewish Jerusalem, those of the emperor Charles V, of Spain, and of New Spain. In their turn Spain and New Spain beseech the Roman curia to pray for them. The pope responds first by sending Santiago to help the Spaniards, then St. Hippolytus to help New Spain, and finally St. Michael to advise the Moors that they are doomed. The army in the castle of Jerusalem finally surrenders; after according a royal reception and swearing fealty to the emperor by kissing his hand, the sultan then humiliates himself and his army before the pope and Eucharist, who is of course the god who sent the saints into battle. Real, unbaptized "Turks or Indians" suitably produced for the occasion were then actually baptized as part of the capitulation.

The most noteworthy aspect of this play is that it included a native army among its dramatic persons. Though obviously headed by a Spanish viceroy played by a Tlaxcalan, this army was otherwise composed of ten squadrons of as many native tribes, foremost among which were those of Tlaxcala and Tenochtitlan. Again, all these squadrons marched under the imperial and viceregal flag but each was costumed in its native dress.[102] Thus, alone among the military plays I have found, this one held out the promise that one day the American nations would be part of the final Habsburg victory over the Moors and Jews.[103] No matter how improbable on its face, this Mendicant scenario did argue the moral superiority of the Indians over even converted Moors and it did ostentatiously represent the tribes in their distinctive clothing rather than reducing them to sameness.[104]

Yet the very fancifulness of such a future warns us away from overemphasizing either the integrative impulse of the Christian-Habsburg vision in the play or the significance of the pluralistic ethnographic representations of the tribes. First, take the interesting casting of the whole spectacle. An Indian played Don Antonio Pimentel playing the head of the Spanish Army; Pimentel lived in Spain and was the person to whom Motolinía dedicated his *History,* which contains the play's description.[105] Other Indians played living conquistadores: Andres de Tapia was the field master, the contemporary viceroy Mendoza the head of the Army of New Spain, while Cortés was the Sultan and Alvarado the head of the Moorish or Turkish Army. Scholars have rightly puzzled over what one called the "dishonorable" fact that "Cortés" and "Alvarado" played hated Moslems but it is more important to remember that Indians played both conquistadores just as, in Ponce's journeys, Indians played welcoming Spaniards.[106] Both sets of natives ended their plays doing obeisance as did all the Indians in this theatre.

A second reason for questioning the apparent ecumenicism in the Tlaxcalan play is that it was full of the same humiliating paternalism encountered elsewhere; that paternalism was more or less equally applied to all the variously dressed native squadrons. Thus the unit of the West Indian Isles, part of the Army of New Spain, was smashed by the Turks "because they were not apt at arms nor did they carry defensive arms nor did they know how to call for god's help."[107]    But an angel then explains to the remaining squadrons of this "Army of the Nahuas or of New Spain" that they too were being defeated by the Turks because, tender in the faith, they had tried to fight before first praying to god. "You were defeated so that you would know that without his help nothing helps. But now that you have humiliated yourselves," the angel concludes, "god has heard your prayer, and now he will send the lawyer and patron of New Spain St. Hippolytus to help you, on whose day the Spaniards, with you the Tlaxcalans, conquered Mexico."[108]

The squadron of Tenochtitlan stood alongside the Tlaxcalans and heard the angelic address, so that when the now-unconquerable army started the war cry "St. Hippolytus!" the "Mexican" squadron, whose real-life counterparts had been conquered by that saint, chimed in. So did the Indians playing the Habsburg minions in the Army of Spain when the cry of "Santiago!" went up. The honor paid natives allowed to play Spaniards was neither less nor more illusory than the dishonor of "Cortés" playing the Sultan for, as Motolinía tells us, all the actors were Tlaxcalan "signores and principals"[109] who had lost their liberty just twenty years before. In the end all those variously dressed tribes fell to their knees; ethnographic particularism serves scholarship but also magnifies the glory of lords. The Sultan "Cortés" spoke for all in admitting that Charles V was "the sole captain of [god's] armies" and that "the whole world ought to obey god, and that you [the emperor] are his captain on earth."[110]

## THE POLITICS OF ETHNOGRAPHY

Tribal cultures were thus transformed by imperialism into what the mestizo national state will call "popular culture." I have emphasized the dominant Spanish role in that transformation, paying no significant attention to the undoubtedly important role of the natives in creating the same theatre. For a politics of domination and subjection motivated this theatre; the Spaniards, not the natives, had the power. I have shown that the Spaniards, certainly at times with the cooperation of the natives, had as their prime intellectual aim in this theatre establishing paradigms of honor and dishonor in their New World.

Yet historians still explain the theatre of New Spain as the result of understandings about the Indian character. I have suggested that in the beginning there was a politics of ethnography; yet pedagogical theory, the staple of the intelligentsia, continues to mask political goals. In concluding, I shall comment on the theatrical and rhetorical distancing of life and politics that forms part of the politics of the ideological industry we call popular culture. I make these comments about today's scholarship in relation to the similar phenomenon of distancing encountered in the ethnographic theatre of early modern Mexico.

The traditional explanation of missionary theatre holds that its purpose was to teach doctrine and, the Indian character being what it was and is, the best way to accomplish that was through theatre. What clerics had said about the European laity they now said about the Americans, with the same passionate confusions. The natives learned through seeing rather than hearing – but our sources also say that they did not learn what they saw.[111] While it was claimed that the natives did not forget what they saw (thus being vengeful), the Spaniards also found them incapable of remembering anything.[112] Since the Indians were innocent, one said, they were credulous enough to accept what they saw as reality – and that implied that they were incapable of deceit. But every time the Americans revolted the Spaniards accused them of being the most duplicitous people on earth.[113]

Our scholar-playwrights said that in their gentility the natives had been the most reverential people on earth, yet it was also said that they were incapable of distinguishing the sacred from the profane. Not only did they insist on reverencing the devil but the extent of their so-called sacred activity was dances and songs. The Christian clergy, on the contrary, knew that their mass was sacred; it was the intellectual incapacity of the natives to understand this that early missionaries gave as a reason for incorporating dances and songs. The natives were therefore naturally drawn to externals; everyone agreed on that.[114] Most scholars, in fact, still do. Today we know that perhaps the oldest extant play in the repertory of missionary theatre had allegorical characters — so much, one would think, for the assertion that the natives could not understand abstractions. Yet modern scholars, objectively conspiring with their clerical ancestors, distinguish between a nonabstract or "ritual" native theatre and the abstract autos or colloquies of the colonial Spaniards. Needless to say, such marginalization is possible because the religious behavior of the European settlers has not been studied, and has the effect of insuring that it will remain so.[115]

I have passed this sorry array of past and present assertions in review for a particular reason. On examination, these assertions about the "Indian" character, here used to justify theatre, were also used to explain why the natives revolted. I have described a set of cultural forms being created from the top down and yet, from the beginning, I stressed that a full understanding of the theatre would have to examine the Indians' preservation of their own cultural forms through this theatre: the "signores and principals" who played theatrical roles, for example, clearly had a class interest in preserving their hegemony through the new theatre.[116] Yet when we study the Spanish clergy's description of the Indians revolting against that theatre from the outside, so to speak, we see that the psychological characterizations of the Indians have a political function which helps us understand the assertedly pedagogical reasons for the theatre itself. This link between revolt and theatre is best examined by studying the last common denominator of the psychology attributed to the natives, their designation as either "children" or "barbarians."

In the early decades of the conquest these terms could be used indiscriminately if contradictorily: one and the same nation might be called infantile and "grown old in evil."[117] But soon a clear distinction became imperative. If the natives were "naturally" barbaric or "childlike," they could not be punished with the full rigor of Spanish law for their "idolatry." The Yucatan prelate Sanchez de Aguilar managed to avoid that eventuality by the following examination of these stereotypes. Citing Las Casas at one point, he stressed the pre-Columbian achievements of the Mayas and thus cast doubt on the stupidity of which others accused them. Full of surprises, the same Sanchez might nonetheless admit that at that point in history the natives had been like children but he then insisted that over the Christian decades they had grown up intellectually and could thus be punished as adults.[118]

In this schema, it became imperative to establish that the "idolatrous" Christian Mayas knew what they were doing. At this point his exposition becomes crucial. Sanchez's prime evidence for his conviction about Mayan consciousness was their revolts: the calculated planning and malice that these revolts manifested proved beyond doubt that the natives were not innocent children but adult traitors.[119] Sanchez's reasoning is significant not because it marks a new departure nor because it is consistent — which it is not — but because, more clearly than his predecessors, he enumerated a body of psychological stereotypes used to explain revolt. The same corpus was used to justify missionary theatre.

The essence of what we may call the revolt psychology is that the natives were unstable or "movable." But here is not the place to detail this language and *its* contradictions: that, for example, Indian rebels were "the most traitorous and cautious people the world holds" *and* that they were uncautious, tricked by the devil into taking appearances for reality.[120] Every statement about externality used in the language characterizing revolt has its corollary in that describing Indians in theatre.[121] Nor need we emphasize that in the Mexican national tradition, the nativists who have wanted to preserve indigenous customs do so with an unwanted revolt of "the people" in mind.[122] It is, however, necessary to realize that this common language when used to describe the natives in revolt pictures those peoples driven by a specific psychology to activities dangerous to the state; whereas when the same language is used to explain missionary theatre, the mode is pedagogical rather than political. The same *movimiento* the pedagogue seeks through his theatre, the citizen regrets in revolt. This combination suggests that the operative understanding of both revolt and theatre was similar. Theatre was a counterrevolutionary act of the missionaries, who hoped to reshape through

behavior and contain through psychological violence the insur-
rectionary opposition to Spanish domination.

Like most histories of popular culture, Mexico's has its myth
of decline: the theatre of the missionaries was originally pure
but was later contaminated by immorality.[123] In fact, that theatre
incorporated from its beginning the sacred and profane, because
the missionary theatre was a total public system of mutual manipulation, not a one-way street. In the 18th century, the archbishop of Mexico summarized the matter forthrightly:

[The plays] have [always] been dissonant, and they violate . . . a general
repeated prohibition two and a half centuries old because of the grave sins,
imponderable consequences, ridicule, vain observances, irreverences, superstitions, and other things . . . which motivate them. We [also] declare . . .
prohibited . . . the representations of the Pastors and the [Three Magi] Kings,
because of the irreverences and profanations of vestments and sacred ornaments that accompany them.[124]

The archbishop understood that theatre had imponderable consequences in fact, whatever the pedagogical ideology that was said
to motivate the plays. If the Tepeguanes had in open revolt used
sacred chalices sacrilegiously, so did the theatre of the missionaries.[125] Even as the missionaries encouraged the natives to insult
themselves in their plays, so they understood that the same plays
and the preparations for them could be and were ideal occasions
for insurrections. The military theatre itself at times showed the
"Spaniards" mocked by brave if doomed "Chichimecas."[126]
The friars and priests accepted the risk of insurrection but it was
not one they talked about, nor one subsequent scholarship has
confronted in studying theatre. The actors have remained what
the playwrights wanted them to appear — a distinct, subject,
distant race.

Is there a relationship between the rhetoric or choreography by
which the missionaries laid the groundwork for the so-called
popular culture of today's Mexico and the rhetoric by which
today's students preserve those forms? The early ethnographers
heightened dominance through freezing the customs of the vanquished at the moment of their humiliation. They praised the
mechanical genius of the natives yet they scorned "mechanics";
the new interest in manual occupations in early modern Europe
accompanied the growth of the modern intelligentsia and its
patron states. These missionaries created a picture of happy

natives who were ideally a self-contained and distant culture, so perfectly theatrical that one could forget about the Spanish and native power that suffused it.

It is this vision of a self-winding culture that inspired both the missionaries and their latter-day epigones. Historical writing remains, after all, a partly theatrical undertaking comparable to the military theatre I have described, convincing in its characterizations of past peoples when they are self-contained. The rhetoric of the best historical writing is already found in the missionary historian Mendieta, when he describes a Palm Sunday procession in Tlaxcala in a way that leaves no room to doubt the relation between a dream of dominance and the conviction of a separate, lower, cultural sphere:

To stage this, the friars did not have to lose sleep either in hunting up cloth or tapestries or other ornaments. For in each pueblo of Indians, those who governed it — *alcaldes, regidores,* and principals — took care of it themselves in their own persons along with the necessary people, and they put [the play] together and organized it. God be praised! For it is clear in this [fact] that [the Indians] are not like the Moors of Granada, but rather true Christians.[127]

Fanon understood this mentality and, in the surviving military theatres of the Americas, the vanquished still can follow the story. In Santa Fe, New Mexico, the Caballeros de Vargas still recreate the conquistador's military triumph over the pueblo in 1692. Today's Indians refuse to participate and they resent the children of the Caballeros who play Indians because the pueblo adults will not.[128]

Here is a popular culture that is kept alive along with the humiliation that informed its creation. Increasingly, Americanists call such performances involving native Americans "popular culture"; they are now assuming the conceptual and methodological heritage of historians who have long studied "popular culture" in the European world. How then does my analysis relate to this development in American studies; what light does the view from America throw on the field of so-called popular culture at large?

The early history of such cultural forms demonstrates that some of what Americanists call popular culture today was in its inception part of the politics of conquest. Some of those forms evoke pre-Columbian cultures and serve other interests and solidarities than those of the mestizo or tourist audiences. But conquest through behavioral control, which was a function of the missionary theatre of the 16th century, remains today a motive of the mestizo national states in their assiduous cultivation of the *cultura popular*. There were politics to the play then; they continue today.

The modern myth of popular or "indigenous" culture as a self-contained body of behaviors turned up in a frankly political context in the 16th-century *History* of the missionary scholar Mendieta. Mendieta of course saw this "self-winding culture" as a credit to the missionary effort that he thought had created a native willingness to organize their own Christian representations; moderns tend to think of native theatre as nature itself. There is history in the play now, as there was then.

Finally, this early history of Mexican "popular culture" has shown that the early ethnographers were no mere recorders of native life but, through their theatrical efforts, the very creators of its lushly varied yet conceptually unified and marginalized "culture." These theatrical productions of "native culture" may even at times have been the very sources for the scholars' written descriptions of the mores of the Indies. Perhaps modern students of this fabricated popular culture are no longer masters of ceremonies as were their spiritual ancestors the missionaries; they may now be truly the mere scribes of the masters who sit in the ministries of popular culture.

This study of how missionaries applied stereotypes about one segment of European society to whole tribes of Americans allows a concluding observation about the study of European "popular culture." My analysis suggests that, in part, that field's tendency to describe "popular culture" as something apart from elite culture stems from a poor theory of theatre or representation. Whether played in the court, city halls, or in the streets, Western theatre is not defined as behavior that creates triumph and humiliation, honor and dishonor. Thus it is not surprising that the elements of "popular culture" are rarely viewed as parts of such political exchange systems. Students of so-called popular culture and representations need to create a theory of theatre that the theoreticians of theatre have not.

Students of so-called popular culture in Europe should remember that the earliest ethnographers of Europe and the Americas were contemporaries. To a still uncertain extent, European commentators thought of their rustics as "our Indians," as comparable in their diverse oneness to the curious American "Indian." It remains to be seen whether the early ethnographers of the European peasantry were as frankly choreographers as they were the recorders of that popular culture of subjection they wanted. But it is clear to me that today's missionary zeal to discover the essence of the populars, of Europe and the Americas, serves more than scientific ends.


## NOTES

1. St. Helen wishing her son Constantine well in a missionizing play; M. de los Santos y Salazar, *Cómo llegó á descubrir la Santa Cruz la bienaventurada Santa Elena,* trans. F. del Paso y Troncoso (Mexico, D.F.: 1890), p. 32.

2. A missionary describing the natives; M. Ekdahl Ravicz, *Early Colonial Religious Drama in Mexico: From Tzompantli to Golgotha* (Washington, D.C.: 1970), pp. 25, 163.

3. See my "Historiography Sacred or Profane? Reverence and Profanity in the Study of Early Modern Religion," in K. von Greyerz, ed., *Religion and Society in Early Modern Europe, 1500–1800* (London: 1984).

4. On the creation of "the Indian," see B. Keen, *The Aztec Image in Western Thought* (New Brunswick, N.J.: 1971), pp. 156ff and passim.

5. The previous work is by R. Ricard, "Contribution à l'étude des Fêtes de 'Moros y Cristianos' au Mèxique," *Journal de la société des américanistes,* n.s. 24 (1932), pp. 51–84; "Les Fêtes de 'Moros y Cristianos' au Méxique (addition)," ibid., pp. 287–91; "Encore les fetes de 'Moros y Cristianos' au Méxique," ibid., n.s. 29 (1937), pp. 220–27; A. Warman Grije, *La danza de moros y cristianos* (Mexico, D.F.: 1972). For Peru, see N. Wachtel, *La vision des vaincus* (Paris: 1971), pp. 65–98. Las Casas says that natives played all the live parts in the theatre he saw: *Apologética historia sumaria,* ed. E. O'Gorman, 2 vols. (Mexico, D.F.: 1967), 1:333ff. In a modern example of this military theatre, Indians ideally play Indians: R. Grimes, *Symbol and Conquest: Public Ritual and Drama in Santa Fe, New Mexico* (Ithaca, N.Y.: 1976), pp. 170–74.

6. *The Libro Cerimoniale of the Florentine Republic by Francesco Filarete and Angelo Manfidi,* ed. R. Trexler (Geneva: 1978), pp. 27–31. The known Franciscan authors of theatre are reviewed in M. Pazos, "El teatro franciscano en Mejico, durante el siglo XVI," *Archivo Ibero-Americano,* n.s. 11 (1951), pp. 129–89.

7. B. Diaz del Castillo, *The True History of the Conquest of New Spain,* trans. A. Maudslay, 5 vols. (Nendeln: 1967), 4:8 (chap. 137); R. Trexler, "Aztec Priests for Christian Altars: The Theory and Practice of Reverence in New Spain," *Scienze, credenze occulte, e livelli di*

*cultura* (Florence: 1982), p. 183. On the Flemish cap sent to the lords of Tlaxcala, see C. Gibson, *Tlaxcala in the Sixteenth Century* (Stanford, Calif.: 1952), p. 18.

8.  On that convention see my *Public Life in Renaissance Florence* (New York: 1980), p. 432. The text of a surviving Nahua play shows Cortés, desiring to enter grandly into Tenochtitlan, demanding jewels and other valuables from Moctezuma; B. McAfee and R. Barlow, eds., "Un 'Cuaderno de Marqueses,' " *México Antiguo* 8 (1947), pp. 394ff.

9.  In addition to the Conquest printed by McAfee and Barlow ("Un 'Cuaderno,'") see the famous spectacle of 1556 on the meeting in J. de Torquemada, *Monarquia Indiana*, 3 vols. (Mexico, D.F.: 1969), 1:629–31. J. Rojas Garcidueñas mentions a 1595 play: *El teatro de Nueva España en el siglo XVI* (Mexico, D.F.: 1935), p. 112. For the Dance of the Conquest, see Ricard, "Contribution," pp. 70ff. Wachtel, *Vision*, . pp. 84–91, and B. Bode, "The Dance of the Conquest of Guatemala," in *The Native Theatre in Middle America* (Middle American Research Institute, Tulane University, publication no. 27 [New Orleans, 1961]), pp. 205–92, analyze modern texts of modern performances.

10. J.M. Póu y Marti, ed., "El libro perdido de las platicas o coloquios de los doce primeros misioneros de México" (by Sahagún), in *Miscellanea Francesco Ehrle* 3 (Vatican City: 1924), p. 297; F. López de Gómara, *Historia Géneral de las Indias*, ed. E. de Vedia, in *Historiadores primitivos de las Indias* (Madrid: 1946), pp. 404ff. G. de Mendieta, *Historia eclesiástica Indiana* (Mexico, D.F.: 1971), p. 211, and Torquemada, *Monarquia*, 3:21, compare the Apostles' entry to that of Christ into Jerusalem on Palm Sunday, which apparently explains the presence of the apostles in Palm Sunday theatre in Tlaxcala; Mendieta, *Historia*, p. 433.

11. Mendieta, *Historia*, p. 93.

12. Ibid., p. 211; Torquemada, *Monarquia*, 3:21. Córtes ordered the Indians to receive the friars as he had: Toribio Motolinía, *Memoriales e Historia de los Indios de la Nueva España* (Madrid: 1970), p. 286. Diaz del Castillo took pride in having taught them the same; *True History*, 5:266 (chap. 209).

13. A later colonial governor repeated Cortés' procedure with his natives; A. Pérez de Ribas, *Triunfos de nuestra santa Fé*, 3 vols. (London and Mexico, D.F.: 1944), 3:41.

14  Pazos, "Teatro," p. 130.

15. Mendieta (*Historia*, p. 211) and Torquemada (*Monarquia*, 3:21) considered it the "firm foundation," and P. Sanchez de Aguilar noted that "en México los sacerdotes y en especial los frailes, son reverenciados en sumo grado de los indios, por imitar al cristianísimo capitán Don Fernando Cortés"; *Informe contra idolorum cultores* (Merida: 1937), p. 79. Since the Spanish "humillarse" is stronger than "kneeling," I subsequently translate it as "humiliate."

16. Note that St. Michael was the patron (*capitán y caudillo*) of the Twelve

Apostles, so that they effectively became Good Angels: Motolinía, *Historia,* p. 207. For the colloquies, see Póu y Marti, "Libro," pp. 301, 316–20.

17. See, e.g., Antonio de Ciudad Real, *Tratado curioso y docto de las grandezas de la Nueva España,* 2 vols. (Mexico, D.F.: 1976), 2:115, 185. A native god could also be the Antichrist, as the (unnamed) penitential god Quetzalcoatl seems to have been in a Last Judgment play: Ravicz, *Early Colonial,* pp. 149, 151, 157.
18. *La 'Conquête spirituelle' du México* (Paris: 1933), chap. 5.
19. Motolinía, *Historia,* p. 239; for Zumárraga, see R. Padden, *The Hummingbird and the Hawk* (New York: 1970).
20. "Toda su adoración dellos a sus dioses era cantar y bailar delante dellos"; Ghent's letter of 1556 recalling 1526, cited in M. Cuevas, *Historia de la iglesia en Mexico* 2 (Tlalpam, D.F.: 1919), pp. 201ff. Cf. Zumárraga writing in 1544 or 1545: "Lo tomarian por doctrina y ley, que en estas tales burierias consiste la santification de las fiestas"; cited in J. Garcia Icazbalceta, ed., *Coloquios espirituales y sacramentales y poesías sagradas del presbitero Fernan Gonzales de Slava* (Mexico, D.F.: 1877), p. xxviii.
21. "Y en aquella que es pública y sin perjuicio de nadie hay menos inconvenientes que en otras, que podrían hacer a sus solas, si les quitasen éstas": J. de Acosta, *Obras* (Madrid: 1954), p. 208. Cf. Pérez de Ribas, *Triunfos,* 2:340. But see also Sanchez de Aguilar, *Informe,* p. 172, indicating that the missionaries also aimed at converting the domestic shrines into Christian ones. For the European lay-clergy typology, see my "Legitimating Prayer Gestures in the Twelfth Century: The *De Penitentia* of Peter the Chanter," *History and Anthropology,* 1 (1984).
22. The epideictic function of native processions is examined in my "La vie ludique dans la Nouvelle-Espagne: L'empereur et ses Trois Rois," in *Les jeux à la Renaissance,* ed. J.-C. Margolin (Paris: 1982), p. 85.
23. J. Garcia Icazbalceta, "La fiesta del Pendon en México," in his *Obras* 2 (Mexico, D.F.: 1896), pp. 443–51 (starting with an ordinance of 1528); Santiago as captain is in Motolinía, *Historia,* p. 244.
24. For Oaxaca, see *Epistolario de Nueva España, 1505–1818,* ed. F. del Paso y Troncoso, 3 (Mexico, D.F.: 1939), pp. 243ff. See below for the other celebrations.
25. Cited subsequently as Ciudad Real, *Tratado.*
26. Charges that Ponce did have the pallium are in Ciudad Real, *Tratado,* 1: 170ff. An enormous file containing all the judicial accusations against Ponce is in the *Archivo General de Indias,* Mexico, 2606. Ponce as an apostle is in the *Tradado,* 1:12, where his entry is also compared to that of some Spanish grandee.
27. The structure of the entry is similar to that in Europe, for which see my *Public Life,* chap. 9. Caution against seeing what may have been simpler forms with eyes used to European panoply was expressed by A. Bandelier, *On the Social Organization and Mode of Government of the Ancient Mexicans* (New York: 1975), pp. 120–23.

28. The ships were used in Mexico City in 1539; Diaz del Castillo, *True History*, 5:91 (chap. 201); Las Casas, *Apologética historia*, 1:334.
29. Ciudad Real, *Tratado*, 1:37; 2:18,69ff., etc., and for European measurements Trexler, *Public Life*, pp. 307ff. For the noises Ciudad Real, *Tratado*, 1:143; 2:56, 85, etc. The size of the party was usually six; *Tratado*, 1:180. Ciudad Real comments regularly on the reception "by the Indians as well as by the friars"; our interest is exclusively his measurement of the former's devotion. The visitors said throughout that the natives were delighted to see them but they knew the form of the reception was the clergy's; e.g., "recibióle el clérigo con música de trompetas"; Ciudad Real, *Tratado*, 2:71.
30. Ciudad Real, *Tratado*, 2:82.
31. Ibid., 1:12, 141; 2:79, 81.
32 Ibid., 1:12, 2:85. I study the triumphal theme in my "Vie Ludique."
33. The measurements of a large *ramada* are in Ciudad Real, *Tratado*, 2:368; see also my *Public Life*, p. 309. Clowns are in Ciudad Real, *Tratado*, 2:152; an auto, in *Tratado*, 2:122; Francis, in *Tratado*, 2:78, 147; Death, in *Tratado*, 2:152; altars with gifts, in *Tratado*, 2:125; choirs, in *Tratado*, 2:366.
34. On Luigi di Leone, the only secular person known involved in these triumphs, see Ricard, *Etude et documents pour l'Histoire missionaire de l'Espagne et du Portugal* (Louvain: 1930), pp. 161–68. The Mexican "savages" are in Diaz del Castillo, *True History*, 5:190ff. (chap. 201). The only Moors and Christians mentioned in Ciudad Real are in *Tratado*, 1:105 (Puebla), and 2:326 (Yucatan).
35. Ciudad Real, *Tratado*, 2:83.
36. Ricard, "Contribution," p. 71, and p. 70 for a modern play in which the Christians lost. Wachtel, *Vision*, pp. 88–92, analyzes modern plays for such inversions. Further on baptisms below.
37. The Christian representations mentioned in Ciudad Real, *Tratado*, are 15 different comedies at Cholula (1:14); SS. Peter and Andrew living statues (2:78); Stigmata of St. Francis "as in the pictures," a living statue (2:147); St. Michael and the Dragon, living statues, and the Assumption performed in Nahuatl (2:148); History of the Avaricious Rich Man, in Nahuatl (2:152); Dance of the Name of Jesus (2:363); flying angels (2:5); many representations (2:20). There were also many enactments of Passion stories. One encounters occupational mimes, such as that of the smiths (2:69), and of course native dances the visitors thought areligious, like the *zano* in Yucatan (2:330ff).
38. Ciudad Real, *Tratado*, 2:119. One Chichimeca submission was more clearly a tribute than a gift: "Presentaron en señal de paz y subjeción tres manojos de flechas aderezadas y puestas a punto": ibid., 2:114. Normal pueblo submissions, on the other hand, were disguised as "devotion," and the exchange of property as gifting.
39. Ciudad Real, *Tratado*, 2:146. "Les son muy obedientes y hacen muchas limosnas"; *Tratado*, 1:67. "Todos son devotísimos de nuestro estado, y hacen a aquel convento muchas limosnas muy de ordinario"; *Tratado*,

1:101. Gifts functioning as an exchange for mass celebrations are common; see, e.g., the *Tratado,* 1:183; 2:21, 68, 105.

40. The approach and previous authorities are summarized in Rojas Garcidueñas, *Teatro.* On the pre-Hispanic theatre in America, see Ravicz, *Early Colonial,* chap. 1. The background to the military theatre has been well studied by Ricard, "Contribution," where on pp. 60ff he gives Ceballos Novelo's morphology of the military dance; see also Warman, *Danza,* pp. 17–65. An ethnographic analysis of similar Peruvian theatre is in Wachtel, *Vision,* pp. 65ff. Wachtel (*Vision,* pp. 64ff, including photographs) and Grimes (*Symbol*) have considered similar theatres as humiliation and raised questions as to their continuing impact on today's indigenous peoples.

41. Spanish priests also practiced their own indigenous theatre of humiliation, the self-humiliation of flagellation: I. Clendinnen, "Disciplining the Indians: Franciscan Ideology and Missionary Violence in Sixteenth-Century Yucatan," *Past and Present,* no. 94 (1982), pp. 28ff. But this theatre of humiliation differs from the political, social, and cultural humiliation which is our subject.

42. Las Casas, *Apologética historia,* 1:334ff; Motolinía, *Historia,* p. 237; Sanchez de Aguilar, *Informe,* p. 79.

43. Ciudad Real, *Tratado,* 2:149, 71ff. In such cases, the Indians then greeted at the patio: *Tratado,* 1:192ff.

44. E.g. the *Tratado,* 2:145. Garrisons of Aztecs sometimes participated in pueblos they secured for the Spaniards; e.g., *Tratado,* 1:193.

45. Ibid., 2:150, 152; also 2:20, 82.

46. Ibid., 1:231, describing Nicaraguans.

47. E.g., ibid., 2:82, 152.

48. Ciudad Real spells out the contemporary prohibitions against Indians riding horses, using saddles, etc.: *Tratado,* 1:130. Some indications of numbers: 1 horse vs. 12 "Chichimecas" (*Tratado,* 2:150); 30 vs. 20 (2:79); 40 vs. 30 (2:125). References to the "Spaniards" "corriendo sus caballos" against the foot warriors are in the *Tratado,* 2:127, 145, 152. This Spanish custom was the more useful because it terrified the natives, who had not known horses before the conquest.

49. Ciudad Real, *Tratado,* 2:82; the autos and liturgical chants were also donc in Nahuatl, whatever the language of the pueblo: e.g., *Tratado,* 2:71, 152. The interpreters accompanying Ponce were for Nahuatl: *Tratado,* 1:12 and passim. Spanish is the language of all actors in the modern Guatemalan Dance of the Conquest: Wachtel, *Vision,* p. 75. The inculcated sense of degradation of native language and culture moved Ponce when an Aztec student in Tlatelolco welcomed him first in Latin and then in Castillian, saying: "Es muy gran verdad, muy reverendo padre, que cerca de la opinión de muchos, nosotros los indios de esta Nueva España somos como pegas o urracas y como papagayos, las cuales aves con trabajo se enseñan a hablar, y muy presto olvidan lo que se les enseñó; y esto no se dice en balde, porque a la verdad, nuestra habilidad es muy flaca, y por tanto tenemos necesi-

dad grande de ser ayudados para que vengamos a ser hombres cabales":
    *Tratado,* 1:16.
50. Ciudad Real, *Tratado,* 2:82ff.
51. Ibid., 1:217, referring to those of Nicaragua.
52. Chichimeca wigs are mentioned in the *Tratado,* 2:79 in an interesting
    formulation: "en traje de chichimecas con sus arcos y flechas y cabel-
    leras." Masks are in *Tratado,* 2:70 and passim. At one point, the writer
    seems to distinguish between Spaniards, who are not masked, and
    Indians, who are: "Otros salieron danzando como espanoles, y otros
    enmascarados haciendo meneos y visajes muy vistosos y de reir";
    *Tratado,* 1:123, cf. Wachtel, *Vision,* p. 75. F. Scholes and R. Roys
    noted the Yucatan Franciscans' attack on masks, which these modern
    scholars saw as an attack "in the interest of a higher form of culture":
    "Fray Diego de Landa and the Problem of Idolatry in Yucatan," in
    *Cooperation in Research, by Staff Members and Research Associates,*
    *the Carnegie Institution of Washington* (Washington, D.C.: 1938), p.
    587. My sources did not say the "Chichimecas" used body paint.
    Seventeenth-century friars themselves did, however, use it in the
    theatre of the Nativity (G. F. Gemelli Careri, *Viaje a la Nueva España*
    [Mexico, D.F.: 1976], p. 70) just as some Europeans used masks to
    play the Three Kings coming to Bethlehem (brought to my attention
    by Edith Cooper).
53. Pérez de Ribas also noted that when the natives then let their hair
    grow long, it was a sign of impending revolt; *Triunfos,* 2:227. See also
    Mendieta, *Historia,* p. 755, on the question of facial hair or its absence
    among the natives.
54. Ciudad Real, *Tratado,* 2:82.
55. Ibid., 2:81ff. Other humiliations of "Spaniards" were done from foot
    and had a charivaresque flavor: *Tratado,* 2:79, 124. At Ahuacatlán
    (Nay.), Ciudad Real (*Tratado,* 2:125) speaks of "Indians" on horse,
    but "indios coanos" on foot, the one tribal characterization of the
    foot I found. The Coanos were from the sierras and not pueblo resi-
    dents. In real life they fought with the "Chichimecas de guerra" though
    the author calls them "domestic and docile." Earlier in the conversion,
    they had themselves fought the Spaniards and killed missionaries;
    *Tratado,* 2:107ff.
56. Ciudad Real, *Tratado,* 1:27. On fruit contests, see the *Tratado,* 2:328,
    330ff., 363, the last seeming like a Battle of Good and Bad Angels as
    well. Among the "Chichimecas": *Tratado,* 2:112, 114ff., 120f. The
    author never indicates the ages of those in Chichimeca contests.
57. Ravicz, *Early Colonial,* p. 73. She also notes on p. 250 that the techni-
    que of shaming remains a way of changing behavior. Spanish dances
    by natives are in Ciudad Real, *Tratado,* 2:57, 123. Less common were
    dances feigning Portuguese (*Tratado,* 1:104) and blacks (2:114, 141).
58. Motolinía, *Historia,* p. 246. On drinking in pre-Hispanic formal con-
    texts, see W. Taylor, *Drinking, Homicide, and Rebellion in Colonial*
    *Mexican Villages* (Stanford, Calif.: 1979), pp. 28 seq.

59. This play has usually been interpreted as an attack on (unmarried) prostitutes; Ravicz, *Early Colonial*, p. 141; Garcia Icazbalceta, *Colloquios*, p. xxii. But the object of the play is to encourage Christian matrimony against polygynous husbands and their (lascivious) wives. On why women and not men are the object of attack, see J. Cornyn and B. McAfee, eds., "Tlacahuapahualiztli (Bringing Up Children)," *Tlalocan* 1 (1944), p. 317.

60. I.e., "How St. Helen Found the True Cross"; Santos y Salazar, *Cómo llegó*, p. 32. See Ravicz, *Early Colonial*, pp. 250, n. 3, and 184 for the Eagles. The Destruction of Jerusalem is regularly compared to that of Tenochtitlan, e.g. by Motolinía, *Historia*, p. 205, and in n. 10 above.

61. For example, the devils in Last Judgments insisted that their Christian god hand over those who were foolish enough to follow the native gods; see especially Ravicz, *Early Colonial*, pp. 153–56. The Destruction of Jerusalem contains Quetzalcoatl masked as the Antichrist, Moctezuma masked as the unbaptized ruler, and several other unnamed Mexican figures. The tension between the native "demons" and the wise demons deserves further attention.

62. See my "Vie ludique," p. 85.

63. Ciudad Real, *Tratado*, 2:57; further, 2:35, 81, 87ff., 122, 165, 334, and 1:240 ("Era mucho de ver y estimar su devoción, porque casi todos eran principales").

64. Ibid., 1:210; 2:51, 63, 156. Couriers informed villages in advance of the visit: 1:135.

65. Ibid., 2:57, 287ff.

66. Ibid., 2:136ff.

67. Ibid., 2:155, 387.

68. Motolinía, *Historia*, p. 241.

69. Ibid., p. 244; Mendieta, *Historia*, p. 433.

70. See nn. 9 and 60 above.

71. Gibson, *Tlaxcala*, pp. 28 seq.

72. López de Gómara, *Historia*, p. 370; trans. by L. Simpson, *Cortés* (Berkeley, Calif.: 1966), p. 227.

73. See the description in F. Cervantes de Salazar, *Cronica de la Nueva España* 1 (Madrid: 1971), pp. 257–70, esp. p. 259 for the comparison to the siege of Mexico.

74. Cervantes de Salazar, *Cronica*, 1:257, 270. The description on p. 260 is so theatrical as to suggest that the author may have gotten some of his information from a performance.

75. The manuscript is in Spanish, and Rojas Garcidueñas thinks it is late 16th century: *Teatro*, p. 134.

76. Rojas Garcidueñas, *Teatro*, pp. 195, 196, 193. Ravicz's suggestion (*Early Colonial*, pp. 72ff.) is the more probable because Motolinía describes Indian mushrooms' (Spanish: *hongos*) hallucinogenic qualities with reference to the Nahuatl word *teonanacatl*, "que quiere decir carne de Dios, del demonio que ellos adoraban": Motolinía, *Historia*, p. 208; R.G. Wasson, *The Wondrous Mushroom* (New York: 1980), pp. 212–14.

77. Ravicz, *Early Colonial*, p. 73.

78. The pictures in "la casa real, donde se reciben los visorreyes," are mentioned by Cervantes de Salazar, *Cronica*, 1:281. Ciudad Real's account is in *Tratado*, 1:102ff.

79. Ciudad Real, *Tratado*, 1:102.

80. Cervantes de Salazar, *Cronica*, 1:259 seq., shows the Zempoalans aiding the Spaniards. Note that Cervantes de Salazar saw "Chichimecas," whereas López de Gómara, probably referring to the same type of theatre, assumed that "Spaniards" and "Tlaxcalans" took part.

81. Ciudad Real, *Tratado*, 1:103.

82. "En unos sonetos en lengua castellana . . . en un tablado cuatro indios viejos, vestidos a lo antiguo, con coronas . . . los cuales representaban a los cuatro reyes . . . de Tlaxcalla que ayudaron al marqués del Valle [Cortés] . . . y se hicieron vasallos": Ciudad Real, *Tratado*, 1:103.

83. Rojas Garcidueñas, *Teatro*, pp. 211ff.

84. On which see Cervantes de Salazar, *Cronica*, 1:277ff. Also Rojas Garcidueñas, *Teatro*, pp. 216, 218.

85. Rojas Garcidueñas, *Teatro*, pp. 214ff., for the mourning of the demon. A modern challenge matching the Muslim gods vs. the Christian ones is in Ricard, "Contribution," pp. 58ff.

86. Pérez de Ribas, *Triunfos*, 2:40.

87. Ibid., 3:197ff. How these deaths and interments were used to create a cult of martyrs is examined by R. Trexler, "Alla destra di Dio. Organizzazione della vita attraverso i santi morti in Nuova Spagna," *Quaderni Storici*, no. 50 (1982), pp. 112–46.

88. Pérez de Ribas, *Triunfos*, 3:214ff; also 3:58.

89. Ibid., 3:214ff.

90. Ibid., I italicize "they" to show the author identifies the processants with the rebels.

91. My italics emphasize that the feast was celebrated annually thereafter; *Triunfos*, 3:216. Another case of crushed rebellion celebrated annually afterwards is in M. Huerta and P. Palacios, eds., *Rebeliones indígenas de la época colonial* (Mexico, D.F.: 1976), p. 31.

92. Pérez de Ribas, *Triunfos*, 3:215.

93. Huerta and Palacios, *Rebeliones*, pp. 281, 289, quoting J. de Arlequi, O.F.M. See also Ciudad Real, *Tratado*, 2:109 for rebellious Indians using chalices mockingly. Keep in mind that the Spaniards fundamentally identified the natives as those who before baptism had spoken with the devil, and Christians as those who spoke with god: Sanchez de Aguilar, *Informe*, p. 143; *The Incas of Pedro de León*, ed. V. von Hagen (Norman, Okla.: 1959), pp. 26, 32ff., 65, 67, 72, 94ff., 116, 151, especially 152, and passim. Thus every aspect of the conquest has a theatrical quality of deception both for those who wore masks and for the Christians who found devils and natives regularly "in the dress of" each other. On deceit, see my "Aztec Priests."

94. Ricard describes the *retos* ("Contribution," pp. 55 seq.) but does not see the military theatre as such as a *reto*. For these frontier areas, see

Ciudad Real, *Tratado*, 1:136ff; 2:69, 150; also pp. 69 and 159ff. (Acámbaro), where natives with bows and arrows guarded the borders against Chichimecas so Holy Week services could proceed undisturbed. On his entry to Acámbaro, Ponce had witnessed the standard theatrical battle with "Chichimecas." The Chichimeca battles the commissioner witnessed were almost all in Michoacán and Jalisco; the battles in southern Mexico and in Central America, areas Ponce traveled extensively, are not characterized as of Chichimecas.

95. Ciudad Real, *Tratado*, 1:13, 27: 2:81ff. References to the exotic nature of the native submissions are common: see *Tratado*, 1:238; 2:35; 83, and passim.

96. Ibid., 2:120, 151. The Chichimeca play as frontier theatre may explain why the play of the Moors and Christians later replaced the Chichimeca plays in most areas; Ricard, "Contribution," p. 80.

97. Misdated 1538 by Warman, *Danza*, passim. The news of the Truce of Nice (17 June 1538) and/or the interview at Aigues-Mortes (16 July 1538) arrived in Mexico City in January, certainly on or near the 23d, when the viceroy announced the happy news to Oaxaca with no indication that any celebration had yet transpired in the capital; *Epistolario*, pp. 243ff. Ash Wednesday that year was 19 February. The Mexican feast contained races by women, a festive activity in Europe.

98. "El cual pronóstico cumpla Dios en nuestros días"; Motolinía, *Historia*, p. 240. These words are put into the mouth of a correspondent from whom Motolinía allegedly took his account but most authorities believe this was a humble ruse; see, e.g., Pazos, "Teatro," p. 160. Spanish clerical use of conjuration is vividly described by Sanchez de Aguilar, *Informe*, pp. 117ff.

99. "The Marquis Cortés was their commander and the Grand Master of Rhodes": Diaz del Castillo, *True History*, 5:191 (chap. 201); "El soldan . . . que era el marques del Valle Don Hernando Cortés": Motolinía, *Historia*, p. 241. Previous scholarship has mistakenly looked to the past to contextualize these plays instead of to the future.

100. Diaz del Castillo, *True History*, 5:190ff (chap. 201).

101. Motolinía, *Historia*, p. 241. Pazos ("Teatro," p. 161) notes the "primordial" role of the Eucharist.

102. Motolinía, *Historia*, p. 241.

103. The Army of Spain had squadrons from all the Habsburg possessions.

104. This standard opinion is mirrored in the absence of such converts in the Spanish or imperial armies, whereas the besieged are described as "a people well united and differentiated from everyone else, since they wore some bonnets like those used by the Moors": Motolinía, *Historia*, p. 241.

105. Ibid., p. 194.

106. Garcia Icazbalceta, *Colloquios*, p. xvii.

107. Not "si" but "ni sabían el apellido de llamar a dios, no quedó hombre que no cayese en manos de los enemigos": Motolinía, *Historia*, p. 242.

108. "Pero ya que os habéis humillado, dios ha oído": Motolinía, *Historia*, p. 244.

109. Ibid., p. 241.
110. Ibid., p. 244.
111. Thus Mendieta says one friar "represented" the mysteries, etc., "porque mejor lo pudiesen percebir y retener en la memoria, segun son gente de flaca capacidad y talente": *Historia,* p. 624. He also cites without exception Zumárraga's statement that the (native) ignorant were deceived by what they saw: *Historia,* pp. 636ff; Garcia Icazbalceta, *Colloquios,* p. xxvii. The classical formulation by Vetancourt is cited in Pazos, "Teatro," pp. 188, 142, and was repeated constantly thereafter. On seeing and hearing in the European Middle Ages, see my "Legitimizing."
112. On native vengeance, see Huerta and Palacios, *Rebeliones,* pp. 56, 86; bad memory is noted above, n. 49.
113. Huerta and Palacios, *Rebeliones,* pp. 98, 248. Further, see my "Aztec Priests."
114. Pazos, "Teatro," pp. 138, 159, 188; Garcia Icazbalceta, *Colloquios,* pp. xxii, xxvii.
115. The Last Judgment has allegorical Death, Penitence, Time, and Confession as dramatic persons; Ravicz, *Early Colonial,* p. 143. The sacramental autos are the "fruit of civilization" over and against the theatre of evangelization: Rojas Garcidueñas, ed., *Autos y Coloquios del siglo XVI* (Mexico, D.F.: 1939), pp. xix, xx. The distinction between abstract and ritual autos is in M. De Bopp, "Autos Mexicanos del siglo XVI," *Historia Mexicana* 3 (1953), p. 114. It is not only unfounded to write as did Ravicz (*Early Colonial,* p. 79) that "the Indians [were] not particularly capable of ... abstract symbols," thereby implying that the Spaniards were. It is in any case ironic that those things the Indians could not understand but the Spaniards did are commonly labeled "mysteries."
116. A tribal hierarchy may, for example, explain the tribal distinction between the "Spaniards" and "Chichimecas" referred to above, n. 55.
117. Infantilism is alleged by Sahagún because the natives worshipped female deities: *Florentine Codex* 1 (Santa Fe, N.M.: 1950), pp. 27–30; Motolinía, *Historia,* p. 316. The Roman who put on the 1539 theatre in Mexico City said the Spaniards and Indians were "two people as different as men are from children"; Ricard, who shared this view, cites Leone in his *Etudes,* p. 164. In 1951, Pazos says the natives were "niños grandes, nada mas": "Teatro," p. 161. Clendinnen has recently analyzed this characterization in "Disciplining," pp. 41ff.
118. Sanchez de Aguilar, *Informe,* pp. 134ff (citing Las Casas); pp. 144, 151 (not as barbaric as the Chichimecas). The children argument is on pp. 22–25, 71, 127ff, 131, 134, 152, while the barbarian argument is stated and then denied on pp. 24, 57, 140, 154, where the fact they learned their prayers so quickly proves they are not barbarians.
119. The author refers specifically to insurrections in 1546 and 1597: *Informe,* pp. 137–140, 153ff.
120. Huerta and Palacios, *Rebeliones,* pp. 248, 291, 283.

121. For example, the Europeans had the natives act because they were unreflective; the same lack of reflective power explained why they revolted against a religion that was obviously superior. Thus only their "depraved nature" could explain why native children reared by their loving fathers would "forget the love they had for the [padres] and join their *parientes*" in revolt; Huerta and Palacios, *Rebeliones,* p. 285. See further R. Trexler, "From the Mouths of Babes: Christianization by Children in 16th Century New Spain," in *Religious Organization and Religious Experience,* ed. J. Davis (London: 1982), pp. 116–35.

122. I do not question their commitment to "the people" but only observe its functionality. The cult of the pueblo in contemporary Mexico as an instrument of the national state's power centers needs no more evidence than does its importance to the preservation of pueblo identity and solidarity.

123. See e.g. Pazos, "Teatro," p. 188.

124. Cited in ibid., p. 138.

125. See above, at n. 93. On Epiphany in Europe, "le Roi-Boît" was a common figure among the Magi.

126. See above, at nn. 55 and 56. The celebration of the Epiphany among the blacks was feared as a seedbed of revolt: Trexler, "Vie ludique," pp. 90ff. Insurrections hatched in fiesta are mentioned in Huerta and Palacios, *Rebeliones,* pp. 136, 139; the subject needs further study.

127. Mendieta, *Historia,* pp. 433ff.

128. Grimes, *Symbol,* pp. 171ff.

# Culture as Appropriation: Popular Cultural Uses in Early Modern France

ROGER CHARTIER

For the last twenty years, historians of French traditional society have concentrated on identifying a popular culture radically different from that of the ruling class, the clergy, and men of letters. Such research assumed that these two cultures were separated by a changeable but definable boundary. The distinction between high culture and popular culture was basic; it could characterize cultural units differently according to their place in time, but its own relevance was so obvious as to be assumed. Debate as to whether it was permissible to describe such-and-such a cultural form as "popular" was lively, but no one questioned the basic assumption of the antagonists – namely, that it was possible to identify popular culture by describing a certain number of corpora (sets of texts, gestures, and beliefs). It is precisely this assumption and the distinction on which it is based that I shall put to the question. Many discussions of popular culture have given the impression that they are not true discussions at all because they made no critical examination of the categories and the intellectual distinctions on which they were based.[1]

My example is France under the *Ancien Régime.* Its popular culture has been identified in two sources: a set of texts such as the chapbooks sold by peddlars and generally known as the *Bibliothèque bleue* and a set of beliefs and rituals considered a constituent part of a popular religion. In both cases the popular

is defined by contrast to what it is not: that is, scholarly literature and post-Tridentine normative Catholicism. In both cases,
historians aimed to count and describe the different themes that
composed a culture they considered popular. But the social
attribution of the form under consideration — chapbooks and
popular religion — seems less clear now than it was once thought
to be.

Is "popular" religion the religion practiced by peasants, or
by the dominated (as opposed to the dominating elite), or by the
laity (as opposed to the clergy)? Our indecision in the face of such
questions reflects the fact that historians have accepted as a
definition of popular religion the one that the clergy themselves
made. What theologians and pastors did in the Middle Ages, and
more so under the Catholic Reformation, was dual: they defined
a whole body of practices and beliefs as contradicting legitimate
Christianity and qualified as "popular" the practices and beliefs
they considered superstitious. By adopting these distinctions
historians have made themselves victims of an inherent ambiguity.
The clergy's definition of superstition is always a compromise
made between theological references, which since Saint Augustine
have characterized superstitions by assimilating them within the
category of idolatry, and the inventory of practices that embody
these idolatrous beliefs in everyday life. The listing of kinds of
superstition is therefore an endless undertaking that catalogues
"another" religion, both condemnable and condemned. In the
opposition between popular religion and legitimate Christianity,
the historian imitated this basic distinction made by the clergy,
who distinguished between what was allowed and unlawful practices. Historians, thinking that they had identified popular religion, had in fact merely described in different words the fundamental distinction that the Church made to "disqualify" a set of
thoughts and practices.

But the definition of what was "popular" did not have the
same immediately social meaning for ancient theologians that
it has for modern historians. For the theologians, "popular"
opposes "catholic," which means that these practices are not
universal but vary indefinitely, that unlike legitimate behavior
allowed by Scripture or tradition they are not based on authority, and that they are rooted in the life of particular communities and are not shared by the entire congregation. The people is

a plural concept for theologians, therefore, and their writings aim not so much to describe the religion of the lower classes as to define particular communities (those of cities, parishes, or women) that fail to respect clerical jurisdiction. By reproducing a distinction that the clergy made so as to impose their own idea of religious conformity, historians have twisted its meaning by describing as "popular" beliefs and behavior of groups that were conceived of more in a geographical than in a social sense.[2]

It is not an easy task to identify those who read the *Bibliothèque bleue.* Three hypotheses have been formulated since the rediscovery in 1964 of these booklets, printed at Troyes and in other cities. In the classic hypothesis, Robert Mandrou suggested that this literature was intended for the common people; like haberdashery, it was sold by peddlars.[3] On the basis of rather limited evidence indicating that these texts were read in the 18th century at evening gatherings (*veillées*), he asserts this literature's "essentially popular usage." Two groups of argument render this initial interpretation doubtful.

Peddling does not necessarily imply popular buyers. In France during the 17th and a large part of the 18th century, the book peddlar was above all an urban figure; his clientele did not necessarily differ from that of bookshops. In the provinces' small cities and market towns, peddlars replaced shops for potential readers; in Paris, they circulated prohibited books printed outside the kingdom. Elsewhere, numerous texts indicate the ownership of *livrets bleus* among the middle and lower bourgeois classes. The diaries of numerous "petits bourgeois" often mention almanacs and prognostications, and for Molière the reading of chapbooks and *"contes bleus"* helps to identify a bourgeoisie whose material ease runs hand-in-hand with cultural poverty. Therefore, the *Bibliothèque bleue* could be understood as the reading matter of a public that was neither cultured nor popular, a public made up in the city of merchants and wealthy artisans and, in the countryside, of low-ranking officials and the richer farmers and laborers.

It is also possible that the *livrets bleus* did not have a specific public but constituted reading matter for different social groups, each approaching it in ways ranging from a basic deciphering of signs to fluent reading. In any case, it no longer seems possible to equate the *Bibliothèque bleue* with popular culture or assume that an inventory of the books printed in Troyes gives us immediate insight into the culture of the dominated classes.[4]

Therefore it is not as easy as was thought to identify a specifically popular cultural level from a set of texts or religious practices. But this is not all; in fact, all cultural forms in which historians thought they could identify the culture of the masses now appear mixed corpora, containing elements of diverse origins. This is so for the *Bibliothèque bleue,* which includes four kinds of texts. First, devotional literature was represented both in a traditional hagiographic form and also in new forms brought about by the Catholic Reformation, which increased substantially the number of guides and exercises for a new piety. Second, a stock of medieval texts (particularly chivalric novels) had found a definitive form in print in the 16th century, just as the educated elite was losing its taste for them. Third, 16th and 17th century texts by Quevedo, Corneille, Scarron, Perrault, and others were adapted for "mass editions." Finally, new works based on oral tradition (stories, songs, hymns, and recipes) had already been printed before the Troyes printers took over the market; they were not necessarily "popular." These were the four basic sources for the authors of the *livrets bleus,* who were true professional rewriters, cutting, adapting, and simplifying texts for a public that differed from the learned elite — which does not mean that it was popular. These booklets are the results of adapting learned works, rewritten to be read by readers who were not learned.

When examined closely, "popular" religion shows a similar cultural complexity. On the one hand, it is clear that the folkloric culture on which it was based had been transformed, "worked over" by the Church. The Church not only prohibited, regulated, and purged collective behavior (e.g., processions and feastday celebrations) of all that was contrary to decency and legitimate belief but also persuaded adherents to condemn their own practices. In this way, the Catholic Reformation was, perhaps above all, the gradual enforcing over an entire society of a clerical definition of what was permissible or not, of the clerical distinctions between religious and superstitious, Christian and diabolical. The religion of the masses, whether "popular" or not, was determined by censorship that aimed to interiorize a system of perception created by the clergy.[5]

But this observation should not make us eliminate everyday experience from the normative discourse that wants to regulate it.

New spiritual models suggested by the clergy to the faithful did not act as imperative conditioning. Collective piety does not accept new kinds of devotion without adaptations, trespassing, and subversion. For example, the devotion of the Holy Sacrament, imposed by the clergy after the Council of Trent through pastoral practice and iconography, was contaminated by the ancient cult of relics and transformed by a need for outward expression through such practices as benedictions, processions, and other forms of sacred gesture.[6] In the same way the devotion of the Rosary recovered the cult of the Virgin's traditional meanings as protective and merciful. The interplay between the institution and the community, between a standard model and everyday experience, is always dual. "Popular" religion is at the same time both acculturated and acculturating; therefore it cannot be identified either as radically different from the religion of the clerics or as completely molded by them. We must replace the study of cultural sets that were considered as socially pure with another point of view that recognizes each cultural form as a mixture, whose constituent elements meld together indissolubly.

Consequently, I argue that it is pointless to try to identify popular culture by some supposedly specific distribution of cultural objects. Their distribution is always more complex than it might seem at first glance, as are their appropriations by groups and individuals. A sociology of distribution implying that the classification of professional groups corresponds with a classification of cultural products and practices can no longer be accepted uncritically. It is clear that the relation of appropriation to texts or behavior in a given society may be a more distinctive factor than how texts and behavior are distributed. The "popular" cannot be found readymade in a set of texts that merely require to be identified and listed; above all, the popular qualifies a kind of relation, a way of using cultural products such as legitimate ideas and attitudes. Such an argument evidently changes the work of historians, because it implies identifying and distinguishing not cultural sets defined as "popular" but rather the specific ways in which such cultural sets are appropriated. In a few privileged cases, such relations are immediately accessible in the form of individual accounts. Thus, Carlo Ginzburg was able to reconstruct what Menocchio, a miller from Frioul arrested by the Inquisition at the end of the 16th century, read. The books he read were in no way especially designed for a popular audience – the Bible, *Il Fioretto della Bibbia,* Mandeville's *Voyages, Il Decamerone* – but the way in which he read them was not that of a learned man. He breaks the texts up into individual sections that acquire their own meaning, he changes the hierarchy of themes and radically alters their meaning, he makes analogies out of fragments that another reader would not have done, and he takes metaphors at their face value. Neither literate nor illiterate, Menocchio exemplifies a way of reading that characterizes nonlearned readers and can also be found in cities among those who produce the culture of the "public square," to use Bakhtin's expression.[7]

Inquisition trials give us one insight into how the people read; the way texts are organized, visually and typographically, give us another. For example, the narrative line in the *Bibliothèque bleue* novels is broken up into numerous, minute segments, with many repetitions and references to previous sections. It follows a small number of narrative schemas and from one section to another continuously reorganizes a text that is never definitive.[8] This textual organization inscribes in the object itself the kind of reading of which Menocchio provides an example. Can this way of reading be considered "popular"? By contrast, a learned reader grasps texts in their overall meaning, understands the hierarchical importance of themes, and decodes any work he comes across by classifying it in the accepted repertory of genres and by understanding as literary the "literary" forms of writing.[9] What is needed is a historical approach not unlike that of sociologists when they try to identify cultural types not from a group of objects supposedly characteristic of a particular group but rather from the relation each group has with shared objects, knowledge, or practices.[10]

To ask whether "popular" is merely what the people create or what is designed for them is to mistake the character of the problem we face. Cultural consumption, whether popular or not, is at the same time a form of production, which creates ways of using that cannot be limited to the intentions of those who produce. This perspective gives a central place to the "art of doing" and "doing with," as Michel de Certeau wrote, and it gives cultural consumption a new status – it is no longer seen as passive or dependent and submissive but as creative, and it sometimes resists suggested or imposed models.[11] In no way can the user's intelligence be reduced to a soft wax on which the ideas and representations of the dominating classes could be inscribed with absolute legibility. For too long the acculturating force of messages manipulated by the dominant elite has been overestimated, whether it concerns "mass culture" in the 20th century or the culture of the Catholic Reformation and the Absolutist State in early modern France. These messages, seen as all-powerful, were supposed to have destroyed an older popular culture, once dynamic and alive, and changed men's minds to conform to their ideology, which is submission or consumption.

Twenty years ago Richard Hoggart warned against such a point of view. In England in the 1950s, working-class culture, far from being identified as mass culture, seemed to him to be characterized above all by relations of suspicion and self-defense. Widely circulated newspapers, songs, advertisements, and horoscopes were subject to a reading that made for belief and disbelief, that encouraged belief in what was read (or heard) without completely eliminating doubts as to its authenticity.[12] Modern mass media do not therefore, as was often thought, forcibly level some popular identity that must be sought in a world we have lost. How the message is received depends on the intellectual and cultural habits of those on the receiving end. What is "popular" is neither culture created for the people nor culture uprooted; it is a kind of specific relation with cultural objects.

Popular attitudes toward the culture of the Counter-Reformation and Absolutism must be understood in similar terms. The determination to impose cultural models does not guarantee the way in which they are received and used. Historians may describe at length the new standards to which the people were supposed to adhere but they should not think that these standards completely and generally shaped the behavior of the popular class. On the contrary, they should suppose that disparities between the behavior the models prescribed and the ways in which the people lived left room for the popular classes creatively to appropriate and adapt those models. Thus, to question the distinction between popular and learned enables us to assess cultural functions in a new way. The search for a specific and exclusively popular culture, often a disappointing quest, must be replaced by the search for the differentiated ways in which common material was used. What distinguishes cultural worlds is different kinds of use and different strategies of appropriation. In the 16th century, for example, Protestant reformers proposed a new faith and new practices; but, as the Lyon example shows, masters and journeymen did not assign the same functions to faith and practice or incorporate them into their scale of values in the same way. For the masters, the proposals seemed to assure an infallible unity for the social body by creating a completely homogeneous community of faith and work; for journeymen, they were experienced differently, outside the economic struggle. The journeymen, in sharp distinction to their masters, found Protestantism conducive to a dual adhesion: on the one hand, with the masters in the new church, on the other with their fellows, who remained Catholic in the professional confraternities.[13]

French historians have perhaps taken a wrong turning in trying to describe the contents of a category such as "popular culture" without first questioning the validity of the distinction. This does not diminish the value of past research but it does make the distinction on which it was based questionable.[14] These critical considerations of the foundation of earlier work suggest that research on popular culture should be conducted in a different, more theoretically informed manner. In the following pages I illustrate the implications in a case study of publishing strategies and "popular" reading in early modern France.

This "case study" is founded on three basic ideas, which tie together the history of publishing and the history of the circulation and reading of printed materials.

First, between literacy and illiteracy there exists a wide range of reading abilities, which depend on the length, structure, and forms of the written or printed text. Previous quantitative studies devoted to literacy have aggregrated, rather than distinguishing among, these abilities; as a result, they have unfortunately limited their understanding of the cultural contexts of literacy.

Second, between private, individual reading and passive listening to spoken words there exists a wide range of attitudes toward print culture, collective and utilitarian, rooted in the basic social experience of the popular urban classes, developed in the workshops, the festive confraternities, and the Protestant conventicles. Here I argue against a too-simplistic opposition between oral culture and scribal or print culture.

Third, between learned books and simple images there exists a wide range of printed materials that merge texts and pictures. Their deciphering necessarily involves decoding the imagery and reading the texts that comment on or explain it. I shall focus upon products of the print culture generally neglected in the classic history of books, that is to say in France *images volantes, placards, occasionnels, livres bleus;* in England *popular prints, broadsheets,* and *chapbooks;* and in Spain *aleluyas, cartelones de feria,* and *pliegos de cordel.*[15]

It is obvious that publishing strategies depend largely on the public that at a given moment constitutes the printers' potential clientele. The decision to print a particular text, the choice of format, and the production run are determined in the first place by the possible market (or at least the more or less plausible idea the publisher has of the market). But the circulation of printed books modifies the cultural balance. By offering a new instrument of learning and entertainment, by multiplying the possible uses of the written word, by encouraging new forms of social exchange, printing transformed the perception and cultural practices of those who used its product. E. Eisenstein has recently compiled a list of the deep-seated changes that the increasing use of printed texts caused in the intellectual habits and mental equipment of high or learned culture.[16] Here I address another, difficult problem: that of the circulation of books and other forms of printed matter in social strata other than those of the elites. In the period between the first third of the 16th century and the mid-17th century, is it possible to identify a "popular" usage of printed matter that simultaneously offered a new and widespread market for publishing and transformed the culture of the mass of the people? This inquiry points the way to a better understanding of the publishing decisions made by printers and booksellers, and to a richer appreciation of what we have come to call "popular culture."

Did the popular classes play a dominant role among owners and buyers of books in 16th and 17th century France? Here I take "popular classes" to mean, by default, readers who did not belong to "the three robes," as Daniel Roche put it: the black robe of the clerics; the short robe of the nobility; and the long robe of a varied group of low- or high-grade officials, lawyers, and attorneys, to which must be added the medical profession.

Thus I identify the following as belonging to the "popular" class: peasants, master craftsmen and their journeymen, and merchants, including those who have retired from business and style themselves "bourgeois." It is not easy to determine if such groups were familiar with printed texts and for the moment it is only possible to do this in a systematic way in certain towns. I shall take the example of Amiens in the 16th century, a middling town of 20,000 inhabitants whose book-owning habits have been brought to light in a study by A. Labarre.[17] It is clear that book owners constituted a minority: out of 4,442 inventories made after death for the years 1503–1576, only 887 (20 %) mention the presence of books. In a society where book owners were a minority, 259 merchants possessed books, as did 98 craftsmen or artisans – respectively 37 percent and 14 percent of the total number of inventories with books. It is clear from the earliest period of printing that book ownership (the incidence of which is far greater than manuscript ownership in Amiens) was not merely the exclusive privilege of the nobility; it also involved a population of modest readers situated at the lower end of the social ladder.

However, this observation calls for a few qualifying remarks. First, the percentage of inventories with books tends to vary by social category: it is highest in the medical profession, with 94 percent (but here the total number of inventories is only 34), and remains high in the legal profession (73 %) and the nobility and clerics (72 % in both groups). According to Labarre's data it was only 11.6 percent for merchants and craftsmen when the two groups are combined. Within the merchant and craftsman population only a small minority owned books. On the other hand, book ownership was far from equal: the Amiens merchants, who made up 37 percent of book owners socially identifiable, possessed only 13 percent of books owned and the artisans, who made up 14 percent of book owners, possessed only 3 percent. The "popular" classes boasted rather paltry "libraries." While the average number of books owned is 37 for the legal profession, 33 for the medical, 23 for clerics, and 20 for the nobility, it drops to 6 for merchants and only 4 for craftsmen. In fact, more often than not, craftsmen possessed just one book. (This is the case for 53 % of artisans' inventories that mention books and 44 % for those of merchants.) Only 16 merchants and only 2 artisans – a wine-loader and a carpenter – possessed more than 20 books. If the popular classes are not entirely divorced from book ownership in the 16th century, the example of Amiens demonstrates that only a small fraction of them owned books, that books remained exceptional for them, and that they owned them in at best very small quantities.

The Amiens example requires one further observation concerning the unequal distribution of books within the group of artisans and craftsmen. Among the 98 who owned books, three groups were particularly deprived: agricultural workers who lived within the city walls, those in the "food" professions, and masons. (They account respectively for only 6, 6, and 3 of the inventories including books.) Those who work in the wood trades seem to be more familiar with books (15 inventories including books); while metal workers account for 10 inventories, as also do leather workers. The textile industry is well represented (22 inventories including books) but it played such a major role in the Amiens economy that the figure must be interpreted as a rather low percentage of book owners. This hierarchy of book owners in Amiens corresponds to the one based on the ability to sign one's name that N. Z. Davis noted in Lyon during the 1560s: metal workers come first, then the leather and clothing trades, and at the lowest level building workers and agricultural laborers.

What kind of books were bought? In 16th century Amiens merchants and artisans possessed books that were for the most part religious, especially *livres d'heures*. Even though the *livres d'heures* constituted 6 percent of all books mentioned in inventories, they represented 15 percent of those possessed by craftsmen. *Livres d'heures* are often the only kind of book owned: 124 merchants out of 259 (48%) only possessed *livres d'heures,* 91 had one, 23 had two, 7 had three, 1 had four, and 2 had five, which comprised the sum of their "library." Thirty-two artisans out of 98 (33%) were in the same situation: 28 only possessed one, 3 owned three, and 1 had five. Ranked behind the *livres d'heures,* but in smaller numbers, are the *Légende dorée* (a dozen owned by merchants, 10 by artisans), Bibles (7 and 5 respectively, all apparently in French), breviaries, and missals. Religious books, therefore, clearly dominate. The only other coherent group is what the inventories describe as books of "*pourtraicture,*" which are collections of models, patterns, and plates used in the exercise of a craft. They are to be found in the inventories of two painters, two illuminators, two glassmakers, one bin-maker, one carpenter, one mason, one gunsmith, and three goldsmiths.

The inventories from Amiens indicate that the reading matter of merchants and artisans was limited to two areas: professional and religious. And obviously the latter was more in demand, particularly liturgical books. The *livres d'heures,* which included texts of the services and fragments of Scripture, constitute the most important kind of devotional literature and they were printed in enormous quantities — as the inventories of bookshops show. In 1528, bookseller Loys Roger had 98,529 copies of *livres d'heures* in his shop out of a total of 101,860 books; in 1545 his colleague Guillaume Godard possessed a stock of 263,696 books of which 148,717 were liturgical works. So the *livre d'heures* represents the basic market for publishing in the 16th century, because it attracted at the same time the notables and the "popular" readers, for whom it was the most frequent and often the only purchase. According to Amiens figures, the costs of these books reflected this twin social market: 43 percent of the *livres d'heures* cost fewer than 18 *sous,* 42 percent between one and four *livres,* and 15 percent between four and twenty *livres.* These inventory prices usually only concern bound books and, therefore, give an inaccurate picture of the real accessibility of *livres d'heures;* they usually did not cost more than one *sou,* making them one of the cheapest kinds of books and well within the range of the poorest readers.

The Amiens inventories of books confirm that "popular" readers were only a minority among the book-owning public, a minority that usually limited its purchases to one or only a few books. The evidence does not suggest that those on the lowest rung of the social ladder constituted a special market: they did not, by any means, read everything read by the notables but the books they acquired were not specific to their class. Liturgical books, devotional books, school books, and even *"pourtraicture"* books (a category that also included books illustrated by Alberti or Holbein) were products shared by all readers. It would seem, therefore, that there is no special "popular" public for books in the 16th and 17th century, and that publishers do not focus on "popular literature" because of socially differential demand factors; they merely printed certain books in large quantities and at cheap rates for an audience consisting primarily but not exclusively of merchants and artisans.

Still, two questions must be raised regarding these conclusions. On the one hand, can one discern the popular classes' relation to books exclusively on the basis of the possession of books found in postmortem inventories or the registers of booksellers? And, on the other hand, can the relation vis-à-vis "printed culture," to use Eisenstein's expression, be identified only through the reading of *books*? In the 16th and 17th centuries, a relation to printed matter did not inevitably imply individual reading, reading did not necessarily imply possession of books, and familiarity with printed matter did not necessarily imply familiarity with books. Without taking account of these qualifications, it would be impossible to understand publishing activity.

Among urban popular classes the use of printed texts can sometimes be collective or can be mediated by reading aloud. There are three basic social situations that give rise to these kinds of usages. First comes the workshop, where technical books are consulted by the master and his apprentices to help in their work. In the Amiens inventories they are often anonymous works: "a book concerning the craft of binmaking including several patterns," "a book containing several drawings for the carpenters' trade," 8 volumes including several *pourtraictz*. At Grenoble in the mid 17th century, the bookseller Nicolas sold an *Arithmétique* to the merchant potter Rose and a *Praxis medica* to the apothecary Massard.[18] These technical collections, often written by master craftsmen, were part of the printers' publishing activity: for example, *La Fidelle ouverture de l'art de serrurier* and *Le Théâtre de l'art de charpentier* written by Mathurin Jousse, "merchant key maker in the town of La Fleche," and published in 1627 by Georges Grivaud, a printer in the town.

A second collective use of printed works is to be found in assemblies held in town and also sometimes in the countryside, by Protestant proselytes. Because the Reformation aimed at attracting even the most humble, even illiterates who only had access to the written through the spoken word, it depended largely on these meetings where psalm singing and the reading aloud of the Scriptures brought together those who could read and those who listened, those who taught and those who learned. Such assemblies were supplied by the clandestine trade in books printed in Geneva and brought into the kingdom by pedlars and haberdashers such as Jehan Beaumaistre, Hector Bartholomé, and

Pierre Bonnet, who were some of the clients of Laurent de Normandie, a Genevan bookseller who provided them with Bibles, psalm books, and booklets by Calvin.[19] Protestantism made possible a sustained apprenticeship with the printed word for a disparate universe composed of men and women, literates and illiterates, and persons of virtually all professions. In the houses and barns of the towns of Flanders and the Hainaut, such groups prepared for the outburst of iconoclasm in the summer of 1566 by reading Scriptures and singing psalms together. They got their books through pedlars who stocked up at Antwerp. For example, at Lessines, a small town situated to the east of Tournai, a witness of the Protestant assemblies reported that "the greater part of their psalm books were bought in this town from an itinerant dealer from Antwerp."[20] Read and commented on by ministers and preachers, owned and handled by the faithful, the printed book permeated the entire religious life of the Protestant communities, where a return to the true faith could not be separated from access to the civilization of print.[21]

Third, printed works celebrating festive occasions were circulated and read in the various fraternal organizations that sprang up in the workplace or the neighborhood. At Lyon the confraternity of journeyman printers called *Confrerie de La Coquille*, or Fraternity of the Misprint, produced this sort of printed material. The confraternity of La Coquille took part in neighborhood parades that parodied certain domestic arrangements, displaying "mottos printed in Latin and French." It also produced a written commentary on these rites (for example, the *Recueil faict a vray de la chevauchée de l'asne faicte en la ville de Lyon et commencée le premier jour du mois de septembre 1566*, and the *Recueil de la chevauchée faicte en la ville de Lyon, le dix-septieme de novembre 1578*). During the carnival period, these printers published small booklets such as *Les plaisants devis des supposts du Seigneur de la Coquille*, which reported the comic remarks supposedly exchanged by the three henchmen of the festive dignitary at the head of the parade on Shrove Sunday. At Lyon similar texts "printed by the Lord of La Coquille" have survived for the following years: 1558, 1581, 1584, 1589, 1593, 1594, and 1601. Similar printed material existed at Rouen during the festivities of the Abbaye des Conards and in the towns of the Languedoc region during the carnival parades. It constituted a sort of acculturation to the written word, elaborated and deciphered collectively, read aloud to the illiterate by those who were able to read.[22]

Thus between the individual reading of a book, a private act, and the mere hearing of the written word as, for example, in a sermon, there existed, at least in the towns, another kind of relation to the printed word. The printed word was familiar even to those who could not read, in workshops, in the Protestant churches, and in the festive confraternities. Addressed in common, taught by some and deciphered by others, deeply integrated into the life of the community, the printed word laid its mark on the urban culture of the popular masses. And it thus created a public, and therefore a market, beyond those who were literate and even those who read books. In fact between 1530 and 1660, for the majority of the popular urban classes, the relation to the printed material is not a relation to books or at least not to books sufficiently "noble" as to be kept for a lifetime and cherished as an inheritance. The "typographic acculturation" of popular urban classes has other, more modest, and short-lived foundations. In all of these kinds of materials, which constituted an important part of printing activity, the text and the picture form a set in various relations. Among the genres that represent different stages of transition in print rather than wholly autonomous forms are popular prints, broadsheets, chapbooks, the *livres bleus*. I examine first the typographic form that appears furthest removed from written culture: prints or engravings. In this form the printed word is always present; it includes titles, captions, and commentaries. One example is to be found in the engravings of the craft or devotional confraternities.[23]

Engravings were always printed on large sheets that displayed both text and pictures: in some, the engraved design is the more important element while in others, for example broadsheets for pardons and indulgences or lists of members, it is the printed text that dominates. In the latter cases a head and tail piece usually accompany the text while the large engravings give an increasingly large place to the written word: the title of the confraternity, the name of the church where it was established, prayers in honor of a patron saint, historical review of the confraternity or its statutes. As a print of a confraternity of the Holy Sacrament shows, this material can always be read on two levels: "He who

places this text in a place where it can be read and who reads it —
those who cannot read must genuflect — will gain full indulgence"
(B.N., Est. Re 19). These images are destined at the same time
for public and for private use. The members receive one each
year when they pay their annual subscription; they hang it on
their bedroom wall or in the workshop. Some statutes make this
an obligation, for example that of the confraternity of the Holy
Sacrament of Rueil, which states that members "must have a
picture showing this mystery in their house." During the festival
of the patron saint, pictures are distributed in the town and
exhibited in the church. For example, the Parisian carpenter
journeymen who belong to the confraternity of Saint Joseph in
the parish of Saint Nicolas des Champs "have a high mass sung
with the deacon and subdeacon and the chapter, organs and
bells, tapestries both inside and outside the church with the
*pictures* of the confraternity whereon it is written that King
Robert, 37th king of France, is the founder and the indulgence
bulls were given in the month of March in the year 1665 by
Pope Alexander VII." These prints, which offer prayers and
pious formulas, indicate the names of masters and churchwar-
dens and give a sensitive and figurative illustration of the community devotion (the Holy Sacrament, the Rosary, the patron saint).
They encourage the piety of those who can read and those who
cannot, and one can see how their familiar presence in the heart
of everyday life gradually makes the printed word familiar to all
those who had not learned their alphabet in the town schools.

    Part of this production is printed from plates that belong to
confraternities: the confraternity of carpenter journeymen, for
example, owned "two copper plates which are used for printing
the pictures belonging to the confraternity" and "a large copper
plate which was made in 1660." But more often the confraternity gets help from artists, engravers, and print makers. In Paris,
throughout the 16th century, the workshops in the rue Montor-
gueil near les Halles controlled the market for large mural images
engraved on wood. Their work was completed by copper-plate
engravers in the rue Saint-Jacques near the Sorbonne, who also
made illustrated books. Orders from confraternities evidently
constituted only a part of these picture makers' activity, which
was long dominated by religious pictures. According to a survey
made of engravings preserved in the Bibliothèque Nationale,

religious prints constituted 97 percent of wood engravings at the end of the 15th century, 80 percent at the end of the 16th, and around 50 percent at the beginning of the 17th in the works produced by the printers of the rue Saint-Jacques.[24]

The discontent of book publishers, confronted with the proliferation of engravings with texts, suggests that this production of religious pictures should be considered a kind of "publishing." It presents several noteworthy characteristics. First is its magnitude: each plate can make multiple prints over a long period of time. The engravings preserved only represent, therefore, a minute part of those that circulated, were fixed on walls above the bed or over the hearth, were kept in coffers or drawers, and, sometimes, were placed in the coffin. On the other hand, religious pictures change: large wood engravings, which often composed "series" and could be colored, were followed by small copper-engraved pictures, the same size as the books to which they could be added as illustrations. This twofold usage of prints — the print by itself and as a plate in a book — is merely one example of the many varied uses of engraved pictures.

Broadsheets, printed on the recto of a single sheet, are somewhat different.[25] Commonly the layout reveals from the top to the bottom of the sheet the title to be read and announced aloud, then a wood engraving and a descriptive text of approximately ten to twenty lines. Here again picture and text combine to describe celestial wonders (*Le pourtraict de la comète, Qui est apparue sur la ville de Paris depuys le Mercredy 28e Novembre 1618, jusques à quelques jours ensuivans,* Paris, M. de Mathonière, 1618), the misdeeds of sorcerers (*Mort et trespas de Monseigneur le Prince de Courtenay, par la malicieuse Sorcellerie d'un miserable Sorcier qui depuys fut exécuté,* n.p., n.d.), or monstrous creatures (as in the two broadsheets of identical form printed in 1578 by F. Poumard at Chambery, *Briefz discours d'un merveilleux monstre né a Eurisgo, terre de Novarrez en Lombardie, au moys de Janvier en la présents Année 1578. Avec le vray pourtraict d'icelluy au plus prez du naturel* and *Vray pourtraict, et sommaire description d'un horrible et merveilleux monstre, né à Cher, terre de Piémond, le 10 de Janvier 1578. A huit heures du soir, de la femme d'un docteur, avec sept cornes, celle qui pend jusques à la saincture à celle qui est autour du col sont de chair*).

Some sheets concerning political events followed the same
pattern, printed on only one side so they could be posted. One
example, drawn from 1642, is *Le pourtraict de Monseigneur le
Cardinal de Richelieu sur son lit de parade, avec son Epitaphe,*
printed in Paris by Fraincois Beauplet. The text is longer than
that of a popular print. This kind of sheet in folio is an intermediary form between different short-lived typographical forms that
could reach those who did not buy them. "Placards" were less
popular, because they only contained a written text, but they
could nevertheless contribute to the culture of the masses because
they were posted on town walls and could be read by the literate
to the illiterate. This is undoubtedly what the religious reformers
of 1534 hoped for in Paris when they posted on the walls the
placard against the mass composed by Antoine Marcourt and
printed by Pierre de Vingle, both refugees in Geneva. In January
1649 the Queen and Mazarin at Rueil had a placard posted; it
was later printed as a satirical pamphlet with the aim of winning
over the population. Throughout the 16th and 17th centuries,
in different forms that almost always made a twofold reading
possible, there circulated widely an abundant printed material
intended for walls of houses and churches, bedrooms, and workshops. This led to a great change in a culture that had previously
been divorced from written material. Such a change helped to
make the written word familiar, necessary for a complete understanding of the pictures that were shown; it was undoubtedly
decisive for urban literacy and created, in the long run, a "popular" market for books.

If postmortem inventories make no mention of this market
until the mid 17th century, it is because the reading matter of
the lowest classes was based on booklets that were considered
worthless as objects and, therefore, were not included in the
inventories. This is true from 1530 onwards for the chapbooks
(*canards*) distributed by urban pedlars, the *"porte-paniers"* or
*"contreporteux"* mentioned by Pierre de l'Estoile.

One chapbook in four contains a text accompanied by a wood
engraving, usually small in size and from various sources. The
same piece of wood, touched up or not, could be used for several
editions: a monstrous snake from Cuba easily converted into a
dragon flying in the Parisian sky. Texts as well as pictures were
reused in successive series of chapbooks. For example, the same

text successively recounts the death of Marguerite de la Rivère, executed at Padua in December 1596, that of Catherine de la Critonnière, executed in the same town in September 1607, again that of Marguerite de la Rivère executed at Padua (but this time in December 1617), and lastly the same heroine executed at Metz in November 1623, J. P. Séguin gives five other examples of such reuses concerning two, four, or six chapbooks published by the same printer or by different printers; and Pierre de l'Estoile mentions several times the existence of such "scraped off" pieces disguised to appear as new editions. Chapbooks were based on a limited repertory of intrigues and used a small number of narrative formulas. Out of 517 editions of *canards* made between 1530 and 1630, six themes dominate: crime and capital executions (89 editions), heavenly apparitions (86 editions, to which we can add 8 editions of the vision of the Great Turk), sorcerers and diabolic possessions (62 editions), miracles (45 editions), floods (37 editions), and earthquakes (32 editions). This is reading matter for the literate, because the written word dominates, but some space is given to illustrations. So these chapbooks feed the imaginations of town dwellers by stories of excess: of moral dissoluteness or natural disorders, of natural or miraculous or diabolical breaks with the monotony of everyday life. Printed in large numbers, the chapbooks, along with almanacs, comprise the first collections of printed texts aimed at the largest and most "popular" readership, though this does not imply that they were only bought by artisans or merchants, or that their reading produced the same effects in each case. Pierre de l'Estoile testifies to the taste of the urban elite for this kind of literature and, at the same time, their distance from what they called "nonsense," "twaddle," "idle stories," and "*couonneries,*" which the naive and simple-minded believe to be true.

The success of these cheap booklets, but also the Parisian printers' control of their publication, gave Nicolas Oudot, a publisher based at Troyes, the idea of producing similar works for the same public but with different contents. Reusing woodcuts abandoned because of the success of copper engraving, using wornout fonts of type, printing on second-class paper made in Champagne, Oudot started in 1602 to publish low-price booklets that were soon given the name of "*livrets bleus,*" an allusion to the color of their paper or cover.[26] In the "rue Nostre Dame, au

Chappon d'Or couronné" he published them until his death in 1636—52 editions, according to A. Morin's catalogue.[27] Chivalrous novels, with 21 editions, constituted almost half of his production. Oudot also published 10 editions of the lives of saints in cheap booklet form. Unlike the novels of chivalry, which often ran to 100 or even 200 pages in quarto format, these saints' lives were published in small octavo booklets. Finally, his new editorial formula enabled him to circulate widely learned works such as French tragedies with subjects similar to those of chivalrous novels.

Oudot's son, Nicolas II, continued his work. His main activity was publishing texts that his father had neglected, though using forms with which he had experimented. He published 17 books of instruction and practice (such as *Civilité puérile et honnête pour l'éducation des enfants*), models for conversation (the *Cabinet de l'Eloquence francaise* or the *Fleurs de bien dire*), books giving everyday knowledge (the *Cuisinier francais* by Varenne or the *Maréchal expert*), medical recipes (the *Médecin charitable enseignant la manière de faire et préparer en sa maison avec facilité et peu de frais les remèdes propres à toutes maladies* or *l'Operateur des pauvres, ou la fleur d'opération nécessaire aux pauvres pour conserver leur santé et soy guérir à peu de frais*), and, finally, astrological collections (the *Palais des Curieux ou l'Algèbre et le Sort donnet la décision des questions les plus douteuses et ou les songes et les visions nocturnes sont expliquées selon la doctrine des Anciens*, the *Miroir d'Astrologie Naturelle* or *Pronostications generalles* by Commelet, of which he made five successive and different editions). On the other hand, Nicolas Oudot Jr. gave an important place to the burlesque that characterized the mid-17th century and published, for example, the *Fantaisies de Bruscambille*, Scarron's *Oeuvres burlesques,* and the *Tracas de Paris en vers burlesques.* Lastly, he introduced into the *Bibliothèque bleue* catalogue, but only on a small scale, devout literature produced by the Catholic Reformation: for instance, *Sept trompettes spirituelles pour resveiller les pecheurs et pour les induire à faire pénitence,* by the Recollet Bartholomé Solutive. The Oudot formula, in its second generation, kept the same characteristics as far as the type of edition was concerned but widened the choice of texts published by circulating, at low prices, fashionable literature, guides to the new spirituality, and everyday booklets.

It is not easy to locate the readers of these booklets, mass produced at Troyes or later in other towns such as Rouen. However, two propositions can be suggested. First, the *Bibliothèque bleue,* including almanacs, during its first hundred years seemed to reach a basically urban public. That the cheap books printed by the Oudots were circulated by pedlars should not lead us astray: in the 17th century it appears that book peddling was strictly limited to urban areas, where it was regulated and sometimes limited because it competed against bookshops and encouraged the diffusion of forbidden books. The book pedlar was, therefore, an urban figure who offered chapbooks and official texts, almanacs and *livrets bleus,* pamphlets and gazettes. I offer as support for this claim a text that dates from 1660. It mocks the pedlars, "who carry here and there almanacs, ordinary and out-of-the-ordinary gazettes, legends and little novels of Mélusine by Maugis, the four sons of Aymond, by Geoffroy la grand-dent, by Valentin and Ourson, fashionable songs, dirty and sordid ones, dictated by indecent thoughts, vaudevilles, court songs, drinking songs."[28] The contents of this mixed bag betray different forms and reveal differing cultural expectations. All works were apparently printed on small sheets with a small number of pages, bound only in paper and cheap. Only with the turn of the 18th century would pedlars venture outside the city walls, taking not only the *livrets bleus* but other books, including prohibited works, to small towns and villages that lacked bookshops.

Another indication of the urban circulation of printed matter from Troyes printers is the agreements passed between them and booksellers in the capital. Nicholas Oudot Sr. was the first to experiment with such a formula, with the Parisian bookseller Jean Promé. In 1627 he printed a *Nouveau Testament de Nostre Seigneur Jésus Christ,* of which A. Morin found one copy with an engraved title glued over the original: "At Troyes, and to be sold in Paris at Jean Promé rue Frémentel au petit Corbeil 1628." One of Nicolas Jr.'s sons settled in Paris in 1664 and married the daughter of Promé's widow. In the last third of the 17th century the Paris booksellers Antoine Raffle and Jean Musier circulated books printed at Troyes on a large scale. It is clear that from the start the publisher of the *Bibliothèque bleue* considered the Paris market to be essential.

The *"littérature bleue"* that circulated in towns was probably
not read exclusively by the lower urban classes. It seems certain
that the almanac was a text read by all strata of society. The
almanac, by its very conciseness, was capable of encouraging a
plurality of readings, with the text to be read by the literate
and signs and pictures to be deciphered by the illiterate. The
almanac provided information about the dates of law cases and
fairs and about the weather. It offered predictions, horoscopes,
precepts, and advice.[29] An everyday book to be used in a multitude of ways, intermingling in a unique way signs and text, the
almanac is an ideal book for a society where there exists a multiplicity of relations to the printed word, ranging from cursive
reading to hesitant deciphering. Such a remark also applies to the
*livrets bleus,* although to a lesser extent because their text is
rarely accompanied by pictures.[30] The few indications we have
concerning their reading public in the 17th century allow us to
suggest a double hypothesis. On the one hand, the *livrets bleus*
stand out in a society where readers are neither the lower urban
classes nor the clientele of learned books but a midway world of
semiliterates, small notables, town bourgeois, and active or retired
merchants, who enjoyed reading classical texts, and the agreeable
and practical works that constitute a large part of the Troyes
stock. On the other hand, they suggest that in the world of urban
crafts these books could be used collectively, like other texts,
in the workshop or confraternities. This was probably the first
public for the *Bibliothèque bleue* before the rise of rural peddling,
the growth of literacy, and the disdain of notables, made them
reading for the popular classes alone.

The years 1530–1660 mark a decisive step in the history of
publishing in France. It is during this period, despite the fact that
illiteracy remained high even in the towns and that individual
ownership of books remained an elite privilege, that a "popular"
market was created. The way was prepared by the circulation of
a wide assortment of printed materials, both texts and pictures,
thus rendering the written word familiar even to those who could
not read. This new relation to the printed word was largely forged
in and accelerated by networks of popular sociability in the workplace, at prayer, or in festive celebration. Yet the way the popular
classes received the printed word did not create a specific literature but enabled them to handle texts also read by the notability,

whether small or great; for example, almanacs, broadsheets, and *livrets bleus*. In the 16th century in Paris and Lyon, and in the 17th at Troyes, printers concentrated on publishing these books, which cost little but had a wide audience. In this way they created or reinforced cultural divergencies that were previously less obvious. The first differentiates towns and countryside. Traditional rural culture gives very little room to the printed text whereas in towns familiarity with the printed text is widespread, because books are present, because pedlars sell *canards* and *livres bleus,* and because walls are covered with pictures and broadsheets. In a world where the oral and the gesture predominate, the towns become islands of a different culture in which the whole urban population participates directly or indirectly.

To this first divergence, the "popular" diffusion of printed matter and books adds another. The new publishing practices that produce cheap books do not focus equally on all kinds of texts. Essentially they help to circulate texts that no longer belong to the elite culture, and books that the notability has begun to despise. And this leads to a contrast that will grow between two bodies of texts, those that feed the richest or most learned and those that aim to feed the curiosity of the popular classes.[31] In the 17th century these two literatures do not have radically different publics because, as I have said, much of their reading matter is shared; however, it still remains true that they define two kinds of material published by printers for their clienteles, with itineraries of circulation and uses that are no longer one. It is in the material aspect of the book that these contrasts become manifest: on the one hand a noble object refined, bound, and preserved, and on the other an ephemeral and cheap object. By its form and content, the book becomes a distinguishing sign; it is a marker of a cultural identity. Molière is a good example of this sociology that characterizes each social group by the books it reads. For him the presence of *contes bleus* or an almanac suffices to define a cultural horizon (which is neither that of the popular classes nor of the elite). Thus "popular" printing has a complex meaning. For it is a recovering and reuse for a new public of texts that once belonged entirely to an elite culture before they fell from fashion. Simultaneously it tends to stigmatize the texts it uses; they thus become, in the eyes of the cultured, unworthy reading because they belong to the popular classes. Publishing strategies therefore create not a progressive enlarging of *one* book-oriented public but systems of appreciation that culturally define the products of printing, that fragment the market, and that draw new cultural boundaries.

NOTES

1. J.-C. Schmitt, "Religion populaire et culture folklorique," *Annales E.S.C.* (1976), pp. 941–53.
2. R. Chartier and J. Revel, "Le paysan, l'ours et saint Augustin," in *La découverte de la France au XVIIe siècle* (Paris: 1980), pp. 259–64.
3. R. Mandrou, *De la culture populaire aux XVIIe et XVIIIe siècles: La Bibliothèque bleue de Troyes* (Paris: 1964, new edition in 1975).
4. I agree with the conclusions of H.-J. Martin, "Culture écrite et culture orale, culture savante et culture populaire dans la France d'Ancien Régime," *Journal des Savants* (July-December 1975), pp. 225–82, and J.-L. Marais, "Littérature et culture populaires aux XVIIe et XVIIIe siècles: Réponses et questions," *Annales de Bretagne et des Pays de l'Ouest* (1980), pp. 65–105. Cf. R. Chartier, "La circulation de l'écrit," *Histoire de la France Urbaine*, vol. 3: *La ville classique* (Paris: 1981), pp. 266–82.
5. An example of this process is given by C. Ginzburg, *I benandanti: Stregoneria e culti agrari tra Cinquecento e Seicento* (Turin: 1966); cf. R. Chartier, "L'histoire au singulier," *Critique* 404 (1981), pp. 72–84.
6. M.-H. Froeschlé-Chopard, *La religion populaire en Provence orientale au XVIIIe siècle* (Paris: 1980), particularly the preface by A. Dupront, pp. 5–31.
7. C. Ginzburg, *Il formaggio e i vermi: Il cosmo di un mugnaio del'500* (Turin: 1976), and M. Bakhtin, *Rabelais and His World* (1940; Cambridge, Mass.: 1968).
8. G. Bollème, "Des romans égarés," *La Nouvelle Revue Française* 238 (1972), pp. 191–228.
9. From this point of view, it is possible to generalize the propositions made by H. R. Jauss in *Literaturgeschichte als Provokation* (Frankfurt: 1974).
10. P. Bourdieu, *La Distinction: Critique sociale du jugement* (Paris: 1979), especially pp. 365–81.
11. M. de Certeau, *L'invention du quotidien*, vol. 1: *Arts de faire* (Paris: 1980).
12. R. Hoggart, *The Uses of Literacy* (London: 1975).
13. N. Z. Davis, "Strikes and Salvation at Lyons," in *Society and Culture in Early Modern France* (Stanford: 1975), pp. 1–16.

14. R. Chartier, "Intellectual History or Sociocultural History? The French Trajectories," in *Modern European Intellectual History: Reappraisals and New Perspectives,* edited by D. LaCapra and S. L. Kaplan (Ithaca, N.Y.: 1982), pp. 13–46.

15. For a comparative study, see M. Spufford, *Small Books and Pleasant Histories: Popular Fiction and Its Readership in Seventeenth-Century England* (London: 1981); J. Caro Baroja, *Ensayo sobre la literatura de cordel* (Madrid: 1969); M. Cruz García de Enterría, *Sociedad y poesía de cordel en el Barroco* (Madrid: 1973); J. Marco, *Literatura popular en Espana en los siglos XVIII y XIX (Una aproximación a los pliegos de cordel)* (Madrid: 1977); R. W. Scribner, *For the Sake of Simple Folk* (Cambridge: 1981).

16. E. Eisenstein, *The Printer as an Agent of Change: Communications and Cultural Transformations in Early Modern Europe* (Cambridge: 1979).

17. A. Labarre, *Le livre dans la vie amiénoise du seizième siècle: L'enseignement des inventaires après décès, 1503–1576* (Paris and Louvain: 1971).

18. H.-J. Martin and M. Lecocq, *Livres et lecteurs à Grenoble: Les registres du libraire Nicolas (1645–1668)* (Geneva: 1977), 1:244–45, 215.

19. H.-L. Schlaepfer, "Laurent de Normandie," *Aspects de la Propagande Religieuse* (Geneva: 1957), pp. 176–230.

20. Quoted by S. Deyon and P. Lottin in *Les casseurs de l'été 1566: L'iconoclasme dans le Nord* (Paris: 1981), pp. 19–20.

21. N. Z. Davis, "The Protestant Printing Workers of Lyons in 1551," *Aspects de la Propagande Religieuse,* pp. 247–57, and "Printing and the People," in *Society and Culture,* pp. 189–226.

22. *Entrées royales et fêtes populaires à Lyon du XVIe au XVIIIe siècles* (Paris: 1978), pp. 279–82, 337–44.

23. J. Gaston, *Les images des confréries parisiennes avant la Révolution* (Paris: 1910).

24. P. Chaunu, *La mort à Paris XVIe, XVIIe et XVIIIe siècles* (Paris: 1978), pp. 279–82, 337–44.

25. J.-P. Seguin, *L'information en France avant le périodique: 517 canards imprimés entre 1529 et 1631* (Paris: 1964).

26. On the Oudots see L. Morin, "Les Oudot imprimeurs et libraires à Troyes, à Paris, à Sens et à Tours," *Bulletin du Bibliophile* (1901), pp. 66–77, 138–45, 182–94.

27. A. Morin, *Catalogue descriptif de la Bibliothèque Bleue de Troyes (almanachs exclus)* (Geneva: 1974).

28. D. Martin, *Parlement nouveau ...* (Strasbourg: 1660), quoted by Marais, "Litterature," p. 70.

29. G. Bollème, *Les almanachs populaires aux XVIIe et XVIIIe siècles: Essai d'histoire sociale* (Paris and The Hague: 1969).

30. G. Bollème, *La Bibliothèque Bleue: Littérature populaire en France du XVIIe au XIXe siècle* (Paris: 1971), and *La Bible bleue: Anthologie d'une littérature "populaire"* (Paris: 1975).

31. As an example, see the literature on roguery, *Figures de la gueuserie,* edited by R. Chartier (Paris: 1982).

# Forms of Expertise:
# Intellectuals and "Popular" Culture
# in France (1650—1800)

JACQUES REVEL

Our knowledge of the subcultures or "popular" cultures of preindustrial Europe seldom comes from immediate and spontaneous accounts by participants. Instead, as it has become commonplace to admit, learned people gathered most of the available
information on the premodern period. Often from extremely
diverse milieux and educational backgrounds, they nonetheless
all belonged to the legitimate, recognized, literate culture of the
old regime; I shall refer to them here as "intellectuals." Such a
designation is not meant to indicate a rigorously defined social
or socioprofessional group (even though, as we shall see, the
problem of the professionalism of expertise is not unimportant);
I shall be dealing with theologians, men of letters, doctors, travelers, and administrators. Nor do I wish to imply that premodern French society recognized a clearly identifiable category
for those whose social activity is defined by their mastery of
knowledge.
    While the characterization "intellectual" is anachronistic when
applied to premodern France, its use is justifiable. Whatever their
background, learned commentators and observers of popular life
all described a cultural sphere remote from them. They defined
that world as different and thereby established a relationship
that tended to reinforce the coherence of their own culture. Thus
their writings persistently resonated on two often quite indis-

tinguishable registers: observation (in its largest sense) and the
vision of society within which the authors at least implicitly situated themselves. Moreover, when these writers drew on an established
form of knowledge to describe, explain, classify, and judge popular practices, they more or less explicitly appealed to forms of
authority (with their own occasionally concurrent and contradictory strains) that invested them with a kind of social and
cultural magisterium. This gave rise to a double coherence and to
an interdependence between those who described popular culture and what they described. Given this interdependence, I aim
here to investigate the production of a certain kind of discourse
and knowledge and, more precisely, the relationship between the
use of this discourse and the production of a particular object:
"popular culture."

This relationship was not stable — on the contrary, it evolved
between the 16th and 18th centuries. Recent historians of the
relationship between dominant and popular cultures (as represented
very differently by G. Cocchiara or R. Muchembled) have generally
interpreted its evolution in linear terms.[1] They have argued that,
between the end of the Middle Ages and the dawn of industrial
society, the rift between the two cultures widened and popular
culture continued to be both repressed and marginalized. The
folklorists of the 19th century would only rediscover the charms
of popular culture after it had been reduced to an inoffensive
curiosity.[2] Similarly the rationalism of the Enlightenment, so it
seems, simply continued the effort of both Reformations, Protestant and Catholic, as well as of the absolute monarchy, to norma-
lize such practices and beliefs. Limiting myself to an analysis of
the forms of expertise, between about 1650 and 1800, I shall
show that this evolution was less linear and more complex than
has been thought.

In the period leading up to roughly 1750, one can identify two
kinds of attitudes, of manipulations, of discourse, all of which
moved in opposite directions. In the mid 17th century, those who
dealt with popular practices were, for the most part, intellectuals
who derived their status as experts from their profession: mainly
theologians, but also some doctors, jurists, and astronomers. All
relied on both the authority of knowledge and professional skill.
The closer one gets to the first half of the 18th century, however,
the more the competence of those who discussed popular culture

seems to dissolve; they are deprofessionalized, divested of authority. A cultural and social consensus founded on common sense and convention begins to appear and, as a result, a gradual shift can be discerned in attitudes toward popular practices: in 1650 the object of study by a qualified body of professionals, after 1700, little by little, they began to be treated as a distinct sociocultural phenomenon.

This movement was reversed after the middle of the 18th century. Slowly, in a complex and sometimes contradictory fashion, a systematized approach to popular culture was reconstructed and conditions of observation were to an ever greater extent codified. Consequently, forms of expertise and competence were redefined, leading to the establishment at the end of the century of a new scientific and autonomous discipline: anthropology. The future of this discipline seemed uncertain but the nature of its object of study, its methods, and its criteria was becoming clear. I turn now to examine these three successive stages in more detail.

I use the term "popular" for that set of practices which had no legitimate status in the culture of traditional society. These practices take shape through a series of attributes that, item for item, oppose the attributes of established culture.

These oppositions were set up on the basis of three criteria that had a cumulative effect but did not neatly overlap. The first and the narrowest, rooted in tradition, was the criterion of truth: true knowledge was opposed to false knowledge, knowing to unknowing. This was the position of the theologian, for example, who used the opposition to distinguish licit from illicit. The second was a criterion of rationality. It contrasted practices and attitudes that were coherent and understandable (from a moral, intellectual, social, or even theological point of view) with those that were not; that is, with the products of nefarious passions. The third and broadest criterion can be called "convention": it was based upon the recognition of a more or less explicit social code that determined what was culturally acceptable and what was not. Between the mid-17th and the mid-18th century, these three systems of opposition functioned simultaneously. But the hierarchy of criteria gradually altered; the last and most approximate — but by no means the least effective — system of opposition substituted for the first and most rigorous criterion (true/

nontrue). By about 1750, more attention was being paid to identifying the propriety of certain practices where the preoccupation a century earlier had been to establish whether they had a basis in truth. As a consequence, the object of expertise was also transformed.

Abbé Jean-Baptiste Thiers, the most famous of the theological writers of tracts on superstitions, is a convenient example of the first of these positions. In addition to his *Traité des superstitions* (published in 1679, significantly expanded in 1702, and reprinted several times in the 18th century), Thiers devoted innumerable pamphlets, essays, and commentaries to denouncing false beliefs and practices and the misuse of religion. This moralist parish priest, affiliated with a large network of "Jansenist" priests and unhappy in his relationship with the Catholic hierarchy, was a man in the field whose pastoral preoccupations informed an indefatigable theological militancy. However he approached his subject, he measured the forms of behavior he was analyzing against the standards of truth. The *Traité des superstitions* was based entirely on the confrontation of the imprecisely defined world of actual practices with a body of theological references (a corpus borrowed for the most part from Augustine by way of Aquinas and the conciliar and synodal authorities, which distinguished between true religion and idolatry).[3] In his polemical exchanges with, among others, Mabillon in the late 17th and early 18th centuries on the authenticity of the relics of Saint Firmin d'Amiens (1699) or of the Sainte Larme de Vendôme (1699), this destroyer of false cults conducted a twofold critical examination.[4] Thiers verified the canonical conformity of tradition: thus the Larme de Vendôme was a belief, but a *false* belief, since the tradition that attested to it was "neither divine, nor apostolic, nor episcopal or ecclesiastic, and there are only these three sets of true traditions." On the other hand he criticized, in the name of the proper use of knowledge, the proofs adduced by those who argued in favor of the relic: "All these events are presented in such a way that they might pass for true, if they were not without proof. But the historian who recounts them does not have sufficient authority for us to take his word. He has neither command of style, nor erudition, nor genius, nor enlightened discrimination. His reasoning goes astray; he is given to believing blindly in fables; he writes only out of interest or passion; and I would not have much trouble demonstrating that, of all the facts he presents, there is not one single one which is not extremely uncertain or absolutely false. . . ."[5] In this text, one can already perceive the criterion of the rationality of practices (e.g., "enlightened discrimination," "command of style" vs "fable") but the reference to an authority of knowledge, be it scriptural or historic, remains dominant and is the basis of the condemnation.

Moreover, Thiers's characterization of "popular culture" does not refer to any social or sociocultural attribute or to any intellectual quality. Popular belief is opposed to Catholic belief as the particular to the universal ("every kingdom, every province, every diocese, every town, every parish has its own beliefs"); popular belief has no foundation in canonical authority. "Popular tradition" (and Thiers was one of the first to use this expression) is by definition unacceptable because it confuses belief and tradition: "Belief in the Larme de Vendôme is neither a divine Tradition, nor an apostolic Tradition nor an ecclesiastic Tradition. It is nothing more than a popular tradition which does not deserve to bear the name of Tradition, as it is not based on any truth."[6]

The line of demarcation between knowledge and ignorance was constantly shifting in the second half of the 17th century and the first half of the 18th. The criteria that served to establish the distinction were becoming relatively secular. The oratorian P. Lebrun, a contemporary of Thiers and a disciple of Malebranche, published in 1702 a *Histoire critique des pratiques superstitieux qui ont séduit les peuples et embarrassé les savants.* As the title indicates, Lebrun closely examined superstitious practices according to the standards of science and faith. The methods of expertise were meant to be systematic and scientific – as they were even more explicitly in Fontenelle's *Histoire des Oracles* some years later. But the trend was neither simple nor linear; it was not merely an indiscriminate secularization bent on discrediting, or attempting to disqualify, the clerical experts. The reason for the complexity of the trend is twofold. On the one hand, the clerics themselves adopted the new criteria, at least in part, and this retained something of their claim to a cultural magisterium. This was the attitude of Catholic rationalism. Second, even when rationalism was militant, its proponents were careful not to encroach on theologians' territory. The work of Dom Calmet reflects the first attitude.[7] Dom Calmet was a Dominican and a well-known victim of Voltaire's sarcasm during the height of the Enlightenment. In 1746 he published a *Dissertation sur les apparitions des anges, des démons et des esprits et sur les revenants et vampires de Hongrie...*, which was reissued several times. His untiring and sometimes clumsy attempts to settle the question of faith and reason led him to oppose what he terms the "real" (i.e., reasonable) supernatural against the entire range of popular superstitions, which he attributes to ignorance and does not hesitate to criticize. "One notices that the greater the ignorance in a country, the more superstition reigns, and that the spirit of darkness exercises a power proportionate to the amount of error and disorder in which the people live."[8] In this analysis there is hardly a trace of the demon that obsessed Thiers. But, on the other hand, one can observe the prudence of rationalism. It has recently been noted that even in the bastion of enlightened militancy, the *Encyclopédie,* the articles dealing with the various forms of superstition are characterized by a cautious discretion.[9] These articles, most of which were authored by the Chevalier de Jaucourt, generally refer to the works of traditional theologians (Thiers in particular). They more readily invoke the practice of "sound reason" than the requirements of secular rationalism. The *encyclopédistes* turned to the theologians to set limits to reason. Even the definition of superstition indicates a kind of division of tasks: it is "a cult of religion, false, poorly supervised, full of illusory terrors, contrary to reason and to the healthy notions one ought to have about the Supreme Being." The article on spells is even more explicit: "Spells are a part of what we call magic; but they are particularly aimed at harming men, either their person, or their cattle, their plants, or the fruits they have gathered from the earth. Only theologians are capable of dealing with such a delicate matter." No doubt this is an example of the *encyclopédistes'* caution but it also suggests that a solidarity existed among the custodians of the proper use of reason when they came up against those who reasoned poorly or not at all. This brings me to a second system of opposition, which was identifiable well before the age of the *Encyclopédie.*

Beginning in the first half of the 17th century, another kind of division appears between high culture and popular culture. The 16th century had seen a diversity of interest in the products of subculture (most particularly in regional expressions, language, and proverbs, which were carefully collected and compiled); but French classicism clearly defined the distance between the two cultural levels.[10] Admittedly, collections of proverbs were still being published, though to a lesser extent, and collections of popular tales made their way into high literature with the *Contes de ma mère l'Oye* of Charles Perrault (1697). These landmarks, however, do not reflect the general trend. Following René Pintard, J. M. Goulemot rightly insists on the decisive role played in this evolution by the circle of *libertins érudits*.[11] Though it constituted a minority and was ultimately marginal, this group advocated a kind of social and cultural control very different from that of the custodians of the *bon usage* described above. The pretension to a sociocultural magisterium was no longer founded on professional status. This group involved alliances far wider and more diverse than those that united, for example, the theologians with the abbé Thiers. These "free-thinkers" were neither coopted nor identified themselves on the basis of a normative competence; nor did they claim to possess the truth. What they held in common was a desire for the free and beneficial application of critical reason.

No doubt the paths to reason were by definition accessible to everyone; but the ability to use reason was an unequally distributed privilege. It was the sign by which an emerging elite that wished to establish a new aristocracy distinguished itself. At the very time that the notion of *raison d'Etat* was being developed, this elite was expecting the young absolute monarchy not only to recognize and confirm its talents and privileges but to turn the State into an agent of the social institutionalization of "sound reason." The relationship between knowledge and politics – to be revived and developed in the 18th century – was thus proposed early in the evolutionary process. Once again, however, it would be a mistake to oversimplify. The battle for reason was fought on several fronts in the 17th and the first half of the 18th centuries. Great debates arose as to what should be accepted as credible: from 1630 to 1660 they centered on the reality of cases of sorcery and possession by the devil; from 1650 to 1680, on the nature and meaning of comets. All of these debates pitted libertines versus "ignorance," but also clergy versus laity, scientists versus amateurs, different professional groups against one

another, all of them using infinitely complex and shifting strategies and alliances.[12] It was thus that the clergy, with an eagerness
tinged with reticence, gradually joined the camp of positive
knowledge: they were threatened on the one side by the tenacity
of popular beliefs and on the other by the denunciation of libertines, as well as by the technical competence of such professionals
as doctors and astronomers.

In any case, to be denounced for error or false belief now
meant to be socially discredited. Popular beliefs were no longer
the sign of epistemological nonconformity, as they had been in
the preceding stage; they had become the source of obfuscation
and misunderstanding. This is what the *intendant* of fortifications,
Petit, clearly expressed in his *Dissertation sur la nature des comètes*
(1654). He was commissioned by the monarchy to give a rational
description of the astronomical event that shook a credulous
Europe: "All of Europe was struck with terror, *I am talking about
the ignorant people,* to the point of believing that this was the
end of the world. . . ."[13] A generation later, at the time of the
comet of 1680, the terms were even more explicit: false belief
was a "popular illness." The people were seen as carriers of this
fossilized trace of a social and cultural archaism; it was both an
indication of their subservient status and its justification. Popular
practices, therefore, represented a bygone age, nothing more than
a repository of the erroneous beliefs of humanity and the infancy
of mankind (the theme was to be an enduring one). The *Journal
des Savants* clearly reflects this attitude as it traces an astonishing
trajectory from Aristotelian astronomy to the netherworld of
popular beliefs:

Ancient philosophy believed, because it wanted Comets to be sublunary and
wanted their nature to be that of a mass of fumes from the Earth, that when
the fumes happened to catch fire, which could only indicate a great disorder
in the Elementary Region, some grand and considerable revolution must
therefore follow, according to that opinion. But since we have learned that
Comets are celestial bodies we have had our eyes opened to this error, which
is nothing more than a popular error.[14]

It is clear how the imperceptible shift took place: what had been
denounced in the name of accepted reason or of scientific knowledge was now invalidated by being labeled the product of an
inferior social group. Thus one can identify a third dividing line.

I shall only outline briefly the reorganization of cultural references that characterizes the age of French classicism — a period roughly spanning the century from 1650 to 1750 — because the phenomenon is well known. With the support of the monarchical State and its new institutions, and thanks to the efforts of the post-Tridentine Church, a many-faceted cultural normalization was carried out. Its effects were evident everywhere: in the codification of works and in the criteria of taste, in the reformulation of social conduct and licit forms of sociability, and in the prescriptions of a collective morality. A broad range of elitist models of behavior and elitist values, generally urban in origin, were now offered; they were contrasted with popular forms, which were mostly considered to be of peasant origin. Purification and control of religious practices was systematically carried out, for the most part by professional experts, as we have already seen. But the very success of their enterprise — for their books came into fashion and were soon elevated to the rank of collections of *curiosa,* repeatedly republished for 18th century *amateurs* — shows that the effects of ecclesiastical (i.e., theological) and rationalist discrimination were compounded among a larger public of *honnêtes gens* by social ostracism (there is more than adequate evidence of this in the correspondence of Mme de Sévigné, for example). At the same time, the workings and the usage of language underwent a twofold treatment: inventory and scientific analysis on the one hand, and social codification on the other. Public institutions like the Académie Française, grammar specialists, and compilers of dictionaries determined the rules of proper usage of the language; this preferred usage was considered exclusive of all others (that is, bourgeois, popular, regional, professional, technical, etc.), which were thus invalidated. Henceforth, the propriety of legitimate practices was set against the marginality of nonregulated uses of language (which were, of course, the uses of the majority). The norm had become classificatory; while the term "popular" remained socially pejorative, it lost all reference to a specific social identity. It still included the superstitions of the countryside and the slang of the Parisian streets, of course, but now it could also include the outmoded corpus of "elite" literature of the past, reprinted in the Bibliotheque bleue, the *balourdises* (blunderings) of the *Bourgeois Gentilhomme,* and "la vieille chanson," work of *"nos pères tous grossiers*," which Alceste in contrast with prevailing fashion praised so much. The domain of the popular was now the negative world of illicit practices, odd or erratic conduct, unrestrained expressiveness, and nature versus culture — the same nature that so many 18th century explorers of deeper France thought they had discovered.

We can thus establish the existence and simultaneous application of criteria that were all the more general for being loosely defined. In fact, between 1650 and 1750 the least rigorous, and therefore the most exclusive, criteria gradually came to prevail. These criteria were, moreover, manipulated by groups whose competence and expertise were more strictly defined as their principles of reference were made clearer. Demonologists like Bodin, theologians like Thiers or Lebrun, doctors, and, even more so, astronomers were professional experts in a specific area of knowledge; they mastered particular techniques and applied them to a well-defined field of interest. While the role of these professionals declined across the 17th and 18th centuries, a social and cultural code of legitimation and exclusion asserted itself. The code was all the more socially effective as its methods of operation remained obscure: it presented itself as a compendium of common practices but its mastery remained limited to the few. This code did not have its own body of specialists; rather, it was appropriated by those who considered themselves to be qualified insiders. Where there had been a body of knowledge, however arbitrary one may judge it to have been, there was now a system of tacit agreement.

These developments had obvious consequences on the very definition of the object in question, "popular culture." Like most theologians writing on superstition, Thiers in his *Traité* has difficulty choosing between the rigor of a ready-made, peremptory definition (religion versus superstition) and an imprecise, empirical inventory of concrete manifestations of evil that he intends to expose — of illicit practices that must be identified, described, and classified. It is for this reason that the act of classification takes on such great importance for Thiers. That act was ultimately more important to him than the actual gathering of data or an examination of the principles of classification — a classification that could not be questioned because of its divine and ecclesiastical origin. Curiously enough, Thiers's correspondence with his fellow parish priests shows hardly anything more than bibliographical references and bookish data, and no attempt to verify in the field the quality of the sources and the validity of the data. There is never a sense that the practices he records might have a coherent significance in and of themselves. A posthumous account of Thiers at work gives us an idea of his methods:

When he had decided to write on a subject he had chosen, one that was always extraordinary or bizarre, he would leaf through the list of his books – he had quite a few unusual books – and continue his quest at the best libraries or in the libraries of friends, in order to gather material for his projects; he then put his discoveries on paper.[15]

It is not surprising to find the absence of "ethnographic" preoccupations in the work of a writer whose interest does not lie in that kind of analysis. His vocation and expertise certainly put him in daily contact with popular practices but his calling was the defense and illustration of a norm.

Still, he believed in the existence of truth and falsehood and in the rules that determine them. His interest was not popular culture, it was true faith, which he felt it his duty to preserve and impose on others. If we place ourselves at the other end of the spectrum, where the discourse of social exclusion was more general and less explicit, this discourse appears to have neither author nor object. This does not mean that it did not operate extremely effectively in society. It was perpetuated anonymously by a collective voice whose identity was derived from the use of the discourse, independent of any technical capacity for expertise. The group used the discourse to define itself, not to illustrate or apply a norm or to indicate a professional competence. The object of the discourse was to qualify or disqualify practices in terms of a social position. While Thiers wore himself out composing taxonomies of unending complexity and Lebrun tried to establish a sure way to distinguish truth from falsehood, the abbé Lenglet Dufresnoy proposed in 1751 a *Recueil de dissertations anciennes et nouvelles sur les apparitions, les visions et les songes,* a very useful compilation of "extraordinary stories," of which he boasts: "I shall not be accused of believing all that is printed here."[16] As author, he keeps a safe distance from the body of texts, which he has arranged in as neutral a manner as possible – chronologically – and which he presents to the curiosity of his readers without expressing any judgment or providing rules of interpretation. In so doing, however, Lenglet Dufresnoy left no room for expertise; apparently there was no longer any need for it.

Toward the middle of the 18th century, at the very time when the old system of oppositions used to define popular culture was apparently in a state of decomposition, a movement in the opposite direction seems to have developed. Before the end of the century, in the space of two generations, this movement would lead to a redefinition of the object of observation (popular practices) and to new forms of professionalization, founded both on the accumulation of a body of knowledge and on a new codification of observation.

Unlike the texts just described, the aim of which was to distinguish illicit or illegitimate cultural productions from dominant or authorized forms of culture by prohibition or disqualification, another series of texts indicates a decisive change in attitude. They can be roughly characterized as "pre-ethnographic," not in the sense that they contain rudimentary ethnographic data (one could say as much for 17th century treatises on superstition, 18th century collections of *curiosités,* and many medieval documents as well), but because of the attitude their authors adopted toward the object they proposed to investigate. These writings are diverse: reports of trips into the provinces, statistical documents, administrative reports, descriptive monographs; most of these varieties flourished after 1750 and they were followed by the great collective investigations of the last third of the century. Diverse as they were, they shared certain features. In varying degrees, they reveal the discovery and recognition of a different cultural level, foreign and strange (or, as they often put it, "curious"). But that "curiousness" was no longer an argument for avoiding the study of popular practices; instead, it made a new type of investigation possible. For the acknowledgment of another culture as being different was possible – and herein lay the novelty – only when a very strong sense of identity existed between "us" and "them," between the observer and the observed; and this identity served to affirm a fundamental unity among the varying forms of humanity. The description and understanding of the characteristics of the "other" had to be incorporated into a history of the collective origins of humanity.

One is immediately reminded of the great theoreticians of the century, like Rousseau or Buffon.[17] But it is more interesting to

examine the mass of efforts made, often modestly and in a hapha-
zard way, to reconstitute, piece by piece, the social and cultural
genealogy of humankind — that is, the efforts to rediscover the
substructures of the past that give coherence to human activity
and human history. Every *"curiosité,"* every vestige, every fragment of popular practices that was uncovered now provided a
clue to an archaic stratum and provided evidence of a buried
past. "Archaic" no longer marked a bygone and downgraded
past but, rather, a chain of being that had to be understood in
order to make modern society intelligible. No doubt, fact-collect-
ing was still the gathering of insignificant data and objects, and
would remain so for some time, but the enterprise became significant as the gathered information was integrated into a larger
scheme that 18th century thinkers set out to discover and understand.

Popular culture was perceived at this point as conserving the
memory of past ages. It was to be understood as a social artifact
produced in particular conditions, not as the negative product of
a system of invalidation. Destutt de Tracy expressed this idea at
the very end of this intellectual movement, in his *Eléments de
l'Idéologie* (1801–1804):

The savage often gives us an opportunity to consider that men so unenligh-
tened might be able to create structures that are so refined and, in doing so,
might also be utterly incapable of creating others which seem to us to be less
complex. In civilized societies, the class with the least extensive and varied
means of communication offers analogous phenomena. Peasants living in
remote mountain areas are remarkable for the exactitude they display in a
small number of structures, their absolute ignorance of a multitude of others,
and their inability to create new ones.[18]

This text is remarkable on two counts: first, because, in spite
of the simplistic contrast it makes between the savage and civilized man, it serves to relativize the order and the hierarchy of
cultural productions; second, because it does not suggest that one
civilization be considered in opposition to another. Rather, it
emphasizes the importance of social status within each civilization. The parallel of the savage and the peasant, a true commonplace in Enlightenment Europe, does not introduce a negative
value judgment; rather, it refers back to a hierarchy of forms of
social life that are intelligible within a history. During the 18th

century, this was the object of value judgments that were, to say the least, contradictory.

Destutt de Tracy is in no way an isolated example. On the contrary, he comes at the end of an extraordinarily diverse period of "genetic" research, which lasted thirty or forty years. Antoine Court de Gébelin, for example, departed on a quest for the *Origine du langage et de l'écriture* in his *Monde primitif analysé et comparé avec le monde moderne, considéré dans l'histoire naturelle de la parole* (1775). Starting with the postulate that one can "trace all languages to a single language, of which all others are but nuances," he attempts to identify the primitive language of all humanity, then to identify the language of Europe (i.e. Celtic, "the language which serves as the foundation of our French origins"), and to retrace the history of its progressive differentiations. The aim of the scientific approach is clear: to exorcise the "terrifying phantom of the multitude of languages" – which is also the phantom of social heterogeneity – and make their differences comprehensible from a historical point of view. Almost contemporaneous with Court de Gébelin's work is the analysis by Legrand d'Aussy in his *Histoire de la vie quotidienne des Français depuis l'origine de la nation jusques à nos jours* (1782), informed by a similar concern. While the author deals in a highly original way with the diversity of nutritional practices and is constantly preoccupied with localizing and dating them, he also wants to understand multiplicity from a genetic perspective because that multiplicity, as his title indicates, results from a history.

More generally, the 18th century obsession with Celtism can be understood as manifesting the desire to build an anthropology founded in history. Nothing testifies to this more clearly than the work of the Académie Celtique, at the very beginning of the 19th century, and, in particular, the preparation of a questionnaire by Dulaure and Mangourit in 1807, recently studied by Mona Ozouf.[19] The members of the Académie drew up a detailed set of questions aimed at producing as systematic a survey as possible of the still observable features of traditional French culture.

It has been rightly emphasized that the data gathering was in principle an open-ended task; the questionnaire could be expanded and, moreover, it defined "less the object than the territory to be staked out." But it is the social and cultural territory that was the true object of the inquiry. The enterprise rested on two postulates, which determined its method: first, it sought to establish the unity of the French nation culturally (at the very time when political unity was being sought); second, every detail collected, every "trace" observed, had to find its place in a coherent cultural system, whose reconstruction was proof of that sought-for unity.

Thus perspectives had reversed themselves and the relationship of intellectuals to popular culture had changed. What seemed to resist cultural assimilation had now become the principal object of study and the focus of interest. Educated travelers in the 17th and even in the first half of the 18th centuries would visit towns and monuments that attested to an already constituted history; they became acquainted with works of art, discovered the dominant cultural practices, and learned to recognize the forms of sociability of the local elite. Their counterparts at the end of the 18th century followed a completely different course. It was approximately between 1770 and 1780, according to M. Vovelle, that visitors to Provence began to display greater curiosity and to explore the interior of the province more systematically. The traveler's interest now took him where there was no marked monument, no recognized history, and no identifiable practices. He went to the outskirts, the out-of-the-way places, mountains, and islands (Brittany, the Pyrénées, and the Alps were very much in vogue). This domestic exoticism was both a return to origins and a social exploration. In the heyday of Ideology, De Gerando gave a perfectly explicit theoretical justification of this phenomenon: "The *philosophe*-traveler who navigates to the ends of the earth passes through the succession of epochs; he travels in the past; each step he takes he covers another century. The unknown islands that he reaches are for him the cradle of human society."[20]

The cultural project was profoundly linked to political projects. The connection would become patent at the time of the Revolution and the First Empire, but it dates back farther than the 18th century. A major part of the literature on the discovery of popular life was the work of administrators, doctors, and economists. They did not invent the genre of administrative description, which had existed in France since the 17th century. But their texts, which were incomparably more numerous than previous writings, were distinctive because they were obsessed with the desire for social intervention and practicality. Most of them reflect a central question: in what ways could society be better managed? What was the best way of introducing improvements and innovation? But the will to innovate often ran up against the resistance of tradition. Whether through the recurrent reproaches in physiocratic literature concerning the inertia of peasant customs, or Grégoire's apprehension about the penetration of revolutionary creed into the countryside during the first years of the Revolution, whether through François de Neufchateau's survey of the public mood throughout the provinces under the Directory, or the correspondents of the *Société royale de médecine,* the managers of the Enlightenment discovered the obstacle of popular mentality and behavior. Here again, they were certainly not the first to identify rural France – the convenient symbol of both social opacity and cultural traditionalism – with the greatest obstacle to their enterprises. But things had changed.

For one thing, these men were much more concerned with empirical efficiency than their predecessors had been. One has only to compare the survey on the state of the realm, carried out in 1697 by the duc de Beauvilliers for the Dauphin, with other administrative or medical surveys from the second half of the 18th century. Administrative efficiency cannot do without a pedagogy intended for the popular classes; moreover, it implies that what determines the popular classes' obstinate rejection of progress has already been located and explained. And thus, rather than perceive its behavior as an erratic and peculiar trait associated with inferior status, one tries to comprehend its *coherence*; that is, what not only forms a system but also (in the mind of those pioneers of ethnography) permits in the same framework the association of geographic data (soil, climate, etc.), modes of human settlement, codes of sociability, a particular physiology, consistent psychological features – in short, all the factors whose interaction must, in the last analysis, account for a certain intellectual backwardness and a resistance to innovation. In 1790 the abbé Grégoire designed a questionnaire with a view to preparing measures to generalize the use of French and reduce regional languages; the impulse is characteristic of this new approach. The Revolution added another rupture, even more explicitly political in character; for the people who had lagged behind the Enlightenment now became the official protagonist of the Revolution, entrusted henceforth with the destiny of the nation. Not only was that people located at the source of all humankind but hereaf-

ter it would also embody the human future. At the very moment
when its hesitations about following the revolutionary course
created the worst problems for the politicians, it was the object
of the greatest ideological celebration. Hence the urgent need to
understand it, for through comprehension it would be incorporated into the collective scheme.[21]

Obviously, any distinction between culture and politics cannot
but be artificial: the two factors intermingle, at times even in one
and the same expression. But it is important to note, in conclusion, that corresponding to this new appearance of the people in
both the Enlightenment and the Revolutionary eras was a new
status for the observer and a new form of expertise. True, this development occurred at times within traditional institutions (the network of the *académies* for instance) or within old literary forms
(such as the *voyage littéraire*); but neither dominates. Topographic
studies and medical reference books, statistical research, administrative reports, and above all surveys, which increased rapidly
in number during the last thirty years of the old regime and even
more so during the Revolution, all represented the official framework in which the new interest in the popular classes developed.
The information gathered is often more austere than the more
general discussions of the *philosophes,* but its specific purpose
in these publications was to accumulate positivistic data concerning the *peuple.*

New institutions arose whose organization displays the recently
defined scientific aim. The new literary genres had already inspired
writers to efface themselves behind a display of learning that was
both cumulative and communicable: all systematic data could
thus be considered as contributing to the collective survey, designed to present the French orbit according to more or less standardized rules. But the revolutionary *sociétés de pensée* (for example,
the Société des Amis de la Constitution, which provided Grégoire
with so many of his correspondents), and in particular specialized
organizations, endowed these enterprises with both a framework
of scholarly sociability and a clearly defined scientific purpose.
I have already mentioned the best known, the Académie Celtique.
Perhaps even more significant was its predecessor, the Société des
Observateurs de l'Homme (1799–1805), which has recently been
studied.[22] The latter perceived itself as a learned circle, operating
collectively while gathering researchers from entirely different

fields. Here one found both doctors and geographers, linguists and naturalists, historians and philosophers, publicists and *voyageurs,* all concentrating on the same scientific purpose — the "physical, intellectual and moral study of man." Its fifty members shared their various specialized skills in order to elaborate the doctrine of research (*Idéologie* is the generic title of the sect) as well as to codify a common method. For in the framework of their loosely defined objective — the study of man — the Ideologues proposed a reorganization of disciplines, supervision over the professional use of scientific observation, and even a special pedagogy of research. Standardizing, codifying, professionalizing, systematizing the study of popular culture, all were used in establishing the scope and criteria of expertise. Indeed, for the first time popular ways were the object of a coherent study, in the context of the earliest elaboration of the human sciences, and were no longer judged according to criteria taken from other cultural or social realms. As we know, however, the project had no immediate success. The Ideologues were soon to be dispersed, and in the early 19th century the study of popular culture would once again be torn between an often-normative *statistique morale* and Romantic folklorism.

NOTES

1. G. Cocchiara, *Storia del folklore in Europa* (Turin: 1971); R. Muchembled, *Culture populaire et culture des élites dans la France moderne* (*XVe-XVIIIe siècles*) (Paris: 1978).
2. M. de Certeau, D. Julia, and J. Revel, "La beauté du mort: Le concept de culture populaire," *Politique aujourd'hui* (December 1970), pp. 3−23.
3. R. Chartier and J. Revel, "Le paysan, l'ours et St. Augustin," *La découverte de la France au 17e siècle* (Paris: 1980), pp. 259−64.
4. J. B. Thiers, *Dissertation sur la Sainte Larme de Vendôme* (Paris: 1699); *Dissertation sur le lieu où repose présentement le corps de S. Firmin le Confès, IIIe Evesque d'Amiens* (Paris: 1699).
5. *Dissertation sur la Sainte Larme* (Amsterdam: 1751), p. 125.
6. Ibid., p. xxxix.
7. B. Kopeczi, "Un scandale des Lumières: les Vampires," *Thèmes et figures du Siècle des Lumières: Mélanges offerts à Roland Mortier,* ed. by R. Trousson (Geneva: 1980), pp. 123−35.
8. Calmet, *Dissertation sur les apparitions,* p. 178.

9. The following is based on a recent study by J. M. Goulemot, "Démons, merveilles et philosophie à l'âge classique," *Annales E.S.C.* (6/1980), pp. 1223–50.

10. N. Z. Davis, *Society and Culture in Early Modern France* (Stanford, Calif.: 1975), chap. 8, "Proverbial Wisdom and Popular Errors," pp. 227–67.

11. R. Pintard, *Le libertinage érudit dans la première moitié du XVIIe siècle* (Paris: 1943).

12. R. Mandrou, *Magistrats et sorciers en France au XVIIe siècle: Une analyse de psychologie historique* (Paris: 1968); M. de Certeau, *La Possession de Loudun* (Paris: 1971); El. Labrousse, *L'entrée de Saturne au Lion: L'éclipse du 12 août 1654* (The Hague: 1974).

13. Quoted by Goulemot, "Démons," pp. 1226–27. My emphasis.

14. Ibid., p. 1227. My emphasis.

15. Bibliothèque municipale, Grenoble Ms. 227, Recueil de lettres de D. Bonaventure d'Argonne, ff. 28–29.

16. N. Lenglet Dufresnoy, *Recueil,* avertissement; Goulemot, "Démons," p. 1234.

17. M. Duchet, *Anthropologie et histoire au Siècle des Lumières* (Paris: 1971).

18. Destutt de Tracey, *Eléments de l'Idéologie* (1801; Paris: 1970) I: 295.

19. M. Ozouf, "L'invention de l'ethnographie française: le questionnaire de l'Académie Celtique," *Annales E.S.C.* (2/1981), pp. 210–30.

20. J. M. De Gérando, *Considérations sur les diverses méthodes à suivre dans l'exploration des peuples sauvages* (Paris: 1800); republished in J. Copans and J. Jamin, *Aux origines de l'Anthropologie française: Les Mémoires de la Société des Observateurs de l'Homme en l'an VIII* (Paris: 1978), p. 131.

21. M. de Certeau, D. Julia, and J. Revel, *Une politique de la langue: La Révolution française et les patois. L'enquête de Grégoire (1790–1794)* (Paris: 1975).

22. Copans and Jamin, *Aux origines;* J. Jamin, "Naissance de l'observation anthropologique: La Société des Observateurs de l'Homme (1799–1805)," *Cahiers internationaux de sociologie,* 1980.

# On the Use and Abuse of Handicraft: Journeyman Culture and Enlightened Public Opinion in 18th and 19th Century Germany

HANS-ULRICH THAMER

"A dog cannot have as many fleas as the guilds have abuses," complained the Bavarian Chancellor, Baron von Kreittmayr, in 1768.[1] His voice was only one in a great chorus of enlightened officials, lawyers, economists, and writers who, frequently using stereotyped formulas, attacked the so-called abuses of handicraft (*Handwerksmissbrauch*) in their official evaluations and decrees, in their prize-essays, articles, and reform pamphlets, throughout the 18th century. They called the customs of handicraft ridiculous, foolish, cruel, dangerous, and anachronistic, and they saw themselves as the vanguard of enlightened culture.

Their grievances seemed the more justified because the Imperial Patent of 1731, to Remedy Abuses among the Guilds, had failed to work. The older type of economic and constitutional history has studied extensively the reasons why attempts at reform had failed. The failure of those reform initiatives was seen as proof for the decline of the old handicraft.[2] Historians have, however, almost entirely ignored the fact that the history of trade policies and guild battles was also a chapter in the conflict between two cultures. This conflict between the dominant culture of the Enlightenment and popular culture was, indeed, an important part of the concept of the reform of popular culture. Seen from this perspective the decline of handicraft takes two contrary forms: on the one hand, it appears as degeneration and stubbornness, on the other hand as a last attempt to ensure the social and political autonomy of the corporate guild system and a part of handicraft culture's resistance against the bureaucratic state and its policy of police (*Policey*). What the authorities and enlightened public opinion regarded as abuse was for the guilds the basis of their craft honor.

The greater part of what we know about handicraft culture does not originate from artisans. It comes from laws, decrees, memoirs, juridical dissertations, prize-essays, and journals – that is to say, from the culture of the educated classes. These sources reflect a certain form of perception that we must distinguish from the perception of the world of handicraft itself. Therefore, research on the perceptions of the educated classes must be part of an analysis of popular culture itself. In the case of German journeyman culture the problem of sources does not seem insurmountable. For the German intelligentsia of the 18th century did not live totally separated from the world of handicraft. For example, one important author, Johann Andreas Ortloff, professor on the Faculty of Law at Erlangen, had himself been a journeyman in his youth; he knew the problems of a traveling journeyman from personal experience.[3] Anyway, the research of Friedrich Frisius, rector at Altenberg, who in 1708 used the most modern methods of inquiry, provides ample evidence that the culture of the educated classes (*Gebildete*) was not always hostile to and contemptuous toward popular culture.[4] On the contrary, his work shows the first intimations of a scientific interest in the world of the common man.

The world of handicraft, as defined in social and legal terms and as accentuated by customs and rituals, forms a specific and discrete segment of the broad spectrum of popular culture. Shaped by the guild system, urban handicraft culture differed from that of the peasants. Handicraft culture was distinguished by its own tradition, its own myths, and its own rituals. The guilds organized both the working life and the leisure of their members. The internal structures of the guilds were characterized by egalitarian as well as by hierarchical patterns. Their collective organization, their pride in their work and their own skills, together with a high degree of literacy, created and strengthened the self-consciousness of craftsmen who thought themselves an elite in the world of work.

But handicraft culture also shared many manifestations of popular culture. The life of peasants as well as of craftsmen was based on an economy of subsistence, organized as a family economy of the "whole house" (*Ganzes Haus*). The logic of this family economy combined economic processes and values with a specific form of social and moral behavior. Economic and social processes were regulated by symbolic and ritualistic forms of behavior and perception. Craftsmen as well as peasants saw no contradiction between a sparse regime for everyday life and conspicuous expenditure for festivals and rituals.[5] Therefore the reform of handicraft culture, promulgated by the educated classes and the authorities, was directed not only against a specific form of economy but also against a specific form of popular culture.

Corresponding to rural popular culture, urban handicraft culture was shaped by a particularism of a regional as well as an occupational aspect. Indeed, within the world of handicraft one should speak of a variety of craftsmen cultures, distinguishing shoemakers from printers and so on.[6] Every craft had its own culture, determined by its own skills and occupational customs and by a different degree of literacy. Every craft had its own rituals, festivities, and patron saints. The work that the craftsmen did determined their forms of behavior and consciousness: printing, for example, demanded a disciplined cooperation and favored self-consciousness and solidarity among the workers. Thus, as N. Davis has shown, collective work turned printers to a union earlier than journeymen in other crafts who worked alone.[7]

The journeymen, too, had their own culture. On the one hand, they shared occupational customs and skills with the masters in their craft; on the other, journeymen had their own organizations and traditions. Their brotherhoods were secret societies characterized by initiation rites and myths about the founders, by self-jurisdiction and autonomy. They formed a closed culture within handicraft, parallel to masters' guilds as well as to popular culture as a whole. Their particular organization and culture were the basis for their specific forms of refusal and resistance. The customs of handicraft were particularly strong among journeymen, whose rules of behavior were characterized more by tradition and customs than were those of the masters' guilds. The journeymen regarded themselves as the guardians of guild custom, for their careers were more threatened by the taint of dishonor than were those of established masters. Therefore, journeymen persistently defended their autonomy and tradition, and interventions by the authorities and the enlightened public concerned the journeymen above all. This is one reason why we know more about the customs of journeymen than about those of their masters.

But within the life of a craftsman, journeymanship and journeyman brotherhoods were a temporary phase. Journeymen hoped to become masters and, since they believed in the chances of such a promotion, they accepted the rules of the game within the guild. Moreover, masters and journeymen worked together in the same workshop and usually lived in the same house. Because of these similarities one should not exaggerate the differences among the various branches of handicraft. The different guilds cooperated during the major urban festivals and journeyman strikes were often supported by members of other crafts. For the purposes of analysis, therefore, we may construct an ideal type of handicraft culture and, in particular, of journeyman culture.

The German 18th century was the century of journeyman rebellions and strikes in spite of or, perhaps, because of the restrictive legislation of the Empire and the territorial states. The journeyman became nearly synonymous with rebellion; the fact shows that the reality of the Old Empire was characterized not only by quietism and silent decline but also by political and social conflicts with egalitarian aspects.[8] Moreover, journeymen's strikes give the historian of popular culture the chance to analyze more directly the patterns of behavior and values in journeyman culture, for "actions speak louder than words."[9]

The rebellious journeymen, their rituals and riots, were the main cause for all complaints about the abuses of handicraft and provoked the laborious process of Imperial legislation concerning the guilds. The strike of the journeymen shoemakers of Augsburg in 1726 not only received great publicity, it convinced even the Emperor and territorial princes that they could rid handicraft of abuses only by far-reaching and generally supported regulations. The main object of the Imperial Patent of 1731, which was supported at best half-heartedly by the smaller territories and Imperial cities, was the abolition of the guilds' autonomy.[10] The authorities, seeking to centralize and to rationalize government on Colbert's model, tried to deprive the guilds of their semiofficial character as elements of a corporate tradition and to reduce them into instruments of economic regulation, a sort of occupational grouping. The handicraft community was threatened not only by the authorities' economic and political measures but even more by the insurmountable problem of excess recruitment in the trades. The handicraft community reacted with a policy of closure to ward off intruders from the outside as well as journeymen from within the trade.[11]

This double pressure, which was increasing in the second half of the 18th century, formed the background for the stubborn resistance of the masters' guilds and of the journeymen in defense of their corporate autonomy. Their resistance followed traditional patterns of action and value and, therefore, from the perspective of enlightened culture, looked like abuse and barbarity.

The definition of abuse was a function of the authorities' ideas about political and economic organization and of the enlightened elites' cultural values. The lawyer Kulenkamp defined the term in 1807: "All customs which are not confirmed by the authorities or which are repugnant to law or morality are abuses. They concern all parts of the guilds."[12]

Even if enlightened administration and public opinion agreed in defining the most important forms of abuses, their struggle against them was extremely difficult because use and abuse were mixed beyond recognition. Moreover, the culture of the *Gebildeten* failed to comprehend the characteristic interdependence of economic, social, moral, and legal standards within handicraft culture.

The subject of the *Imperial Patent of 1731 to Remedy Abuses among the Guilds* was not new. Imperial policies since the early 16th century had aimed to prohibit various handicraft customs. Obviously their effect was not very great, since every new decree justified itself by the failure of its predecessors. The catalogue of abuses, of course, had significantly lengthened from the 16th to the 18th century. Beside the prohibition of luxury, social legislation in the 16th century was directed against the exclusiveness of the so-called gift trades ("*geschenkte Gewerbe*"), those that gave subsistence money as a gift to the wandering journeymen. Other targets were the practices of public defamation (*Schmähen*), ostracism (*Unredlichmachen*), and disseminating libelous news (*Auftreiben*). In the *Imperial Decree* of 1672 other customary behaviors were forbidden: the violation of contracts, the strike, the secret ceremony in which one was made a journeyman (*Gesellenmachen*), and the rituals of wandering – which were all characterized as "some odd, ridiculous, irritating and dishonorable customs, called planing (*Hobeln*), polishing (*Schleifen*), preaching (*Predigen*), christening (*Taufen*), putting on unusual clothing, leading them around the street or sending them around and such things," and further, "their guild-greetings (*Handwerksgrüsse*), their silly turns of speech."[13] Moreover, excessive festivities and neglect of work, as on Saint Monday, were forbidden; some magical customs were also affected. Guilds punished members who worked with dogs' skins, or killed cats or dogs, or had touched carrion, even though the laws prohibited the guilds from punishing their members for such things. Finally, all supraregional forms of communication between craft guilds were prohibited, in particular the high guilds (*Hauptlade*) and the correspondence of journeymen brotherhoods. Some new regulations aimed to counteract the tendencies of isolation and seclusion: the fees for apprenticeship were to be diminished; in order to facilitate entrance into the craft guilds some occupations traditionally defined as dishonorable were to be declared honorable; moreover, the high fees for application for mastership usually caused by a masterwork, which was as expensive as it was unprofitable and old-fashioned, and by the costs of excessive food and drink for all the local masters were to be abolished or at least reduced. Finally, the authors hoped to break the masters' tendency to form cartels by forbidding all price and production agreements.

The *Imperial Patent of 1731* largely replicates this *Decree* of 1672. The only new point introduces a wandering certificate (*Kundschaft*), which was to ensure control over the journeymen during their wandering years. Nevertheless, the *Imperial Patent* of 1731 marked the culmination of German handicraft policy and of the suppression of autonomous guild rights in the 18th century because it permitted the territorial states to issue supplementary ordinances.[14]

The other addition to this decree of 1731 was the threat to dissolve the guilds in case of disobedience. However, the authorities, until the end of the Old Empire, steered a middle course between involuntary recognition of corporate autonomy and dissolution of the guilds, a course expressed in 1672 as "*Maneat usus, tollatur abusus.*"[15]

From the perspective of the early modern state, abuses were all tendencies toward corporate autonomy. The director of the Chamber of the Prussian province of Neumark, Hille, one of the most determined advocates of a rigid handicraft policy, complained about the artisans' wish for independence: "These people flatter themselves with a chimerical independence, like the students in the time of fagging. And they continue their absurd craft customs contrary to all rational territorial law, which is designed for their own conservation; they have nothing else in mind but their imaginary point d'honneur."[16] The insignia and symbols of guild autonomy, the guild chests, journeymen boards, and other ceremonial utensils passed in Hille's view for "idols" whose surrender to the administration he registered with satisfaction.[17] In 1793, during a wave of journeymen strikes, the Prussian finance official, Count Hoym, proposed to regard journeymen "only as paid workers, who do not form any legal corporation."[18] He did not weary of attacking their stubbornness and foolishness. "This class of people rebels against every reasonable order and law, is deaf to all remonstrances, and forms a state within the state with impunity."[19] It was the lawyers' ideas of *étatisme* and mercantilism, and their conviction about the superiority of enlightened government and communication, that shaped the endless quarrel with the craft guilds.

Although these efforts achieved a new intensity and a new theoretical basis in the Age of Enlightenment, the continuity with similar policies dating from the early 16th century is evident. Therefore we have to challenge Peter Burke's thesis. He described the reform of popular culture as a two-stage development: in the 16th century a reform based on theological and moral considerations, and from the latter half of 17th century on secular considerations.[20] As far as German handicraft culture is concerned, we observe from as early as the 16th century a strong secular motivation that accompanies the religious one.

Theological criticism was aroused by the adoption of Christian ceremonies, and that of journeyman baptism caused particular offense. The preacher of Oderberg in Prussia complained about this ceremony among the potters, and their disdain for God and his gospel. He thought them to be anti-Christians and tempters.[21] When questioned by the authorities the potters denied "that they abused or denounced the Holy Sacrament and the Ministry" and they called attention to the fact "that this ceremony was in use in the whole Holy Roman Empire, in Poland and Denmark."[22]

Handicraft festivals also caused offense. At the end of the 17th century the ministry at Frankfurt constantly demanded the abolition of festival customs that were regarded as desecrations of Christian feasts. In 1672 the reformers attacked the bakers' dance, in 1695 the fishers' ritual stabbing, in 1727 the "atrocities" of the *Sachsenhausen* feast-day festivals. "Not only did they eat greedily, guzzle and revel in their houses, but they are used to have a public procession with music and banners, whereby they set up desks for dice and gambling, where there is a lot of fraud and where a lot of useless money is wasted loosely by foolish people. Not only do they spend the day with a lot of luxury, but they continue their godless excesses until late in the night or early in the morning."[23]

The complaint of Christian Gerber, preacher at Loschwitz near Dresden, about the "Unknown Sins of the World" received much publicity. In his "best-seller" he dedicated a whole chapter to "abuses and disturbances in every craft." He was shocked to have found in the course of his investigations so many "absurdities, foolishness and un-Christian customs, that I would not know where to begin, I could devote an entire book to it."[24] Therefore he only gave a "brief impression" of this un-Christian behavior of the journeymen, and decided to leave the rest to the authorities. With outspoken disgust he described journeyman baptism and castigated the blasphemous character of this custom. "They defame and desecrate the ceremonies of the Holy Christian Church, abusing the Bible and making a mockery of it. They defame the servants of God by repeating their formulas *alloquendi* and phrases which they have picked up from the apostles. . . . To say nothing of their way to make journeymen, which offends Christian love and honor, because the journeyman is treated as a fool, vexed, pushed, pulled, thrown, wetted and given an insulting nickname. Finally they booze him up and harm his health."[25] Finally, the report of a "damned, infernal" journeyman Shrove Tuesday sermon made him fear for his own salvation. "I myself worry that these insulting and blasphemous phrases will come into my mind and will entangle me, when I shall speak with God seriously and piously."[26] Therefore he confined himself to an annotated selection of some blasphemous phrases and summed up: "Our entire service of worship, with sermons, prayers, pleas, and thanksgivings, was blasphemed."[27]

In the Age of Enlightenment, however, such complaints became rare while learned dissertations about the statutes and customs of handicraft increased. Written by lawyers or economists, they stressed the constitutional or economic aspect. During the first half of the 18th century, juridical essays were superior in numbers. Later contributions came from the cameralists, who beside the legal aspect censured the abuses of the handicraft trades from the point of view of economic *dirigisme* and economic utility.[28] While the cameralists followed a moderate course, seeking reform and not abolition of the craft guilds, the few German partisans of physiocracy like Schlettwein doubted the chances of guild reform and demanded their radical abolition.[29]

To the first category belongs the voluminous *Dissertatio juridica de abusibus qui in Germania nostra in Collegiis vigent opificum,* written by Christian Heinrich Hiller in 1729, which is part of the debate about the Imperial Trade Edict.[30] Hiller drew up a list of all abuses named in police ordinances since 1530, which demonstrated the development and extension of the legislation concerning handicraft statutes. The lawyer Joseph Lomberg in his *Historisch-politische Staatsrechtliche Abhandlung* of 1779 called justified any handicraft custom that the authorities had confirmed and that served the public welfare.[31] Those that were illegal and inappropriate, and that were detrimental to the livelihood and property (*Nahrungs- und Vermögensstand*) of the community, he termed abuses. Sharing the institutional and economic viewpoint of cameralism, he wanted to maintain the guilds as economic instruments and occupational groups.

Economic *dirigisme* as a characteristic feature of enlightened despotism was a topic in several journals of the German Enlightenment, which made the idea of the *bonum commune* and sometimes of free labor the criterion of their economic and social articles. The anonymous author of an article in the *Schleswig-Holsteinsche Provinzialberichte* regarded the guilds as an anachronism. "The idea of the guilds remains one of the greatest inconveniences . . . because they form a class of citizens, who isolate themselves, and who finally abuse the concentration of power to the damage of the public and who sometimes usurp an authority which violates the law."[32] The economic aspect becomes more evident in an article written by Baron von Seckendorff, who proclaims the freedom of labor. "Livelihood (*Nahrung*) has to be free, not regulated by any guild. This will be a harsh lesson for the craft guilds."[33]

Both authors agreed with the policy of the absolutist state, which regarded the prejudices and abuses of the craft guilds as a contradiction of the idea of "culture and perfection" and which asserted their "pernicious influence on the moral and economic condition of this class of citizens."[34]

The idea of utility was also a criterion for the classification of abuses from the pen of Johann Heinrich Firnhaber, whose *Historisch-politische Betrachtungen der Innungen und deren Zweckmässigkeit* of 1782 answered the challenge of the economic theory of physiocracy.[35] Firnhaber's position was that of conservative reform. He admitted that the radical critique of the craft guilds was justified but he tried to avoid their abolition through the reform of abuses. Firnhaber distinguished four categories of handicraft abuses: first, impediments to access to apprenticeship; second, impediments to application for mastership; third, those abuses that were detrimental to the masters themselves; and fourth, those that were detrimental to the cities.

In the first group he numbers the exclusion of people born illegitimate or as sons of craftsmen from dishonorable trades, the long duration of the apprenticeship, the humiliating treatment of apprentices, the unjustifiable increase of the price of the certificate of birth and apprenticeship, the refusal to issue such documents for the pettiest of formal reasons, and, finally, the humiliating and superfluous ceremonies during admission to the group of journeymen (*Gesellenmachen*).

To the second category, impediments to application for mastership, belong the obligation to make a useless masterpiece, the payment of high fees, excessive and expensive celebrations while the candidate presented his masterpiece, the preference for masters' sons or those who married a master's widow or daughter, and finally the long years of wandering and their precise justification, and the exclusion of those who had not been trained in the guilds.

In the third group one finds several customs that signal increasing social conflict between masters and journeymen: the journeymen's "bad practice" of leaving the master's workshop without observing the regulations of work and the threat of journeymen to leave the master and to boycott his workshop by denouncing him.

In the fourth category Firnhaber numbers "the journeymen's mischievous behavior" during their wandering, especially begging and, in particular, their participation in riots and strikes.[36]

The debate over the abuse of the handicraft trades in the 18th century generated certain recurrent arguments and criticisms. These were, first, corporate autonomy and jurisdiction, second, the customs of work and those of fraternity, and third, their celebration customs. From the economic perspective of utility, which was the dominant view at the end of the century, the efforts toward monopoly and the cartel agreements of the masters' guilds were condemned as much as the disturbance of production by journeymen's strikes and boycotts. Even the moral argument, directed at the excessive celebrations and banquets, had taken on an economic hue because drinking bouts caused an "inability to work for one or more days."[37] But all critics agreed in condemning the journeymen and their abuses as the main danger.

Before discussing journeyman culture in greater detail, I address the instruments with which the authorities and publicists wanted to combat the abuses of handicraft in general and the journeymen in particular. First of all, they recommended an extension and strengthening of governmental control: no meeting of a craft guild was to be held without knowledge and surveillance by the local authorities. Guild punishments were only to be legal if the verdict were reached in the presence of the authorities. At the end of the 18th century the territories, and in particular Prussia, tried to regulate the wandering of journeymen and put the journeymen hostels (*Herbergen*) under public supervision.

The limited effect of these ordinances and controls confirmed the reformers in their hope for the influence of education and refinement. One should strike the evil at its roots, Firnhaber announced, and, believing in reason and enlightment, he was of the opinion that journeymen should be taught to think rationally.[38] The reformers' interest turned to the journeymen's wandering, whose advantages were to be preserved by reform and rationalization. In order to ensure a better preparation for the wandering they proposed better private and public instruction and the planning of the wandering-route with the help of books on geography and trade. During the wandering the journeymen were to be supported by welfare institutions, in order to avoid the pernicious hostels.[39]

The number of pamphlets of advice increased at the end of the century; they were part of an educational offensive by the popular Enlightenment.[40] And the authorities also relied on education and training as well as on control and repression. The wandering patent of the small principality of Öttingen-Wallerstein in South Germany tried to apply the discussion about reform in order to improve regional trade.[41] Enlightened Prussia, too, hoped to make use of the supervised guilds as instruments of education. The *General Patent* for all craft guilds demanded school training before or during apprenticeship and, as part of the apprentice's final examination, a basic knowledge of the catechism, reading, writing, and arithmetic.[42]

Firnhaber and the others knew that the reform of journeyman culture would require long, arduous learning: one would have to deal with "common people upon whom usually a rational argument makes little impression, since they think it would offend their rights."[43]

This remark reflects two fundamental perceptions. First, there was a gap between popular culture and enlightened culture in regard to their way of thinking and perceiving. Second, the reference to rights (the old law) was the main legitimation and argument of the craft guilds in their conflict with the authorities. The customary behavior of masters and journeymen expressed this old law as well as their perception of their environment. The craft customs regulated all social and working relations within the guild and secured the coherence of the group. How well aware craftsmen were of this integrative function of handicraft custom is illustrated by the defense of a journeyman baker from Berlin in 1702: he feared "that the result of the abolition of this or other customs would be the total dissolution (*Zernichtung*) of the brotherhood and the bakers' guild."[44]

Enlightened culture saw these customs as anachronistic, morally reprehensible, and politically dangerous. By the end of the century journeymen were also doubting the legitimation of handicraft customs and criticized the pressure to conform to group standards. Beside individual petitions to the authorities, some evidence exists that there were protests coming from a minority that resented control of its affairs by the brotherhood.[45] In 1768, sixty-two journeymen joiners from Berlin complained about the federation's increasing fees (*Auflage*) and about the fact that they were compelled to join in carousals and banquets.[46] Every evening at the hostel collective festivities would be held; every journeyman would be listed by the chest journeyman (*Ladengeselle*). He would collect the carousal fees, would stay away from work, and live in idleness during the tenure of his office. Whoever refused to pay would be treated by the *Ladengeselle* "in the most humiliating way" and mistreated by his indignant companions; so that most meetings would end in violence.

The bookbinder Adam Henss confirmed in his memoirs of wandering at the end of the 18th century this complaint about the pressure of handicraft customs. Supraregional communication was, in the opinion of Henss, the main reason for their persistence. "When I go elsewhere, I risk them breaking my arms and legs; when I return home to become a master, then they will reject me and the authorities do not protect me."[47]

Three abuses of journeyman culture are commonly identified: the customs of federation and wandering, the customs of celebration, and journeymen jurisdiction and strikes. These three phenomena depend on one another just as the craft world is characterized by the interdependence of economic, social, and moral functions, of technological and anthropological processes. The main motive for the constitution of journeymen federations was the organization of the wandering, which had been an obligation since the 16th century. Wandering required the supraregional validation of the group's patterns of value and the strict control of their members. Critics of the abuses of journeyman culture point out that the "foreign" journeymen in particular were the main actors in meetings and strikes.[48] Indeed, wandering promoted the journeymen's group consciousness.

On the other hand, the obligation to wander confirmed the increasing competition within the guilds and the defensive policy of the masters against pressure from below. For the real function of the wandering was not to train journeymen but to ease the labor market.[49] Therefore, the abuses of journeymen resulted from the very social and economic coercive measures that had provoked the expansion of the wandering. The abuses of journey-

men largely reflected mounting social conflicts within the handicraft.[50]

Critics regarded as the extreme moral danger during the wan-
dering-years the seduction of begging and idleness, which they
traced back to the liberality of the handicraft's gift (*Handwerks-
geschenk*). This gift was given to wandering journeymen on their
arrival or departure. According to the reformers, it came from the
various arbitrary fines the guilds collected, and, they continued,
the gift was wasted on drunken celebrations. This would cause the
loss of working hours and fights as well as an increasing laziness
and begging. The generous support of the gift would seduce young
men into evading harder work.[51]

The many efforts of the authorities to reduce the amount of
the gift and to ensure that only the over-journeyman might
dispense it were repugnant to the collective character of the journeymen. The absence of this act of welcome was seen as a sign of
poverty of the craft guild.[52] In order to ensure social integration
and distinctiveness, handicraft culture – like popular culture as
a whole – spared no conspicuous expenses, even if they caused
pecuniary damage.

The arriving journeyman had to prove his membership to the
group by the standard greeting (*Gruss*) and he had to ask for the
gift, which means that he demanded the assistance of the group in
finding a place of work (*Umfrage*). While the strict observance of
the greeting formula served, in a nonliterate culture, as a severe
control of membership, the gift was also a proof of integration
into the local group and their living and working environment.
This symbolic act, performed after fourteen days' probation
during the *Auflage*, required the presence of the whole group. The
fact that the gift was also handed to journeymen who did not
find work and had to wander again demonstrates the hostel's
function as an employment agency as much as the continuity of
group surveillance during the wandering.

The right to control hiring was stubbornly defended by all
journeymen because control of the labor market was the basis
of their social influence. As long as the journeymen held control,
they had a weapon against their masters. When, at the instigation
of the masters, the joiner journeymen of Berlin became the target
of an ordinance aimed at the abuses of meetings (*Auflage* and
*Umfrage*) four hundred of them left the city.[53]

The *Auflage* had been an offense since the 16th century. Its
ritual was held to be ridiculous and anachronistic, and it was
attacked as stimulating excessive carousals that were obligatory
for all journeymen. The fact that the *Auflage* usually took place
on Saint Monday was an additional affront. The *Auflage* itself was
of great importance in the conformity and integration of the
group. It served to control moral conformity and self-government in the group. A constituent part of the *Auflage* was the
collection of fees.

The *Auflage* at the hostel followed a severe ritual with standardized phrases.[54] After a ceremonial opening of the chest, which
formed the symbolic center of the group, a ritual inquiry began in
order to screen the social and moral behavior of those present and
to sanction, if necessary, that of deviators. The legitimacy of this
jurisdiction rested on the opening of the chest as a symbol of the
validity of the old law and the submission of the group under its
traditional norms. When the chest was closed a collective carousal
began; this was an integral part of the rite, for the powers of
jurisdiction during the *Auflage* remained valid during the subsequent banquet. (This is proved by complaints about compulsion,
provocations, and arbitrary penalties during the banquet.)[55]
Another form of collective constraint was the so-called "burn-
off" (*Abbrennen*), which meant that deviators were forced to
observe Saint Monday and to pay for drink.[56] The counter-measures
taken by the Prussian government in the 1790s first reduced the
fees of the *Auflage*. Then the abolition of the *Auflage* and the
collection of social fees in the workshop were decreed. Eventually,
all these measures were directed against the hostel culture and
favored the substitution of their social and occupational function
by rational and controlled institutions.

The hostels were identified as the "main cause of all the abuses"
and the place of "the real seduction of all tidy journeymen."[57]
The hostel was a place of collective festivals and banquets as well
as a place of self-jurisdiction and an employment agency. It was
a center of social influence and social protest for the journeymen
as much as a place of socialization into the moral standards of
the group through initiation rituals. The abolition of the hostels
would have struck at the center of social and normative action.[58]
Just as the journeymen should be regarded as ordinary paid
workers, the reformers demanded that "having abolished all

ceremonies" the hostel should be treated an "ordinary inn for wandering journeymen or even better an institution for out-of-town invalids and the poor."[59] In reducing the hostels to a function of social welfare, authorities and masters hoped to strike journeyman culture at its heart, to erase its autonomy and the locus it provided for a network of supraregional communication.

Controlling the hostels was also a means to combat Saint Monday, included in every catalogue of abuses. A Prussian functionary calculated that this abuse, which was said to lead to idleness and excesses, cost two months' work in any one year, let alone the losses of the masters and the journeymen themselves.[60] A Prussian decree against Saint Monday forbade entrance to hostels before Monday evening and recommended higher wages for additional work done on Monday.[61]

In the view of the authorities and public opinion Saint Monday was an opportunity to reduce the number of working days and to prolong the Sunday carousals, while the journeymen believed that Saint Monday served for "their diversion on occasion of the *Auflage.*"[62] They saw the connection between "fête" and organization. Folklorists could prove the nexus between Saint Monday and the self-government of the brotherhood.[63] Monday was the day of the *Auflage* as well as the beginning of the wandering. The increasing numbers of Saint Mondays, originally four in one year and eventually fourteen, was the consequence of the extension of wandering. There was another reason to choose the Monday: it was the best time to collect fees after the payment of wages on Sunday. Both acts, the *Auflage* as well as departures, demanded the presence of all members and, therefore, this day had to be free of work for all.

At the same time Saint Monday expressed the journeymen's disposition to arrange their work themselves.[64] To divide work from leisure strictly was unknown in a world of production marked by an inchoate division of labor and a high degree of independence in working. Undone work could be made up by extra work. Praising the time of nonwork was standard in journeymen's songs but it did not contradict their pride in their work. Both were often praised in the same song.[65]

Preparation for wandering and training in the norms of the group was the object of the initiation rituals, especially of the so-called *Gesellenmachen*, one of the highlights in the hostel culture.

The ritual of *Gesellenmachen* was extremely rich in those trades where wandering was obligatory (*geschenkte Gewerbe* or gift trades). While the Enlightenment regarded this ceremony as the quintessence of ridiculous customs, folklorists since Friedrich Frisius collected as much information about this secret procedure as possible. In contrast to the Enlightenment, the brothers Grimm regarded the ritual of *Gesellenmachen* as a proof of the "cheerful, tender, awkward and sensuous character" of craft guilds, which the Enlightenment had been wrong to reform.[66]

The initiation rituals of the journeymen followed the classical pattern of all archaic social movements. They were divided into three phases: division, transition, and incorporation.[67] Every act in this rite had a symbolic function and taught the participant to join a closed, hierarchical, but fraternal, group. Entering the journeyman's rank was an important change of status, as the humiliating rites emphasized. They signified purification from the former status and stressed the necessity of absolute conformity with the norms of the group.

The first phase, the division, was performed in the darkness of the admission room by such purification rituals as the removal of a blotch or a cow's tail, which had been affixed before the ceremony. In the second phase, the transition, the novice had to suffer tortures that symbolized his submission to the rules of the group. The giving of a new name and a three-fold baptism meant the transition to a new status, which was completed by an oath and incorporation into the standardized speech patterns of the group. Now the member was called brother.[68]

At the same time this ceremony served as training in the social norms of the group and the specific norms of behavior during the wandering years. Arrival and departure, entrance into the hostel, conduct in the master's house, and the notice of intention to leave the master were rehearsed in standardized phrases and, thereby, impressed on the journeyman's mind as token of his membership. To observe these minute formulas in an illiterate culture was of great importance for access to a strange labor market. Conversely, the observance of the values of the group ensured their main function — control over the local and supraregional labor market.

These complicated ceremonies were incomprehensible to the partisans of utilitarianism. But they were indispensible for integration into the craft world. The disproportion between symbolic action and the social framework was even more evident in the case of the journeymen's strikes. An increasing wave of such strikes in the last third of the 18th century was seen by the public as an abuse and a great danger to law and order.[69] From the point of view of the journeymen it was an increasingly unsuccessful use of their traditional forms of protest against the decline of their social status.

All the journeymen's strikes of the 18th century, and those of the French Revolution, had a reactive character. They reacted against a real or supposed violation of common law or status by members of the guild themselves or by the authorities. Their object was the restoration of corporate honor, either as a traditional magical purification after an act that had disgraced the group or one of its members or as restitution of the group's autonomous jurisdiction and control of the labor market. The reference to the old law also legitimized strikes over wages, whose object was the restitution of the old reward and the just price.

The execution and the success of a strike depended on the journeymen's supraregional communication, solidarity, and discipline. The normative conformity of its members was the precondition for a boycott of a workshop or a whole city, which was regulated by an interurban exchange of letters (*Laufbriefe*). This was the real meaning of all symbolic actions — they were to ensure the solidarity and discipline of the members. So long as the brotherhood preserved these essentials and so long as the organization of wandering and the control of the labor market were maintained, the journeymen were equipped with remarkable social power. In this respect, wandering had a function beside training and improvement of the labor market: it was an instrument of social protest.

The most symbolic action in the strike was to take along the chest. Apart from its practical function as a strike-fund, the chest had a magical importance as the symbolic center of the group. After its removal from a city under boycott, no honest work could be performed there. A violation of this boycott, which would have been communicated in all directions, would have meant disgrace and danger for the strikebreaker's career.[70]

In contrast to the riots of the urban lower classes the journeymen's strikes were anything but spontaneous, emotional protests.

There are many indications that there existed a conscious timing of the strikes to make use of a given economic situation.[71] The greater part of strikes was planned by the journeyman group at the hostel in a democratic decision-making process. (Thus the difference between preindustrial conflict behavior in the handicrafts and industrial forms of strike was not so great as it was supposed to be.)[72]

In spite of their loss of status, journeymen were conscious of belonging to a trade elite with a clear code of honor and behavior; it did not permit them to make common cause with the urban lower classes. Records of the strikes of the 1790s attest, in spite of their critical attitude toward journeymen's actions, to their "refusal of violence, excesses, or insults."[73] At Hamburg, one observer related, the journeymen still "conducted themselves with honor and respect for the laws" and they "scornfully rejected the offer of the mob to support them in looting or plundering or in attacking the guards."[74]

Their traditional behavior, which reacted against the violation of old rights and was, therefore, more restorative than revolutionary, remained vital even during the French Revolution, whose influence was reduced to the formal inclusion of some of its watchwords. The joiner journeymen at Hamburg in 1791, during the ritualized act of a toast to health, drank not only to the welfare of their guild but also to the welfare of freedom and revolution. But the toast was as much motivated by a wish to provoke and by sensationalism as another toast during the same strike to the health of the "convolution." "Whether this meant revolution or constitution," the observer noted, "will remain unknown."[75] Only with difficulty could the journeymen conceal the persistence of their old corporate liberties behind their demand for freedom. And they did not invent the use of revolutionary concepts of freedom and human rights for their own corporate interest: the idea that the journeymen's strikes of the 1790s represented an increasing political consciousness was held by the educated classes and the authorities. But this interpretation missed the main issue of the journeymen's behavior as much as it missed the meaning of journeyman culture in general. The procession during the strike is also evidence for traditional patterns of protest. They observed the traditional divisions between the guilds and maintained the essence of traditional festival behavior. They carried their insignia, generally tools, as a sign of their pride in their labor, in a solemn ceremonious procession through the city, passing the hostel and the city hall as the centers of opposed positions of right, in order publicly to represent their claim.[76] This strike procession recalls the general processions of journeymen.[77] Their conflict behavior reveals the close connection between *"fête et révolte,"* which was inherent in several forms of popular culture.[78] The conflict potential in festival customs became apparent not only in the ceremonies of the procession but also in the rhymed addresses of the over-journeymen who constantly alluded to their determination to defend their rights and autonomy.[79]

The validity of these traditional value patterns within the craft guilds had already been weakened and the social distance between master and journeymen had increased; it was the masters who stimulated the repression of the federations of journeymen and their hostels at Berlin as well as at Frankfurt. At Frankfurt and elsewhere the journeymen's chest was abolished, their leader (*Ladengeselle*) removed, the *Auflage* and other meetings forbidden.[80]

Nevertheless, complaints of the authorities and measures against the abuses of handicraft persisted during the first half of the 19th century. An 1823 decree of the King of Hannover named the same abuses of journeymen as had other decrees a century earlier.[81] Public discussion about the problems of the trades brought the same complaints about the abuses of handicraft that the publicists of the 18th century had recited.[82] In 1839 the authorities in some states of Northern Germany discovered an interurban network of journeymen masons, who had boycotted the masonry of Hamburg.[83] Their conflictual behavior proved the persistence of the traditional norms and patterns of action. But combat against the journeymen's federations took on a political aspect with the 1830s, for the revolutionary German democratic or socialist intelligentsia succeeded in politicizing and organizing some journeymen. The traditional struggle against the abuses of handicraft assumed an antirevolutionary turn, and the authorities forbade wandering in those states where revolutionary workers' associations existed.[84]

Apart from pauperization and loss of status, one precondition of this process of political organization was the collectivist tradition of crafts guilds and their latent conflict potential. Those journeymen who now called themselves "workers" (*Arbeiter*) meant to rediscover their corporate tradition in the promising watchword "*association*." This password suggested the old principles of solidarity, the moral quality of organized work, and mutualism. The journeymen's reception of the idea of association demonstrates the revolutionary potential inherent even in old-fashioned, corporate forms of thinking and living.[85]

Nevertheless, the intellectual agents of early socialism recognized the fundamental difference between the patterns of value and perception in the culture of the educated classes and those in popular culture. In this respect they stood in the tradition of the Enlightenment and its effort to reform popular culture.

While enlightened public opinion and the authorities made continuous efforts to treat the guilds as purely economic institutions and to interpret the guilds' actions from a utilitarian perspective, the guilds regarded themselves as corporations with their own privileges and dues, their own values of behavior and customs, and with a specific organization of work. The interdependence of economic, social, and moral processes is a characteristic feature of the guilds and especially of the culture of journeymen, who regarded themselves as the guardians of this culture. The values of such a culture, which correlates with an "embedded economy,"[86] lead the social activities of its members to extra-economic fields and norms. Social appreciation depends on the observance of those moral values. They regulate the social conduct and the integration of the group. Customs were the symbolic expression of these patterns of values, their function to stabilize the normative system of the group, ensure its conformity, and regulate social and economic relations within the group. Therefore, the way of acting often took a symbolic character. The legitimation of the craft customs rested on an appeal to the old law. The power of integration, mediated by customs, depended on the custom's general validity. Mutual control and sanctions ensured the coherence of the group.

The focus of this normative system of handicraft was the idea of honor. The observance of this corporate notion of honor determined the logic of crafts' customary behavior. Corporate honor meant decent living and working, observing the norms of mutualism and solidarity and the rules of the guild. The notion of honor was bound to the honest practice of work and to honest social, legal, and human behavior. The high standard of this corporate morality is characterized by a curious stock expression: "The guilds must be as pure as if they had been gathered together by doves."[87]

A good deal of the journeymen's social activities were directed by the observance of this corporate honor in the field of noneconomic action, even at the cost of economic disadvantage. The division of life into a public and a private sphere, proposed by the authorities and public opinion, meant for the guilds a fundamental attack on its tradition. It was an attack against a polyfunctional order, where work and social interaction could not be divided.

In the view of the journeymen any attack on their corporation was a violation of honor. They perceived and reacted to social, economic, and human problems through the notion of honor and its restitution. The journeymen's strikes, too, did not serve primarily economic interests. They were, even in disputes over wages, mediated by the idea of honor. And therefore the strikes too were a ritual of purification and followed forms of symbolic action.[88]

Reinforcement through ritual action within the journeymen's group, which in the view of enlightened public opinion passed for brutalization and an increase in abuses, rested in the logic of their traditional behavior. It reflected the increasing discrepancy between the normative system of the journeyman group and their environment. The greater the pressure from outside became, the more stubbornly they defended their customs. The expenses of maintaining this traditional value pattern and behavior became disproportionate compared to the benefits and the protection the group could offer. Thus an increasing number of its members interpreted the traditional forms of integration as compulsory and an abuse.

NOTES

1. Wigulaus X. A. Kreittmayr, *Abhandlung vom Handwerksrecht* (Munich: 1768). I want to thank Michael Beer (Erlangen), who is preparing a dissertation about the wandering journeymen of the 18th century, for this reference.

2. For example Moritz Meyer, *Geschichte der Preussischen Handwerks politik,* 2 vols. (Minden: 1864–66); Johannes Heinrich Gebauer, "Das Hildesheimer Handwerkswesen im 18. Jahrhundert und das Reichsgesetz von 1731 gegen die Handwerksmissbräuche," *Hansische Geschichtsblätter,* 1917–18, pp. 157–87. The best modern study is Wolfram Fischer, *Handwerksrecht und Handwerkswirtschaft um 1800: Studien zur Sozial- und Wirtschaftsverfassung vor der industriellen Revolution* (Berlin: 1955); also, Mack Walker, *German Home Towns: Community, State and General Estate 1648–1871* (Ithaca, N.Y.: 1971), pp. 73–108.

3. Johann Andreas Ortloff, *Corpus Juris Opificiarii, oder Sammlung von allgemeinen Innungsgesetzen und Verordnungen für die Handwerker* (Erlangen: 1804); J. A. Ortloff, *Beantwortung der Preisfrage: Wie können die Vorteile, welche durch das Wandern der Handwerksgesellen möglich sind, befördert, und die dabey vorkommenden Nachteile verhütet werden?* (Erlangen: 1798).

4. Friedrich Frisius, *Der vornehmsten Kunstler und Handwerker Ceremonial- Politica, in welcher nicht allein dasjenige, was bey den Aufdingen, Lossprechen und Meister werden nach den Articuls-Briefen unterschiedener Oerter, von langer Zeit her in ihren Innungen und Zunften observiert worden, sondern auch diejenigen lächerlichen und bisweilen bedenklichen Actus wie auch Examina bey dem Gesellenmachen ordentlich durch Fragen und Antworten vorstellen und mit nutzlichen Anmerckungen zufälliger Gedanken ausführen wollen* (Leipzig: 1708); on Frisius see Georg Fischer, "Friedrich Friese, ein Wegbereiter deutscher Volkskunde," in Fischer, *Volk und Geschichte: Studien und Quellen zur Sozialgeschichte und Historischen Volkskunde* (Kulmbach: 1962).

5. See Hans Medick, "Plebejische Kultur, plebejische Offentlichkeit, plebejische Ökonomie: Über Erfahrungen und Verhaltensweisen Besitzarmer und Besitzloser in der Ubergangsphase zum Kapitalismus," in Berdahl et al., *Klassen und Kultur: Sozialanthropologische Perspektiven in der Geschichtsschreibung* (Frankfurt: 1982), pp. 157–204.

6. Peter Burke, *Popular Culture in Early Modern Europe* (London: 1978), pp. 36–42.

7. Natalie Z. Davis, "A Trade Union in Sixteenth-Century France," *Economic History Review* 19 (1966), pp. 48–69.

8. See Karl H. Wegert, "Patrimonial Rule, Popular Self-Interest and Jacobinism in Germany 1763–1800," *Journal of Modern History* 53 (1981), pp. 440–67.

9. Burke, *Popular Culture,* p. 75.

10. The text of this Patent is in Hans Proesler, *Das gesamtdeutsches Handwerk im Spiegel der Reichsgesetzgebung von 1530 bis 1806* (Berlin: 1954).

11. See W. Abel et al., *Handwerksgeschichte in neuer Sicht* (Gottingen: 1970).

12. E. J. Kulenkamp, *Das Recht der Handwerker und Zünfte nach den Reichs- und Kurhessischen Landesgesetzen* (Marburg: 1807), p. 93.

13. Proesler, *Gesamtdeutsches Handwerk,* pp. 35–37.

14. For Prussia see Meyer, *Preussische Handwerkspolitik,* vol. 2.

15. Proesler, *Gesamtdeutsches Handwerk*, p. 36.
16. Meyer, *Preussische Handwerkspolitik*, 2:34.
17. Fischer, *Handwerksrecht*, p. 25.
18. Quoted in Rudolf Wissell, *Des Alten Handwerks Recht und Gewohnheit*, 2d ed. (Berlin: 1981), 3: 193.
19. Ibid., p. 204.
20. Burke, *Popular Culture*, pp. 207–34.
21. Quoted in Wissel, *Des Alten Handwerks Recht*, 3:249.
22. Ibid.
23. Quoted in Heinz Lenhardt, "Feste und Feiern des Frankfurter Handwerks," *Archiv für Frankfurts Geschichte und Kunst*, 5th series, 1 (1950), p. 76.
24. Christian Gerber, *Unerkannte Sünden der Welt*, 5th ed. (Dresden: 1708), p. 1319.
25. Ibid.
26. Ibid., p. 1326.
27. Ibid.
28. See Mack Walker, "Rights and Functions: The Social Categories of Eighteenth Century German Jurists and Cameralists," *Journal of Modern History* 50 (1978), pp. 234–51.
29. Johann August Schlettwein, *Die wichtigste Angelegenheit für das ganze Publikum oder die natürliche Ordnung in der Politik*, 2 vols. (Karlsruhe: 1772–73); on the guilds, especially Schlettwein's criticism in *Ephemeriden der Menschheit*, August 1776.
30. Christian Heinrich Hiller, *Tractatus Iuridico Politicus de Abusibus qui in Germania nostra in Collegiis Opificum vigent* (Tubingen: 1729).
31. Joseph Lomberg, *Historisch-politische Staatsrechts Abhandlung von der Abstellung der Missbräuche bei den Zünften und Handwerkern* (Bonn: 1786), p. 19.
32. Quoted in Kai Detlev Sievers, *Volkskultur und Aufklärung im Spiegel der Schleswig-Holsteinschen Provinzialberichte* (Neumunster: 1970), p. 127.
33. Ibid., p. 128.
34. Ibid.
35. Johann Heinrich Firnhaber, *Historisch-politische Betrachtung der Innungen und deren zweckmässige Einrichtung* (Hannover: 1782).
36. Ibid., p. 268.
37. Ibid., p. 291.
38. Ibid., p. 224.
39. See, beside Ortloff, *Beantwortung der Preisfrage*, especially Karl Friedrich Mohl, *Über die Frage: Wie können die Vortheile, welche durch das Wandern der Handwerksgesellen möglich sind, befördert und die dabei vorhandenen Nachteile verhütet werden* (Erlangen: 1798), and *Vom Wandern der Handwerksgesellen: Eine Abhandlung aus der Gewerbepolicey und dem Handwerksrecht* (Nuremberg: 1800).
40. See Reinhart Siegert, "Aufklärung und Volkslektüre: Exemplarisch dargestellt an Rudolph Zacharias Becker und seinem 'Noth- und Hilfs-

büchlein," " *Archiv für Geschichte des Buchwesens* 19 (1978), pp. 566–1347.

41. The text appears in Michael Stürmer, ed., *Herbst des Alten Handwerks: Zur Sozialgeschichte des 18.Jahrhunderts* (Munich: 1979), p. 211.
42. See Meyer, *Preussische Handwerkspolitik,* passim.
43. Firnhaber, *Historisch-politische Betrachtung,* p. 313.
44. Wissell, *Des Alten Handwerks Recht,* 3:257.
45. F. Fuhse, "Die Tischlergesellen-Bruderschaft im 18.Jahrhundert und ihr Ende: Nach den herzoglichen Polizeiakten," *Braunschweigisches Jahrbuch* (1911), pp. 1–45.
46. Quoted in Wissell, *Des Alten Handwerks Recht,* 3:203.
47. Adam Henss, *Wanderungen und Lebensansichten des Buchbindermeisters Adam Henss* (Weimar: 1845), p. 143.
48. See Ortloff, *Beantwortung der Preisfrage,* and Mohl, *Über die Frage.*
49. See Klaus J. Bade, "Altes Handwerk, Wanderzwang und Gute Policey: Gesellenwanderung zwischen Zunftökonomie und Gewerbereform," *Vierteljahrsschrift für Sozial- und Wirtschaftsgeschichte* 69 (1982), pp. 1–37.
50. Hermann Lenzen, *Lehrlinge und Gesellen in der Reichsstadt Köln* (diss. phil., Cologne: 1920).
51. "Abhandlung von Handwerks-Geschenken und geschenkten Handwerkerkern," *Leipziger Sammlungen* 5 (1749), p. 244.
52. See Wissell, *Des Alten Handwerks Recht,* 3: 266.
53. Andreas Griessinger, *Das symbolische Kapital der Ehre: Streikbewegungen und kollektives Bewusstsein deutscher Handwerksgesellen im 18. Jahrhundert* (Frankfurt and Berlin: 1981), p. 267.
54. See Frisius, *Der vornehmsten Künstler,* passim, and "Rede des Laden-Gesellen unter den Schneidern zu Nurnberg, bey ihrer vierwöchentlichen Auflage," in C. W. Gatterer, *Technologisches Magazin* (Memmingen: 1792) 2: 128–31, reprinted in Stürmer, *Herbst des Alten Handwerks,* p. 219.
55. See Wissell, *Des Alten Handwerks Recht,* 3: 205.
56. See Griessinger, *Symbolisches Kapital,* p. 259.
57. See Wissell, *Des Alten Handwerks Recht,* 3: 210.
58. Quoted in Griessinger, *Symbolisches Kapital,* p. 260.
59. *Leipziger Sammlungen* 5 (1749).
60. Quoted in Wissell, *Des Alten Handwerks Recht,* 3: 204.
61. *Edict wegen Abstellung einiger Missbräuche besonders des sogenannten Blauen Montages bey den Handwerkern* (Berlin: 1783).
62. Quoted in Griessinger, *Symbolisches Kapital,* p. 270.
63. Karl Koehne, "Studien zur Geschichte des blauen Montags," *Zeitschrift für Sozialwissenschaft,* n.s. 11 (1920), pp. 268–87, 394–414; in addition, H. F. Singer, *Der blaue Montag: Eine kulturgeschichtliche und soziale Studie* (Mainz: 1917).
64. Griessinger, *Symbolisches Kapital,* passim.
65. Oskar Schade, "Vom deutschen Handwerksleben in Brauch, Spruch und Lied," *Weimarsches Jahrbuch für deutsche Sprache, Literatur und Kunst* 4 (1856), pp. 214–44.

66. *Altdeutsche Wälder durch die Brüder Grimm* (Cassel: 1813), 3: 83.
67. See Van Gennep, *Les rites de passage* (Paris: 1909).
68. See Frisius, *Der Vornehmsten Künstler*, passim.
69. For the strike movement see Griessinger, *Symbolisches Kapital.*
70. For example Fuhse, *Tischlergesellen-Bruderschaft.*
71. For example the remarks of J. C. Händler, *Biographie eines noch leben-
den Schneiders von ihm selbst geschrieben* (Nuremberg: 1798), p. 72.
72. See Griessinger, *Symbolisches Kapital*, p. 425.
73. Ibid., p. 119.
74. J. A. Günther, "Über den Aufstand der Handwerksgesellen zu Hamburg
im August 1791, nebst einigen Reflexionen über Zunftsgeist und Zunft-
erziehung," *Journal von und für Deutschland* 8 (1791), p. 517 n. 7.
75. Griessinger, *Symbolisches Kapital*, p. 117.
76. Ibid., p. 115.
77. See Lenhardt, *Feste und Feiern.*
78. See Y. M. Berce, *Fête et révolte: Des mentalités populaires du XVI$^e$·
au XVIII$^e$ siècle* (Paris: 1976).
79. For example *Ruhm und Ehrengedächtnis bey dem Oberherrlich gnädig
erlaubten Aufzug der löblich und weltberühmten Schreinerzunft in der
Heil: Röm. Reichs Kaiserlichen freyen Stadt Nürnberg nebst einer
Lobrede welche ein Gesell abgelegt* (Nuremberg: 1768).
80. Griessinger, *Symbolisches Kapital*, p. 272.
81. Quoted in Wissell, *Des Alten Handwerks Recht*, 3: 215.
82. Hans-Peter Franck, *Zunftwesen und Gewerbefreiheit: Zeitschriftenstim-
men zur Frage der Gewerbeverfassung im Deutschland der ersten Hälfte
des 19. Jahrhunderts* (diss., Hamburg: 1971).
83. *Die Verbindung der Maurergesellen oder authentische Darstellung der bei
diesen Verbindungen üblichen Gebräuche* (Lubeck: 1841).
84. Josef Bopp, *Die Entwicklung des deutschen Handwerksgesellentums im
19. Jahrhundert unter dem Einfluss der Zeitströmungen* (Paderborn:
1932).
85. Hans-Ulrich Thamer, *Zunftideal und Zukunftsstaat: Zur Ideen- und
Sozialgeschichte des Frühsozialismus in Frankreich und Deutschland*
(Habilitationsschrift, Erlangen: 1980).
86. K. Polanyi, *Trade and Market in Early Empires* (Glencoe, Ill.: 1957),
p. 6.
87. Quoted in Helmut Möller, *Die kleinbürgerliche Familie im 18. Jahrhundert: Verhalten und Gruppenkultur* (Berlin: 1969), p. 208.
88. See Griessinger, *Symbolisches Kapital*, p. 389.

# Notes on the Contributors

Roger CHARTIER is a member of the Ecole des Hautes Etudes en Sciences Sociales whose Center for Historical Research he directs. He is co-author of *L'Education en France du XVIe au XVIIIe siècle* (1976), *La Nouvelle Histoire* (1978), *Histoire de la France urbaine*, volume III (1981), and *Histoire de l'Edition Française* (1983). He has also published *Figures de la gueuserie* (1982) and is working on a book devoted to popular reading in early modern France.

Carlo GINZBURG is Professor of Modern History at the University of Bologna. He is the author of *The Cheese and the Worms* (1980) and *The Night Battles* (1983). He is now writing a book on the witches' sabbat.

David D. HALL is Professor of History at Boston University. He has edited *The Antinomian Controversy, 1636–1638: A Documentary History* (1968) and is author of *The Faithful Shepherd: A History of the New England Ministry in the Seventeenth Century* (1972). He is presently writing on popular religion and popular culture in early New England.

Clive HOLMES is Professor of History at Cornell University and associate editor of the journal *Law in Past Time*. He is author of *The Eastern Association in the English Civil War* (1974) and of *Seventeenth Century Lincolnshire* (1980). His most recent work focuses upon the interaction of central government and local societies through the common law system in early modern England.

Steven Laurence KAPLAN is Professor of European History at Cornell University and founding editor of *Food & Foodways: Explorations in the History and Culture of Human Nourishment.* He is the author of *Bread, Politics and Political Economy During the Reign of Louis XV* (1976), *La Bagarre: Galiani's "Lost Parody"*

(1979), and *Le Complot de famine: histoire d'une rumeur au dix-huitième siècle* (1982). The Cornell University Press will publish his *Provisioning Paris: Merchants and Millers in the Grain and Flour Trades During the Eighteenth Century* in 1983–84.

Jacques LE GOFF is the former President of the Ecole des Hautes Etudes en Sciences Sociales, where he remains Directeur d'Etudes. He is also an editor of *Annales: Economies, Sociétés, Civilisations* and *Ethnologie Française.* Two of his many works on the Middle Ages have been translated into English, *The Intellectuals of the Middle Ages* (1974) and *Time, Work and Culture in the Middle Ages* (1980).

Günther LOTTES teaches history at the University of Erlangen-Nürnberg. He has written a book on English Radicalism in the late 18th century and is currently engaged in a study of the Enlightenment and the origins of conservative thought in Western Europe.

H. C. Erik MIDELFORT is Associate Professor of History at the University of Virginia. He is the author of *Witch Hunting in Southwestern Germany, 1562–1684: The Social and Intellectual Foundations* (1972), and translator of *Imperial Cities and the Reformation* by Bernd Moeller (1972) and of *The Revolution of 1525* by Peter Blickle (1981). He is currently working on a history of madness in sixteenth-century Germany.

Mary R. O'NEIL is Assistant Professor of History at the University of Washington in Seattle. Stanford University Press will publish her dissertation, "Discerning Superstition: Popular Errors and Orthodox Response in Late Sixteenth Century Italy." She is currently working on a study of Inquisition trials for superstitious offenses in 16th and 17th century Italy.

Jacques REVEL is Directeur d'Etudes at the Ecole des Hautes Etudes en Sciences Sociales and one of the editors of the *Annales: Economies, Sociétés, Civilisations.* He is the co-author of *Une Politique de la Langue* (1975) and of *La Nouvelle Histoire* (1978). He is currently working in early modern Europe socio-cultural history, with special attention to the relationship between high and popular culture.

Hans-Ulrich THAMER is Professor of Modern History at the University of Erlangen-Nürnberg. He is the author of *Revolution und Reaktion in der französischen Sozialkritik des 18. Jahrhunderts. Linguet, Mably, Babeuf.* (Frankfurt/Main, 1973) and co-author of *Faschistische und neofaschistische Bewegungen. Probleme empirischer Faschismusforschung* (Darmstadt, 1977). He is now working on a history of the Third Reich.

Richard C. TREXLER is Professor of History at the State University of New York at Binghamton. His most recent book is *Public Life in Renaissance Florence* (1980). His present research concerns the social history of the cult of the Magi, medieval prayer postures, and early colonial New Spain.

# Index

Aarne, Antti, 20, 26, 27
Abbrennon, 289
Absolutism, 235
Academie Française, 263
*Aeneid,* 23
Agassa Trial, 42
Aguilar, Sanchez de, 213
Alberic of Settifrati, 28
Alberti, Domenico, 240
Alceste, 264
Amiens, 238, 239, 240, 241
Anderson, Lord Chief Justice, 91
Animal Metamorphosis, 47
Anjou, 42
*The Antiquities of the Country People,* 6
Apparitions, 6, 12
Arab Medicine, 116–17
Aristocracy, 21
Aristotle, 116, 262
Armenian Church, 41
*Armer Konrad,* 162
Assyro-Babylonian, 23
Aquinas, Thomas, 32, 258
Auflage, 287, 288, 289, 294
Augustine, 32
Aussy, Legrand d', 268
Aztec Religion, 193
  Theatre, 208
Azzolini, Girolamo, 68, 69, 71

Bakhtin Mikhail, 234
Ballotta, Gasparina, 62, 63
Basel, 43, 44
Bartolomeo, Don, 74
Battista, Gian, 68
  Trial of, 67
*Benandanti* (Friulian), 45, 46, 47
Benedetto, Fra, 69, 70
Bercé, Yves-Marie, 165
Bern, 43, 44
Bernard, Richard, 92, 97, 102
*Bibliothèque bleue,* 30, 229, 231,

232, 234, 248, 249, 250, 263
Bibliothèque Nationale, 245
Black Death, 43, 44
Bodenham, Ann, 89
Bodin, Jean, 264
Bologna, 55, 56, 72
Bolognese Plan of 1577, 60
Borromeo, Cardinal Federigo, 73
Bourdieu, Pierre, 20, 21
Bourgeois, 12, 21
Bourne, Henry, 6, 7
Broadsheets, 243, 245
Buffon, 266
Burke, Peter, 6, 10, 11, 12, 113, 125, 147, 148, 172, 281
*Burkudzäutä,* 46

Calmet, Don, 260
*Calusarii,* 46
Calvinism, 16, 137, 139, 177, 242
Camporesi, Piero, 30, 31
Carnival, 11, 12, 16, 20, 148, 242
Carpo, Gasparino da, 69, 70
Cathars, 41, 44
Catholic Magic, 179
Celtic, 24, 268
Certeau, Michael de, 234
Chapbooks, 12, 15, 230, 243, 246, 247
Charivari, 14, 20
Charlemagne, 24
Charles V, 192, 194, 204, 209, 210
Charles The Fat, 24
Chartier, Roger, 6, 7, 13, 30, 229, 253
*The Cheese and The Worms,* 10, 12
Chichimecas, 193, 195, 196, 198, 199, 200, 204, 207, 208, 214
Christian Church, 6, 21
Christianity, 33
Christianization, 28, 31
Christians, 41

Church of England, 6
Ciudad Real, António de, 207
Classes, 5, 20, 86
Classicism, 6, 7
  French, 261, 263
Cocchiara, G., 256
Cohn, Norman, 39, 40, 41
Colbert, Jean-Baptiste, 278
Coleridge, Samuel, 7
*Compendio dell'arte essorcista*, 54
Confrerie de La Coquille, 242
Corpus Christi Dramas, 11
Correggi, Antonio de, 57, 58
Cortes, Hernán, 191, 192, 194,
  198, 202, 203, 204, 205, 208,
  209, 210
Cosmopolitanism, 8
Cotta, John 104
Council of Trent, 32, 174, 233
Counter-Culture, 21
Counter-Reformation, 235
Court de Gebelin, Antoine, 268
Crema, Aurelio da, 72
Criminal Law (English), 86
Cult of the Virgin Mary, 175, 177,
  178
"Culture as Appropriation," 13
"Culturalism," 149

*Daemonologie*, 104
"Dances of the Conquest", 202
Darcy, Brian, 88, 90, 91, 98
Darrell, John, 90
Davis, Natalie, 11, 14, 148, 149,
  165, 239, 277
Delcambre (Lorraine), 70
*De morbo Saturnino seu melancho-
  lia*, 123
*De Praestigiis Daemonum*, 139
"Destruction of Jerusalem," 202
Devil, 10
*Dialogues of Gregory The Great*, 34
Directory (French), 270
*Disquisitionum Magicarum Libri
  Sex*, 139
*Dissertation sur la nature des
  comètes*, 262

*Divine Comedy*, 32
Donatist, 72
"Dorfweistumer," 156
Dreyfus Affair, 42
Drinking, 169, 289
Dufresmoy, Lenglet, 265, 266
Durán, 202
Dürer, Albrecht, 115
Duvernoy, J., 42
Eagle Warriors, 200
Egyptian, 23
Egalitarian Tradition (in Germany),
  163
Eisenstein, E., 237, 241
*Eléments de l'Ideologie*, 267
Elisha, 28
Elizabethan Statute of 1563, 87
Emerson, Ralph Waldo, 7
*Encyclopédie*, 260
Endres, Robert, 161
Eneas, 23
English Ballads, 10
English Judicial System, 91
Engravings (French), 243–45
Enkidou, 23
Enlightenment, The, 16, 181, 256,
  260, 267, 270, 271, 275, 281,
  283, 286, 291, 295
*Epic of Gilgamesh*, 23
Estoile, Pierre de l', 246, 247
Ethnography (Mexico), 202, 211–
  17
  (France), 265–6
Euchitians, 44
*Europe's Inner Demons*, 39
Exemplum, 20
Exorcism, 60, 61, 73, 74, 101,
  135

Fabliau, 20
"Fairfax Girls," 88, 89
Feldgeschworenen, 175
Firnhaber, Johann Henrich, 284,
  285, 286
First Empire (France), 269
*Flagellum Daemonum*, 74
Fletcher, "Widow," 88

Foljambe, Godfrey, 90
Folklorization, 29
    Romantic, 272
Forbicino, Camillo, 67, 68
*Formicarius*, 44, 47
Fournier, Jacques, 42
Franciscan Tertiary, 68
French Revolution, 269, 270, 271, 292, 293
Freud, Sigmund, 16
Fries, Lorenz, 116, 117, 118
Frisius, Friedrich, 276, 291
*Fuga Daemonum*, 75

Galenism, 118, 119, 122, 124, 125, 140
Gasparina, 65
Gatto, Giuseppe, 27, 33
Geertz, Hildred, 85, 86
Gemeinde, 153, 155, 156, 157, 159, 160, 162, 164, 165, 166, 169
Gélis, Arnaud, 45, 46
General Patent, 286
Gerard (abbot), 29
Gerber, Christian, 282
Germany, Early Modern State in, 167–181
    Socioeconomic Crisis of 16th Century in, 170
Gesellenmachen, 291
Gifford, George, 87, 92, 97, 102, 103
Ginsburg, Carlo, 9, 10, 12, 30, 94, 233
Glanville, 97, 98
Godard, Guillaume, 240
Gomara, Lopez de, 203
Goodcole, Henry, 93
Graf, Arturo, 33
Gramsci, Antonio, 9, 147
Grégoire, 270, 271
Grimm Brothers, 291
Gruss, 288
Guido, 29
Guild Punishment, 285
"Gutswirtschaft," 152, 166

Hall, David, 2
Handicraft, 275, 288
    Culture, 276, 277, 281
Handicraft Festivals, 282
Harsnett, Samuel, 90
Hatfield Peveril Witches, 100
Herbalism, 115, 124
Herodotus, 47
Hille, 281
Hiller, Christian Heinrich, 283
Hippocrates, 122
Hispanicism, 208
Hoggart, Richard, 235
Holbein, Hans, 240
Holmes, Clive, 10
Holt, John, 90
Holy Roman Empire, 282
Honor (in Handicraft), 295
Hospitals (of Haina), 126, 128, 129, 130, 132
Humoral treatment, 125
Hunt, Robert, 90

*Images Volantes*, 237
Imperial Decree of 1672 (Germany), 279, 280
Imperial Patent of 1731 (Germany), 275, 278, 279, 280
Industrial Revolution, 19
Insanity and Religion (in Germany), 134
Inquisition, 12, 55, 56, 58, 59, 62, 67, 71, 74, 233; Trials, 42, 56, 60; Modenese, 57
Inquisitor of Evian, 44
Ireland, 26

Jacobean, 87
James VI, 104
Jansenist, 258
Jaucourt, Chevalier de, 260
Jesus, 31
Jesuits, 135, 205, 206
Jews, 42, 43, 44, 135, 209
Jewish Conspiracy, 41–44
Jezebel (Queen), 95

John of Ojun, 41
*Journal des Savants*, 262
Journeyman Culture (German), 276,
    277, 278, 279, 280, 284, 285,
    287, 291
Journeyman Strikes, 292, 293
Journeys in the otherworld, 23–25
Junkers, 152, 153, 154, 166

*Kallikantzaroi*, 46
Kammen, Michael, 2, 3
"Kammergericht," 153, 154
Kaplan, Steven, 1–3
Kemp, Ursley, 91, 97, 102
*Kerstniki*, 46
Kieckhefer, Richard, 86, 91
King Arthur, 32
King of the Underworld, 23
Kirch Weihkuchle, 173
"Klöpfleinsnachte," 158, 159, 180
Krüger, K., 161, 168
Kuhn, Johann, 120, 121, 122

Labarre, A., 238
Ladengeselle, 287, 294
Lamburano, Don Giacomo Bernardo, 71
Lancashire Trial of 1634, 99
*Land of Cokaygne*, 27
Land of Cokaygne, 25, 26, 31
Ladurie, Emmaniel Le Roy, 165
Lebrun, Pierre, 264, 265
*Légende Dorée*, 239
LeGoff, Jacques, 8, 9
Lepers' Conspiracy, 41–43
Livizzano, Margarita, 62, 63, 64
*Livrets Bleus*, 5, 13, 237, 248,
    250, 251
Loomis, Grant, 9
Lottes, Gunther, 7, 10
Luther, Martin, 134, 137
Lutherans, 135, 137, 138

Macfarlane, Alan, 85
Madness, 14, 114
Magic, 7, 8
Magic Flight, 47

Maleficium, Maleficio, 54, 55, 58,
    60, 61, 62, 64, 65, 68, 70, 71
Malpiglia, Camillo, 65
Manasses (King), 95
Mandrou, Robert, 231
Mantuanus, Battista, 202
*Margarita Medicine*, 115
Mariani, Maria de, 63, 70
Masks, 197
Melancholy, 114, 115, 117, 123,
    124, 132, 140
Melanchthon, Philip, 118
Mendicant Scholars, 190
Mendieta, G. de, 201, 205, 216
Menghi, Girolamo, 54, 55, 58, 61,
    72, 73, 74, 75
Menocchio, 12, 30
Methodism, 15
Mexico, 16 and 17th Century,
    189–227
Michelet, Jules, 42
Midelfort, Erik, 6
Milan, 73
"Military Theatre," 190, 191, 192–
    197, 202, 205, 208
Miracles, 6
Moctezuma, 191, 198
Modena, 56
Modernization, 28
Moegling, Daniel, 120, 121, 122
Molière, Jean Baptiste, 231, 251
Monte Cassino, 29
Monter, E. William, 94
Moordike, Sarah, 95
Moors, 196, 198, 201, 208, 209,
    215
Morin, A., 248, 249
Moses, 28
Moslem Kings, 42
*Motif Index of Folk Literature*, 20,
    25, 26
Motolinía, 201, 202, 208, 210
Muchembled, R., 256
Murray, Margaret, 39, 40
Mythology, 9
National Centralization, 190

*Navigation of St. Brendan*, 25, 26
Nergal, 23
Neufchateau, François de, 270
Nider, Johannes, 44, 45, 47

Oath, 20
Occasionnels, 237
Occident, 22
"Old Law," 162, 164, 166
*On the Operations of the Demons*, 41
O'Neil, Mary, 12, 15
Oneiric Universe, 31
Oral Tradition, 7, 8, 10, 12, 15, 24, 28
Ortloff, Johann Andreas, 276
Osiander, 176
Oudot, Nicholas, 247, 248, 249
Oudot, Nicholas Jr., 248, 249
Our-Nammou, 23
Owen, 24
Ozouf, Mona, 268

Pagan, 24
Paganism, 34
Palm Sunday, 201, 215
Paracelsus, 134
Parma, Basileo da, 71, 72, 73, 74
Paulicians, 41, 44
Peasants' War of 1525 (German), 149, 157, 158, 162, 166
Peddling (in France), 231
Perkins, William, 92, 94, 96, 104
Perrault, Charles, 261
Perry, William, 88
Peter of Ghent, 193
Peter the Deacon, 29
Petit, 262
Philipp The Magnamimous, 161
Philip The Tall, 42
Phrenesis, 121–122
Piper of Niklahausen, 163
Placards, 237, 246
Ponce, Alonso, 194, 195, 197, 198, 199, 201, 204, 210
Ponce, Fougeyron, 44
Pope Alexander V, 44

Popular Culture (defined), 1, 2
Popular Festivals, 113
Portents, 6
Possession (Diabolic), 101, 114, 130, 134
Powell, Justice John, 89, 90
Prophecy, 6
Propp, V., 46
Psellos, Michael, 41
*Purgatorium Sancti Patricii*, 24

Quetzalcoatl, 200

Rationality, 8
Rationalism, 256, 260
    Liberal, 85
Ravicz, M. Ekdahl, 203
Reductionism, 85, 118
Reformation, 53, 60, 94, 136, 159, 167, 173, 174, 176, 178, 180, 241, 248, 256
    Catholic Reformation, 230, 231, 235, 256
Religious Resistance, 179
Renaissance, 25, 30, 94
Revel, Jacques, 6
Ribas, Perez de, 205, 206
Rivère, Marguerite de la, 247
Robinson, Joan, 88
Roche, Daniel, 237
Richard, Robert, 193
Roger, Loys, 240
Roman Church, 53, 75
Romantic Nationalism, 7
Romanticism, 7
Rousseau, 266
Rural Culture, 7
Ryff, Walter, 115

Sahagún, 190, 202
Saint Augustine, 230, 258
Saint Joseph Confraternity, 244
*Saint Patrick's Purgatory*, 24, 32
Salamus, Thomaso, 71
Sassolo, Sebastian, 62
Satan, 92, 93, 97, 99
Sawyer, Elizabeth, 93
Scarron, 248

*Schembartlaut*, 169, 176
Schmitt, Jean-Claude, 9, 27, 32
Schoner, Johann, 116, 117
Schulze, Winfried, 164, 165
Scott, Reginald, 90, 104
Scotland, 86
Scott, Sir Walter, 6, 7
Scribner, Robert, 149, 176
Seguin, J. P., 247
Senioretto, 29
Shrove Sunday, 242
Simonini, Margarita, 65
Smith, Mary, 93
Social Discipline, 169, 171
Social Localization, 7
Socialism, 295, 296
Song, 20
Spanish State, 190
Spatialization, 32
State, 261
    Monarchial State, 263
Strasbourg, 43
Sumptuary Legislation, 170–171, 172
Superstition, 8, 10, 53
Sutton, Mary, 95, 104
"Swimming," 104

Tale, 20
*Táltos*, 46
Tarécuato, 196
Tenochtitlán, 191, 192, 193, 194, 200, 202, 203, 204, 209, 210
Teocacingo, 203
Tepeguanes, 205, 206, 207, 214
Thamer, Hans Ulrich, 6, 8
Thiers, Jean Baptiste, 6, 258, 260, 261, 264, 265
Thompson, E. P., 11, 85, 86, 100, 148, 149, 156, 165
Thompson, Stith, 9, 20, 25, 26, 27
Thomas, Keith, 9, 30, 63, 85, 86, 95, 103
Thrakian Bogomiles, 41
Tlaxcalans, 193, 194, 201, 202, 203, 204, 205, 208, 209, 210, 215

Tnugdal, 24
Toledo, 43
Tollat, Johann, 115, 116, 117
Tracy, Destutt de, 267, 268
Traditionalism, 270
*Traité des Superstitions*, 6, 258, 264 (Thiers)
Trevor-Roper, Hugh, 39
Tridentine, 55, 151, 179, 230, 263
Tridentine Church, 76
Turchill, 33
Turks, 135, 139, 208, 210
Twelve Apostles of the Indies, 191, 192, 194
*Types of the Folktale, The*, 20

Umfrage, 288
*Understanding Popular Culture*, 5, 8, 10
Udine, Geremia da, 57, 58, 59, 60, 66, 67, 68

Valais Witches, 45
Varenne, 248
Vargas, Caballeros de, 215
Vauderie, Arras, 47
Vaudois Witches, 47
Venice, 56, 60, 72
Vergil, Polydore, 23, 202
Vesalius, 115, 118
Vidal, J. M., 42
Vincenzo, Francesca da, 61
Vision, 20, 23
*Vision of Tnugdal*, 32
*Vision of Wettinus*, 31
Voltaire, 260
Vovelle, M., 269
*Voyage of Bran*, 25, 26

Wagstaffe, John, 94
Waite, Margaret, 88
Wasson, R.G., 203
Weistümer, 161
Wenham, Jane, 89, 90, 95, 101
Weyer, Johann, 123, 138–141